REV'D MATTHEW CLARK.

HERITAGE BOOKS
AN IMPRINT OF HERITAGE BOOKS, INC.

Books, CDs, and more—Worldwide

For our listing of thousands of titles see our website
at
www.HeritageBooks.com

A Facsimile Reprint
Published 2025 by
HERITAGE BOOKS, INC.
Publishing Division
5810 Ruatan Street
Berwyn Heights, MD 20740

Manchester, N.H.
Printed by the John B. Clarke Company
1908

— Publisher's Notice —
In reprints such as this, it is often not possible to remove blemishes from the original. We feel the contents of this book warrant its reissue despite these blemishes and hope you will agree and read it with pleasure.

International Standard Book Number
Paperbound: 978-1-55613-682-5

MANCHESTER HISTORIC ASSOCIATION COLLECTIONS

Volume V

1908

Edited, with Introduction,
Notes, and Index by

George Waldo Browne

HERITAGE BOOKS
2025

INTRODUCTION.

In finishing the work upon Volume I, Early Records of Londonderry, N. H., it seems fitting that we should give here a few words of explanation and description. The sources from which we have drawn are Volumes I and II of the old town books. The first is devoted to records of town meetings, homesteads, and vital statistics, with a sprinkling of advertisements. About one hundred and seventy-two pages of this book are filled with vital statistics and records of the boundaries of homesteads and outlying lots. The time covered is from 1719 to 1726. Page 60 gives the Articles of Incorporation, followed by a list of the proprietors; then succeed records of roads and earmarks.

Reversing the book, it begins with the "First Planting," April 11, 1719, following with forty-six pages of political records. In addition to these are two pages of records and two of acts given out of chronological order. Volume I contains in all two hundred and twenty-two pages. Much of the writing is faded and difficult to decipher, and the book shows its age.

Volume II is written from both sides, with a change of the book at different places between these transcripts, as if the recorders tried to bring the different classifications of subjects together and miscalculated on the space needed by the parts. Thus the three or four classes are mixed and somewhat difficult to separate. The records in this volume extend from 1727 to 1770. This book contains about six hundred and fifty pages, and is in a better state of preservation than the first.

In order to bring the political records of the town together, to form a continuous narrative, we have thought best to take these as we found them scattered throughout the books, omitting the transcripts of homesteads, roads, and vital records. To include them all, and in the order, or lack of order in which they were written, we should have had nothing complete or systematized so as to be of easy access. Another volume would comprise all of these and possibly bring the political records to about 1780, thus covering the colonial and revolutionary war periods. It would be difficult to imagine two volumes of early history of greater value.

It is only proper to say here that while the greatest care has been taken in deciphering the writing, which has often been read through a magnifying glass, there are places which seem impossible of correct transcription. In a few cases it has been thought safest to insert a question mark, thus (?). The use of capitals is frequently a mooted point, but an attempt has been made to be as uniform as possible. Wherever there has been a doubt the author or person writing the word has been given the benefit of the same.

In preparing the index it has been impossible when of the same name to discriminate between father and son. This is noticeably the situation with John Wallace. Usually, where no distinction has been given in the Records, the credit has been plaçed to that of the name which would indicate the senior member of the family. We have adopted the modern form of spelling the names in the index, with reference in some cases to the spelling as given in the Records.

In the body of the work we have tried at all times to reproduce the original in style, spelling, punctuation, and language as near as it is possible on the printed page. The copy and proof have been read as many as five times, by three persons, and is believed to be as correct as it is possible to transcribe a work of this kind. The editor is sorry to find that an error found its way in a footnote on page 157, and the reader is requested to supply *James* instead of *Robert*, where mention is made of the decease of Londonderry's first minister.

While the first settlers of Londonderry had received from Governor Shute, through their agent, the Rev. William Boyd, assurance that they might have any portion of territory within his jursidiction that they wanted, they came to this country with only a vague idea of the location of their future homes. About seventy-five landed in Boston August 4, 1718, and of these the following broke the wilderness of Nutfield in April, 1719: Rev. James McGregor, Alexander McGregor, Alexander Nichols, James Nichols, James Blair, Alexander Walker, Robert Boyes, Samuel Graves, Joseph Simonds, David Cargill, David Cargill, Jr., Archibald Clendenin, James Nesmith, James Clark, Elias Keyes, John Barnett, James McKeen, James Gregg, James Morrison, John Morrison, Allen Anderson, Thomas Steel, and Robert Weare. The seven last named went to Casco, Me., before coming to Londonderry. To this list of twenty should be added John Goffe, Esq., who acted as agent for the immigrants. It will be noticed that the list of twenty first settlers, as given upon page 22 of this volume, varies slightly from this; but this was made nine months after the first arrival. It is proper to say here that it is impossible to make out this list complete with certainty, though we have given the benefit of Mr. McMurphy's copy, which was made by him before the book had become as worn as it is to-day.

The earnest purpose of the first settlers of Londonderry is shown by the fact that within a year a two-story dwelling house was built for the minister. This house was standing not many years ago, occupied by John Morrison, a descendant of the Morrisons who figure in these Records. Within two years a meeting house was built, and less than two years later four school houses, all speaking in unmistakable terms of the sincere devotion to Christian principles of the builders. Within five years this church had two hundred and thirty members. Mills were erected within two years of their settlement, and their owners became the pioneer manufacturers in this country. The manufacture of linen was an important industry in their day. There were no public means provided for the support of the poor, and when one became reduced to poverty through sickness or misfortune he became an object of uncertain charity, as shown by the votes referring to one.

The grant of the township, which had been named Londonderry in memory of the old home of the majority of the pioneers, was made June 21, 1722, by Gov. Samuel Shute to John Moor and one hundred and seventeen others, whose names appear upon page 41.

There is no gainsaying the fact that these new-comers were a fearless, hardy race. While determined efforts have been put forth to show that they were of Irish ancestry, there does not seem to be any sustained argument to show it. They were of Scotch descent, with a character founded during the stormy period of early Scottish struggles, confirmed and strengthened after their emigration to the north of Ireland in 1612 by their long and sanguinary conflicts against royal and ecclesiastical tyranny. Profound in their convictions, inflexible in their will and of strong sensibilities, they were indeed a hard people to crush. The story of sufferings and persecutions in religious and civil liberties had become such a stern influence in their lives, from generation to generation, it was small wonder if they displayed a continual spirit of obstinacy that seemed to contradict their love of liberty and fair play. Yet that very trait served to develop that faith in fair doing, which has so marked the race. The outspoken opinions of the individuals and the fearlessness in giving these expression is shown by the frequent protests made at the town meetings against the prevailing actions.

In one respect the pioneers of Londonderry were fortunate. They did not suffer at the hands of the Indians. This, too, during the period when that fearful uprising and bitter struggle between the races known as Lovewell's war occurred before they had fairly entered upon their settlement. This immunity from harm has been explained in two ways. One explanation accounted for this peace through a friendship existing between Rev. Mr. MacGregor and Marquis de Vaudreuil, the French governor of New France. It is even claimed that the former, owing to this friendly relation, had induced the Catholic priests not to allow the Amerinds to molest the Scotch people, as they were different from the English. Another reason explains that a fair and acknowledged Indian title, secured through the Wheelwright deed, had gained for them the friendship of this race. It is possible both of these claims had some bearing upon the situation. But there are two other reasons more potent than these. The towns nearest to the rivers, which were the natural highways of the red men, were always the ones to suffer first and most. While Londonderry was not far removed from that important war-trail, the Merrimack, yet it lay out of the regular line of travel. This, coupled with the fact that the English settlers of Old Dunstable and Exeter were constantly beating back the enemies through their scouting parties, kept the Indians from entering their territory. Again, the Scotch had not been in this country long enough to have formed any enmity to the aborigines, especially when in order to do this they must ally themselves with a people against whom they had long cherished a bitterness of heart. One man from Londonderry, Samuel Moore, was with Lovewell in his second expedition.

During King George's War, 1744-1748, however, we find Londonderry beginning to participate in the struggle. Early in the summer of 1746 Capt. Samuel Barr, at the head of seventeen men, marched through the wilderness of the "North Country." Later in the season Capt. Andrew Todd went with twenty-three men to Canterbury, hoping to find some of the enemies and put them to rout. Some of the followers under these leaders were from Londonderry, but neither of the bands seemed to have met with foes, who had become too wily to be caught napping as they had in the days of Lovewell. Between the homes of these hardy pioneers and the headquarters of their enemies lay a wide belt of wilderness, the White Mountain range forming a natural barrier behind which the Indians found a common resort with the French. Thinking to meet them upon their own ground, Governor Shirley planned his Quixotic campaign, which has passed into history as "The Expedition to Canada." Londonderry furnished her share of the soldiery of this march into the wilderness as far north as the shore of Lake Winnipesaukee, where the heavy body of foot soldiers rested, hunted, and fished without finding an Indian. While this was being done the Indians were active where they could be the most effective, and on the whole they got the best of the border warfare; but the day of reckoning came only a few years later. Several Londonderry men were with Major Rogers and his Rangers during the Seven Years' War, though I do not think any great number were in the service. Their activity was most noticeable in the American Revolution, and at Bunker Hill, Bennington, and elsewhere they performed heroic parts.

It seems proper to insert here the Muster Rolls of the men employed in His Majesty's service, scouting in the woods, by order of the Governor, under Captains Barr and Todd, all of whom I think were from Londonderry.

Muster-Roll of Capt. Samuel Barr.

Samuel Barr, Captain,	David Thompson,
Thomas Gregg, Sergeant,	George Clark,
John Wallace,	Samuel Center,
James McGregor,* Clerk,	William Smith,
John McDuffie	Edward Aiken,
James Adams,	John Aiken,
William Robertson,	James Duncan,
James Paul,	Samuel Bell,
Adam Dickey,	John Anderson.

Enlisted the men the 16th of May, began our march 20th of May, and discharged them the thirtieth of said month.

Sam'l Barr, Capt.

*** Son of Rev. James McGregor, the first minister of Londonderry.—Ed.**

Muster-Roll of Capt. Andrew Todd.

Andrew Todd, Captain,	Samuel Morrison, Sent.
William Holmes, Sergeant	John Reside, Sent.
James Wilson, Sergeant,	Hugh Thompson, Sent.
William Brownlee, Sent.	William Caldwell, Sent.
Thomas Hogg, Sent.	Adam Wilson, Sent.
John Miller, Sent.	Archibald Miller, Sent.
Joseph Ayers, Sent.	David Alexander, Sent.
Alexander Gault, Sent.	Joseph Hamblee, Sent.
John Grimes, Sent.	Samuel Marston, Sent.
James Boyce, Sent.	Hugh Boyd, Sent.
William McMaster, Sent.	Joseph Stewart, Sent.
James Leggett, Sent.	Arthur Boyd, Sent.

Captain Todd and his men were scouting at Canterbury and vicinity fourteen days from the 14th of July, 1746.

The town was divided into two parishes by an act of the court approved February 25, 1740, after the matter had been agitated by the town for six years, and a vote taken December 1, 1735, but which was strenuously opposed by a good-sized minority. Petitions and counter petitions followed, until at last it was decided to make the division.

The southern portion of the grant was set off into a parish to be called Windham, February 12, 1742, the first meeting of which was called March 8, 1742, by Robert Dinsmore, Joseph Waugh, and Robert Thompson.

September 3, 1751, another part was severed from the original body and joined with a tract from Chester and ungranted land about Amoskeag falls and incorporated under the name of Derryfield.

A portion of Londonderry was annexed to Nottingham West, now Hudson, March 6, 1778.

Though we are passing the limit of the period covered by the following records, it may be well to state here that Windham received the estates of several persons from Londonderry September 26, 1777. November 26, 1778, Samuel Clark and his estate were annexed to Windham. The line between the towns was not established by the courts until November 22, 1782. After this, December 25, 1805, Windham received another portion of Londonderry.

July 2, 1827, the remaining township was divided by an act of the legislature, the east half incorporated under the name of Derry.

Moderators, 1719-1762.

The moderators for this period acting at the annual meetings were as follows: James McKeen, 1719-1721; James Gregg, 1722; James Nichols, 1723; Robert Boyes, 1724; John Blair, 1725; Robert Boyes, 1726-1727; James Gregg, 1728; James McKeen, 1729; James Nesmith, 1730; James McKeen, 1731; Robert Boyes, 1732; Robert Wear, 1733; Robert Boyes, 1734-5; John Blair, 1736; Nathaniel Weare, 1737; Andrew Todd, 1738; Robert Boyes, 1739; John Morrison, Sen., 1740; Andrew Todd, 1741; Hugh Wilson, 1742-1748; Robert Boyes, 1749; Hugh Wilson, 1750-1752; John Mitchell, 1753; James Clark, 1754; Samuel Barr, 1755; James Clark, 1756; Andrew Todd, 1757-1762.

Clerks, 1719-1762.

During the period of the records given here there were five town clerks, viz.: John Goffe, 1719-1722; John McMurphy, 1723-1736; John Wallace, 1737-1742; Moses Barnett, 1743-1749; James Nesmith, 1750-1753; Moses Barnett, 1754-1771.

Representatives, 1719-1762.

James McKeen, 1727-8; Lt. John Goffe, 1729-30; John McMurphy, 1731-2-3; Robert Boyes, 1734-5; James Gregg, 1736; Robert Boyes, 1737; Hugh Wilson, 1738; Robert Boyes, 1739-40; Samuel Barr, 1741; Andrew Todd, 1742; no election for 1743-4; John Wallace, Jr., January to June, 1745; John McMurphy (elected in June), 1745-54; Robert Clark, 1755-7; Matthew Thornton, 1758-60; Samuel Barr, 1761-7.

G. W. B.

TOWN OF LONDONDERRY.

In the warrant for the annual meeting of the town of Londonderry, held March 14, 1905, appears the following article:

ART. 6. To see if the town will vote to raise the sum of two hundred dollars ($200) to be expended by the selectmen for printing the early and Proprietors' Records of Londonderry, provided the town of Derry shall vote to raise an equitable amount for the same purpose.

On the above article the following action was taken:

ART. 6. Upon motion it was voted that the article be adopted.

A true record. Attest:

WILLIAM H. CROWELL, *Town Clerk.*

A true copy. Attest:

WILLIAM H. CROWELL, *Town Clerk.*

TOWN OF WINDHAM.

Town warrant, Windham, N. H., March 14, 1905.

ART. 4. By request. To see if the town will vote to raise one hundred dollars, to be expended by the selectmen for the printing of early proprietors' records of Londonderry, provided that Londonderry and Derry shall vote to raise equitable amounts for the same purpose.

Voted, To raise one hundred dollars for proprietors records, provided Londonderry and Derry do likewise.

A true record. Attest:

JOHN E. COCHRAN, *Town Clerk.*

A true copy of record. Attest:

JOHN E. COCHRAN, *Town Clerk.*

TOWN OF DERRY.

The warrant for the annual town meeting of the town of Derry, N. H., under date of February 25, 1905, contained the following:

Art. 10. To see if the town will vote to raise and appropriate the sum of three hundred dollars for the purpose of publishing and preserving the early town records, said appropriation to be conditional upon similar action by the town of Londonderry.

At the above annual town meeting, held March 15, 1905, it was voted:

Art. 10. Voted to raise and appropriate the sum of three hundred dollars for publishing and preserving the early town records, if the town of Londonderry takes similar action.

A true record. Attest:

W. H. BENSON, *Town Clerk.*

A true copy. Attest:

W. H. BENSON, *Town Clerk.*

STATE OF NEW HAMPSHIRE.

Hillsborough, SS.

I, the undersigned, Chairman of the Publication Committee of the Manchester Historic Association, to whom has been assigned the task of compiling and editing the Early Records of Londonderry, the original township of Londonderry, Windham, and Derry, N. H., certify that the following transcript of the political records included in Volume I, complete, and Volume II as far as page 375, is a true and correct copy.

GEORGE WALDO BROWNE.

Subscribed and sworn to before me, this tenth day of September, A. D. 1908.

HARRY T. LORD, *Notary Public.*

FIRST FRAMED HOUSE IN LONDONDERRY.

EARLY RECORDS

OF THE

TOWN OF LONDONDERRY, N. H.

The Record of the Town of Nutfield from the first planting of it Apriel y^e 11th anno Domini 1719

M^r. James Mac Gregor minister James Nickel Alexander macgregor Alexander Nickel James Blaier Alexander Walker and divers oathers having arived at boston August ye 4th 1718 from Ireland presented a petition to the General Court of the massachusetts Bay met at boston in the month of october 1718 for a tract of land for a Township in som of the unapropriated Lands and the Court having Redily granted their Desire James MacKeen James Greg James Moreson John Morison Alan Anderson Thomas Steel and Divers oathers of the People of Ireland came up from Cascobay to Haverel in order to setel at Nutfield about the begining of Apriel 1719] The said James Mac Keen James Greg James Morison John Morison Alan Anderson Thomas Steel Robart Wier and Divers oathers of the People of Ireland for the forwarding their said plantation presented a Call to the Revd Mr James Mac Gregor to be their minister for his salery and maintanance besids lands they obledged them selves in their Call to pay him yearly and every year twenty shilings out of every lott in the said Town for them selves and oathers that should take up lotts in the said Town accordingly the said Mr Mac Gregor preached with them on the 12th Day apriel Anno Dom 1719 and accepted their Call about the begining of may 1719 and since that time hath Continued with them as their minister Those who planted since that time have laid them selves under the afore said obligation to pay twenty shilings pr lott to the minister and the Town agreed that each lott should Give a Dais work to the ministers setelment

The first famelis that arived at Nutfield planted them selves in the moneth of Apriel 1719 on either side of a small Brook Runing westward into Beaver River and may be Called west Runing brook they agreed that their home lotts should be thirty perches broad fronting on the Brook and the same bredth to be continued backward on a south and north line untill it make up sixty acres to each lott and if aney lott wanted of sixty acres it was to be made up of the most conveneant common lands the first lott on the south side of west runing brook begining begining the Reconing at Haverel line is posesed by

In the month of June 17th 1719 The Town ordered A saw mill to be built on beaver River and the tener of their agreement with the undertakers viz Robert Buys James Greg Samuel Graves and Joseph Simonds is as folloeth Samuel Graves Robert Boyes Joseph Simonds & James Gregg hath oblidged them selves to build a saw mill upon beaver River to be Redy som time in the month of September and that the said streem is granted to the above named men and a lott of land to them and their heirs for ever only the above named James Gregg shall have full previlidge to build a grist mill upon the said streem that is to say upon beaver River and that the said Samuel Graves Robart Boyes Joseph simonds & James Gregg shall have the prevelidg of the said streem from the fut of the falls to the uper end of beaver pond

The Town ordered September 1719 James Greg and Robart Wyer to present A petition to the Court of Newhamshire to obtain a power of Government and Town priviledges the said petition was presented and the answer of it Delayed untill the next spring session

The Town understanding that it was needfull to make an agreement with Coll John Wheelwright of Wells about the sail of nutfield ordered october 1719 Mr James Mac Gregor and Samuel Graves to wait upon Coll Whealwright for that end they accordingly obtained a Deed from Coll Whealwright to an agreement with him The Coppye of the Deed is as folloeth

These presents wittneseth that I John Wheelwright of Wells in the County of yorke in the province of the Massachusets Bay Do for me my self my Heirs Executors Administrators & Assigns by virtue of a Deed of Grant made to my Grand Father a minister of the Gospel and oathers named in said Grant by sundrey Indian Sagemores with the Consent of ye whole tribe of Indians between the Rivers of Merimake and pescatequa tó them and their Heirs for ever full power for for the laying out bounding and Granting these Lands into suetable tracts for townships unto such numbers of People as may from time to time offer to setle and Improve the same which Deed beareth Date may the seventeenth one thousand six hundred twenty and nine and is well Executed Acknowledged and approved by the authority in the Day as may at large more fully appear pursuant there unto I Do by these presents Give and Grant all my Right title and Intrest therein Contain (ed) for the ends uses above said unto m^r^ James Mac Gregor Samuel Graves David Cargill James MacKeen James Greg and one hundred more mentioned in A List to them and their Heirs for ever A Certain tract of Land bounded as folloeth not exceding the quantity tenn miles square begining at a pine tree marked which is the south west Corner of Cheshier and Runing to the north west Corner of the said Cheshire and from the north west Corner Runing upon a due west line unto the River Merimack and Down the River Merimack until it meets with the line of Dunstable and then turning Eastward upon it Dunstable lyne untill it meet with the Line of Dracut and Continuing Eastward upon Dracut Line untill it meet with the Line of Haverill and Extending northward upon Haverill Line untill it meet with the Line of Cheshire unto the pine tree first mentioned where it began in wittness whereof I have here unto set my hand

and seal this twentyeth Day of October one thousand seven and nineteen

John Wheelwright O

Signed Sealed and Delivered in the Presence of
Daniel Dupee
John Hirst

Suffolk Sc

Boston October ye 20th 1719

John Wheelwright Esqr personaly appearing acknowledged the above Instrument to be his volluntary Act and Deed

Cer Wm Welsteed Just peece

Province of Newhamsher

Entred and Recorded in the 11th Book of the said Records Page 138: 139 this 24th of Octob^r^ 1719

Pr Sam^ll^ Penhallow Recorder

Recorded this 9th Day of Janua^ry^ 1719/20

Pr John Goffe Town Clerk

The Coppie of ye Agreement is as folloeth

These presents witnesseth that the Revd Mr James Mac Gregor and Samuel Graves Do in the name of the People of Nutfield and by virtue of being a Committe from them agree the Honble Lt Governour John Wentworth of Portsmouth and Coll John Wheelwright of Wells and their Heirs for ever should have and posess two Lotts with them in Nutfield lying to the northward of and butting upon beaver pond to wit L Governer Wentworth to have the third and Coll Wheelwright the fourth in order upon that Range to gather with what second divisions will fall to the said lotts through out the said Town, and each of these Gentlemen and their Heirs to have besides the said Lotts five hundred acres apece for ever Laid out in farms where they shall think fit in the said Town

Recorded this 9th Day of January 1719/20

pr John Goffe Town Clerke

The people of Nutfield do acknowledge with all gratitude the obligation they are under to the above mentioned Gentlemen particularly to the Honourable Co[l] John Wentworth Esq Liet. Governour of Newhampshire. They remember with pleasure that his honour on all occasions shewed a great deal of civility and real kindness to them being strangers in the Country and cherished the small beginnings of their Settlement, and defended them from the incroachment and violence of such as upon unjust grounds would disturb their Settlement, and always gave them favourable ear and easy access to the Government and procured Justice for them and established order and promoted peace and good agreement amongst them, giving them always the most wholesome and Seasonable advice both with respect to the purity and Liberty of the Gospel and the management of their secular affaires, and put Arms and Ammunition into their hands to defend them from the fears and dangers of the Indians, and contributed liberally by his example and influence to the building of a House for the worship of God So that under God we owe him for the Patron & Guardian of our Settlement and erect this Monument of gratitude to the name and family of Wentworth to be had in the greatest veneration by the present generation and latest Posterity.

Att a Town meeting November y[e] 9th 1719 The Town voated m[r] James Mac Keen for moderater on the said Day was voated for Town Clerke John Goffe

att a publick Town meeting November y[e] 20th 1719 The Town voated that seven men should be Chosen as a Commite for the managing the publick affaiers of this Town and the names of the members are as followeth

Com[te]

M[r] Cargil	John Morison
James Mackeen	Samuel Graves
James Greg	John Goffe
Robart Weir	

Com[te]

December y[e] 25th 1719: at a meeting of the Commite it was then agreed upon by the said Commite that the first Comers to this town which is the number of twenty shall each of them have one lott to Dispous of to aney person whom they shall see Caus to setle on it provided the person be capable of and will make a present setlement thereon: the names of ye men are James Mac Keen James Greg Samuel Graves the rest of the names are in the margin

David cargil Robt Wier John morison James Anderson Thomas Steel Allen Anderson John Gregg John barnard Archbel: Clendenin Jams Clerk James Neasmeth John Goffe Elias Keyes Joseph Simons James Mc Keen James Mc Keen* on the said Day it was farther agreed upon by the said Commite that if their be aney lott not Dispoused of within the number of one hundred and five it shall be alowed for a saw-mill lott, but if the 105 lotts are all filled up then their shall be a lott laid out in the undevided Lands for a saw mill Lott

at A Generall Town meeting January ye 11th 1719/20 the Town voated that all persons that have Lotts laid out to them in Nutfield shall com and setle in the said Town so as to be proper inhabetants in the said Town of nutfield on or be fore the first Day of apriel next ensewing the dat above written but if they or aney of them shall neglect and Refues to Com and setle here by the said first Day of apriel that then the said Lotts shall be Dispoused of by the town to aney person or persons that will make a present setlement upon them

at a Generall Town meeting Janvary ye 19th 1719/20 The Town voated that four men shuld be Chosen as a Commite for the vewing and laying out the meddows and the names of the members are as followeth

Mr Mac gregor
Thomas Steel
James Mac Keen
James Gregg
John Goffe
Commite

* This list is one name short. Mr. Jesse McMurphy in his sketch of "The Double Range in Nutfield" adds to this list the names of James Alexander, James Sterrat and Samuel Allison.—Ed.

on said day voated that if aney meddows shall fall within aney mans lotts ye land above half an acre by mistake (?) it shall be setled for by the propreators as other meddows are

It was allso on the said day voated that the above said commite shall have four shilings pr day for their work in vewing and laying out the meddows on the Day above said the Town voated that Mr James Gregg shall have his Grist mill Lott laid out to him upon the southeast side of beaver River

At a generall Town meeting Apriel ye 4th 1720 whereas the above said Grist mill Lott was intended for william Greg the Town hath on the above said Day for som Good reason voated that the said William Greg shall not have the said lott or aney oather intrest in the Town of nutfield

At ageneral Town meeting Apriel ye 15th 1720 on the said Day the Town voated that three men shall be Chosen to wait upon the Generall Court at the bank* the names of the men are as followeth

M^r^ mac Gregor m^r^ James Mackeen and m^r^ Samuel Graves

At a generall Town meeting June ye 1st 1720 The town then voated that m^r^ Cargill shall be Town treasuerar

on the Day above said the Town voated that John Hunter shall not have a Lott in this Town on the Day above said the Town voated that their shall be a small hous built that may be conveneant for the inhabetants to meet in for the worship of God and that it shall be built as sune as it can with Conveneancy allso that the hous shall be built as near the senter of the one hundred and five lotts as can be with Conveneance

At ageneral Town meeting June ye 29th 1720 the town then voated that the meeting hous shall be built within tenn Rhods of a black stake set up either upon or near unto m^r^ m^c^ Grigors Lott

* Strawberry Bank, now Portsmouth.—ED.

on the above said day the town voated tht if aney of the medows laid out so aney lotts in this town shall fall within aney farms not belonging to this town or within aney other town bounds so as to be leagealy taken from them the town Doth then here by oblege them selves to make up the loss by giving them oather meddows in the prime (place) of those that are so taken from them

At a generall Town meeting when there was a party in the town that weir troubled at the actions of the Commite upon July ye 25 and mett then for to endeavour to Divide the Differance it was then voated that the present Commite be Dismised and not Capable of acting as a Commite aney further in this town

On the said Day their weir a partie at the Meeting who manefested their Displeasuer at their being a number of lotts asigned to a certain number of men in this town they weir for having the said lotts to lye Common the moderater then asked whether they weir willing to leave it to a voate of the town but they refuesed it exept the men that weir intrested in said lotts weir all out the Commite then agreed to leave it to the Generall Court at the bank on the said day the town voated that the above said Commite shuld act as before with regard to the lotts notwithstanding the aforesaid move

At a Town meeting held ye July 25 1720 ye town then voated that Hew M^nt^ Gumery shall be (written) unto to see whether he will come to this Town and make a present setlement upon the one half of Cap^tt^ Wainwrights Lott the said Cap^tt^ Wainwright to keep the oather half him self

On the said 25 of July a Greived party appeared against the Commites assignining twenty lotts to 20 men of ye first coming the Commite offered them a voate of the town which they refused until they set a side all men intrested in said lotts upon voat the Commite with the oather part of the Town have left the whole matter to be Desided by the Generall Court at their next sessions at the bank

At a Town meeting September—1720 the Town voated that his Excelency Governer shall shall have Laid out to him within this township a farme of five hundred acres for his Lott of Land of sixty acres with the common rights belonging there unto

October ye 14th 1720 Lieve Governer Wentworth being present in this town he ordered that Insign Blair John Mc Murphy and Hew M^{nt} Gumery should joyn with the Comite in the management of the publick affairs of this town

At the same Day it was ordered by the Governer aforesaid that the Commite shall have full power to lay out highwais in this town the wais to be laid out not to be under four rhod wide

at a generall Town meeting November ye 4th 1720 It was voated by the town that thirty acres of Land shall be laid out to each propriator in this town in the most Conveneant Common or undevided Lands

January ye 11th 1720/21

at a Generall Town meeting the Town voated & Choes for moderater m^{r} m^{c} Keen on the Day above said it was voated that a meeting hous shall be built in this town as spedely as may be and that the above said hous shall be fifty foot in lenkth fourty five broad and so hygh as may be Conveneant for one set of Galeryes on the Day afore said voated that two men be Chosen as a Commite to agree with the Carpinter for building the meeting hous and oather afairs relaiting to said hous

The members Chosen for said Commite are

Mr James m^{c} Keen
Mr Sam^{ll} more

The Commite of this town having ben some time since petitioned to by Will Aiken John Bell Andrew Todd John Wallis James Aikin and Benjamin Willson for the Grant of a streem or brook which commonly goes by the name of Aikins brook in order to the seting up a saw mill there on) and allso one acre of land adjoining to said brook that will be conveneant for a yard to said mill th Commite having taken the pettition into Consideration and thinking that it may tend to the publick good of this town to have more saw mils set up in it) wee there fore the said Commite by virtue of the power trust Commited to us by the inhabetants of this town for the mannagement of the publick affairs there of have thought fit and do hereby grant the said streem or brook with one acre of land for a yard unto the above named Willm Aikin Andrew Todd John bell John Walis James Aikin and Benjamin Willson for the uses afore said and the part of the streem pettioned for and granted is from a spruce swamp down to David moresons Lott

David Cargill
James m^{c} Keen
John Goffe
John m^{c} neel
James Gregg
Rob^{tt} Wear
Committ

and wee the said William Aiken John Bell James Aiken andrew todd John Wallis and Benjamin Willson do hereby prommis and ingage that what boards wee have to Dispous of the inhabetants of this town shall have the refuesall of at the rate of thirty shilings pr thousand and sawing at fifteen shilings pr thousand in wittnes where of we have here unto set our hands and seal

Willm Aikin
John Walis
Andrew Todd
James Aikin
John bell
Benjamin Wilson

Recorded this 23rd of march 1720/1
Pr John Goffe Town Clerk

october ye 28 1720 the Commite being then mett with regard to the —— officers of this town it was then agreed upon by the said (?) Commite that John Given and abraham Rouns shall have time alowed them untill the first of January to setle upon their Lotts, but if they refues and neglect to setl Such by the said first of January it may be in the power of the town to Dispous of said Lotts to those who will make a present setelment thereon

upon the said Day the Commite Choes four persons for saveers of the by ways the names of the men are as followeth

Alexander Nicols
John m^{c} neel
William Akin
John Goffe
James Gregg

saveers

Nutfield March ye 25th 1721

All the Lotts in this Town have ben raited thirty shilings pr Lott from the first setlement there of unto this present Day march ye 25th 1721 upon the said Day the Commite Chozen for the setling the towns accompts mett and adjusted and setled all the accompts in this Town and the names of thoes that remain in Debt and what each person oweth to make up his thirty shilings is as followeth

John Barnard Dr........
James Anderson Dr 0-13-2

The names of the persons that have money Due to them from the Town and what Due to each person is as followeth

May 11 : 1722 the accompt at the right hand being alowed in raits or paid other wise: ye remaindure is under this

The names of thoes that have money due from the

	£
To m^{r} m^{c} gregor	1—12— 9
To m^{r} Gregg	6— 9— 3
To m^{r} m^{c} Keen	2—16— 7
To John moreson	0—10— 6
Cap^{tt} Cargill	0—18— 8
To John m^{c} morphy	0— 4—10

town to you

Due to m^{r} Gregg	4— 5— 6
To m^{r} m^{c} Gregor	0— 0— 9
To m^{r} m^{c} Keen	0— 6— 9
To arbel Clandenen	0— 8—10
To hew mn^{t} Gummery	1— 1— 6
To James m^{c} neel	1— 0— 0
To John mitchel	0— 1— 6
To Cap^{tt} Cargill	0— 3— 7
To John m^{c}morphy	0— 4—10
To John Jno Goffe for service as Clerk in full for 1721	0—10— 0
To m^{r} Barnard	0— 7—10
To m^{r} Wear	2—11— 6
To m^{r} mn^{t} Gummery	1— 6— 6
To m^{r} James m^{c} neel	1—14— 5
Samuel Hewston	0— 0— 7
To Abel merrel	0— 5— 0
To John Goffe	3— 4— 3
To m^{r} Graves	0—14—10
To m^{r} John Blair	0— 0— 7
To mr James Blair	0— 3— 0
	— — —
	£26— 3— 8
To m^{r} Aleck Nicols	8— 9

on the above said 25st of march accounted with robert wear and their remains Due to the town, 11— 0— 0

At a Generall Town meeting march ye 25 1721 for the Chuesing Town of esers the Town voated that 3 men be Chos as a Commite for the publik affairs of this town

for Commite

Samuel more
John Sentr
John Coughevin

John Bell
Joseph Simons
John more
Hew m^{nt} Gumery
Seveyers

may ye 8th 1721 m^r^ m^c^ Keen by vertue of an order from the Governer of this province the town being then mett did make choys of seven men for a Commite to manage the prudenshall afairs of this town and the naims of the Commite are

Samuel more
James Gregg
James alexander
Jams m^c^ neel
Sam^ll^ Graves
John Coughrin
John Goffe
Commite

may ye 24th 1721: the Commite being then mett three men weir Chosen by ye Commite to valu the lotts in this town that are Complained of (viz)

Thomas Steel
James m^c^ neel
Elias Keyes

march ye 25th 1721

m^r^ James m^c^ neel then appearing and making som Complaint to the Commite of the greveances that he was under by reason of the threatening that haveril people gave him with regard to the land which he is now settled upon) the said Commite having considered the matter and not Knowing what trouble and Charge the said m^c^ neel may be at in defending the land which he is now at work upon supoused to be within haveril) they the said Commite by vertue of the pour and trust Commited to them by the inhabetants of this town for the mannagement of the public affaiers thereof, have thought fit and do here by prommis and ingage unto the said m^c^ neel that he shall have a lott of land equall to oather lotts made out to him within this Township where he shall think Conveneant in the undevided land and allso that if he doth defend the land which he is now upon within haveril line that then he shall have one hundred acres of the said land for him self where he is now setled

Done by order of the Commite afore said and Recorded this 29th Day of march 1721

Saml Graves
Hugh mntt Gumery
John Goffe

David Cargill
James mc Keen
James Gregg
Robtt Wear
Commite

March 25th 1721

John Woodbourn then made Complaint to the Commite of the badness of his lott of land which was laid out to him the said Commite inquiering into the matter and finding the said lott to be very ordinery do therfore all agree that the said woodbourn shall have an oather lott laid out to him in the Common lands provided that the said woodbourn letts the lott he now posseses drop but never the less if he doth let that lot drop wholy the town shall pay him what may be thought reasonable for his labor but if the town refueses to do so that then the said woodbourn shall have the liberty of taking the said lott in his second devisions

June ye 19th 1721

The Commite being then mett they agreed to mak sale of the half lott which hew mnt Gumery hath refuesed to setle acording to his agreement

June 26. the Commite made sale of the above said half lott unto Willm Gillmore and James Roger and Recd tenn shillings ernist of mr Samll more on accompt of ye said Gilmor and Rogers

on the above said Day the Commite mad Coys of three men for to value the lotts (viz) James Gregg Samll Graves Tho Steel) and all persons that have a mind to Complain of their lotts may repair to the three men above named paying them for their time they are by them to have their lotts valued and a recompence made them according to their want provided they make their Complaint by the 10th of may next ensewing and no alowance after that time on the above said

Day the Comite alowed John moreson to git what land he wants to make up his lott by reason of by ways beng taken out of his lotts and all other wants to be laid out with his second Devisions alowing him quantety and qualety as other Devisions have the said moreson to have the said lands along with m^r^ Gregs lott which he hath the liberty to exchang for a lott in the undevided land

July 2^nt^ the Commite upon the Complaint of m^r^ m^c^ Keen of his meddow and others to the number of seven in the thirteen acre meddow have upon Consideration agreed that the vewers of meddow shall lay out two acres of meddow to the said Complainers in the undevided meddows and that they shall have liberty of cuting two acres in teverels without Disturbance from the town untill the said two acres be laid out on the said Day the Commite agreed that Willm Gregg shall have the liberty of taking his second devision of land in any lott above Captt Cargils to Chester line

August 14 at a meeting of the Commite the said Commite voted that the common land at the east of beaver pond should be laid out for a ministerel lott it was allso don by the consent of a number of the propriators who were to have the said land to make up their lotts they having their lotts made up els wheir) on said day the commite agreed to lay out that land which goes by the name of haveril land in second devisions to aney of the propriators of this town that have a mind to take their second devisions their provided they will make a present setlement there on according to the orders of the commite or els consent to lues their devisions els wheir if they lues them in the above said land threw neglect of setling them by aney stranger coming in and setling or in aney leagal way

At a Generall Town meeting september ye 18th 1721
there was Chosen for moderator m^r^ James Mc Keen
on the said day voated that the land which goes by the name of leverits farm shall be laid out in second devision to such persons as will make a present setlement there on or luse

their second devisions of land els wheir in this town if they lues their land in said farme after it is given to them: there neglect of setling them

at a meeting of the Commite november ye 21 1721 agreed upon by the said Commite that John moreson shall have what land he wants to make up his own lott laid out to him in that part of the undevided land at the eastward of beaver pond which is nearist to his own lott

at a meeting of the Comite January ye 15th 1721/2 their being a lott of second devision land lying in that land which goes by the name of haveril it being in debate btwen four men (viz) Jams Greg Rob^tt^ Wear Alexander Nicol & old m^r^ moreson ordered by said commite that the said moreson shall have said lott

January ye 22: 1721/2

The Commite being mett in order to take som proper methods for giting in the ministers salery, ordered by said Commite that a list be drawed forth with of the arears and the town clerk to annex a warrant their to in order so the cunstables distraining thoes persons that neglect or refues to pay their rate to the minister

ordered on said day that the town clerk draw a paper and set it up at som publick place to for warn the in habetants of this town from cuting aney timber on aney part of the land which goes by the name of haveril land untill the said land be laid out it being all redy assigned to a number of the propriators of this town on the above said day the commite agreed to lay out in second devision an other quarter of a —— of the land which goes by the name of haveril it was the major voat of the commite James Gregg is to have three devisions in said land where he shall improve it (?) and the rest of said land to be laid out to the persons that (?) are under written as they follow

*1—2 Rob^rt^ Wear 3 John Barnard 4 alxndr Nicols 5 James Nicols 6 Daniel Aiken (?) 7 Sam^ll^ Graves (?)

* A portion of this page is so worn and soiled it is impossible to decipher all the names.

8— 9 Robart H—— (?) 10—11—12—13— 14 Tho: Steel 15 John Barnd

The town of Nutfield hath ben Raited this present year 1721 by the Commite 15 Shillings pr lott which amounts to 81 £ 3^{s} 0^{d} and It hath ben dispoused of in the folowing manner: allso 15£—0—0 Recd of Gilmore for half a lot sould by ye town, allso 5£—0—0— Recd of ye Governer: of ye town money & 11£ due from cunstable wear to the town in al £112—0—0

Alowed to m^{r} m^{c} Gregor for the rait of one Lott	0—15— 0
To m^{r} James Greg for 4 lotts and saw-mil lott .	4— 8— 9
To m^{r} m^{c} Keen for 4 lotts	3— 0— 0
To Alexand Walker for going with m^{r} Greg on Chester line	4— 0
To John moreson for seting ye Commite . . .	0—10— 6
To John Barnard for the rait of 2 lotts . . .	1—10— 0
To hew mn^{t} Gumery for one lott	0—15— 0
To John m^{c} neel for his rate & comite work. .	1—14— 5
To John Goffe for his raits & commite work . .	3—17— 0
To Alexander Nicols 4£ he paid 8^{s}—9 due to him from the town 11^{s}—10^{d} m^{r} m^{c} keen paid for him 10^{s} for his going down for the clements for the salvement	2—10— 7
To James m^{c}neel for his rait	0—15— 0
To James m^{c} neel for going to ye bank on the towns businis	1— 5— 0
To Archebel Clandenen 1£—1^{s}—0 for work at m^{r} m^{c} Gregors at his flanker & 3 ^{s}—10^{d} due from the town	1— 4—10
To Robart Wear for Caring the prisoners to the bank caling the court a cunstable staf and Charges at Chester	2— 8— 0
To Robart Wear for paper 2^{s} for david beard 8^{d}	0— 2— 8
To Robert Wear for the charges of the prisoners at his hous	0— 4— 8
To m^{r} m^{c} Keen when he went to the sessions at the bank when he got the promis of a gift to the town twords the building the meeting hous	0—19— 8

To Jeremiah osgood b^{d}	15—12— 8
To m^{r} Graves for busines don for ye town . .	0—14—10
To Sam^{ll} Graves for the saw mill	0—10— 0
To m^{r} m^{c} Gregor & m^{r} m^{c} Keen when they went to Governer usher	0—10— 9
To m^{r} Jams m^{c} nell when he went to the bank with the Governer and m^{r} leverets leters & time	1—12— 6
1721 april 14: 17	
To Cap^{tt} Cargill	3— 3—11
To Elizebath moreson	5—11— 0
To Daniel m^{c} fee for going to the bank with the prisoners and making ye town stok of bulits .	0—14— 0
To James Axexander for ledd	0— 2— 0
To m^{r} Keen	2—10— 4
To John Walies part of his note from osgood .	2—10— 5
To Alexander m^{c} neel for his note from osgood .	1— 0— 0
To m^{r} osgood by Andru todds note	1—12— 8
To James blair for going with the prisoners to the bank & 3 shilins ye town owed him . . .	0—13— 0
To Cap^{tt} Cargill by osgoods note	1—10— 4
To m^{r} osgood by note to James more	0—16— 5
To m^{r} osgood by note to Sam^{ll} hewston. . . .	0—10— 4
To m^{r} osgood by note to samuel Graves . . .	0—15— 0
To m^{r} osgood by note to mathew Clerk . . .	0— 7— 0
To m^{r} osgood by note to John Stewart	0— 5— 0
To m^{r} osgood by note to James m^{c} neel . . .	1— 4— 0
To m^{r} osgood by note to Robort Wear	1—10— 0
To m^{r} osgood by note to William Akin or Jno Goffe	0—15— 0
To Cap^{tt} Cargill mony due from ye town . .	0—15— 0
To m^{r} osgood by note to John Crumey . .	4— 8— 9
To m^{r} osgood by note to Robart m^{c} Keen . . .	0—15— 6
To m^{r} James m^{c} neel for going to the bank for the mony the Gentelmen at the bank promised to bestow on the town tword the building of ye meeting hous time & expence	2—10— 0

To m^{r} James m^{c} neel the mony due to him from the for former servis don for the town . . 2—15— 6

To Archbel Wear by his note to James m^{c}neel . 0—12— 0

To Archbel Wear for John bars sons work at m^{r} m^{c}gregor . . . . 1— 3— 0

To Abel merrel for mony due from ye town & hors hyer . . . . 0—12— 6

To James Neasmoth for his hors . . . . 0— 8— 0

To Robart Wear for mony due to him from ye town on old accont: for making ye bar for ye metin hous and drawing the boards to ye meting hous . . . . 2— 3— 0

To Edward Prockter for boards for ye meting hous . . . . 0—15— 0

To William Gregg for sawing stuff for ye meeting hous . . . . 4—10— 0

To Governer wintworth m^{r} penhalow Coll Whealwright and Governer shute mony not to be had in this way . . . . 3— 0— 0

To John mitchel . . . . 0— 8— 6

To what was abated to axnder m^{c}neel for cuting the hyway . . . . 0— 2— 0

To John Barnard . . . . 0—19— 0

To Cap^{tt} Cargill due from the town . . . . . 0—18— 0

To what was abated to cambil for cutin the hyway . . . . 0— 2— 0

To John Senter by note from m^{r} osgood . . 100—12— 4

To edword Prockter by note from osgood . . . 0—15— 0

Apriel ye 18th 1722

Then Reconed with Constable Wear and their Remains due to the town from him in all . . 11— 7— 8

To Hew mn^{t} Gumery . . . . 0—11— 0

To m^{r} m^{c} Gregor . . . . 0—15— 0

To Benjamin Kidder . . . . 0—12— 0

To the comishoners that go to the bank on accounpt of the Town Grant or Charter . . . 0— 7— 0

To Thomas steel under pinin the meting hous . 0—15— 0

John moreson dito	0—10— 0
Sam^el aleson work on ye metin hous	0—15— 0
To John Bell dito	0— 5— 6
To Randal alexander by note from osgood . .	0— 7— 0
To William humphry for drawing boards to the metin hous	0—14— 0
To John [unintelligible]	0—15— 0
To archbel meril by note from osgood . . .	0—10—10
January ye 18th Reconed with Robart Wear remains to the town	3—12— 3
paid to James akin for going to boston & ——	3—17— 8
To James clerk for diging the well at the metin hous	— 9— 6

At a generall town meeting februry ye 14th 1721/22 the town voated for moderater m^r m^c Keen

Chosen for Commite to vew the Common meddows in order to a second devision } Thomas Steel, Stephen Pearce, John Bell

on the above said the Town agreed to chues a suetable number of men for a commite on their next generall meeting to vew the first devision of meddows for such as complain of being wronged in said devision the complainers paying the commite for their labour and the said commite to right thoes that it appears are wronged and to make them equall with their nighbours that have good lotts and so no reason to complain or els to ad so mutch of the common meddows to each devision that wants as to make them sufficiant to mow after the rate of three good load of hay upon each devision

March ye 24 1721/2 the Commite being met to hear the reasons from the persons that have their second devisions in haveril land why they do not setle them and they have heard their reasons) and have given them orders to setle them foarth with or els they may expect to run the hazard of luesing them acording to the agreement of the Commite as it is recorded on said day voated by the commite that William Gilmore shall have his meddow in the white rock meddow

on the said day the commite having cast up how many dais they have sat upon the publick afaiers of this town and finding it to be 20 dais to six of said comtt and ten dais to Joseph Simons and the com[tt] agreed to take their pay in work from the town

paid to m[r] engals for webster	5— 6
to elias kees for webster	5— 0

September y[e] 7th 1722 Then Reconed with Constable Rob[tt] Wear for the year 1721 their remains due to y[e] town	2— 0— 0
paid to Rob[tt] Doak out of his note from osgood .	0— 8— 0
To Robart boys for going to the bank alowed by y[e] comite	10— 0
To Samuel hewston by not from osgood . . .	5— 8
To James Clerk over rated	7— 0
paid to Sam[ll] Aleson by David Crage for ½ lot .	0— 7— 6
paid by m[r] m[c] greger the arears of Jn[o] Clerks half lot	2— 0
paid by will[m] Thompson by note on osgood . .	3— 6

At a Generall Town meeting march y[e] 26th 1722 for Chuesing their town ofisers and they are chosen as followeth

for moderater James Gregg

for Commite Elias Keyes John m[c] Morphy James Gregg Alin Anderson John Wallis Hew mn[t] Gumery James Lindsey

for Clerk John Goffe

men to account with the town John Blair Stephen peirce James neasmoth David Cargill

men Chosen to setel the constabls salery with the Commite Cap[tt] Cargill Jams nicol m[r] more Tho steel John Bell Jams Lassley Joseph simonds

for seveyers of Hy ways Benjamin Willson Alexander nicols Jams Clerk Sam[ll] Graves John m[c]neel for Hog reaves Henery Green John Goffe

for fens vewers John Moreson John Anderson

on said Day the town voated to ad two men to the Commite formerly Choese for laying out the secund devisions of meddows and that the five men so chosen shall have power (after they were chosen and swoarn) to vew and valu the meddows in this town boath devided and undevided and to lay out every mans meddow as conveneant to every propriator as they can find it and the said Cmomite are to have four shilings pr day for their work, and the two men chosen to be aded to the Commite allredy chosen are John more David Cargill

on said day the commite so chosen did appear before the Justis and weir swoarn to the faithfull discharg of their ofis

voated on said day that esekels pond shall be put to a cant to this town Mr More hath bid seventeen pound for Ezekiels pond, on said day the town voated to Give m^r^ more one acre of land by the brest of the above said pond

it is also votted that m^r^ more and partners shall have Ezekiels pond at w^t^ they have bid, the Commite for bounding s^d^ pond is James Alexander John Barnat John Stewart

on said day the town voated that the pond near merrils lott shall be put to a cant m^r^ Graves hath bid 37 pound for said pond

It is also votted that Mr Graves and those w^t^ he has for his partners shall have the afores^d^ pond at w^t^ Mr Graves bid for s^d^ pond

The Commite for bounding, and signing the s^d^ ponds transcript is as followeth

James m^tt^ Keen
James alexander
Thomas Stiel

GEORGE BY THE GRACE OF GOD OF GREIT BRITAIN FRANCE AND IRELAND KING DEFENDER OF THE FAITH &c

To all People to whom these presents shall come Greeting

Know ye that wee of our especial Knowledg and mear motion for the due incuragement of setling new plantations by and with the advis and consent of our Councel Have Given and Granted and by these presents as far as in us lies do Give and Grant in equall shares unto sundry of our beloved subjects whose names are entered unto a schedule hereunto annexed that inhabit or shall inhabit within the said Grant withinin our province of newhampshier all that tract of land within the following bounds being ten miles square or So mutch as as amounts to ten miles squair and no more begining on the north East Angle at a Beach tree marked which is the south east angle of Chester and runing from thence due south on Kings town line Four miles & half & from thence on a west line One mile an three quarters & from thence south six miles and half and from thence west north west nine miles and an half and from thence North Eleven miles and an half from thence north North East Three miles from thence East South East one mile and from thence South South West to the South west angle of Chester and from thence on an East South East line bounding on Chester ten miles unto the Beach tree first mentioned and that the same be a Town Corporate by the name of London Dery to the persons afore said for ever provided never the less and the true intent and meaning of these presents is aney thing to the contrary notwithstanding that nothing in this our sd Grant shall extend to or be understood to extend to Defeet prejudes or make nul and void aney Claim title or pretence which our province of the Massachusets Bay may have to all or any part of the Premesses Granted as afore said or the right Claim property or Demand of aney privet person or persons by reason & means of all or aney part of the sd Granted premesses Falling within the line or boundaries of our said province of the Massachusets To have and To Hold the s^d^ Land to the Grantes their Heirs & Assigns for ever upon the following Conditions (viz)

1st that the propriators of every shier build a dwelling hous within three years and setle a famely their in & brake up three acres of Ground & plant or sow the same within four years and pay his or their proportion of the town charges when and so oftin as occasion shall requier the same

2^{ly} that a meeting hous be built within four years

3^{ly} that upon ye default of aney particular propriator in complying with the condition of this Charter on his part such delinquent propriator shall forfit his share to the other propriators to be dispoused of by voate of the maj^{r} part of the propriators and in case of an indin war within the said four years the said Grantees shall have four years more after the said war is ended for the performance of thoes Conditions

The said men and inhabetants allso rendering and paying for the same to us and our sucsesors or to such ofiser or ofisers as shall be appoynted to recive the same the annual Quit rent or acknowledgment of one peck of potatos on the first day of october yearly for ever reserving allso unto us our Heirs & Sucesers all mast trees Growing on said tract of land according to the acts of Parliment in that behalf made and provided

and for the beter order rule and Gournment of the said Town wee do by these presents Grant for us our Heirs & successors unto the said grantees that yearly & every year upon the fifth day of march for ever except on the lords day and then on the monday next following they shall meet to Elect and choose by the major part of the electors present all Town offisers according to the laws and usage of the other towns within our sd province for the year ensewing with such powers priviledges and authorities as other Town ofisers in our province afore said do injoy

as allso that on every wensday in the weke for ever they may hold keep and injoy a markit for the selling and buying of goods wares marchantdizes and all kind of creatures indowed with the usual prevelidges prophits and imunities as other markit towns usualy hold posses and injoy

and two fairs annually for ever the first to be held or keep within the said Town on the eighth day of october next and so de anno in annum for ever and ye other on the eighth of may in like manner provided that if it should so hapin that if at aney time either of thoes daies fall on the Lords Day then the said fair shall be held and keep the day following and that the sd fair shall have hold and posses the liberties privilidges

& immunities that other fairs in other towns usuly posses Hold & injoy,

in witness whereof we have caused the seal of our said Province to be hereunto affixed witness Samuel Shute Esqr our Gouernor and Commander in cheef of our said province the twenty first day of June anno Domini seventeen hundred twenty two and in the eighth year of our Reign

Samuel Shute

By advice of the Councel Richard Waldron

Cler: Con

A SCHIDULE OF THE NAMES OF THE PROPRIATORS OF LONDON DEREY

	Share.		Share.
John More	1	Thomas Steel	1
Robt Wilson	1	Samuel Allison	1
Saml More	1	John Moreson	1
John Asbel	1	Robt Wear	1
James Doak & John Doak,	1	Alin Anderson	1
Henery Green	1	Mr Mc Gregor & sons	3
Abel Merrel	1	James Neasmoth	1
Randal Alexander	1	James Clerk	1
Robt Doak	1	Wm Gregg	1
Alexander Walker	1	John Gregg	1
John Clerk	1	James Gregg & sons	2
James Anderson	1	Wm Wilson & John Riche,	1
James Alexander	1	David Cargil Ju^{r}	1
James Moreson	1	Wm Thompson	1
John Mitchel	1	Hugh mn^{t} Gumery	1
Archebel Clandenin	1	Robt Moreson	1
John Barnard	1	Alex^{r} M^{c}neel	1
James McKeen & son	2	Robt Boyes	1
Jona Tyler	1	John m^{c} murphe	1
Alexandr Nicols	1	John m^{c} neel	1
James Nicols	1	Wm Cambil	1
Wm Nicols	1	Capt David Cargil	1
Wm Humphery	1	John Asbel Ju^{r}	1

John Bar & sons . . . 2
David Crage & Wm Gilmore, 2
John Stewart 1
Edward Procter . . . 1
Ben Kidder 1
John Gray 1
Joseph Kidder 1
John Goffe 1
Sam^{ll} Graves 1
John Crumey 1
Mathew Clerk 1
James Lindsey 1
James Lassley 1
John Anderson 1
James Blair 1
John Blair 1
James more 1
John Shields . . . . ½
James Rogers . . . . ½
Joseph simonds 1
Elias Keyes 1
John Roby 1
John Senter 1
Rob^{tt} M^{c} keen 1
Jenet Sam^{ll} & John m^{c} ken, 1
Wm Coghran 1
John Peter & Andrew Coghran 1
David Boyle 1
James Greg Saml Graves & Robt Boyes . . . 1
James Aikin 1
Wm Aiken 1
Edward Aiken 1
John Walis 1
Ben^{j} Wilson 1
James m^{c} neel 1
Danl m^{c} dufe . . . . ½
Sam^{ll} Hewston 1
Col John Whealrit . . 1
Andrew Todd 1
John Bell 1
David moreson 1
Sam^{ll} moreson 1
Abraham Holms . . . 1
John Given 1
Willm Aiers 1
Tho: Boyle 1
Eliz Wilson & mary her dater . . . . . . ½
Sam^{ll} Graves Ju^{r} . . . 1
John Goffe Ju^{r} 1
Stephen Peirce 1
Andrew Spauldin . . . 1
Alexander m^{c}murphy & James leget . . . . ½
James m^{c} gregor for servent . . . . . . ½
Capt Cargill for two servents 1
Georg Clerk . . . . . ½
Tho Clerk . . . . . ½
Nehem Giffing . . . . ½
James m^{c} gloughlen . . ½
parsonage lot 1
John barnard Ju^{r} . . . 1
John m^{c} conoghy . . . 1
John m^{c} clurg . . . . ½
John Woodbourn . . . 1
Bening Wentworth . . 1
Richard Walden Ju^{r} . . 1
L Govr Wentworth . . 1
Rob^{tt} Armstrong . . . 1
Rob^{tt} Acmuty 1

The full number of Proprietors in our Charter is one hundred & twenty four and an half personage lot and all 124/½

Memorandom over and above what is all redy given in this schedule is added to

m^r^ m^c^ Gregor . .	250	acres
m^r^ m^c^ Keen . .	250	"
m^r^ David Cargill .	100	"
m^r^ James Gregg .	150	"
John Goffe . .	100	"
	850	"

and to the two last mentioned (viz) Gregg & Goffe a mill streem within the said Town for their good servis in promoting the settlement of the Town

Rich: Waldin Cler Con*

New Hampshier June y[e] 21: 1722

admited propriators & Commoners in the Town of London Derey with the persons mentioned in this sheduel

His Exelensy Gover: Shute a home lot & . . .	500	acres
his honer L Gour Wentworth a home lot & . .	500	. .
Sam[ll] Penhalow	1	share
marke Hunking	1	
Georg Jeffry	1	
Shad[a] Walton	1	
Richart Wiberd	1	
Tho[s] Westbrook	1	
Tho[s] Perker	1	
Archi m[c] pheadres	1	

Rich Waldron Cer Con

May y[e] 31 1722 the Commite being mett they have for good reasons agreed that the half lott which was given to Capt[tt] Wainright shall be given to David Criage

the Commite Cosen to lay out the second Devisions of Commons are as followeth

David Cargill
John m[c] morphy
Will[m] Aikin

* Clerk of Council.—ED.

at a Town meeting July ye 9th 1722 voated for moderater Sam^{ll} more

on said day voated that m^r Gregg shall be no longer in the Commite

on said day voated that three men shall be aded to the Commite

for Commite John more James Nicols Sam^{ll} Graves

on said day voated that 5 men be Chosen as a commite to look out the land for the men that are to have land in this town mentioned in the Charter the names of the Commite are

John more
Joseph Simonds
Sam^{ll} Graves
John mitchel
Alexander Nicols

Memorandom it is to be noted here by that all the transactions of the above mentioned meeting upon July ye 9th 1722 is wholey void

Londonderry July 1723

Wheras the town thought fit march 1723 to chuce us for the regulation of their meadows and for the bounding and limiting meadows and fences of meadows we therefore for the conveniency of sundry fences have Given Liberty to cut a cross neeks of Land where no propriety is to hinder wth meadows will be known upon Inquerey yet notwithstanding S^d Liberty y^t no person pretend to Claim any mans propriety or the town Commons further then two Rhods up any swamp further then what is Laid out to them for meadow

David Cargill
John Bell
alen anderson
John Mitchell
Committe

Recorded this 26th of february 1723/4

Pr John M^{tt} Murphy Town Clark

At a Generall town meeting march ye 5 1722/3 for the Chuesing their town ofisers and they are Chosen as followeth

for moderater James Nicols

on said day voated that five men shall be chosen to agree with the select men for their wages on the towns afaiers

for select men

Sam^ll more
James Nikols
John Blair
Benjamin Willson
Rob^tt Boyes

for Town Clerk John Mc Murphy

for Constable James Neasmoth

the above said James neasmoth being a comishon ofiser refueseth to serve their is an other to be chosen in his room

for Constable James Clerk

for serveyers James Aikin Willm Humphery Rob^tt Doak Sam^ll Graves Willm Thompson

fens vewers Sam^ll Aleson Willm Caldwell

for Hog Reaves Sam^ll Graves Willm Humphery

the Com^tt to set the selectmens wages Tho Steel James moreson Whi^m Aiers John Goffe David Cargill

on said day voated that hogs shall be yoaked from the 15 of march to the last of october

voated that the select men shall have power to agree with the commite that have laid out the second devision to lay out thoes that yet remain to be laid out

voated to lay out the land given in the town Charter to m^r m^c Gregor m^r m^c Keen Cap^tt Gregg m^r Cargill & John Goffe

Commite for laying out the farms to the men above named John more Elek Nicols John mitchel Sam^el Graves wil^l Aiken

Mr Mc Keen

voted the selectmen shall have power to agree with the com^tt to lay out the above said farms voated that the selectmen shall have power to chues a serveyer and lot layers to go with the said commite to lay out the above said farms

voated also that the diferance betwen m^{r} m^{c} Keen and his nibours about the hy-way to go threw the 13 acre meddow shall be left to the select men to deside

on said day voated that Jeremiah osgood shall have a tract of land alowed him in the common lands in this town as a consideration for his loss in his work about the meeting hous in this town

voated that the said Jeremiah osgood shall have one hundred acres in satisfaction for his work

On said day the town voated that the fairs and markits shall be held at the meeting hous

voated that the pound shall be made by the meeting hous

voated that the pound shall be built this spring before June next ensewing

voated that a commite shall be chosen to vew the home steed meddows and valu them and amend them out of the common meddows as it is recorded in page ye 24th and in page ye 20

the men chosen for the com^{tt} as above said are

John Bell
Sam^{ll} Graves
Alin Anderson
John mitchel
Hugh mn^{t} Gumery

John Walis hath got the pond above senters one acre meddow upon a cant for 4£—5^{s}—0^{d} and hath obledged him self to pay it in boards for the use of the meeting hous white pine at the rate of thirty five shilings pr thousand and pitch pine at the usual rate voated that all persons shall have the liberty to bring in catle to the town so as to make up the mumber of six with his own catle & no more and thoes that have catle of their own have the liberty to bring in the number of ten if they bring a bull with them other wise to bring in none voated that the select men shall have power to take what methods they shall think fit for the securing the fishery at ameskeeg

a commite chosen for setling the accompts of the town with constable Wear and John m^c murphy upon the 6 day of this instant march and the Com^tt so chosen are

David Cargil
John Blair
James neasmoth

voated that Jese Criste shall be cleared of the publick raits of this town for two years from the time of his purchising his land of the town except the ministers rate

At alegale atown meetting held at Londonderry aprill the 29th 1723 the town Chuse for moderator Ro^t Boys

the said town meetting is consentibly adjurned to may the 13th 1723 at 9 of the cloak in the forenoon

The town meet according to adjurnment

The said Day the town votted that three men shall be a Comttee to Lay out the wants of homesteads and what amendments the town wants,

the names of the Committee is ass followeth (viz)

David Cargill Jur
Will aiken
John m^tt murphy

the said day votted that the men for Laying out the above Land the men y^t wants sd Land have it to repair and know of them when they shall met

The said day voted that the select shall disposs or Improve the ash swamp that Lyes to the east of the Beaveor River to the towns Benefit

At aGenerall town meetting June the 27th 1723

The town Chuse for moderator Mr M^tt Keen at a Town meeting october the 25th 1723 The town Chuse for moderator Samuell moore the said day the town voted that all persons thats presed upon the publick conserns of the town by the constable shall be allowed in wages two shill and six pence and no more pr day the said day the town votted that the select men shall have power to agree with every proprietor that the town takes of their Land for High ways with respect to the fencing and that the town will be oblidged to build and keep up and that they are to allow them the usuall prise of stone wall, and said price of stone wall to be allowed in their town rats till it is payd up from year to year this present rate and the ministers rats only excepted

At a Town meeting held at Londonderry January the 20th 1723/4

The town Chuse for moderator Robert Boys

The town then Chuse that day fo a Committe to joyn Chaster Committe to adjost the town line and Chuse a Sirvayor as also to run the towns south line betwen us and Haverhill

Capt Gregg
David Cargill
John mt murphy

also the town voted that their should be some men Chosen to try at what prise they can have the lover story of the meetinghouse silled and the house seated at the publick Charge of the town

also voted Said day that the proprietors shall have agenerall lot for their Seats according to their propriety they paying equall Cost and Charges for the same

also the town voted to Chuse four men to make the aforesaid tryall the men are these

Capt Gregg
Lev:t Goffe
James Alexander
alexander nickels

also voted that the lover story shall be seated all alike with pews

also voted that the town is willing to give land for what High ways takes of their lots as also land for what nesisary fences these High ways ocasions to all Such as will take up with the same also the town voted yt the town shall make up the fences that the High ways ocasione at the publick Charge of the town that goes throu the thirtine acre meadow upon the Commons as also all other quarters of the town that has arod of like priviledge of arod upon the Commons S^d rod shall be pay'd by the town and they shall have arod

also the town voted that the Committe that was Chosen to lay out the second divisions wants of homesteads and mendements shall lay out wants of homesteads and mendments quantety for quality distance and conveniency considered the names of the men are these

David Cargill Jur
William aiken
John M^tt murphy

An Act or By Law made by the Select men and other Persons Chosen by the town at their annuall meeting march the 5th 1723/4 to Joyne with the Select men in makeing Laws for the publik good of our town of London derry in the Prov: of New Hamper:— on the above said day it is ënacted and agreed upon by the S^d Select men and others Chosen as above S^d that all Persons that are Proprietors of our Town shall have liberty of Cutting timber upon the Town Commons so much as they shall need for the makeing of anysort of waires for the use and benifitt of the Inhabitants of S^d Town an no more & all Persons that Stand in need of Timber upon the Common are to apply themselves to the Selectmen as often as they have ocasion to Cut Timber upon S^d Commons for the use afores^d or for fire wood But whereas Great distinction hath been made upon the Good timber in the Town by Reason of some Persons Cutting the timber and letting it ly—upon the Ground and others Improving the Good Timber in making staves for a market out of the Town for their own private advantage so that the Town is like to be Greatly Impovished for want of Good Timber for the Preventing of any further distructione of the timber upon the Commons it is enacted on S^d day that no persons hearafter shall have Liberty to cut any timber upon the Commons to make sale of out of the town for their own Privat

Intrest and all Persons that shall presume to cut any Timber upon the Common Lands Shall forefit and pay to the Select men of our town for the use of S^{d} town twenty Shills for every tree that Shall be found fell and twenty Shills for every thousand of Staves that Shall be found split upon the Commons afores^{d} and if the person that have cut the timber cannot be found then the selectmen are by Virtue of this Law Impowered to seis upon S^{d} timber for the use of S^{d} town

David Cargill
James Alexander
Robert Boyd
John Blair
John Moor
John M^{tt}Murphy
James Greg
James M^{tt}Keen
John Goffe
Andrew todd
James Moreson

Province of New Hampshire
at his majesties Court of Generall Q^{r} sessions of the peace holden at portsmouth the 2^{d} day of June 1724

Present Rich^{d} waldron Sam^{ll} Penhalw George Jaffrey Rich^{d} wibard Shad. Walton John Plaisted Jotham Odiorne Peter Wear & nath^{ll} Sergant Esqr
Justices

The within by Law Being read and Confirmed its ordered by the Court that the same be allowed approved and Confirmed

Theodore Atkinson Cler

Vera Copia Theodore Atkison Cler
Recorded this 10th of march 1724/5

John M^{tt}Murphy Town Clark

Twesday ye 23^{d} of February 1724/5

We the Subscribers being upon oath and being Inployed by the Commits of Chester and Londonderry to run the line betwon the S^{d} two towns, we began at the Beach tree on the westerly side of Kingstown, which is the Corner bounds of y^{e}

above S[d] towns we Run ten miles on a west norwest point without any allowance for Crookedness of way and ran to masabesick River

James Stevens Sirvayer
Benjamin Barker
John Carton
Chair men

The Commite y[t] was Chosen and was along with the above S[d] men, Chaster Commite was

Samuel Ingols
Thomas Smith
Commite

Londonderrys Commite was

James Gregg
David Cargill
John M[c]Murphy
Commite

Recorded this 5th of March 1724/5
John M[tt]Murphy Town Clark

At a Generall Town meeting march the 5th 1723/4 for the Chuseing of their town officers and they are Chosen as followeth

for moderator Robert Boys

the town then aggreed to have five select men for this Enshewing year

for select men
John Blair
Robert Boys
John more
James Alexander
Will[m] Cochran

For Town Clark John m[tt] murphy

also voted yt they shall pay aConstable and his wagess is aggreed upon by the town to be fifty shill pr year also the town Chuse to serve for this enshowing as Constable James Leslie for survayers

Willm Gregg
Thomas Stiele
David Cargill
John anderson
John Senter

for tithing men

John Stewart
Lev^{t} John Goffe

for hawards

Mathew Clark
John Bell
Gabriel Barr

for fence viewers and prizerss

Alexander nickels
Sam^{ll} Graves

also the town voted that they shall Endeavor to make aby Law to preserve the town Commons from being Destroyed by Cutting the timber and other needfull preservations the men that wre voted for and Chosen for making the aforesaid by Laws are these

Mr M^{tt} Keen
Lev^{t} Goffe
Capt Cargill
Capt Gregg
Lev^{t} Todd
Sam^{ll} Graves
John m^{tt} murphy

John m^{tt} murphy

also voted the same day that their shall be aschol house built in this town, the demension of s^{d} house is to be sixtine foot Long and twelve foot Brenth S^{d} house is to be alogg house seven foot side wall

also voted that they shall come to asecond view of the home lots

John Dinsmoore having petitioned the town for atract of Land the town Considered to bestow S^{d} Dinsmore Sixty acres of Good land in some Convenient place and S^{d} man is to Setle this place in the space of a year after the peace is Concluded and if so be that he or his son does not Setle S^{d} place against the perfixt time y[t] then and at y[t] time S[d] land Shall fall to the town or S[d] grantees John mitchell James & John morison and Ro[t] Doak denies S[d] vote

also voted y[t] three men Shall view the homelots and they are to be viewed as at the first view the men are these

John Moore
Thomas Stiele
John Blair

the men for the trying the towns accounts with the sellect men or town assesors are these

James nesmith
David Cargill
John Blair

At atown meeting June y[e] 25th 1724

The town then Chuse for moderator John Blair

Att a Generall Town meetting march y[e] 5th 1724/5 for the Chusing of their town officers, and they are Chosen as followeth

For modrator John Blair

For Town Clark John M[tt] Murphy

The Town votted and aggreed that they shall have for this enshewing year five Select men

For Select men

James Aieken — Sam[ll] Graves
Ro[t] Boys — John Mitchell
James Morrison

For Town Constable James Leslie

For Sirvayers

Patrick Douglas — Robert M[tt] Keen
James Anderson — Gabriel Barr
James Rodgers

For Tithingmen

Thomas Stiel — William Cochran

For Hawards

James Calwell — Thomas Bogle
John M[tt] Conehey

For fence viewers and prizers

John Archibald, South
Alexander Renkine
John Wallace

It is also votted on the aforesaid day that the five men y^t Regulated the meadows before, shall go out again and make as near aregulation as their Judgments afford to all such person as are not yet not made up, the names of the men is as followeth (viz)

David Cargill — Sam^{ll} Graves
John Mitchell — John Bell
Alen Anderson

It is also votted on the aforesaid day that the homesteads Lotts is to be viewed according to the directions y^t y^e Commite y^t viewed the Lots before or according as the nature of their views was, as also it is votted that John Stewarts home Lott shall be the precept to the men that shall be Chosen for the aforesaid viewe the names of the men is as followeth

John Blair
$Will^m$ Aieken
John m^{tt} murphy

It is also votted that their is another man Chosen to viewe in the absence of John Blair the name of the man is as followeth James Clark it is also votted that the wages of the men that are to viewe the home lots is to be three shill pr, lott, and if any person desire to have other lot measured in lenth they shall pay for it themselves

The men for trying the towns accounts with the select men is as followeth (viz)

James nesmith
David Cargill
John M^{tt} Murphy

It is votted on the aforesaid day that John Senter shall be overseer in the building and repairing of the bridge that is to be build at ye Lower end of the pond and he shall be allowed at the rate of two Shill and sixpence p^{r} day, and ye overseer shall warn the sirvayers to Come w^{t} their men as the select men sees the severall town highways are to be repaired by much Labour or litle, and if the sirvayer be delinquent the overseer shall have power to hire men in the sirvayer or sirvayers

It is votted y^{t} two men shall go and view and mark out aroad from this town to tower hill the men is as followeth

Capt Gregg Jo: mitchell

It is votted that their shall no person bring in any strange Cattele to this town w^{t}out Liberty from the select under the pain of forfiting the sume of six shill— for every head that they shall be known to bring

At atown meetting April ye 22^{ed} 1725 The town Chose for Moderator John Mitchell

It is votted on the above S^{d} day that their shal be a school in each quarter of the town if their can be sutable persons found for keeping the same, for six monsths time from their Comencent

At atown meetting Septembr ye 17th 1725 The Town Chose for Moderator—John Mc Neal

on the aforesaid day the Town votted that the Bridge at the Lower end of Beaver pond shall be Built by a rate

It is also votted on the aforesaid day that Robert Boys shall build ye bridge at ye Lower end of Beaver pond sufficiently from hard Ground on each side and further that the afores^{d} Robert Boys shall be oblidged to Keep up in Good repair for the space of two years from the time that he shall finish the same aforesaid bridge, and shall have for his makeing building and Keeping up the same bridge for the time aforesaid the sume of twelve pounds Currant and passeble Bils of Credit, and ten days work out of the publick work of the Town as he shall call for from the severall quarters of the Town, and further that the s^{d} bridge is to be build and repaired w^{t} round pouls, and oak pouls above the arches, and oak streamers above the arches and further that the afores^{d} Ro^{tt} Boys shall have povor to Cutt timber upon the ministeriall Lott to repair and build said Bridge, and that the said Robert Boys shall be oblidged to finish said bridge at or before the first of January next Enshewing

Robert Boyes

It is also votted on the aforesaid day that James Leslie shall be paid for his Carring Belnapp to Dunstable to Co^{ll} Things house

It is also votted on ye afores^{d} day that four men shall sitt w^{t} with the select men to make arate for this Enshewing year and to reviw all Just dew debts y^{t} the town ows as als to add thirty pound in this year's rate to buy stuff for the repairing the meetting house

the name of the men is as followeth

Mr James m^{c} Keen
Lev^{t} Todd
James Linsday
David Cargill

At atown Meeting Nov^{br} ye 29th 1725 the town Chuse for moderator James Alexander on s^{d} day the town votted that two men shall be Chosen to Goo to the Recorder to have the Charter put on Record

The two men that are Chosen to Go with the Charter to have it put upon Record is as followeth James Alexander John M^{tt} Murphy

The town Have votted on said day that their is no school to be Keept in this town for this winter

At A General Town meeting hold at Londonderry March ye 5th 1725/6

The town Chose for moderator

For Moderator Robert Boys

For Town Clark John Mc Murphy

It is also votted on s^{d} Day that five men shall be Chosen for Select men

For Select men

James Alexander.
John Moor.
Robert Boys.
Sam^{ll} Graves.
Abraham Holms,

It is also votted on ye aforesaid day that by his own Consent the town Chuse for town Constable James Leslie

and he is by the vote of the town to have for his wages the time past that he has serv'd and this present year three pound ayear for his raiseing the town rates and the ministers

For Sirvayers

John Wilson
Alexander Walker
Alexander m^c Murphy
John Stewart
Robert Morison

For Tithing-men

John Barrat
Edward Aiken

For Hawards

John Senter,
Samuel Morison,
Thomas Wilson,

For fence veiwers and prizers

James Rodgers,
$Will^m$ Gregg,

It is also voted on the above s^d Day that the proprietors are satisfied and Designed to Lay out athird division of Land and that the third Division be Laid out fivety acres to each proprietor that have afull right in the town and that said land shall be laid out Quantity and Quality to Be Considered by the Committee that shall be Chose to lay out the same and it is further votted on the aforesaid day that that their shall be three men Chosen for a Committee to Lay out the third Division of Land, besides the sirvayer

The names of the men is as followeth

John Mitchell
Thomas Stiel
John m^c murphy,

It is also votted that the town Chuse for Constable

John Mitchell.

It is also voted that the town Chuse for Sirvayers to Lay out the third division of Land David Cargill Junr

It is also votted that there shall be aschool set up in Each quarter of the town for the Learning of the youth

It is also votted that the Committee for the subdivideing of the meadow's shall have three days to finish the meadow's of the town and after wards to be dismised for Ever

The men to setle the town account is

David Cargill
James Nesmith
John m[c] murphy

It is also votted that the select men for the time being shall sign a Quit Claim Deed to James adam's of that Land that he bought from James m[c] Neal

At a Proprietory Meeting held at Londonderry June y[e] 16: 1726

The town Chose for moderator Robert Boys

It is votted on the said day that their shall no person or persons or proprietor whatsovever have any land that is or shall be laid out, for want of homelott or mendements laid out in any part of our township within three miles of merrimack River upon the Common

It is votted on the aforesaid day that their shall be three men Chosen as Committe to veiwe the home lotts in the second veiws & to make Every proprietor's lot in our town Equivolent with the precept that said Committee is to Judge by, which is the home lot of John Stewart & the number of acres that they Judge Each proprietor to want, is Granted & ordered to be laid out to them by the lot layers, of our town, the names of the Com[ttee] is*

Samuel Graves
Hugh Muntgomery
James Rodgers
Comitt

It is also votted on said day that the three men Chosen to veiwe the home lots is to finish the aforesaid veiwe by the tenth day of September next, and make return of their doings to the Select men in alist of what Evry man is to have or whett the said Committe allows them

At atown meetting held at Londonderry July ye 15th 1726.

The town Chose for moderator Robert Boys on the aforesaid Day the town have aggreed to Keep a Gramer School,

Also votted on the aforesaid day that David m^{c} Gregor is Chosen by vote of thetown to Keep aGramer school for this year David m^{c} Gregor,

It is also votted on the aforesaid day that Every person and persons that have any land allowed them by the Committee for viewing the lots, shall have their land by Lott, but no old Grant Demolis'd that have already put in their Claim said Claim to break no form of Land, and no person from the Date of this record is to putt in any Claim untill ye Committee for viewing the Lots make there return

Att atown meeting held at Londonderry octobr ye 24th 1726

The town Chuse for moderator Capt David Cargill,

It is votted on the said day that all wants of homesteads and mendements that are to be laid out is to be laid out, but the land is first to be formed and then made in rangess to the best advantage or Benefit of this town, to the Best of the Committee's Judgment that lays out the aforesaid mendments and wants of homestead's

It is also votted on the aforesaid Day that three men shall be Chosen to lay out Convenient Rods to the several neighbouring towns from the highways already laid out, and said Rods or high ways to be laid out to the benefit of the Common lands that is to be laid out for mendements and want of home steads, the aforesaid Rods is to be laid out in the Convenientest Ground that can be found, Leading straight to the places after mentioned (viz) one Road to Haverhill one to Methewins one to Dracut one to Dunstable and one Road to amiscige, and one to netecook, the names of the men is ass followeth

Capt James Gregg
m^{r} John Moore
m^{r} Willm Aiken
Com^{tte}

*This has been traced in recent years so it is not certain it is an exact copy of the original paragraph.—ED.

It is also votted on the aforesaid Day that James moore that was once proprietor in this town, shall have the land that the several proprietor's Doth bestow upon him the said Moore, of their mendment land and Shall have s[d] Land in a Convenient place where he Shall Chuse, but the said Choise to break no form of land nor Demolish any old Grant

It is also votted on the aforesaid Day that Evry proprietor hear present is willing and satisfied to have the third Division laid out, and bear their Equall shares of all the Charges that shall or may arise by setleing the said third Division of Land, from time to time, and it is aggreed by the persons present that the selectmen shall send out the Com[tte] when they please, to Lay out the third Divisions of Land

at atown meeting Held at Londonderry Nov[r] y[e] 14th 1726!

The town Chuse for moderator James alexander

It is votted on the aforesaid Day that the third Division of Land is to be laid out on the River of merrimack from the Lower End of the Intervaile of Noticook, and so up on the aforesaid River, ass farr ass the Committee that lays out the said third Division shall think Good for the publick Benefit of the said settlement

It is also votted on the afores[d] Day, that Every four proprietors in this town, shall setle one Inhabitant on the one fourth Lott thorowout, the whole setlement, of the third division of Land, and Evry person that will not comply with this vote shall joyn together and take their rights in the one End of the afores[d] setlement and if they lose their rights threw aCouse of Law in their own Default by nonsetleing their third Division, they shall lose it to themselves and the town shall not be obliged to make up their third Division to those men &

It is also voted on the aforesaid day that all proprietors in this town that havenot had their home lott's viewed shall have the priviledge of haveing their lotts viewed by the Committee that was allowed by the town to view the home lotts and they shall have liberty for said views any time before the Last day of Deceber next Enshewing &c

It is also votted on the aforesaid Day, that the return that the Committee for viewing the lotts have made, shall be returned to them from the select men, and they shall make their return to Evry proprietor that have been veiwed by them, or have not veiwed at all acording to the highest veiwe or ——— that any proprietor have, Except those proprietors that was themselves Contented with what was allowed them in the first veiw

At a Generall town meeting held at Londonderry March ye 6th 1726/7

the town Chose for Moderator Robert Boys
For town Clerk John Mc Murphy

It is aggreed and Concluded upon on the aforesaid Day that five — men Shall serve ass select men for the Enshewing year, the names of the men is ass followeth

John Moor
Thomas Stiel
Alexander Renkins
John Woodburn
Samuel Graves

It is also votted on the aforesaid Day that the the town Chose a Constable for this Enshewing year and that he shall have for his service three pounds the name of the Constable is ass followeth

Samuel Barr

For tithing men

Robert Wilson
William Eyers

For Sirvayers

James Morison
John Archibald South

It is voted on the aforesaid day that their shall be a sirvayee in the north side of west runing brook the name of the man is ass followeth

Robert Boys
John Blair
William Adams
John Bell
James Nesmith

For Hawards — Robert McKeen
William Humphra

For fence viewers and prizers — Archibald Clandine
James Lindsay

It is also voted on the aforesaid Day that the second viewe is approved of by the town in Generall, and that the Committees return signed under their hands for ye aforesaid second viewe, Shall be put on Record ass their return is made by them

It is also votted on the aforesaid Day that their shall be asirvayer Chosen and sworn for Laying out the wants of homesteads and Highway Land and mendements that are to be laid out in this town the mans name is David Cargill

It is also votted on the aforesaid Day that three men shall serve ass a Committee for Laying out the wants of homesteads and High way Land and mendements that are to be laid out in this town the names of the men is ass followeth

Andrew Todd
Willm Aiken
John McMurphy

It is also votted on the aforesaid Day that their shall be but one School keept up at the publick Charge of the town for the Enshewing year

It is also votted on the aforesaid Day that their shall no proprietor nor any man that have any share of apropriety have any land laid out, nor an Equall Lott with the rest of the proprietor's untill they pay their Equall share of all the town rates or Charges that are Legally Dew by them.

It is also voted on the aforesaid Day that three men shall be Chosen to try the Select mens account, or towns accounts

David Cargill
James Nesmith
John McMurphy

At atown Meeting held at Londonderry May ye 1st 1727,
The town Chuse for Moderator—John Blair

It is votted and aggreed upon onthe aforesaid Day that

the publick school shall be Keept at the meetinghouse, for five months from the date of this record, and the other six months, the school shall be Keept in the out parts of the town where it shall be thought most Convenient,

It is also votted on the aforesaid Day that their shall be two men Chosen for takeing out what Coppy's of Records they see cause out of the town Books, the names of the men is ass followeth John Blair James Nesmith

It is also votted that their shall be a school house built at the Meetinghouse ass soon ass possible the demensions of said house is to be Eighteen foot besides the Chimney, and that their shall be two fire places in one End ass large ass the house will allow, and it shall be built seven foot in the side wall w[t] logs

It is also votted on the aforesaid day that the Committee that was runing Chester west nor west line shall have no more wages than Committees have formerly had which was four shillings p[r] day.

It is also votted that that artickle of Rateing the town after the manner of the province is dropped at this time.*

At apropprietory meeting held at Londonderry July the 3[d] 1727, the town Chuse for Moderator—John Blair

It is votted on the aforesaid Day that the proprietors of this town is willing to defend the rights of our Charter from all Incrochers, that do not setle in any part of our town legaly, and all trespasses of any soever.

It is also votted on the aforesaid day that the town have Chuse a Committee for for this present year to Defend our Charter rights from all Incrochers, and that three men shall serve ass a Committee for said Ends, the Commi[ttee's] names is ass followeth John Mitchell John Senter—Robert Boys

*In the House of Representatives May the 10th 1727 A. M.

Voted......That Londonderry be Taxed this yeare for the Province Tax the Sume of forty pounds; and that they bring in a list of their Rateabl Estates with the other Towns Next May Sessions in the Same Manner.

James Jeffry Clr assm.

On the aforesaid day the town have Discharged that said Committee of the office to which they were Chosen, and have Committed the trust of said Business to the select men for the time being.

And it is further votted and aggreed upon that any person that will come and Inform, the select men or Constable, of any person trespassing on our Commons, shall have five shillings paid them for their pains.

It is also votted on the aforesaid day their shall no land laid out in this town, untill their be another proprietory meeting.

It is also votted on the aforesaid day that their is a Considerable number of the proprietors of this town that are aggived at the Caryings on of the late Committee (viz) John Macmurphy Willm Aiken, Andrew Todd and David Cargill in their laying out of the mendment land in said town we do theirfore at aGenerall town Meeting on the above said day protest against all their proceedings in laying out of any land in said town Except the second division's which they were sworn too, Either heartofore or for the future.

It is also votted on the aforesaid day that three men shall be Chosen for takeing an Invoice of the rateable pols in this town, ass also to valoue the rateable Estates the mens names is ass followeth.

Lev^t John Goffe
Mr John Moore
Mr John Wallace

It is also votted on said Day that Benjam Wilson shall have the offer of his second Division in the Common land where Samuel Renkine have boxt the pines on the Common's, It is also votted on the aforesaid Day that Governour Wentworth shall have the Remender of his farm laid out according ass the second Division's have been laid out.

Londonderry July ye 3^d 1727.

You are hearby required to warn the proprietors of this town to meet at the meeting house of Londonderry upon

Munday the seventeenth Instant at Eight of the Cloock in the forenoon then and there.

1st To see if the town will Chuse a Committee for the laying out of what land the proprietors of this town thinks fit to lay out.

2ly That the town may hear the Complaints of the proprietors Concerning the unlegall proceedings of the lot-layers and to Corect any unjust act of the Lotlayers.

3ly To see if the town will vote the former Committes acts and records unlegall unjust null and void.

4ly To see if any act of the lotlayers shall be put on record before a return be made and aproved by the town.

5ly To see if the proprietors of this town will make Choise of a new town Clerk.

6ly To see if why the town Clerk refusess proprietors votes.

7ly That the town may see how they will have the meetinghouse finish'd

8 To see if the town will give Mr Butterfield the farm he Claims in this he paying what his artikles binds him too.

John Moore
Samuel Graves
Thomas Stiel

To Samuel Barr town Constable.

At aproprietory meeting held at Londonderry July ye 17th 1727.

The proprietors votted for Moderator.........John Blair.

It is voted on the aforesaid day that the town shall Chuse a Comttee for laying out what lands the think fitt, the said Committee going out when the town and select men think fitt, They being upon oath for the aforesaid busines. The names of the men that is Chuse for a Committee is ass followeth. Thomas Stiele Samll Graves Jon Mitchell

It is voted on the aforesaid day that upon Complaint of the proprietors against John Macmurphy and David Cargill and Wm Aiken as aCommittee to lay out the mendment land, is that they were not lawfully qualified by oath to lay out any mendment lands and that they have laid out very great tracts of lands to themselves Contrary to the minds of the town and to their benefit. It is voted on the aforesaid day that the former Committes acts and records are unlegall unjust null and void.

This may signify to all Concerned y[t] we do hearby decent from and protest against our being concerned in a vote, wherein the town have votted against the proceedings of the Committee, they being legaly Chosen, for laying out of mendments and wants of homesteads, wherein they vote that they have done Contrary (viz)

The said Committe to y[e] mind of the proprietors notwithstanding they Chuse them for that purpose, also against their voting said Committees acts and records to be null and void.

David Cargill
John MacMurphy
James Rodgers
Robert Boyes

It is voted on the aforesaid day that their shall no land be put upon record before a return be made, and aproved by the town.

It is voted on the aforesaid day that the town will not proceed in that at present to Chuse another town Clerk.

It is voted on the aforesaid day that the town will not proceed in that of the town Clerk's refuseing to take proprietors votes

It is voted on the aforesaid day that three men shall be Chosen to lay down amethod to y[e] town with the advise of a workman how the meetinghouse shall be seated and repaired, the names of the men is as followeth Cap[t] Gregg M[r] John Wallace and M[r] John Moore

It is voted on the aforesaid day that M[r] Butterfields farm shall be made up ahundred acres of upland besides his two acres of meadow as soon as the first Committee for Laying out land shall be sent out, and when said land is laid out in full, the select men for the time being are hearby Impowered by this vote to Give the said Butterfield a quit Claim Deed, of said land, Weell Executed in the Law

Londonderry, September ye 2^{ed} 1727

You are hearby required to warn the proprietors of this town to meet at the meetinghouse upon thursday the 5th of october at Eight of the Clock in the forenoon then & there

1st That the town may take some prudent method to regulate the Differances that are and have been in the town about Equivolant land

2^{ly} To see if the town will help those lots that are miserable and what and what method they will take to help them

3^{ly} To see whether the town will order the Committee Chosen for the third Divisions, to lay out what land the town sees Cause to lay out

John Moore
Alex^{r} Renkine
Thomas Stiell
Sam^{ll} Graves
Select

To Sam^{ll} Barr town Constable

At aproprietory Meeting held at London Derry October ye 8th 1727.

The town Chus for Moderator.............John Morison

It is voted on the aforesaid day that the Committee that was Chosen to lay out what land the town thinks fitt shall be Qualified by oath when Called to it by the town.

Londonderry october ye 9th (?) 1727.

You are hearby required to warn the proprietors of this town to meet at the meetinghouse upon wensday the 25th Instant at ten of the Clock in the forenoon then and there.

1st To see if the town will make Choise of a Committee for to Defend the Charter Rights of this town.

2^{ly} To see if the town will allow those proprietors that have not paid to the expence of the meetinghouse building, apart, they paying their proportionable part to the building and finishing said house,

3ly To see if the town will Impower men to aggree for the finishing the meetinghouse and that the town may propose the method to do it.

4ly To see what the town will do about takeing an Invoice.

John Moore
Samuel Graves
Thomas Stiel
Alexr Renkine

To Samuel Barr Town Constable

At apropriety meeting held at Londonderry october ye 25th 1727.

The town votted and Chuse for moderator......John Blair

1st It is votted on the above said Day that three men shall serve ass a Comttee to Defend the Charter Rights of this town the names of the men is ass followeth. John Mitchell, John Moore and John Blair

2ly It is aggreed upon that the second artikle in the warrant is Deferred till afterwards.

3ly It is aggreed and votted on said Day that three men shall serve ass a Committee to aggree with the workman, and give their Bond for the repairing of the meeting house, and that they shall agree with aworkman by the Great, the mens names is ass followeth,

Mr James Mackeen,
Capt Gregg & Mr John Moore,

4ly It is votted on said Day that the town will not take an Invoice.

Londonderry Novbr ye 3d 1727

You are hearby Required to warn the proprietors of this town to meet at the meeting house upon saterday the Eighteenth Instant at Eight of the Clock in the forenoon then and there

1st To see if the town will Choose a Committee to let that house that Pisley Cause build on our town's land together with what land is needfull to be leat and least for one year.

2ly To see if the town will make Choise of athird Committee man to Joyn Thomas stiel and John Mitchell for laying out land

Alexr Renkine
John Moore
Thomas stiell
Samll Graves

To Samuel Barr town Constable.

At apropriietory meeting held at Londonderry Novbr ye 18th—1727

The town Chuse for Moderator............James Aiken

It is voted on the aforesaid day that the town will not Chuse a Committee to let that house that Pisley Caus'd build.

It is votted on the aforesaid day that the town will not Chuse a third Committee man to Joyn Thomas Stiel and John Mitchell for laying out land.

Londonderry Novbr ye 18th 1727,

You the hearby required to warn the proprietors of this town to meet at the meetinghouse the first wensday of December at Eight of the Clock in the forenoon then and there.

1st To see if the town will Chuse aCommittee of Indifrent men to lay out what land the town sees Cause, and to Consider the method that they will lay out said land

2ly To see if the town will Chuse aCommittee to let that house that Pisley Caused build on the Peeik land, with what land is needfull to be lett, or what method the town will take with it.

3ly To see if the town will pass avote, that if any person loos land laid out to them in this town by their not setleing, shall to have it made up by the town

4^{ly} To see what lawshuts the town will allow of, and bearthe Charge of and whether, and whether it be Consistent with the towns Intrest to continue the Committee chosen for to defend the Charter rights or to take some Other Method.

5^{ly} To see if the town will think fitt to take an Invoice of the poles and Estates acording to law.

6^{ly} That the town may make Choise of a Representitive to answer for ye town*

John Moore
Alexander Renkine
Samuel Graves
Thomas Stiel
John Woodburn
Select

*In the House of Represent May 21st 1725

Wheras The Town of Londo Derry hath lived under this Government for Several Years past, and hath neither as yet paid any rates for the Support of the Government nor Sent any person to represent said Town in Genl assembly,

Voted That The Governr be desired to Send a Precept to Said Town of Londo Derry to Send a meet person to represent Said Town in Genl assem at the next fall Sessions, and to bring in a list of their rateable Estates that they may be assessed accordingly.

James Jeffrey Cler assem

In Counl Eod die.
Read and Concurred.

Richd Waldron Cler Con
Journal General Assembly,
—vol. 4 p 172

At a Genl assem hel d at Portsmouth by adjournmt April 12, 1726.

The Selectmen of London Derry prefer'd a Petition to the board directed to ye Genl assem Praying to be Excused from Sending a represen^{t} to ye Genl assem and Exempt from the Province Tax for the Present wch being read and a Vote pass'd thereon for granting the Prayer thereof the Same was Sent down by Shada Walton & Jon Frost Esq^{rs}.

The following year it was recorded

A Message to the Board by Mess[rs] Stevens & Jennis wth a Vote That the Town of Lond[o] Derry be taxed this year for the Province Tax the Sum of forty pounds and that the Treasurer Issue out his Warrts accordingly.

May 13th 1727.

Ja[s] Jeffry Cler assem

To Samuel Barr town Constable.

At atown meeting held at Londonderry the first wensday of December 1727, for the Ends aforesaid.

The town Chuse for Moderator............James Aiken

1st It is voted on the aforesaid day that the town have Chosen three men of indiffrent persons not Interested to lay out what land the town sees Cause the mens names is ass followeth Archibald Stark, Robert Adams, & Patrick Douglas and the town have votted that M[r] George Duncan. M[r] James Adams & M[r] John Hervey shall propose the method that what land the town thinks fitt to lay out, shall be laid out by virtue of this above vote.

2[ly] The town voted on the aforesaid day that the town will not Chuse a Committee to lett that house that Pisley built

As to the third votte Called for in the warrant, the town has votted to pass it at present.

4[ly] It is votted on the aforesaid day that the town will only bear the charge of what lawshuts comes by other town's people Incroching on our town, and no other, law shuts, and it is further voted on the said day that the Committee chosen for the Charter's right Defending, is discharged and have no more power to act ass a Committee for the End aforesaid, and the method proposed to defend our town's right's from all Incrochers from other towns, is y[t] the town votted and Chuse one man for the defence of our town, for the end aforesaid the mans name is John Mitchell

Ass to the fifth artikle in takeing an Invoice is done already therefore we pass it.

6ly It is voted on the aforesaid day that the town have chosen Mr James Mac-Keen Esqr of our town to be our Representitive or assembly man for the time being.*

At ameeting of the proprietors of Londonderry ye 6th 1727

We the subscribers being proprietors of this town do protest against the vote of Chuseing another Committee than what are allready Chosen for laying out land in our town

John Barnat,
John Barr,
Archibald Clandinen.

At ameeting of the proprietors of Londonderry Decembr ye 6th 1727

we the subscribers being proprietors do protest against the vote of leaving the method of laying our land to the Judgement of George Duncan John Hervey and James Adams, and all other votes passed upon said day Except the Chuseing an assembley man.

John Mitchell
Archibald Clandinen

Londonderry February ye 15th 1727/8

You are hearby required to warn the Inhabitants of this town to meet at the meetinghouse upon thursday the fifth of march next Enshewing at Eight of the Clock in the forenoon then and there.

1st That the town may make Choise of town officers.

2ly To see if the town will pay for fencing and high way land upon second Divisions and mendments or what method they will take about it.

3ly To see if the town will bring sirvayer from some other town to sirvay those great tracts of land laid out to some particular men in this town

*In the house of Representatives Thursday December the 14th am

James Mackeen Esqr Return for a Representative not being authentic; one of the Selectmen of Londonderry being psent was called in and Declared mr Mackeen was Legally Chosen and yt the Returns not being Right was thro Ignorance; however the house accepted him and ordered that they Should Send a proper Return.

4[ly] To see if the town will will make Choise of a sirvayer and a Committee to run the lines betwen this town and Hev-erhill and Dracut and Dunstable

5[ly] To see if the town will aprove of the method of De-fending the town from the Incrochers of other towns or take some othr method, and Chuse a Committee for the same.

6[ly] To see if the town will Exempt the strangers that are in this town from rates.

7[ly] To see if the town will have a schooll or schoolls

John Moore
Samuel Graves
Alexander Renkine
Thomas Stiel
John Woodburn

To Samuel Barr Town Constable

At a General town meeting held at London Derry March y[e] 5th 1727/8

The town have Chuse for moderator on the aforesaid day—Cap[t] James Gregg

On the aforesaid day the town voted that their shall be five men Chosen to serve as select men for the Enshewing year,

the names of the men is as followeth

Alen Anderson
John Wallace
James Reed
John Archibald
James Lindsay

On the aforesaid day the town voted for Town Clerk for the Enshewing year—John Mac Murphy.

Londonderry March y[e] 5th 1727/8

at agenerall town meeting we the subscribers and others do protest against the vote of Chuseing John Macmurphy Town Clerk.

John Mitchell
John Morison

On the aforesaid day it is voted that their Shall be two Constables chosen to serve for the Enshewing year the names of the men is as followeth

John Goffe Jun[r]
Sam[ll] Barr.

On the aforesaid day the town have votted that the aforesaid constable, shall have Each of them forty shi[lls] for their service for this Enshewing year. And it further votted on the aforesaid day that Beaver brook shall Divide and be the line betwen the two Constables John Goffe Jun[r] shall serve on the westerly side of Beaver brook and Sam[ll] Barr Constable shall serve on the southerly side of Beaver Brook.

And it is also voted on the aforesaid day that the town have votted for sirvayers for repairing the Roads and high ways of this town for this Enshewing year.

William Nikels. | John Crumey.
Archibald Clandinen. | James Callwell.
John Gregg. | George Duncan.
Robert Boys.

On the aforesaid day the town votted that two men shall serve as tithingmen for the Enshewing year the names of the men is as followeth Samuel Alison David Morison

On the aforesaid day it is also voted that two men shall serve as Hawards for this Enshewing year the mens names is as followeth—David Dickey, James Moore

On the aforesaid day the town votted that two men shall serve as fence veiwers and prizers, for this Enshewing year the mens names is as followeth James Anderson, James Leslie.

On the aforesaid day the town votted that three men shall serve as a Com[ttee] to try the town's acounts for this Enshewing year the names of y[e] men is as followeth. James Nesmith. David Cargill. John Mac murphy

On the aforesaid day the town voted that their shall be afitt person chosen for sealing of weights, measures, leather. and all sorts of Good sufficient linen Cloth that are made in this town for this Enshewing year, the mans name is as followeth—James Alexander.

On the aforesaid day the town voted that two men shall serve as Field-drivers for this Enshewing year, the names of the men is as followeth John Senter. Willm Umphra

On the aforesaid day the town votted that they will not pay for fencing or high way land in any of the second Divisions in this town

On the aforesaid day it is voted that the town will not be at the charge of sirvaying those tracts of land that is mentioned in the warrant

On the afore said day the town voted that their shall be a Committee chosen to run our town lines Betwen our town and Kingstown, Heverhill Methewine Dracut and dunstable, and it is further voted that three men shall serve & is Chosen as a Com^{ttee} to run the aforesaid lines the names of the men is as followeth that is Chosen for the Ends aforesaid.

Robert Boys.
John Goffe Junr
Alexander Walker.

On the aforesaid day the town have aggreed to allow the aforesaid Com^{ttee} four shill^{s} pr day dureing the time that they are out on Said lines

On the aforesaid day the town have votted that their shall be a sirvayer chosen to run the aforesaid lines and that he shall be allowed seven shill^{s} pr day for his wages dureing runing the aforesaid lines, the name of the sirvayer is as followeth: is— David Cargill

On the aforesaid day it is voted that John Mitchell is no longer Continued in that office of Defending our town from Incrochers of other town's.

On the aforesaid day the town have Chosen David Craig to stand our law shuit or represent our town at Ipswigh Court and the town have defered the Chuseing a Committee to Defend our town from incrochers of other towns

On the aforesaid day the town have voted that all the strangers that came in to this town to Inhabit the last fall from Ireland are Exempted from paying any of the rates that are now sesed and returned in a list to the Constables.

On the above or aforesaid day the town have voted that their shall be but one schooll kept at the publick charge of the town this Enshewing year, and that Mr John Herbey shall be the person to Keep the aforesaid schooll, and that he shall have for his salery thirty six pounds pr annum

You are hearby required to warn the proprietors of Londonderry to meet at their Meetinghouse on Munday the 15th Instant at Eight of the Cloack before noon then & there

1st To see what method they will take to raise money to Defray Inpending Charges, and to see what method they will take Concerning the lawshuit now Depending betwen them & Hevirhill

2^{ly} To see if the town aprove of the former select mens acounts as they are Given in to the Committee or not.

3^{ly} To see if they will Chuse men to lay out the land for ye meetinghouse & the Graveyard, and take Deeds for the same, & what restitution they will make for said land.

4^{ly} To see if they will Chuse a Committee to Defend their lines from Incrochers from Neighbouring towns.

5^{ly} To see what method they will take to lay out their Equivolent lands & to see if they will Continue the last Committee Chosen for that End or Chuse another, or any other thing or things that may Concern the proprietors and this shall be your warrant.

Given under our hands this first day of april 1728.

James Lindsay.
Allen Anderson.
John Archbald.
John Wallace.
James Reid.
Selectmen

To Samuel Barr Constable of Londonderry

At apropprietory meeting held at Londonderry Meetinghouse april ye 15th 1728.

The proprietors of Londonderry Chuse for Moderator Capt James Gregg.

1st It is voted on the afore^{sd} day y^{t} their shall be one hundred acres of Good land & two acres of meadow by veiwe, sold for the publick Benefit of the town to repay ye publick Charge of the same, and y^{t} s^{d} land shall be Disposed of & sold to ye best advantage for the town, & it is also voted y^{t} ye select men shall sell & Dispose of and Give Deeds of s^{d} land to the person or persons y^{t} shall appear to buy ye aforesaid one hundred acres, & the afores^{d} two acres of meadow

2^{y} It is also voted on the afores^{d} Day y^{t} the select mens acounts for ye year 1723 1724: & 1725 are approved of by the town, But the select mens accounts for ye rate 1726 is not aproved of by the town at present, ye s^{d} select men serving in ye year 1727: & it is also voted that the select mens accounts for ye year 1727 is aproved of by the town.

3^{ly} It is also voted on the afores^{d} day that three men shall serve as aCom^{ttee} to agree with the particular owners of that land that is to be laid out about ye meetinghouse of Londonderry, as also our Graveyard (viz) two acres about the meetinghous and one acre for a Graveyard, & to allow the owners of said land Reasonable restitution for said land, as also to take Deeds in the towns name for said land the names of the men is as followeth (viz)

John Morison
John Archibald.
David Cargill.

Upon the above said day it is voted that all the Differences Concerning mendements lands High way lands and want of homestead lands is aggreed in the manner following (viz)

1st That all persons that have already Claim'd any land for the wants of the above mentioned lands shall hold their Claims, having them review'd or veiwed over, by a Committee of three men, one of which men shall be one that hath, one of the poorest lots, and another of the men shall be one of them that hath one of the middway lots, and the third man of said Committee a man that hath one of the Good lots, and brought to the method which we shall hearafter Insert (viz) That the man that gets or have Gotten said land above mentioned, at one mile's distance or under, shall have one acre of land made as Good as one acre of the precedent the lots are veiwed by for Every acre they were veiwed or allowed by the Committee Chosen for veiwing the home lots, and so gradualy riseing one quarter of an acre, for each half mile said land lieth Distant from the sundrey lots which is to have said land above mentioned, untill it come to the Quantity of two acres made Good as above, for Every acre that they are allowed for the wants above said, which will be at the Distance of three miles and so rise no more for any distance or Consideration (Whatsoever) and they that have not yet got their above said land or Claims, shall have liberty to put in their Claims, they that wants most or allowed most Coming first, and so on, untill it come to the smalest Quantity which is allowed to any for the wants above mentioned, said land to be formed into ranges that so the Commons may be laid out in order, and the land that is to be reviewed over which is already laid out, shall be done at the Cost of the town, and they that have Bought any of the High way land and is not satisfied with the method, is to return said land and take their money, which they paid for said land again, and when more than one man is allowed an Equall Quantity of the above lands they shall come to the Decision of alot, who shall Claime first Every proprietor is to have twenty acres added to his Claim or mendment

All Differances and Debeats Whatsoever in our town Concerning LAND, is done away in this vote, Note that the twenty acres above mentioned is to be laid out Quantity and Quality only Considered

And it is also voted on the aforesaid day that three men shall serve and is Chosen to lay out the lands above mentioned the names of the men is as followeth

John Mitchell
John Archibald
John Wallace

It is also voted on the aforesaid day that three men shall serve and is Chosen for Defending our town land or lines from Incrochers from other towns, the names of the men is as followeth (viz)

James Clerk.
Robert Boys.
David Cargill.

It is voted on the aforesaid day that all votes and records that are made upon any person or persons, or Committee or Committees, with respect of staining or prejudcing their Good name or Reputation are hearby made null and void. & of none Effect

It is also voted y^t sergant James Moore shall have the land that is allowed him by the several proprietors of this town in the place where it was allready laid out, and that he may setle their when he pleasess untill the Committee go out to lay out said land.

It is also voted that their shall be High ways and Roads laid out in all the Commons that are to be laid out, & that no person's shall have any other allowance of land or fencing, but what is allowed them by the Committee's Judgement that is to lay out said land

Londonderry March ye 8th 1728.

At atown meeting held the Day above for Chuseing a Representitive or assembly man the town Chuse for Moderator Capt James Gregg

On the aforesaid day the town voted for assembly man or Representitive for our town of Londonderry Mr James Mackeen Esqr

You are hearby Required to warn the freeholders & Inhabitants of Londonderry to Conveen at their Meeting house on Munday the Eight of this Instant at seven of the Clock Before noon, then & there to Chuse afit Representitive or person to Represent their town at the Generall assembly which is to meet at Portsmouth on twesday the ninth Instant

Given under our hand this 7th Day of April 1728

Allen Anderson
John Archibald
James Ried
Select Men

To Sam^ll Barr Constable.

You are hearby Required to warn the proprietors of Londonderry to meet at their Meetinghouse on Munday the thirteenth Instant May at Eight of the Clock Before noon then & there

1st To see what Laidout land or meadows the town will aprove of

2^{ly} To see whether the town will take any method to Gratify the nine men that petitioned His Honour the Lev^{t} Governour the Day after the last town meeting held in this town

3^{ly} To see if the town be Satisfied with the method of the selectmen have aggreed upon for setling the school for this present year or any other thing that may Concern the propriety,

And this shall be your warrant Given under our hands this 29th Day of April 1728.

John Wallace.
Allen Anderson.
John Archibald.
James Reid.
Selectmen

To Sam^{ll} Barr Constable

At a Proprietory meeting held at the meetinghouse on the aforesaid Day the town have votted that Capt James Gregg Moderator

On the aforesaid Day the Proprietors by vote have Confirmed and Established all the meadows that are allready laid out & Recorded to Every proprietor in our town of Londonderry, Except the Debeatable meadow's that is betwen Abraham Holms John Macclurg and John Craige

On the aforesaid Day votted that the proprietors aproves of & Establishes and Confirms the home Lotts as they are allready laid out, where they want of sixty acres Either in Quantity or Quality, to be made up according to the vote made by the proprietors of Londonderry bearing Date April the Fifteenth one thousand seven hundred & twenty Eight.

2^{ly} On the aforesaid Day it is voted that the Proprietors of our town will not Gratifie these nine men that Petitioned the Hounourable Governour Wentworth the Day after our last town Meeting April ye 15th 1728

3^{ly} on the aforesaid Day the proprietors voted that the school shall be settled according to the method aggreed upon by the select men for this present year

Pershewant to the Laying out of atract of Land to Robert Boyes & Robert Morison Nov^{br} ye 14th 1726

On the above said Day the proprietors of our town have votted that they aprove of Establishess & Confirms the Laying out & Recording of the aforesaid tract of Land to the persons above named & mentioned (viz)

Robert Boyes and Robert Morison to their own proper use benifit and behoof in fee.

On the aforesaid Day it is votted by the proprietors of our town that there be one man sent to the Honourable Governour & Counsel to Petition them to have the line of our town adjested Betwen our town of Londonderry & Kingstown, and to answer to what Differencess that may arise to the Damage of our town, the name of the person that is Chosen for that End is ....David Cargill. Junr

Voted

On the aforesaid Day that the Proprietors of our town have Chosen a Sirvayer to Joyn the Committee Chosen for Laying out of mendment land High way land & wants of homestead's, as also what second Divisions is yet to lay out in this town, and the said sirvayer is to have for his service six shi^{lls} p^{r} Day, the name of the sirvayer that is Chosen is. ....David Cargill Junr

Purhewant to avote pas'd April ye 15th 1728.

The proprietors of our town do hearby Impower James Clerk Robert Boyes & David Cargill to be their Lawfull attorney's, for to Comence and Defend all Law suits against all Incrochers from any other town Either that hath, or shall, trespass upon any particular mans land or upon the town's Commons, & to Employ one or more attorney's as they shall think fitt for the Ends aforesaid, at the proprietors Charge as ample and full as if the town were their present.

At a town metting held at Londonderry 13 May 1728.

Robert wiare & others protests against John Michell & John Wallace & John Archebald for to be sworn for Laying out aney Land will the town Come to a furder agrement

Att a toun mitting held at Londonderry 13 may 1728.

John Barr and others protests agenest Giving away the touns land by bond to Robert bocyes or aney other without the Consent of vs the proprietors

At a toun mitting heeld in Londonderry 13 may 1728.

william umphra and others protests againist the selling aney Comon land^s unles the selek pay us our proposhen of the money recorded for said Land

att a toun Mitting healld in Londonderry 13 may 1728.

John Morison & others prottests aganest aney Land Confirmed to aney propritor for his homeloatt but sixty Eakers—

You are hearby Required to warn the proprietors of Londonderry to meet at their Meeting house on twesday the Eighteenth Instant then & there at 11 of ye Clock

1st To see what High ways, where & from whence Leading, the proprietors will agree of to be laid out

2^ly To see if they will order the Committee for searching the nearest way to Boston to go to Look said Road Immediatly, or Chuse another Committee if they should decline it

3^ly To see if the proprietors of this town will defend any particular out Lands allready laid out or yett to be laid out from the Incrochments of other towns, provided said proprietors do not setle said out Lands wt such ass shall be allowed them by the town, or any other thing that may Consern the proprietoys Given under our hands this 14th Day of June 1728

James Lindsay.
Allen Anderson.
John Archibald.
John Wallace.
Select men

To Samuel Barr Constable

At a proprietory Meeting Held at Londonderry June y[e] 18th 1728

On the aforesaid Day the proprietors votted for Moderator Robert Boyes

On the afores[d] Day it is voted that the proprietors have aggreed that the Road is to be Determined by the select men that leads to James Reids house they takeing the nearest and Cheapest Road to that place

On the aforesaid Day it is voted that Alexander Nikels & John Mitchell shall Joyn Cap[t] Gregg to try out the nearest way from our setlement to Boston, imediatly.

On the aforesaid day it is voted that all proprietors that will not setle their out lands that is debeatable and liable to Incrochers from other towns at or before the tenth Day of March next Enshewing the date hereof, and if in Case any person or proprietor in our town through their Default or neglect hapen to lose this Land or any particular mans should by not setleing by the time Limited and appointed by the town or proprietors at the time, they shall bear their own Charge in Lawsuits themselves, and lose their land and the town not be obliged to make their land up to them, Excepte that land that Muggett has built ahouse upon, and it is further to be understood by this vote that the lands hear mentioned is homesteads second Divisions twenty acre Lotts and additions.

on the afores[d] day it is voted that their shall be aCommittee Chosen to take the most prudentialest method to setle our out lands Lying on the River Merrimack the Committee that is Chosen for the Ends aforesaid is. James Mackeen. John Mitchell. David Cargill. Alexander Nikels & Robert Boyes, and it is further to be understood by the aforesaid vote that the Committee Chosen shall have full power and authority to Dispose of and Give of that land before mentioned ass they shall think fitt for the preservation of the aforesaid lands, to the benefit of the town of Londonderry and the said Committee shall be upon oath and shall act to the best of their skill & Knowledge &——We James Mackeen John Mitchell David Cargill Alex^r^ Nikels & Robert Boyes do depose and swear in the presence of God that we will act according to the best of our Judgement, and with all Sincerity as Members of the Committee for the Defence & preservation of our land on Merrimack river for the use & benefit of our town So help you God.

Londonderry Agust ye 17th 1728

You are hearby Required to warn the proprietors of Londonderry to meet att their Meetinghouse on Wensday the twenty-Eight Instant att ten of the Cloack then & there &c

1st To see what men they will appoint to take an Invoice of the poles & Estates real & personal within the town

2^ly^ To See what Sum of money they will allow to be assesed & whom they will appoint assesors for this present year

3^ly^ To See whether or not they will Establish the High ways Leading to Boston and Dracut before the lands claimed on that part of the town lying near these places be laid out and this shall be your warrant

given under our hands the day and year above written.

Allen Anderson
John Archibald
James Reid
Select men

To Mr John Goffe Constable in Londonderry.

At apropriietory Meeting held at Londonderry agust ye 28th 1728.

The aforesaid Day the town voted for Moderator Mr James Mackeen

On the aforesaid day it is voted that Capt James Gregg & James Aiken shall take Invoice of the poles and Estates of this town both real & personall

On the aforesaid day it is voted by the proprietors of this town, that the select men shall asses upon the propriety to pay the Charge of repairing the Meetinghouse As Just and full sum of one hundred and forty pounds in bils of Credit—and that the same shall be raised & levied by the Constables of this town as soon as possible for the defraying of the aforesaid Charge

It is also voted on the aforesaid Day that their shall be three High ways laid out from the setlement of our town southerly one high way leading by flat rock towards methewine, & one high way leading towards towrhill, and one high way leading towards Dracut, and however of these three High ways, shall be thought Convenientest to be the leading and best High way from our setlement to Boston by the majority of our town, said High way shall be Clear'd Repair'd and Keept in Good order at the publick Charge of the town, & the other two high ways shall be Clear'd & Repair'd by those proprietors who shall reap and have the benifit and advantage of the aforesaid High ways, & said high ways shall be laid out by the Committee or lotlayers that lays out our mendment lands the mens names of the afores^{d} Com^{ttee} is (viz)

John Wallace,
John Archibald
John Mitchell

You are hearby Required to warn the proprietors of Londonderry to meet at their Meetinghouse on Munday ye 14th Instant at nine of the Cloack before noon then & there

1st To see whether they will sell any more land & what Quantity,

2^{ly} To see whether they will alter the stair Case at their meetinghouse or let it stand where it is and whether they will have two windows in the north side thereof

3^{ly} To see what method they will take to Disanull the old transcripts of Equivolant lands &c that the new may be preparied for aprobation

4^{ly} To see if they will Qualify men to Give transcripts of the meadow laid out to Governour Wentworth & Robert Canady, & this shall be your warrant Given under our hand this 5th Day of october 1728.

James Reid
John Wallace
James Lindsay
John Archibald
Allen Anderson
Select Men

To Samuel Barr Constable

At a proprietory meeting held at Londonderry october ye 14th 1728.

The Proprietors Chus & voted for Moderator—Robert Boys

It is voted on the aforesaid day that their shall be a tract of land sold to defray the publick Charges of the town

It is also voted on the aforesaid day that their shall be one hundred acres of Good land sold and a Quite Claim Deed Given of the same, to Defray the publick Charges of the town, and that the Committee that lays out Equivolant lands shall sell, and lay out said tract of land, and Give a Deed as aforesaid of the same, not Incroching upon any mans Claime It is also voted on the aforesaid day that the stairs to go up to our galliries for the meetinghouse shall be brought to the Inside of the meetinghouse, and it is—voted that their shall be two windows struke out in the north side of the meetinghouse one on Each side of the pulpit,

It is also voted on the aforesaid day that all the Equivolent lands wants of home and high way land that has been allredy laid out & Recorded, shall be Disanulled the person that the aforesd lands has been recorded too, signing the Disanuling of same by signing the underwriteing that the town Clerk shall write with the persons own hand, & the town Clerk attesting the same, shall be authentuk

It is also voted on the aforesaid day that the several transcripts (viz) one transcript to Robert Boyes, and one to Robert Mackeen, one to James Rodgers, one to John Bell, Jonathan Butterfield's farm, & Alexr Mac Neals second Division is all read and approved of by the town

It is also voted on the aforesaid day that the fifty acres that Robert Canady is to have from Governour Wentworth is not approv'd of by the town with the record of one hundred acres of land that said Governour Wentworth rejected after being laid out & recorded be Disanuld, he view'd in full by his own desire one hundred acres in place of the aforesd lands that Robert Canady now lives upon

You are hearby Required to warn the proprietors of Londonderry to Convene at their meetinghouse on Munday the 18th Instant at nine of the Clock before noon there and then

Imp^{r} imus To see whether they will have their prorietory rate lessened or lett the owerplus stand for Contingensess

2^{ly} To see whether they will Defend the men that were apprehended by Heverhill people, or those that apprehended Mugett &c should they be presecuted by heverhill people att Law

3^{ly} To see what wages they will allow the men that have been Imployed by them this year or shall be afterwards Imployed

4^{ly} To see if they will approve of transcripts of Land laid out by the present Committee as they shall from time to time Come before them

5^{ly} To see if they will Chuse a Man or Men to fill up the Com^{ttee} for Defending the town lines

6^{ly} To see what method they will take to Secure themselves from such as have gott or shall gett payment for high ways and fences

7^{ly} To see what sort of Deed they will allow to James Wilson for his land Lately bought from the town, and this shall be your warrant.

Given under our hands this 8th Day of Nov^{br} 1728.

James Lindsay
Allen Anderson
John Archibald
John Wallace,
James Reid
Select men

To Samuel Barr Constable.

At aproprietory meeting held at Londonderry November the 18th 1728.

The town Chuse for Moderator. James Mackeen

On the aforesaid Day the proprietors votted that their shall be Eliven Shi^{lls} and six pence taken of the proprietory rate, and that the proprietory rate shall be thirty shi^{lls} this present year*

*In 1728 Londonderry paid one-fifteenth of the province tax, though so much younger than many of the towns, noticeably Portsmouth, Dover, Exeter and Hampton, which had been settled over a century.—*Editor.*

On the afores^d Day it is votted that the men (viz) John Adams, and James Blair Sam^ll Morison that was taken out of that house that William Mugett Built, shall be left to themselves to Defend themselves in any law shuit that may arise upon them by their being taken by Nathaniell Pisley of Heverhill in the aforesaid house

on the aforesaid Day it is votted that the men for Defending the town's land & the men that took the Invoice of our town this year (viz) James Clerk. Robert Boyes. David Cargill Junr Capt Gregg & James Aiken for what service they have done for the town from the first Day of april to the first Day of october shall have for their wages four shi^lls pr Day, & from the first Day of october to the first Day of april shall have three shi^lls pr Day

on the afores^d Day it is votted that the select men shall take abond of Capt Cargill of thirty pounds penalty to Keep up the Fouling mill for Ever for the town use

on the aforesaid Day it is voted that the severall transcripts or returns made by the present Committee is Read and aprov'd of by the town (viz) one to James Morison one to George & Thomas Clerk one to John Archibald one to David & Thomas Bogle one to Robert Boyes one to Jo^n Crumey, one to Willm Nickels one to Govr Wentworth, two to Jo^n Barr one to Jo^n Anderson, three to Mr MacGregor, one to Jo^n stewart one to Jo^n morison, one to Archibald Clandinene, one to Hendrey Greens right now in the possession of Jo^n anderson one to Alex^r Walker, three to David Cargill sen^r & Junr and the several returns that shall come to hand before next proprietory meeting are to be put on record they being read and aprov'd of by the select men for the time being

on the aforesaid Day it is votted that the men (viz) James Reid & John Macmurphy shall fall in to succeed Robert Boyes and David Cargill to Defend our towns lines or land from Incrochers from other towns,

when the aforesaid Robert Boyes & David Cargill moves themselves out of town, the afore^sd Reid & Macmurphy being upon oath on the aforesaid day it is voted that there shall be a Book provided and Committed to Jo^{n} MacMurphy to Enter in to said Book the payments of high ways both of land and fenceing together with a record of the other Dispursments of our town rates.

It is also voted on said Day that James Wilson shall have a Quite Claime Deed of y^{t} tract of Land that he bought from our town, and if so be that the said land be taken from him by a legall Course of Law or from his assigns he or they setleing said land by the 10th Day of March next Enshewing that then and in that Case said land that he bought from the town shall be made up to him or them in some other Convenient part of our township not Incroching upon any mans Claime.

Londonderry Nov^{br} ye 23^{d} 1728.

You are hearby Required to warn the proprietors of this town to meet at their meeting house on Munday the second Day of December next at ten of the Clock before noon, then & there

1st To Chuse aman to fill up the Committee for laying out the Equivolent land &c in the room of John Mitchell

2^{ly} To Chuse aSirvayer in the room of David Cargill for Carying on the afore^{sd} work

James Reid
John Wallace
John Archibald
Allen Anderson
Select men

To Samuel Barr Constable

At a proprietory meeting held at Londonderry December ye Second 1728

The Proprietors Chuse for Moderator Capt David Cargill

On said Day votted that James Rodgers is Chose and shall serve as a Committee man or lotlayer in the room or place of John Mitchell for laying out of the Equivolant lands that are yet to be laid out &c

On the aforesaid Day the Several Returns is Read & aprov'd of by the town to be put on Record for their owner (viz) one to James Lindsay William Gregg & James Mc-Laughlan one to Thomas Stiel, one to Willm Aiken, one to James Mc Keen one to Robert Morison, one to George Jaffrey now in the possesion of John MacMurphy & partners

You are hearby Required to Warn the proprietors of Londonderry to Conven att their Meetinghouse on Munday the Sixth Day of January next at Eight of the Clock Before noon then and there.

1st To see what method they will take to Dispose of their Seats in the Meetinghouse

2^{ly} To See whether they will admit Such of the proprietors as have not Contributed their Equal Share towards the Building and finishing of the Meetinghouse to alot with such as have, or whither the moveable seats shall be moved at the sacraments at the town's Charge or at their possesers Charge

3^{ly} To See whither they will send a Committee to Run the South line of this town, and this shall be your warrant Given under our hands this 26th Day of December 1728

James Lindsay
John Wallace
Allen Anderson
John Archibald
James Reid
Selectmen

To Samuel Barr Constable of Londondery

At a proprietory Meeting held at Londonderry January ye 6th 1728/9

The proprietors Chuse for Moderator........James Ried

voted on S^{d} Day that Every proprietor that salls his seat in our Meetinghouse afore Seat or aseat of best^{er} Priviledge than others by Lott, Shall pay according as the prise is sett upon the afores^{d} Seats by the Committee Chosen for y^{t} End on the aforesaid Day, and if it Should so happen at any time, that any particular person or persons refuse to pay the several sums sett upon these seats before mentioned, that it shall be in the power of the Select men of our town for the time being, to take said Seats or Seat from such person or persons y^t Refuses to pay what is seas'd upon them for priviledge of s^d seats or seat, and hearby Impowered by s^d vote to Dispose of s^d seat or seats to such proprietor or proprietors as shall or may appear to pay the sum or sums that are laid upon them by the Committee Chosen for that End, and if any person or person Refuse to Give up s^d Seat or Seats peaceably and not pay what is seas'd upon for s^d seats or seat, that it shall be in the power of the town to Distrain such person or persons for the money that are seas'd on them untill they Give up said seat or seats— — — —And it is further to be understood by s^d vote that their shall be no seat in our Meetinghouse of Whatsoever Conveniency or priviledge that they Enjoy, shall be Seas'd or rated above thirty shi^{lls} ayear, and that the Seat of the meanest priviledge & Conveniency shall not pay above ten shi^{lls} ayear

Also voted on s^d Day that their shall be Sevenmen Chosen as aCommittee to valoue all the seats in our Meetinghouse according to their Conveniency & put apise upon them accordingly the men that are Chosen for that End is John Blair, Abraham Holms, James Mackeen James Adams Thomas Stiel Lev^t John Goffe & James Ried

voted on s^d Day that, that artikle in the Warrant annent not leting those proprietors that have not Contributed to the building & finishing of our Meetinghouse have alot for their seat in the meetinghouse is Deffered

voted on said Day that the Committee for laying out our mendment & adition Lands is to go out Directly to measure and run the line of our town on the south side (viz) John Wallace John Archibald & James Rodgers and the sirvayers that is Chosen to go along with them is Capt James Gregg

The several transcripts is Read and by vote approv'd of by the town to be put on Record for their owners (viz) one to $Alex^r$ Walker one to John Barnat sen^r one to Robert Cochran one to Allen Anderson & one to James Nesmith

At ameeting of the proprietors february y^{e} 6th 1728/9

I the subscriber do protest against a vote that pas'd on said Day that their should be arate sett on the seats in the meetinghouse for paying the ministers Salary

James Leslie

Londonderry June ye 14th 1728

Then accounted with the towns Committee for Examining the Town accounts, & I accknowledge to have rec^{d} full satsfaction for all salary due to me from the Begining of our setlement till this 1st Day of may 1723 being four years

Witness my hand James MacGregor

Recorded this 14th Day of January 1728/9

pr John MacMurphy Town Clerk.

WHERAS Robert Wear & John Barr prefered apetition to the Generall assembly on the Eighteenth Instant for themselves & in behalf of twelve other Persons all Belonging to the town of Londonderry showing forth that their was not an Equall: Division and a Just of the land in said town and praying for Relief in the premises & their being an order of the Gen^{ll} Asem^{y} that ahearing on the said petition shoud be had this day, & that the select men of said town should be serv'd with a copy of s^{d} petition, and the said select men having been serv'd with such Copys and having sent several persons in behalf of the town (viz) Masurs James Gregg John Macmurphy Robert Boyes & Andrew Todd to answer to the said petition &c and both parties appearing unitedly Declared that they had settled the Difference amongst themselves and humbly prayeth that the Gov^{t} to give a sanction to their aggreement therefore

In Counsell may ye 23^{d} 1728

Voted

That the said aggreement be & hearby is Established & Confirmed which aggreement is as follows (viz) that the vote pas^{d} at a Proprietory meeting at Londonderry the fifteenth Day of april Anno Domi^{ni} 1728 Concerning the Differences about amendment lands high way lands & want of home stead lands be Good & valid to all Intents & purposes, and in all respects any law usage or Custom to the Contrary Notwithstanding— — — —And that the Petitioners namely John Barr Robert Wear, Sam^ll^ alison Willm Nikels John Anderson James Morison and Arc^d^ Clandinen Jo^n^ Stewart John Morison Willm Umphree Sam^ll^ Barr John Barnat sen^r^ Jo^n^ Barnat Ju^r^ & Gabriell Barr shall have five hundred & ninety four acres of Land within the s^d^ town of Londonderry that is to say the Petitioners shall have the one half of the land that fronts on Cobages pond on the south side & East End of the said pond so begining at the midle of s^d^ Pond & runing out asquare line from the pond three hundred & twenty Rhods if Polisey pond will allow thence Extending East, not to run past the East End of polisey pond Southerly and so runing along the habitable land breaking no form of land untill the aforesaid petitioners Compliment of five hundred & ninety four acres is made up Exclusive of any meadows which is Reserved to The town and further the Committee which shall lay out said tract of land are to have Regard to the Quantity as well as the Quality of the said land as the use & Custom of said town is & has been and lay it out accordingly, the said tract being in full satisfaction to the petitioners for amendment lands twenty acres lots or addition's

Richard Waldron
Clerk Con^ll^

May ye 24th the above Read & Concurd

James Jaffrey
Clerk Asem

Vera Copia
Attests p^r^ Richard Waldron
Clerk Con^ll^

You are hearby Required to warn the proprietors and freeholders of Londonderry to Conven at their meeting house on Wensday the fifth Day of March next at nine of the Clock Before noon then and there

1st To Chuse their town officers for the year Enshewing

2^{ly} To See whether they shall have one Publick Schooll or more as shall be though needfull

3^{ly} To See what method they will take to Defend their town lines from Incrochers

4^{ly} To See after what manner they will lott for their Seats in the meetinghouse, and when they will do it

5^{ly} To See if the proprietors will Chuse aCommittee to Give John Dinsmore a Deed of his land

And this Shall be your Warrant Given under our hands this 21st day of February 1728/9.

Allen Anderson
John Archibald
James Lindsay
James Reid
John Wallace
Select men

To Sam^{ll} Barr Constable

At A Generall town Meeting Legaly Call'd, held at the Meeting house of Londonderry upon wensday the fifth Day of March 1728/9

The Proprietors and freeholders Chuse for Moderator James Mackeen Esqr

Voted on Said day that their Shall be five men Chosen for Serving as Select men in said town of Londonderry for the Enshewing year

The names of the men that are Chosen for the Ends above as Select men is John Wallace John Archibald Allen Anderson James Lindsay James Reid

Also voted on Said Day that John Macmurphy Shall Serve as town Clerk for the Enshewing year — — — John Macmurphy

Also voted that their shall be but one Constable Chosen for our town of Londonderry for y^{e} year Enshewing and his name is as follows John Macneall

For Sirvayers of High Ways Gabriel Barr, Jo^{n} Morison, Solomon Hopkine, James Wallace, $Will^{m}$ Adams James Blair Jo^{n} Bell & Jo^{n} Goffe Ju^{nr}

For tithing men Jo^n^ Senter & Robert Wear

For Hawards Mathew Taylor & James Morison

For fence veiwers & prisers James Clerk & John Anderson weav^r^

For Searching the town accounts James Nesmith Sam^ll^ Barr & Jo^n^ Macmurphy

It is agreed upon that they will Defer that artikle Concerning the meeting house at this present time

voted that the Inhabitants proprietors & freeholders are Satisfied that Mr John Hervey Shall be Schoolmaster for the Enshewing year, provided the Select men and he agree about his salery

Voted that all persons that have land lying on the out Borders of our towns Bound is Exempted from Selling the Same untill after the next proprietory Meeting

You are hearby Required to Warn the Proprietors of Londonderry to Conven at their Meetinghouse on thursday the Seventeenth Instant by nine of the Clock before noon then & there

1st To See what measures they will take as to their sitting in the meeting house

2^ly^ To See what money they will allow to be asses'd to defray Contingent Charges

3^ly^ To See whether they will allow a Convenient place at Cannada for a meetinghouse and some quantity of land for aministeriall Lott,

4^ly^ To See what method they will take to Settle their out Lands

5^ly^ To See whether they will allow the People of the Bank range a Convenient high way to lead them to Heverhill path or let the high way Runing on the line betwen John Barrs land & William Umphra be Demolish'd & have one high way more Centural by which the people of the back Range and the pike Range may be both accomodated

6^ly^ To See if they will aprove of the Several Returns or transcripts given in by the Lott layers or Com^ttee^ for laying out amendments &c and this shall be your warrant Given under our hands this 4th day of April 1729.

James Lindsay
Allen Anderson
John Archibald
John Wallace
James Reid
Select men

To John Mac Neall Town Constable

At a Proprietory meeting held at Londonderry april ye 17th 1729

The proprietors Chuse for Moderator James Mac Keen Esqr

1st votted that the proprietors do agree & Conclude that the Seats in our Meetinghouse shall be Lotted for, according to the method propossed which method is to Continue for three years. Which Method is as followeth (viz) that Every proprietor Shall have one Seat provideing they pay up their Equal proportion in building & finishing of the said meetinghouse, & that their shall be alist taken by the town where Every mans Seat fals or Every proprietor Seat stands, & that it shall be in the power of the Select men for the time being to proportion Every man or proprietor according to the Conveniency or priviledge they Enjoy, the Select men haveing aregard to Several Sums or yearly Salary Sett on the Several Seats by the Committee that was Chosen for that End by the proprietors of our town

2ly voted that their shall be Eighty pounds Currant money or bils of Credit Sessed for the defraying or paying of Contingent Charges

3ly voted that their shall be sixty acres of Good land laid out in a Convenient place where it shall be found for the Incouragement of apresinct or new Erection at Canneeda and the same Quantity of land laid out at Cobats pond for the End aforesaid to Incourage a new presinct

4ly voted that all persons that have land lying on the out borders of our towns Bounds is Exempted from Setleing the same untill after the next proprietory meeting

5^{ly} The fifth artickle deferred at present

6^{ly} votted to be put upon Record the several Returns made by the Committe for laying out amendments & (viz) one for John Wallace one for Sam^{ll} Penhallow & Jo^{n} archibald one for Jo^{n} anderson weaver one for David morison one for Alex^{r} Mac Murphy one for Jesse Cristi one for Daniel Karr one For Sam^{ll} Renkine y^{t} he had of Sam^{ll} Penhallow one to Jo^{n} mitchell one to Jo^{n} ye man Cochran one to widow Cochran Petter & Uinice Cochran one to Sam^{ll} Jo^{n} & Jenat mackeen one to Thomas Cochran & one Return to James Clerk

You are hearby Required to warn the proprietors & freeholders of Londonderry to meet at their Meetinghouse on Munday the 23^{d} Instant presizely at one of the Clock in the afternoon then and there

Imprimus To See what method Shall be taken to pay preachers that may providentially be with us dureing our non setlement and what may be thought a Competency for them

2^{ly} To see after what manner the Select men Shall aploate the money aggred to be Sess'd at last town meeting

3^{ly} To See whom they will Chuse Sirvayer in the room of Gabriel Barr

4^{ly} To See if they will accquit old Robt Gilmore & his son Jo^{n} from paying Rates

5^{ly} To See if the town will Chuse men to take an Invoice of the poles and Estates of our town for ye year 1729

6^{ly} To See if the town will give power to the Select men of our town to aggree for the fencing of our Grave yeard, & what Manner of fence it shall be & to see whether they shall aprove of the returns made by the Lott layers to be read at this time

And this shall be your Warrant Given under our hands this 13th day of June 1729

James Lindsay
Allen Anderson
Jo^{n} Archibald
Jo^{n} Wallace
James Reid
Select men

To John Macneal town Constable

At a Proprietory meeting held at Londonderry meeting house on Munday ye 23^d^ Day of June 1729, The towns Proprietors Chuse for Moderator James MacKeen Esqr

Imprimus voted that the minister that now preaches with us of this town, which is Mr MacKinstrey shall be allow'd thirty shils pr wek besides his boord Lodging & horse Keping

2^ly^ voted that the money aggreed upon to applote shall be Sess'd after ye usuall manner

3^ly^ voted that James Willson & Jo^n^ Senter shall Serve Sirvayers in the room of Gabriel Barr and James Blair

4^ly^ voted that our Select men Shall have no liberty to acquite Ro^t^ Gilmore & his son Jo^n^ from paying Rates

5^ly^ voted that Lev^t^ John Goffe and Willm Moore Shall take the Invoice of our town for ye year 1729, and their pay or wages is to be 2: 8: 0 & no more

6^ly^ voted that the Select men of our town are Impowered to aggree for the fencing of our Grave yeard with a five Raile fence, at the Cheapest Rate that they can have it done for well, and Shall aggree for the Clearing of the aforesaid Grave yeard of the Brush or underwood y^t^ Grows on the same

The severall Returns read & aprov'd off one to Capt Gregg one to James alex^r^ & one to Benj: Wilson

You are hearby Required to warn the proprietors of Londonderry to Conven at their meetinghouse on munday the 25th Instant by six of the Clock before noon then and there, to Concert on Such nesessary and Emergent affairs as Concerns the propriety and this shall be your warrant, & also to See if the proprietors will aprove of the Several transcripts that are Returned by the lot layers Given under our hands this 23^d^ Day of agust 1729

To Jo^n^ Macneal Constable*

At a Proprietory meeting held up on munday ye 25th of

*Evidently the names of the Selectmen were not given in this case on account of lack of room on the page. This same reason applies to frequent cases of abbreviated words and phrases, so given in order to complete the record in that particular space.—EDITOR.

agust 1729 at Londonderry meetinghouse, It was then voted for moderator James mackeen Esqr

voted that James Mackeen Esqr James Reid & John macmurphy shall attend the Genarll Court to be held at Cambridge in behalf of our town to have our Complaint heard & tried, with respect to the abuse and wrongs that we have receiv'd and had from Robert Foord James Heath & Compay (?)

the Severall Transcripts or Returns Read & approv'd of on s^{d} Day (viz) one to Govr Wentworth one to the Rev^{d} m^{r} Philips, one to Jo^{n} Goffe, one to Benjamin Kidder, one to Jo^{n} Goffe Junr, one to Hugh Ramsay one to Sam^{ll} Houston; one to John Mac Clurg, and one to James Anderson

You are hearby Required to warn the proprietors & freeholders of London Derry to meet at their meeting house on Munday the 22^{d} of this Instant Sep^{tr} at Eight of the Clock in the forenoon — — —then and there.

1st To Chuse afitt person in the Room of James Mackeen Esqr to Represent our town of Londonderry at the General Court to be held at portsmouth

2^{ly} To Chuse persons in the Room of James Clerk John Macmurphy and James Reid to Defend our town lines

3^{ly} To See whether they will be Content to Ratify the proposals made by the men that were to Discourse Mr Clerk annent his Setlement in this Congregation

4^{ly} To See what they will do about the prisoners now in new-bury Goal (viz) James Wallace & Willm Hogg of our town

5^{ly} To See whether the proprietors will allow Such as have their Equivolent lands lying in debeatable places to Setle Said lands

6^{ly} To See if they will allow the Com^{ttee} for laying out lands to find out the Bounds of neticook from the River Merrimack River

7^{ly} To See how they will allow the arrears due to Mrs Mac Gregore to be Cessed

8^{ly} To See if they will allow payment for fences throw

mendments and Second Divisions. And this shall be your warrant Given under our hands this ninth day of Sep^{tr} 1729

John Archibald
Allen Anderson
James Lindsay
John Wallace
Select men

To John Macneal town Constable

At atown meeting held at Londonderry Meetinghouse on Munday the 22^{ed} Day of Sep^{tr} 1729. the town Chuse for Moderator Capt Jam^{s} Gregg

1st voted that Lev^{t} John Goffe is Ellected and Chosen to Serve as Representitive for our town of Londonderry in the room stead and place of James Mac Keen Esqr

2^{ly} voted on s^{d} Day that Capt James Gregg Robt Boyes and Sam^{ll} Barr shall Succed as a Com^{ttee} in the defence of our town lines from Incorchers in the Room and Stead of James Reid James Reid James Clerk & John Macmurphy, and if it Should so hapen that Robt Boyes go to Ireland, or Remove any other part out of town, that then & in that Case David Cargill Junr shall Joyn the afores^{d} Com^{ttee} in the Room and place of Robert Boyes aforesaid,

3^{ly} voted that the town hath aggreed with Respect to the Setlement of the Revd Mr Mathew Clerk to be our minister, to pay the S^{d} Mr Clerk ninety pounds p^{r} annum untill another minister Shall be Setled in this Congregation, and from the time of another minister's being Setled hear we are willing to allow the said Mr Clerk Eighty pounds p^{r} annum dureing his being Capable of performing the work of the minis tery, and after that to pay the Said Mr Clerk fourty pounds p^{r} annum provided that he will Save our town from Keeping any other Gramer School Master, our town allways Reserving a Liberty and power to themselves of Calling and Settleing another minister when providence offers and when our town Sees Cause.

4^{ly} Voted on said Day that the Select men shall allow payment to those persons that they Imploy'd to Cut and make any Hay for James Wallace and Willm Hogg, they being prisoners at the same time in newbury Goall as also what money has been sent them for their suport whilest in s^{d} Confinement Shall be at the town Cost & Charges, and the Com^{ttee} appointed in Defence of the town is by s^{d} vote Impowr'd to give Bonds or Bondsmen for the afores^{d} prisoners appearance to s^{d} newbury Court provided they Can obtain the same

5^{ly} voted That the Settleing of our Equivolent lands is deffer'd untill further orders

6^{ly} voted that the Com^{ttee} or lotlayers of our town shall be allow'd payment to search and find the bounds of neticook land and how farr the same Extends from the River Merrimack

7^{ly} voted that the arrears Dew by our town to Mr Macgregors Heirs Shall be Cess'd by precept according to Law

8^{ly} voted that our town will not allow payment for fencing throw mendments and Second Division

You are hearby Required to Warn the proprietors of this town of Londonderry to meet at their meetinghouse on Munday the 10th Instant at ten of the Clock in the forenoon then and there

1st To See whither the proprietors will allow the Select men to applot money to Carry on law Shuits, & what method they will take to Defray law Shuits Cost allready Contract ed

2^{ly} To See whether they will Chuse a Committee to aggree with James Heath and Luther Martine for Damages now Showed for by them in the County of Essex

3^{ly} To See if they will Chuse a Schoollmaster or Schoollmasters in the room of Mr John Harvey for this half year now Runing and this Shall be your warrant Given under our hands this 1st Day of Nov^{br} 1729

Allen Anderson
John archibald
James Reid
Select men

To Mr John Macneal Constable in Londonderry

At a Proprietory meeting held at Londonderry meetinghouse upon Munday ye 10th of Nov^{br} 1729.

The proprietors Chose for Moderator James Mac Keen Esqr

1 voted that the Select men Shall have power to applot so much money as Shall pay the Charges that lies in the propriety by Law Shuits

2^{ly} voted that Lev^{t} Goffe John archibald & James Clerk Shall have power to go to Heverhill to aggree with James Heeth & Luther Martine for the action Comenced by them against James Wallace and Willm Hogg, and that said Com^{ttee} may Give Bonds to Heverhill people for what money s^{d} Wallace & Hogg is Cost in, at the Superior Court at Salem

3^{ly} It is Concluded that the Select men Shall do as they see Cause annent ashoolmaster or Shoolmasters in the Room of Mr Hervey

You are hearby Required to warn the Proprietors of Londonderry to Conven att their meetinghouse on wensday the 3^{d} Day of Dec^{br} Enshewing by nine of the Clock in the forenoon then and there

Imprimus to See what method they will take to Procure aminister

2^{ly} To See whether or not they will Lott for their Seats in the meeting and when

3^{ly} To See what they will do about a Schooll

4^{ly} To See whether they will Chuse aCommittee to Send to the Government for advise about the Debeats with Heverhill, and this Shall be your warrant Given under our hands this 21st Day of Nov^{br} 1729

James Lindsay
John Archibald
John Wallace
Allen Anderson
James Reid
Select men

To John Macneall Town Constable

At aproprietory meting held at Londonderry meetinghouse upon wensday ye 3^{d} Day of Dec^{br} 1729 the Proprietors Chuse for Moderator Robert Boyes

Imprimus Wheras our town have sometime aggo, which

was at atown meeting held at Londonderry meetinghouse on Munday the 22d Day of Septr 1729 pass'd avote for Setling of the Revd Mr Mathew Clerk to be our minister which vote the said Mr Clerk was not willing to take up with Pershewant to Said vote, it is now voted and aggreed upon on ye above said Day that for Mr Clerk's Encouragement to be our minister we have voted to pay Mr Clerk ninety pounds ayear untill another minister be setled in this Congregation, and from the time of another minister's being Settled in this Congregation it is votted and aggreed upon to pay the said Mr Clerk Eighty pounds year

Dureing his being Capable of performing the work of the ministry, and from thence, it is voted to pay the Said Mr Clerk fourty pounds ayear Dureing life allways reserving aliberty of Calling and Setleing another minister when opportunity offers and our town Sees Cause

2ly voted that aforeseat and aBack Seat Shall be Joyn'd together and the persons that falls Sd Seats Shall Conclude to Chuse their partners and aggree among themselves how they Shall sitt in the Said Seats

3ly voted that the Select men Shall do as they See Cause about a Schooll

4ly as to this artikle it is at this time Defer'd

You are hearby Required to warn the proprietors Inhabitants and freeholders of this town to meet at our Meetinghouse of London Derry upon Munday the 15th of this Instant at ten of the Clock in the forenoon then and there

1st To See if the town will Chuse Commissioners in order to give a Call to a minister from Ireland, and what power the town will Invest the said Commisioners with, or whether the town will rather write to the presbetery of Route or to any particular minister or ministers for the Ends aforesaid

2ly To See if they will Chuse a School master or Schoolmasters

3ly To See whether the town will Draw for their seats after the first or the last vote for that End

4ly To See what Incouragement the town will give to the Building of another Grist mill

5^{ly} To See if the town will Chuse aCommittee to Defend our town lines and this shall be your warrant, Given under our hands this 6th day of December 1729

James Reid
Allen Anderson
James Lindsay
John Wallace
John Archibald
Select men

To John Macneill town Constable

At a town meeting held at Londonderry meetinghouse upon munday ye 15th Day of Dec^{br} 1729, the town Chuse for Moderator Capt James Gregg

1st voted on s^d Day that our town will send for aminister to Ireland and that they will Invest Commisioners with a power to give a Call to a minister in Ireland, and transport the said minister from Ireland to new england and said Comisioners is Impowered to apply themselves in the name of our town to the presbetery of Route for their Concurrance and assistance in the $afores^d$ affair, the names of the Commisioners is viz David Cargill Robert Boyes and Hugh Ramsay,

Also voted that the $afores^d$ Commisioners is to apply to the Rev^d m^r John Cochran of Kilrachts, or M^r nathaniel Cochran of Dungonan or to Mr James Dyks of Machera to Know whether any of them will Come to be our minister, and the aforesaid Commisioners is authorized and Impowered to propose for their Salary one hundred pounds a year

2^{ly} voted that it Shall be in the Select men's power to gett a School master or School masters

3^{ly} voted that Mr James Mackeen Shall Prefuor a petitionato the Quarter Sessions of our province to be held at portsmouth to have the method aggreed upon by our proprietors with Respect to our Seats in our meetinghouse Comfirm'd, and made a By Law and if said Mr Mackeens health do not permitt him to go to s^d Sesions then John Macmurphy is to appear at said Sesions for the End aforesaid

also voted that Mrs Macgregore and familey Shall have their

Choise of any two Seats in our meeting house togother, Save one Seat for the Meetinghouse use or ministeriall

as also voted that our Seats in the meeting house Shall be Rated at Higher and Lower prices for the Maintaining of the Gospell as our ministers Salary may Require, and that the prises that the Comm^{ttee} have sett upon them Shall be a Rule for Rateing or Sesing s^{d} Salary And that our Seats Shall be drawn for according to the vote pass'd for that End at a proprietors Meeting Legaly held January ye 6th 1728/9 and that Every person shall Receive his Seat in Good order or Repair at the town's Charge

4^{ly} nothing done about a Grist mill.

5^{ly} voted that James Gregg James Reid and John Macmurphy shall Joyn Kigstown Committee to run our South line and aggree upon the method thereof and are authorized and Impowered to make asetlement and Determine how s^{d} line shall be runn and that m^{r} James mackeen and John Macmurphy shall go to portsmouth to petition the Gov^{t} of our Grivances with respect to Law Shuits that arises from our neighbouring town (viz) Heverhill

The Severall Returns read & approv'd of one to Sam^{ll} morison one to Edward aiken one to Jo^{n} Gregg, and aministeriall lot at Canada.

You are hearby Required to Warn the proprietors of Londonderry to meet at their Meetinghouse upon Munday ye 2^{d} of February 1729/30 at ten of the Clock in the Forenoon then and their &

Imp^{rs} To See whether they will Chuse a Committee for Defending the Bounds of our township and what authority they will Invest them with

2^{ly} To See what method they will take to make Sure the Seats or Exchange that may be made of Seates in our Meetinghouse

3^{ly} To See whether they will make Sale of the vacant room in our Meetinghouse, and whether by Cant or other wise, and any other thing that may Concern the propriety, and this shall be your warrant

Given under our hands this 13th Day of Jan'y 1729/30

Allen Anderson
James Reid
John Archibald
Select men

And all persons that want hire Seats are Desired to be present at the meetinghouse on the aforesaid Day, and they may Expect to be accomodated

James Reid

At a Proprietors meeting held at Londonderry meeting house upon Munday the 2d Day of February 1729/30

The proprietors Chuse by vote for Moderator James Reid

1st voted that their shall be three men Chosen as a Committee in the Defence of our town against all Incrochers and that the said Committee is Invested with full power to appear in behalf of our town against any persons whatsoever that makes any Incrochments upon any part of our township in any Court Spirituall or temporall and use proper methods to Supress any such person or persons above named

The names of Such persons as are Chosen a Comttee for the aforesaid End and Busines is James Mackeen Esqr James Reid and James Nesmith

2ly Wheras we the proprietors of this town of Londonderry have Built and Finished our Meetinghouse Different from the Generall method of other towns in our province haveing paid the publick Charges of our meetinghouse by the propriety, and haveing Drawn for our Seats by Lott the Consentibly that So Every proprietor May have Justice

voted that Every proprietor or other that Buys or Exchangess any Seat or Seats in our Meetinghouse, Shall have the same Confirmed and Established and made Good to them and their Sussessors for Ever, providing that they Signify their Desire for the Ends aforesaid, and Desire that the town Clerk for the time being may Enter Records in our town Book for the Ends a foresaid, the parties Signing to the Said Records, and the same shall be authentick to all Intents and purposess any law usuage or Custom to the Contrary notwithstanding

3^{ly} voted that the vacant Room for Building Seats upon, Shall be Sold by Cant to the Highest Bidder, upon the fifth Day of March in the forenoon before the town meeting Enter and that the Select men Shall have up publick advertisements Constantly from time to time untill the aforesaid Day,

The Severall Returns Read and approv'd of by the proprietors one to m^r^ philips one to James Calderwood, one to Joshua Thorntown & John Macmurphy alies Edward procter, one to John Barr, one to Ro^t^ & Hugh wilson one to Jo^n^ Senter, one to James Gregg and Sam^ll^ Gregg one to Ann Archibald

You are hearby Required to Warn the freeholders and Inhabitants of Londonderry to Conven at their Meetinghouse on thursday the fifth of March next Enshewing at nine of the Clock before noon then and there

Imprimus To Chuse their town officers for the year Enshewing

2^{ly} To See whether the proprietors of the town will oblige such of their number as have y^{tt} settled their Lots to fullfill the Condition of the Charter, as to their Settlement after the Indian Warr

3^{ly} To See what method they will take to prevent tipling housess

4^{ly} To See whether they will Establish a pound or pounds

5^{ly} To See whether they will Chooose a Schoolmaster or Schoolmasters

6^{ly} To See what method they will take to pay the Hundred and Sixty pounds William Hogg and James Wallace were Cast in at Salem Court

and this Shall be y^r warrant Given under our hands this 16th Day of february 1729/30

James Lindsay
John Archibald
Allen Anderson
John Wallace
James Reid
Select men

To Mr John Macneall town Constable

At aGenerall town Meeting held at Londonderry meeting-house March ye 5th 1729/30

The town Choose for Moderator Ensign James Nesmith

Willm Humphra & others do protest against the proceedings of ye 5th day of March, 1729/30 untill we be satisfied w^{t} the disbursements of the towns money these two years past

voted that there Shall be five men Chosen to Serve as Select men for the Enshewing year, the names of the men is as followeth John Wallace James Lindsay Allen Anderson James Reid John Archibald

voted that John MacMurphy Shall be town Clerk for the Enshewing year

voted that their Shall be two Constables Chosen in this town to Serve for the Enshewing year, and that Each of them Shall be allow'd for their Service by the town as Such fifty shi^{lls} the names of the men is ass followeth Willm Humpra for the East side of Beaver Brook, and John Anderson for the westerly Side of the afores^{d} Brook

voted for Sirvayers for the Enshewing year Gabriel Barr John Barnat Junr Willm Gregg Jame^{s} Rodgers James Wallace, Jo^{n} Blair Willm Adams Willm Aiken Capt Gregg

voted for tithing men for the Enshewing year Willm Cochran & Ro^{t} Wear

voted for Hawards for the Enshewing year James Boyes & John Richey

voted for fence veiwers and prisers for ye Enshewing year Jo^{n} Morison & James Leslie

voted for field Driver for ye Enshewing year Alex^{r} MacMurphy

voted for Searching the town's accounts with the Select men James Nesmith John Blair John Macmurphy

voted that all Such persons or proprietors that are not Constantly Inhabiting upon their Lots or putt an Inhabitant upon their Lotts in this town Shall be obliged to Setle their Lotts according to time limetted in our Charter, or Else they may Expect Such Measures will be taken as the Charter of our town Directs voted that all tipling housess that are or may arise in this town are Discharged and forbiden upon penalty of being prosecuted as the Law directs

voted that their Shall be two pounds built in this town and that David Dickey and John Stewart Shall be Constituted and Invested with a power and Liberty to Keep Each of them a pound, and that they Shall have full power and Liberty to be pounders Dureing Such time as they Shall Maintain and Keep up Said pounds in Good and Suficient Repair

voted that Mr Mackeen John MacMurphy and John Morison Shall be Impover'd to treat with Mr Theodw Atkinson anent the lands that he Claims within the Bounds of our town

voted that Jesse Cristie John Barnatt Junr and James Rodgers Shall Serve ass a Committee in the Defence of our town's Bounds

The Severall transcripts Read and approv'd of by the town one to Mathew Clerk one to David Dickey & Mathew Taylor one to Alex^r Renkine one to John Woodburn one to Willm Adam's one to James MacCurdy one to John Richey, one to John MacConechy one to James Lindsay, and one to James Leslie

You are hearby Required to warn the proprietors of Londonderry to Conven at their Meetinghouse on Munday the Sixteenth Instant at ten of the Clock before noon then and there

Imp^s To See what method they will take to raise the hundred and Sixty pounds to be paid for Willm Hogg and James Wallace's Redemption from the Massachusets Courts.

2^ly To hear their accounts Read.

3^ly To make Seale of the vacant Room in the Meetinghouse.

4^ly To Establish a Committee for Defending our town lines.

5^ly To See if the town will aprove of the returns from the lot Layers that are or may be read before the proprietors at the meeting

6ly To See if the proprietors will Confirm the Severall peaces or proportions of Lands that have been laid out by the Severall Committees or lot Layers that have and are Recorded to their heirs & assigns for Ever

and this shall be your warrant Given under our hands this 7th of March 1729/30

James Lindsay
Allen Anderson
John Archibald
John Wallace
James Reid
Select men

To Willm Humphra or John Anderson town Constable's

At a proprietors meeting held at Londonderry Meeting-house March ye 16th 1729/30 The proprietors voted for Moderator Robert Wear

The Said meeting by Consent is adjurned untill Munday ye 23d at ten of the Clock in the forenoon

1st voted that Robert Wear & John MacMurphy are authorized and Commisionated to go to Heverhill and aggree with James Heath and Martine Luther for the damages that they Shew Willm Hogg and James Wallace for, and if they Can make up the Sd aggreement they are authorized and Impovr'd to give bonds to the payment of the aforesd Damagess

John morison Junr Enters his decent against the aforesd vote

2ly after the Reading of the towns accounts for the year 1727 & for ye year 1728, the Sd accounts was approv'd of by the major part of the proprietors by vote

James Morison and John Morison Junr Decents against the afore sd vote

3ly as to the sale of the vacant room in the meeting-house it is defer'd at this time

4ly voted that John Barnat Junr Thomas Stiel and James Aiken Shall Serve as a Committee for the Defence of our town bounds and that sd Comttee Shall Serve in the sd office for the space of six months from the date hearof, and that it shall be in their power to Defend or Commence all Law

Shuits against any trespassors, or Incrochers on our land's within the bounds of our lines and to Employ one or more attorneys as they shall see needfull at the Cost of the proprietors, and the Same shall be as authentick as if the whole propriety had done the same

5ly voted that what Return's is Read that Comes from the Lott layers or Committee appointed for laying out Equivolent land Shall be approv'd of to the owners thereof & their heirs for Ever, there is one Read at this meeting by James Aiken and approv'd of to him & his heirs for Ever

6ly That Wheras their is Severall Return's of land laid out by the Lott layers of our town Read & approv'd of and Recorded only to the Severall persons to whom the aforesd lands was laid out too

It is hearby voted and to be understood that all the aforesd lands that has been recorded as aforesaid, it is to be Construed, that all of the aforesd lands is laid out and Recorded to them and their heirs for Ever any thing to the Contrary notwithstanding

You are hearby Required to Warn the proprietors of Londonderry to Conven at their Meetinghouse on thursday ye 28th of this Instant May at ten of the Clock Before Noon then and there

Imp: To See what method they will take to Raise Money for Defraying William Hogg's and James Wallace's Cost at the Massachusets Courts (viz) the hundred and Sixty pounds they were Cast in

2ly To See whether they will give any Encouragement for Building another Grist mill, on some part of Beaver Brook And this Shall be yr warrant Given under our hands this 8th Day of May 1730

Allen Anderson
James Lindsay
John Archibald
John Wallace
James Reid
Select men

To William Humphra and John Anderson Town Consta-ble's

I have taken Due Care to Warn the proprietors of this town according to the Custom of the s^d town against s^d Day and this is my Return William Humphra Constable.

At a proprietors Meeting held at Londonderry Meeting-house upon thursday ye 28th Day of May 1730 the proprietors Chuse for moderator Robert Wear

1 voted that the proprietors will take no method to Defray William Hogg and James Wallace Cost at the Massachusets Courts

We the under Subscribers proprietors of Londonderry do hearby protest and Enter our Discent against paying any further Charges that may arise from this Day Forward on account of a vote pass'd this day against payment of William Hoggs & James Wallace's Cost at ye Massachusets Courts Given under our hands this 28th of may 1730

John Wallace	David Cargill
John Archibald	James Mackeen
Robert Morison	John Richey
Allen Anderson	James Rodgers
John Macmurphy	James Reid

voted

2^{ly} That Wheraas Benjamin Willson of our town upon the Encouragement that the proprietors offers, is willing to Build agrist mill in the most Convenient place upon Beaver Brook Betwen Robert Doak's meadown now Mr Foye's and the Bridge Called the Lower Bridge upon Beaver Brook, and obliges himself to keep up amill upon s^d place from time to time and for Ever and that in Good Repair upon the following Conditions which is as followeth that the town or propriety will Grant the s^d Benjamin Wilson the priviledge of Beaver brook Stream at the aforesaid place before mentioned, and will purchase if possible with Conveniency that peace of meadow now in the possesion of M^r. Foye or So much of it as will be needfull for a Dam to the Said Grist mill, But if s^d Stream or meadow Ground Cannot be Conveniently purchas'd than the Stream at the falls or place Determin'd to Build s^d mill to be the proprietors as at first, But upon the Contrary if the afores^d meadow Ground Can be purchas'd by the proprietors for the Equivolent of it of meadow in another place then it is hearby to be understood by this vote that s[d] Stream and meadow Ground for a Dam is Granted to s[d] Benjamin Willson, the proprietors always Reserving a priviledge to themselves and their heirs for Ever of haveing their Grain or Corn Ground Before any other person whatsoever as they Shall call for it, and that the said Benjamin Wilson his heirs & Sucesors Shall not detain any proprietor that Comes to s[d] mill any Longer than the Corn that is or may be in the Hopper at the proprietors Entering the mill is Ground out and it is Likevise to be understood by this vote that s[d] Wilson his heirs or assigns is and Shall be obliged to Build and have the said mill fitt for Grinding at or upon the first of June one thousand Seven hundred and thirty one and upon Default of all or Every or any of the afores[d] Conditions to be performed by the s[d] Wilson & his heirs or Succesors from time to time then the s[d] stream with the priviledges Granted thereunto is to Return to the proprietors and at their Disposal as at first, which is the true Intent and meaning of this vote any thing to the Contrary Not withstanding

You are hearby Required to warn the Proprietors of Londonderry to meet at their meetinghouse on Wensday y[e] fifteenth of July next at ten of the Cloack in the forenoon then and there

Imprimus To See what method they will take to Solve the Controversy anent a Lot of Land that John Goffe Jun[r] threatnes to Recover from this town w[e] the proprietors of this town knows nothing off

2[ly] To See if they will Chuse men to take an Invoice of the Ratable poles & Estates of this town

3[ly] To Chuse a Sutable person to take care of our town Charter in the Room of James Alexander

4[ly] To Chuse a Com[ttee] to form a Suplication and present the same to the Generall Assembly at Portsmouth in order to obtain Relief from the Grivancess we are under from the massachusets Province

5[ly] To See whether they will Expose to Sale the falls on

Cohaset Brook Joyning upon Robt & Hugh Wilson's Equivolent land

6^ly^ To See whether they will approve of the Return's of Land Laid out by the Lot Layers and this Shall be your Warrant Given under our hands this 26th of June 1730

James Reid
James Lindsay
Allen Anderson
John Archibald
Select men

To William Humphra & John Anderson Constables

At a Meeting of the Proprietors Legally Called & assembled at Londonderry Meetinghouse July ye 15th 1730

The proprietors Chuse for Moderator John Mac neall

voted that the proprietors have Chosen a Committee of three men (viz) John Morison William Humphra and John Macmurphy to See if they Can Solve the Controversy Betwen the proprietors of this town & John Goffe Junr Concerning aLot of Land that he threatnes to have from this town

voted that their Shall be two men Chosen to take an Invoice of the Ratable Estates and poles in this town, and they are to have for their Service three pounds

The names of the men is as follow's William Moore & William Gregg

voted that Robert Wear of our town is Chosen to Keep our Charter in the Room of James Alexander

voted that Mr James Mackeen Shall be the person that Shall form & present a Supplication to the Gen^ll^ assembly at Portsmouth Concerning the Grivances that we Labour under from ye Massachusets Gov^t^

Voted that the fals at Cohassat Brook Reserved by the Proprietors out of Robert and Hugh Wilson Equivolent land with all the other priviledges Reserved to s^d^ fals Shall be Sold by Cant to the Highest Bidder

The afores^d^ fals being put to Cant and no person appearing to overbid Patrick Douglas in what he proposess to Give for it which is ten pounds in bils of Credit*

voted that Patrick Douglas or his assigns Shall have the Said fals for what he offers which is ten pounds with all the profits priviledges and advantages Reserv'd for the use of Said falls, and Shall have what ass ureance is needfull for the Same when he pleases, he haveing paid the s[d] money at the Same time the vote was pass'd

Their being a Return made by the Lotlayers of Land laid out to Mathew Clerk & John Wallace w[c] Did originally belong to John Shields Right Consisting of one hundred and fifty three acres s[d] Return being Read it is voted y[t] S[d] Return Shall be put upon Record

You are hearby Required to Warn the Proprietors & Inhabitants of London-Derry to Conven at their Meetinghouse on Munday the 24th of Agust next at Eight of the Clock in the forenoon then and there &

Imprimus To hear the List of Defraying M[r] Macgregors funerall Charges Read

2[ly] To See if they will Choose a new Com[ttee] & a Treas-

*To the readers who may not understand the meaning of this term, which appears frequently in the records of those days, a brief description of the financial situation during those periods may not be out of place. Various expedients were resorted to by the colonists in order to effect means of business intercourse. The General Court of Massachusetts in 1690 issued what were known as "Bills of Credit" to the amount of seven thousand pounds. These bills circulated also in New Hampshire, and soon beginning to depreciate in value caused considerable hardship among the people. Late in 1709, in trying to meet the obligations incurred by border warfare, New Hampshire issued bills of credit to the amount of three thousand pounds. These were to be redeemed in five years, and this was the first emission of paper money in New Hampshire. In 1714, the year of their maturity, there was another emission, followed by others in 1717, 1722, 1724, 1725, 1726, 1727, 1729. These bills depreciated so rapidly in value that in 1741 the Government was able to pay only one fourth of the value expressed on their face, and it was more than they were worth on the market.—EDITOR.

urer to Search the towns accounts to the End they may be made Sensible of the disbursments of their money

3ly To See whether the proprietors will allow those that were uneasey about their Equivolent & additionall Lands Laid out or to be laid out, or to Drop their Sd lands or Claims for the Same, and to Chuse in the Commons

4ly To Chuse a Commttee to Give bonds to Mr Clerk for his Salary

5ly To See whether they will Defend those that have their Lands and meadows taken away or threatened to be taken away or let them Defend themselves

6ly To See Whether they will Chuse a Comttee to aggree with a workman to Build a Schooll house and how large they will have it

7ly To See what they will do about the proprietors meeting yt was adjourned till ye 15th of this Instant

8ly To See what they will do about John Moore and this Shall be yr Warrant Given under our hand this 24th Day of July 1730

James Reid
John Wallace
James Lindsay
Allen Anderson
John Archibald
Select men

To William Humphra or John Anderson town's Constables

N. B.—A second copy of this warrant is entered in the Records, which it is not thought necessary to repeat there.—Editor.

At a Town meeting held at Londonderry Meetinghouse upon munday the 24th of agust 1730 The town Chuse for Moderator Robert Wear

1st voted that their shall be a treasurer Chosen

2ly voted that Alexr Nickels James aiken and John Morison Shall Serve as a Comttee to the End the town may be made Sensible of the Disbursments of their money,

We the under Subscribers do hearby Enter our Decent

against the foregoing vote their being a Com^{ttee} legally Chosen for the aforesaid End at our last march meeting

James Rodgers
Allen Anderson
James Lindsay
Jesse Cristey
John Macmurphy
John Archibald
James Reid

3^{ly} voted on Said day that all persons or proprietors that have lands lying in Debeate or Controversy with any other town, or the province line, Shall have liberty to lay down their lands or Claims to the town, and may have what land is due them upon that account in any other part of our Commons not laid out nor allready Claim'd

4^{ly} voted that the town Shall Give bonds to the Rev'd m^{r} Mathew Clerk for his Sallary the persons Chosen by the town in their behalf to Give the aforesaid Bonds is Mr James Mackeen Capt James Gregg Mr Alex^{r} Nikles Mr Jo^{n} Archibald Mr James Reid Mr Edward Aiken James Lindsay

5^{ly} voted y^{t} ye 5th artikle is Defferd only Law Shuts allready Commenc'd to be Carrid on, but if possible to Stop them untill further direction from the Gov^{t}

the 6th artikle Concerning a Schooll house Building is Defferd untill ye 5th of march next

the 7th artikle is defferd at present or lay'd asside

the 8th artikle is deffer'd by reason Jo^{n} Moore is Dead

You are hearby Required to Warn the proprietors & freeholders of Londonderry to Conven at their meetinghouse on Saterday ye 24th Instant at ten of the Clock before noon then and there &c

Imprimmus To Know their minds about Setleing a Second minister

2^{ly} To Know whether they will Choose a Commisioner to attend the next presbetry to be held at Boston in order to obtain the hearing of Some ministers

3ly To See what answer the proprietors will Send to a letter lately sent from mr Achimutey to the Selct men Relateing to Willm Hogs Imprisonments

4ly To See what must be done with Hugh Willson that's uneasey to petter Cochran & others in threatning to abuse their persons and Destroy their Goods

5ly To See if the proprietors will approve of the Severall Returns made by the Comttee for Laying out mendments & adition lands when Read And this Shall be your warrant Given under our hands at Londonderry this 14th day of octobr 1730

Allen Anderson
John Archibald
John Wallace
James Reid
Select men

To Willm Humphra and John Anderson Town Constables

At ameeting of the proprietors and freeholders of Londonderry held at their meetinghouse october ye 24th 1730 they Chuse for moderator John Blair

1st voted that the town will not have a Second minister at this present

2ly voted that they will not send a Commisioner to the next presbetry to be held at Boston

3ly voted that what money Can be Raised to Relieve Willm Hogg Shall be rais'd by way of a Gift

4ly voted that the town hath aggreed to let Hugh Willson be prosecuted for an Idler as the law directs

5ly voted the Severall Returns or transcripts Shall be put on Record to their owners & their heirs (viz) one to Jon archd one for James Clerk one to David Gregg & Alexr maccay & one to John Blair one to Mathew Clerk & Jon Wallace

You are hearby Required to Warn the proprietors and freeholders of Londonderry to Conven at their meetinghouse on wensday the Sixteenth Day of December next at ten of the Clock before noon then and their

1st To See what method the proprietors of this town will take to oblige Such of their number that are non Residents to pay their Rates and Setle their Lots according to the Condition of their Charter

2ly To See what method the town will take to make way for the Setlement of a Second minister according to the Intent of the town as by Record will appear

3ly To See what method they will take in Calling & Setleing a Second minister

4ly To See whether the proprietors will Condesend to have a Door at Each End of the meetinghouse on the South side, for the Conveniency of those that Sitt in the Gallaries

5ly To See if the town will do any thing to hinder the Rigorous prosicution of the Barr's against Thos Stewart in Endeavouring to hinder him to declare his Guilt before the Congregation and this shall be your warrant Given under our hands this 21 of November 1730

Lastly to See if the town will approve of the severall Returns of land laid out by our lotlayers to Some proprietors that have land to lay out which is their due &

James Lindsay
Allen Anderson
John Archibald
John Wallace
James Reid
Select men

At a meeting of the proprietors and freeholders of Londonderry held at their meetinghouse December ye Sixteenth 1730 they Chuse for moderator Mr James Mackeen

1st voted that Alexander Nickols John Moore and John Macmurphy Shall act in behalf of the proprietors as a Committee to notifie the non Residents to pay up their Rates due by them and Settle their lands or else they may Expect to be treated as our Charter obliges them that are Delinquent

2ly voted that in order to have a Second minister for this Congregation we have aggreed and Concluded to have a Supplication Sent to the Presbetry of Roate in the Kingdom of Ireland to help and assist us in this affair namely to help us to one of three ministers which is Either Mr James Dicks Mr James MacCurdy or Mr James Moore

3^ly^ and for the Better Carying on this affair of haveing a Second minister Setled hear it is voted and agreed upon that their shall be a Committee nominated and appointed and Impower'd to advise and Consult with our present minister Mr Mathew Clerk in the properest methods for the obtaining one of the aforesaid ministers and to assist them in that affair, and that said Committee Shall meet Mr Clerk at Ensign Nesmiths house upon friday the Eighteenth Day of this Instant for Said End and purpose the names of the Committee is as followeth (viz) Mr James mac Keen Capt James Gregg Alex^r^ Nickels John archibald Jam^s^ Reid Edward Aiken James Lindsay Capt Cargill Capt Goffe Mr George Duncan John Moore Robert Wear Robert Given Jo^n^ Morison John Macmurphy,

the 4th artikle in the foregoing warrant Deferd

the 5th artikle laid aside and nothing done Concerning it

the severall Returns was Read and approvd of to their owners and their heirs (viz) one to Jo^n^ and Willm Gregg & Sam^ll^ Graves one to James Blair and one to Nathaniel Boyenton of Stephen peirce's propriety

You are hearby Required to Warn the proprietors and freeholders of Londonderry to Conven at their meetinghouse on Munday ye Eighteenth Instant by nine of the Cloack before noon then and there

Imp: To See whether they will approve of the last assessment made by the Select men now in the Constables hands

2^ly^ To See whether they will Send for any of those ministers voted for at last town Meeting

3^ly^ To See whether they will at the Charge of transporting any of the Said ministers

4^ly^ To See what Encouragement they will propose for the obtaining of any of those ministers

5^ly^ To See whether they will Chuse a Com^ttee^ to give bonds to m^r^ Clerk for his Stipends

6^{ly} To See if they will accept of another to Serve as Constable in the Room of John Anderson

7^{ly} To See whether they can fix upon amethod to obtaine aminister to assist Mr Clerk as a Colleague according to the present Constitution of ye Congregation

8^{ly} To See whether they will allow those persons that lately Subscribed for atown meeting to be sett of as a Distinct Congregation

9^{ly} To See if they will Concurr with them in building a meetinghouse

10^{ly} To See whether they will pay a third part of their ministers Salary provided he be allowed to preach with them athird part of the time

11^{ly} To See whether they will allow a Lawer to be Consulted about those persons that are Setleing at amasceegg, & this shall be your warrant Given under our hands this Eight day of January 1730/31

James Lindsay
Allen Anderson
John Archibald
James Reid
Select men

To William Humphra and John Anderson town Constables

At a Meeting of the proprietors and freeholders of the town of Londonderry assembled at their meetinghouse on Munday ye 18th Day of January anno Domini 1730/31

The proprietors & freeholders Chuse for moderator Robert Boys

1st voted that they do approve of the last assesment made by the Select men now in the Constables hands

2^{ly} voted that they will Send for one of those minister's that we voted for at our last meeting

3^{ly} voted that they are willing and have Concluded & aggreed that they will be at the Cost and Charges of transporting any one of the aforesaid ministers that will come to us to be our minister

4^{ly} voted that for the Incouragement of any one of the

aforesaid ministers that will come hear to be our minister we have voted for his Salary one hundred pounds to be paid him in Currant money of newengland pr annum, Besides what private Instructions we Conclude to give our Commisioner or Commisioners for the Incouragement of s^{d} minister

5^{ly} voted that they have Chosen a Committee to give bonds to the Rev^{d} master mathew Clerk for his Stipend according to what our town have Concluded and aggreed with him for as it was voted by the proprietors and freeholders at ameeting December ye 3^{d} 1729 the names of Com^{ttee} Chosen and apponted for Said End is Mr James Mac Keen Alexander Nickels Hugh Ramsey James Clerk & John Morison Junr

6^{ly} voted that they will not accept of another to Serve Constable in the Room of John Anderson

7^{ly} voted that they will Deffer takeing any method at present for the obtaining any other minister to be a Coleguee to Mr Clerk untill they have a further account Concerning those minister's that they have Concluded to Send for to Ireland

8^{ly} voted that they will not allow of those persons that lately Subscribed for atown meeting to be Sett of as a distinct Congregation

9^{ly} voted that they will not Concur with them in Building of a meeting house

10^{ly} voted that they will not Contribute to pay a third part of their ministers Sallary nor have no part of his time

11^{ly} voted that they are willing to leave the Consulting of a Lawyer abot the Setlement that is Carried on at ammasceegg to the Select men and the Com^{tte} that is appointed for the Defence of the propriety

I the under named person do protest against Giveing bonds to the Rev^{d} Mr Clerk

John Blair

Londonderry January ye 18th 1730/31 We the Subscrib-

ers do protest against all the proceedings of a Generall town meeting on the above s^{d} day
Jo^{n} Bell Andrew Todd abraham Holms William Aiken Willm Nutt David Morison Edward Aiken James Aiken Robert Given Sam^{ll} Morison Thomas Bogle

You are hearby Required to Warn the proprietors & freholders of LondonDerry to Conven at their Meetinghouse on Wensday ye twenty Eight Instant at nine of the Clock before noon then & there

Imprimus To See if they will Chuse a Committee to draw up Reasons for transportation of those ministers to be Sent for, & to aggree for their passage thither and to Chuse Commisioners to attend Church Judicatures in order to their transportation

2^{ly} To Chuse a fit person for Representitive or assembly man

3^{ly} To See what the town will do Concerning Mrs Macgregors Rates as it is Set forth in a Supplication presented to them

4^{ly} To See if they will approve of the Severall Returns made by the Lotlayers of this town to be read then

5^{ly} To See if they will allow James Leslie payment for makeing a fire for Mr Clerk

6^{ly} To See if they will do any thing to Reconcile those debeats Betwen Jo^{n} Barr & Thos Stewart

7^{ly} To See if they will allow William Humphra any more Salary then Jo^{n} Anderson on account of the numerouness of the Inhabitants of his District, & this Shall be your Warrant Given under our hands this Eighteenth day of January 1730/31

James Lindsay
Allen Anderson
Jo^{n} Archibald
Jo^{n} Wallace
James Reid
Select men

At ameeting of the proprietors & freeholders of the town of Londonderry assembld at their meeting house upon wensday ye 18th day of January 1730/31

The proprietors & freeholders Chuse for Moderator James Mackeen Esqr

Voted that their Shall be five men Chosen as a Committee to draw up reasons for transportation of one of those ministers that is to be Sent for and to aggree for their passage, as also to Chuse a Commisioner to attend Church Judicatures in order to transportation the names of the Com^{ttee} Is Hugh Ramsey Jo^n Blair Capt Cargill Robert Wearr & James Mac Keen

2^{ly} voted that Jo^n Macmurphy Shall Serve as Representitive or assembly man for this town

3^{ly} voted that in answer to m^{rs} Macgregors petition praying to be Clear'd from Rates, the payer of s^d petition is so farr granted that She Shall be Clear'd from paying Rates for her own Seat in the meetinghouse dureing life or her abode in this town

4^{ly} voted the Severall Return's made by the Lottlayers is approv'd of to their owners & their heirs for Ever (viz) one to James Liggett one to $Will^m$ Campbell two to Jo^n Bell one to James Gregg & Ben: Kidder & Hendry Green one to Randle Alexander, & one to $Will^m$ Eyres

5^{ly} voted that James Lesliee Shall have thirty Shi^{lls} paid him for his past Service & this Winters for makeing afire for m^r Clerk but not to be precedented for the future

6^{ly} voted that the town offers a Refference to Jo^n Barr in behalf of $Thom^s$ Stewart Differences & his

7^{ly} voted that the town will not allow $Will^m$ Humphray any more Salary for being Constable than Jo^n Anderson has

You are hearby Required to Warn the Proprietors Freeholders and Inhabitants of Londonderry to Meet at their Meetinghouse upon Friday the fifth day of March next at nine of the Clock in the forenoon then and there

1st To Chuse their town officers for the year Enshewing

2^{ly} To See Whether the town will Chuse a Committee to

prosecute Capt John Goffe for Recording land to himself when he was town Clerk that he ought not to have done

3^ly To See if the proprietors will approve of the transcripts or Returns made by the Committee or Lottlayers Chosen for that End,

4^ly To See if the town will Chuse a Committee for the Defence of our lands from any Incrouchers that are or may be found Incrouching upon any part of our town ship

5^ly To See whether the town will alter the Fair from the Meetinghouse, and this Shall be your Warrant Given under our hands this Eighteenth Day of February 1730/31

Allen Anderson
John Archibald
John Wallace
James Lindsay
Select Men

To Willm Humphra or John Anderson Town Constables

At a Generall town Meeting of the proprietors Freeholders & Inhabitants of the town of Londonderry assembled at their meetinghouse upon friday the fifth day of March anno Domini 1730/31

Voted for Moderator...............Mr James Mac Keen

voted that their Shall be five men Chosen to Serve as Select Men for the Enshewing year the names of the men is as followeth John Wallace, James Lindsay, Allen Anderson James Reid John Archibald

voted for Town Clerk for the Enshewing year John Mac Murphy

voted that their Shall be two Constables Chosen to Serve for the Enshewing year, and that they Shall have for their Service as Such fifty Shi^lls Each of them and that Beaver Brook Shall be the Divideing line for said Constables the names of Said Constables is James Thomson and William Gregg and that James Thomson Shall Collect the Rates that is to be rais'd upon the Inhabitants that lives upon the Easterly Side of Beaver Brook, and William Gregg Shall Collect the

Rates that is to rais'd upon the Inhabitants that lives upon the Westerly Side of S^{d} Beaver Brook, and it is voted forthwith that William Gregg Shall have power to Execute the office of Constable in that part of the town that James Thomson was Chosen for, as well as in that part that he was Chosen for himself by his own desire

voted for Sirvayers for the Enshewing year Gabriel Barr John Barnat Junr Willm Gregg James Rodgers John Blair Thos Horner Willm Adams Willm Aiken Capt Gregg

voted for Hawards for the Enshewing year John Richey James Boyes

voted for Tithing men for the Enshewing year Robt Wear Robt MacKeen

voted for field Driver for the Enshewing year Alex^{r} Macmurphy and the S^{d} field Driver is to have for his Service in Rideing about through the town to See that no Strange Cattle be brought in upon our Commons to destroy our meadows ten Shi^{lls} Besides what he Can by Law recover for takeing up s^{d} Cattle

voted that their Shall be three men Chosen to Serve as a Committee to Examine the Select mens accoumpts and assessors for the Enshewing year, the names of S^{d} Com^{ttee} that is voted for & Chosen is James Nesmith John Blair John MacMurphy

2^{ly} voted that their is three men Chosen as a Committee to prosecute Capt John Goffe for Recording land to himself when he was Town Clerk that he ought not to have done the names of the Said Com^{ttee} is as followeth Mr James Mac Keen Robert Wear John MacMurphy

But if the S^{d} Capt Goffe do Give the Said Committee Sufficient Security that the town Shall Receive no damage loss nor Disturbance by the Records alledged against him, then the Said Committee is by S^{d} vote Impowered to Make up the matter with him, which Shall be a finall Issue of the same, but if he will not make up the matter with the S^{d} Com^{ttee} then they are to proceed in prosecuting S^{d} Goffe as farr as law will afford

Tho[s] Willson haveing had a Return Read it is voted that the Same Shall be Entred & Recorded for the use of S[d] Willson and his heirs

voted that their is three men Chosen as a Committee to defend our lands from any Incrouchers that are or may be found Incroching on any part of our township the names of the men is as followeth William Humphra John Barnat Jun[r] Sam[ll] Barr

voted that they will not alter the fair from the Meeting-house

voted that M[r] Willson that is our present Schoolmaster Shall be Continued for the Enshewing year, and for the Better accomodation of the Severall Quarters of this town to have the Benefit of our Schoolls it is hearby to be known that it is voted that their Shall be a a Shooll house built in Each Quarter in this town, where it shall be Judged most Convenient, and the Schooll Master to be Remov'd to Each of the said houses and to Continue there by Keeping Schooll according to the Equall proportion of Rates that Said Quarter of the town pays and So from time to time untill further orders, and that Each quarter of the town Shall build their own School house at their own Charge and maintain the Same,

You are hearby Required to Warn the proprietors & freeholders of Londonderry to meet at their Meetinghouse on thursday y[e] 22[ed] Instant at ten of the Clock before noon then & there

Imp:[s] To See whether they will buy Some Small tract of Land, to be Given as a gift to the next minister and his heirs in Perpetuity.

2[ly] To See whether they will have two Door Struck out upon the South Side of the meetinghouse

3[ly] To hear the Disbursements of the Rates for the year 1729

4[ly] To See whether the will be at the Expence of two Cannoos to be Kept at ammasceegg for the Safety of the people at the fishing

5[ly] To See if the town in Generall will be at the Charge of Repairing the pond Bridge

6ly To See whither they will Considering the Weakness of Mr Dallrimple's Congregation allow aSabbaths Collection for his Support

and this Shall be your Warrant Given under our hands this 6th of april 1731

James Lindsay
John Archibald
John Wallace
James Reed
Allen Anderson
Select men

To Mr Willm Humphra or John Anderson or Willm Gregg Constables

At ameeting of the proprietors & freeholders of Londonderry upon thursday ye 22ed of april 1731.

voted and Chosen for Moderator — — — — Mr Mac Keen

voted that the ministeriall Lot Shall be measur'd and Veiwed and the Same made up as other lots in town, as also the mendment of Said lot to be laid out, and the Second Division of the Same and Returns made by the lot Layers of the town, in order to have the same put upon Record for the towns use as they see Cause

2ly voted in Stead of Strikeing out Doors upon the South Side of the Meetinghouse that their Shall be Iron Latchess put upon our meetinghouse doors by the Select men, and a Good Lock put upon the the South Door of our Meetinghouse at the Expence and Charge of the town

3ly voted that the Disbursments of the Rates Collected by John Macneall Constable for ye year 1729 was so farr read as that the were approv'd of by the town

4ly voted that in order to the safety of our towns people at the fishing at ammascegg, the Select men is Impower'd to allow and pay out of the Publick Charge or Rates of the town, three pounds in Bils of Credit to Such person or persons as Shall be oblig'd to make two Good Sufficient Cannos and Capable to manage the sd Cannoos, the Select men obliging the aforesaid undertakers to Serve the Inhabitants of the town the whole time of fishing before any out of towns people, and Shall not Exceed one Shi[ll] p[r] Hundre for all the fish that they Shall ferry over from the Islands and the owner of the fish and his attendants is to be ferried backwards and forwards at free Cost,

5[ly] voted that the Select men & the Sirvayers of High way Sallat our first May fair appoint atime to Regulate the Severall parts of the town, in order to the Repairing of all Difficult places and Bridges that want Repairing & mending in this town, as also to make an Equall Devident of all the Roads & high ways in this town in order that Every quarter of the town may know where they are to Repair

Their was something spoke of Concerning a Collection for M[r] Darimple Congregation but no reall vote pass'd upon it

You are hearby Required to Warn the proprietors of LondonDerry to Conven at their Meetinghouse on Munday y[e] 24th Instant by Six of the Clock in the morning precisley then

To act & do all Such things as may be thought for their defence against a Sutt of Law now Commenc'd against them by John Goffe Jun[r] Relating to aLott of Land he says he wants from them, and this Shall be your warrant Given under our hands this 18th Day of May 1731

James Lindsay
Allen Anderson
John Archibald
John Wallace
James Reid

To M[r] Will[m] Gregg Town Constable.

At a proprietors meeting held at Londonderry upon munday y[e] 24th of May 1731

The proprietors voted for Moderator M[r] John Blair

voted that the proprietors of the afores[d] Londonderry Will Stand the Law Shute with John Goffe Jun[r] that he has Commenc'd against them, for alot of land that he says he wants from the proprietors aforesaid by virtue of his name being Entred in the Schedule annexed to their Charter, and for the further Carrying on the aforesaid Law Shute the proprietors by vote have Chosen John MacMurphy & John Morison Junr as a Committee Impowered by the proprietors to appear in their behalf in the Defence of the aforesaid Law Shute or action, and that all or Each or any one of the aforesaid proprietors Committee, Shall and may act and do Every thing needfull and pertinent to the aforesaid affair with as full and ample authority and Strength as if we the proprietors of London Derry were all personally present, and have voted to Carry on the aforesaid Defences at the proprietors Cost & Charges

Enter my Desent against that Sute of Law with Jo^{n} Goffe Junr

William Humphra

at aproprietors meeting held ye 24th day of may in Londonderry in order to defend John Goffe Junr in alaw Shute that he hath Commenc'd against them for aright that he ought to have by virtue of his name being Entered in aShedule annexed to a Charter for s^{d} town & have proceeded to Chuse aCommittee to Defend him we the Subscriber do therefore Enter our protest against all the votes of Said meeting

John Goffe
Willm Humphra
John Goffe Junr for Andrew Spalding
& Joseph Kidder

You are hearby Required to Warn the Proprietors of Londonderry to Conven at their meetinghouse on munday ye 12th of July next, then and there

Impr^{s} To See whether they will allow the Select men to applott money to Defend the action at Law Commenc'd against them by John Goffe Junr

2^{ly} To See what method they will take to oblige the non Residents proprietors to Setle their Lots, and pay up their Rates in proportion with other Inhabitants Liveing in town, and what Else may be needfull then and there to be acted and done and this Shall be your warrant

Given under our hands this 25th of June 1731

Allen Anderson
James Lindsay
John Archibald
James Reid
Select men

To Mr William Gregg Town Constable

At a Proprietors meeting Held at Londonderry July ye 12th 1731

The proprietors Chuse for moderator Mr James Mac Keen

Wheras their is Severall proprietors whose names are Ent'red in the Shedule annexed to our Charter of Londonderry that have not Complied with the Conditions of the aforesaid Charter by Setleing & Improving upon their Lots, & by paying up their proportion of the town rates when and so often as ocation Required the Same, to the great loss & (last five words marked out) damage of the other proprietors

Voted that all such Delinquent proprietors that will not after fourty Days notice given them, by the Committee Chosen and appointed for that End, Comply with the Conditions of the aforesd Charter, their Lands Shall be Dispos'd of by the major part of the proprietors according to the Directions Given in the aforesaid Charter

The names of the Committee voted and Chosen for that End is

John Mac—neall
William Humphra
Samuel Barr

at the Request and Desire of the proprietors the moderator has adjurned the other affairs of this meeting, untill the Last munday of agust at ten of the Clock in the forenoon

The last Munday of agust 1731 The proprietors meet according to adjurnment,

voted that the Select men have power from time to time to applot and Raise So much money as Shall be Sufficient to

Carry on and Defray the Law Shute Commenc'd against the proprietors of this town by John Goffe Junr

Purshewant to aformer vote pass'd for the Building of a Schooll House, at aGenerall town meeting held March ye 5th 1723/4

voted that their Shall be a Schooll House Built, at the most Convenient place at our Meetinghouse, the Dementions of which is to be Eighteen feet in Length, Sixteen feet in weadth, Seven foot in the Side wall, with a Large Chimney in the one End

Upon the aforesaid adjurnment the said Returns was Read and approved of, to the after named persons and their heirs for Ever (viz) one to Daniel Anderson one to Sam^{ll} Renkine, one to Mr James Macgregors Second Division, one to Robert Morison, one to Willm & Thom^{s} Callwell, one to m^{r} philips John & Alex^{r} MacMurphy

You are hearby Required to Warn the Proprietors and Freeholders of Londonderry to Conven at their meeting-house on Munday the Eight Day of Nov^{br} next by nine of the Clock Before noon then & there

Imprimus To See if they Can Come to an amicable agreement about Laying Down amethod to obtain a Second Minister

2^{ly} To See whether they will make any addition to the Com^{ttee} appointed to Defend the action Comenced by John Goffe Junr against them and what power they will allow them

3^{ly} To See whether or no they will prosecute the non Residents proprietors according to the Condition of the Charter and any other thing or things that may be thought needfull to be done, and this Shall be your warrant Given under our hands this 25th Day of october 1731.

John Archibald
Allen Anderson
James Lindsay
James Reid
Select men

To Mr William Gregg town Constable

At aMeeting of the proprietors and freeholders held at Londonderry meetinghouse upon munday ye 8th Day of Nov^{br} 1731.

voted and Chose for moderator Mr. Robert Boyes

1st voted that the first artickle in this warrant is Defer'd at this present time

2^{ly} voted that Whereas the proprietors of this town at ameeting of the proprietors May ye 24th 1731 Chose a Com^{ttee} impowering the S^{d} Com^{ttee} all or Each or any of them to appear in their behalf in Defence of a Law Shute Comenced against them by John Goffe Junr And for Severall Good reasons have thought it Convenient to make an adition of two men more to S^{d} Com^{ttee} (viz) Ro^{t} Boyes, & James Clerk. to Joyn the Com^{ttee} formerly Chosen at aproprietors meeting in may ye 24th 1731 and that the s^{d} Ro^{t} Boyes & James Clerk they or Either of them Shall and may appear in the Behalf of the aforesaid proprietors at any Court or Courts of Justice with as full and ample power & authority as the Committee that they are added & Joyned too have or whatsoever Else may be needfull and Expedient, to defend the action Comenc'd against S^{d} proprietors by John Goffe Junr

3^{ly} voted that all the Delinquent or non Resident proprietors Shall be prosecuted by the Com^{ttee} formerly Chosen for that End & purpose in the following manner & form (viz) that Every proprietor after being Serv'd by the Com^{ttee} or any one of them with a Copy of the votes that are made against the nonresident proprietors. Shall by the first Day of Ffebruary next pay up all their proportion of the town Charges from the first Settlement of said town and twenty-pounds over & above, and make a Settlement according to the Charter of S^{d} town by the first of May next or Else their Lands Shall be dispos'd of by the proprietors according to the Directions of our Charter

voted that Jo^{n} Archibald Jon Barnard Junr and Hugh Willson Shall be aComittee to meet Daniel Bodwell of Methewine to See if they Can find a Good Comfortable Ground for aRoad Betwen this town & s^{d} Bodwells Ferry & Bring in their Report to the town next proprietors meeting

You are Hearby Required to Warn the Proprietors of Londonderry to meet at their Meetinghouse on Munday the twentieth day of Dec^{br} next at Eight of the Clock in the forenoon then & there

Imprimus To See whether they will allow the Severall proprietors to Setle their Equivolent Lands Especially on the South part of our town

2^{ly} To See if they Can Come to an amicable agreement about asecond minister

3^{ly} To See if they will assist John Anderson in prosecuting William Bolton who possesses his Equivolent Lands & Refuses to pay him for his Intrest there

4^{ly} To See if the town will Empower a Comittee to Dispose of the unsetled Lots, and any other thing needfull, and this Shall be your warrant

Given under our Hands this 23^{d} of Nov^{br} 1731.

James Lindsay
Allen Anderson
John Archibald
John Wallace
James Reid
Select men

To William Gregg Town Constable

At ameeting of the proprietors Held at Londonderry meetinghouse upon Munday ye 20th of Dec^{br} 1731. the Proprietors Chuse for Moderator Robert Boyes

1st voted that Every proprietor Shall Have Liberty to Setle their own Lands

2^{ly} voted that their is a Comittee nominated & appointed to meet at Willm Humphra's House upon tuesday ye 21st of this Instant to Consider of Sending a Call or Calls to Ireland in order to have a second minister for this Congregation (viz) Mr James Mac Curdy, or Mr Fowler

The names of the Comittee is as followeth Capt David Cargill Mr Mac Keen, John Archibald, Jo^{n} Moore Jam^{s} Reid, Allen Anderson, Ro^{t} Wear, Thos Stiel, Jo^{n} Morison Junr Patrick Douglas Mr David Macgregore, Jam^{s} Nesmith, James Clerk, David Craig, Sam^{ll} Barr, Jo^{n} Stewart, Sam^{ll} Allison, Jo^{n} Barnat Senr & Junr Arch^{d} Clandinen Ro^{t} Morison, Jam^{s} Anderson, Alex^{r} Renkine, Sam^{ll} Houston Jam^{s} Morison, Capt Gregg, Willm & Jo^{n} Gregg, Jam^{s} Rodgers, Jesse Cristey, James Adams, James Gillmore, Jam^{s} Willson, James Lindsay Jo^{n} & Jam^{s} Blair, Jam^{s} Lesliey, Jo^{n} & Alex^{r} Macneall, Hugh muntgomery, John Richey, Mathew Tayler, Ro^{t} Boyes & Jo^{n} macmurphy

3^{ly} voted that the third artickle is laid aside and past in the Negative

4^{ly} voted that their fourth artickle is laid aside their being votes formerly pass'd which was Sufficient

voted that Willm Humphra & Alex^{r} Mac neall Shall be a Comittee for takeing the Invoice of the poles & Estates of our town acording to the Directions of the precept that the Generall assembly has sent to our Select men

voted the following Returns or Transcripts to be put upon Record, one to Willm Eayers, one to Jo^{n} macneall & to their heirs for Ever of their Second Divisions

You are hereby Required to Warn the proprietors & Freeholders and Inhabitants of Londonderry to Conven at their Meetinghouse on Munday the Sixth day of March by nine of the Clock in the forenoon then & there.

1st To Chuse their Town officers for the year Enshewing.

2^{ly} To See whither they will allow the people of the north west Range alane besides what they have to the Comons.

3^{ly} To See if ye proprietors will allow afourth Division of Land to be laid out in the Commons and what Quantity of Land Shall be laid out in Every Such Division.

4^{ly} To Chuse a Committee to Defend all Such Lawshuts that may or have been Comenced against the proprietors of this town, and to Impower them as farr as Shall be thought needfull for Executing Such an office

5^{ly} To See whether the proprietors will take up with Such proposalls as Shall then be made to them by William Bolton.

6^{ly} To See if they will pass avote upon a Suplication Sent to them by the Revd Mr Samuel Phillips annent the Setlement of his Lott in this town as also annent the votes pass'd by them in July & Nov^{br} Last.

7^{ly} To appoint a Comittee to Execute a Deed to patrick Douglas, of the Stream he bought of the proprietors.

8^{ly} To See what method they will take to Suppress the many Disorders that Happen about Tavern and Tipling housses in this town and any other thing needfull, and this Shall be your Warrant, Given under our hands this Sixteenth day of February 1731/2

James Lindsay
John Archibald
James Reid
Allen Anderson
Select men

To Mr William Gregg Town Constable

At aGenerall town meeting of the Proprietors Freeholders & Inhabitants of the town of Londonderry assembled at their meetinghouse upon Munday the Sixth of March Anno Domimi 1731/2

voted for moderator Robert Boyes

1st voted that their Shall be Five men Chosen to Serve as Select men for the Enshewing year, the names of the men Chosen is as Followeth John Wallace. James Reid. James Lindsay, Allen Anderson. John Archibald.

voted for town Clerk John MacMurphy

voted that their Shall be two Constables Chosen to Serve for the Enshewing year in this town as such, and that Each of them Shall have for their Service as Such, Fifty Shi^{lls} for the Enshewing year, and the Divideing line betwen S^{d} Constable's Shall be Beaver Brook, the names of the Constables Chosen is Thomas Stiel Thomas Bogle

The aforesaid Thomas Stiel is and Shall be obliged to Serve in the office of Constable in the Easterly Side of Beaver Brook, and Thomas Bogle is and Shall be oblig'd to Serve as Constable in the westerly Side of the afores^{d} Brook.

voted for Sirvayers for the Enshewing year John Huy. Gabriel Barr. Abraham Holms. Mr George Duncan. Sam^{ll} Morison. James Rodgers. John Gregg. Allen Anderson. John Archibald. Patrick Douglas. Thomas Horner. Jesse Cristey.

voted for Tithing men Robert Wear & Sam^{ll} Renkine.

voted for Hawards John Graves & James Morison.

voted as a Com^{ttee} for Searching the town's acounts with the Select men John MacMurphy, James Nesmith & Jo^{n} Blair.

2^{ly} voted the Second artickle to pass in the negative.

3^{ly} voted that their Shall be afourth Division laid out, and that their Shall be thirty acres laid out to Each proprietor in this town, and that the Com^{ttee} or Lott Layers for Laying out the mendment & adition lands in this town, Shall lay out the S^{d} fourth Divisions, and that the Said Com^{ttee} Shall not lay out above four or Five of the afores^{d} fourth Divisions, untill they Bring their Report to the proprietors whether they think the Comons will afford to Lay out to Every proprietor the afores^{d} fourth Division as it's voted, and have the proprietors aprobation for their further proceeding in laying out the afores^{d} Divisions the names of s^{d} Com^{ttee} or Lottlayers is, James Rodgers. John Archibald. John Wallace.

and that it is Left to the S^{d} Com^{ttee} to place S^{d} Division's that they lay out untill further orders from the proprietors.

4^{ly} voted that their is and Shall be a Com^{ttee}. Chosen as a Proprietor's Com^{ttee} to Defend all Lawshuts that may or have been or Shall be Comenced against the proprietors of this town, and that the Said Committee all or Each or any one of them, Shall & may appear in the Defence of the aforesaid proprietors Before any Judge or Judges Justice or Justicess in any Court or Courts, and Shall act and do Every thing needfull in the Defence of the aforesaid Proprietors, in Defending their Rights and priviledgess with as full & ample authority as if we the Whole proprietors of the aforesaid Londonderry were all personally present, and that it shall be in the power of S^{d} Com^{ttee} or any one of them to Constitute appoint make and ordain or Substitutee one or more attorney's under them if they or any of them think meet & Convenient in the Defence of any Law Shute that have been or Shall be Commenc'd against Said Proprietors or any of them, or whatever Else may be needfull and Expedient in the aforesaid affair, and that the Costs & Charges thereof Shall be at the Expence of the whole proprietors.

The names of the Said Com^{ttee} is as follows Robert Boyes. John Macmurphy. John Morison. Junr John Archibald. James Clerk.

5^{ly} Voted Willm Bolton not appearing that this artickle pas in the negative

6^{ly} The petition of the Revd Mr Sam^{ll} Phillips being read it is voted to pass in the negative.

7^{ly} voted that the Selectmen for this present year or the major part of them Shall Give & Execute a Deed to Patrick Douglas of the stream & priviledges thereunto Belonging as it's Entred, of the Fals upon the Brook at Cohassatt

8^{ly} voted that the Select men for the time being Shall furnish the Tithing men, with a Badge of their office in order to supress the Disorders that may hapen at Tavern, or Tipling Housess.

voted and that the Select men Shall aggree with the town Clerk to Enter a Record of all the rates that have been Collected or Rais'd in our town from the first Settlement thereof, if possible they can be found out & how they were Disposs'd of, as near as the Com$^{ttee's}$ account Can make out and Shall pay for Said Entrey's & Records at the town's Charges

The Return of the Com^{ttee} for part of Benjn Kidder's Home Lott was Read & approv'd of, to be put upon Record, for the S^{d} Kidder's or his assigns proper benefit & behoof for Ever

Londonderry March y^{e} 18th 1731/2

You are hereby Required to Warn the Proprietors & Inhabitants of Londonderry to Conven at their meetinghouse on Saturday the Twenty-fifth of march Currant at nine of the Clock before noon then & there.

Imp: To See how they will dispose of the publick Schooll for this year.

2^{ly} To See whether the Proprietors will allow the Com-^{ttee} for Defending the town lines. a power to Commence Law Shuts against Incrochers.

3^{ly} To See if they will approve that Tho: Stiel Substitutee Sam^{ll} Barr as Constable in his behalf, & Impower him for that office.

4^{ly} To hear Constable $Will^{m}$ Humphra's & John Anderson's Reates Dispursments Read and to hear & approve of Such transcripts as may Come before them, and any thing Else needfull, and this Shall be your Warrant, Given under our hands the day and year above said.

John Archibald.
Allen Anderson.
James Reid.
Select men

To Mr Thomas Bogle Town Constable

At ameeting of the proprietors & Inhabitants of Londonderry on Saturday ye 25th of March 1732

voted for Moderator Robert Boyes.

1^{t} voted that their Shall be two Schools Kept in this town as publick Schools for this year, the one Schooll Shall be held & Kept at the meetinghouse, and at, by, or near, Allen Anderson's House, or thereabouts for this year, and acording to the Seasons as it Shall be Held & Kept in Equall proportions of time and space, and Mr John Willson Shall be the Schoolmaster for that part of the town, and the Divideing Bounds in the town for the $afores^{d}$ Schoolls Shall be Beaver Brook, and that their Shall be only fourty pounds Rais'd upon the whole town for the paying of the aforesaid two Schools, and Each part of the town to pay of said fourty pounds according to their proportion of Rates, and the rest of the Charges that Shall arise by Keeping of Said Schools Shall be paid & Rais'd by the Schoolers that Shall be taught at said Schools.

2^{ly} voted that the Comttee appointed & Chosen for the Defending the town lines Shall have power to Comence Law Shute or Law Shutes against all Incrochers.

3^{ly} voted that this artickle pass in the negative.

4^{ly} as to the Constable's Reats Dispursments they being not duley prepar'd Jo^{n} Anderson's Disbursments being only read their was nothing done upon them, the Severall Transscripts being read was approv'd of (viz) one for Mary Wilson of her mendment & adition lands one to Sam^{ll} Alison of his mendment & adition lands, one to John moore of his mendment & adition Lands, one to Sam^{ll} moore of his mendment & adition lands, togother with one to Jo^{n} Barnat Junr and one to Sam^{ll} Penhallow and to their Heirs for Ever.

You are hereby Required to Warn the Inhabitants & freeholders of Londonderry to Conven at their meetinghouse on munday the tenth of July next by nine of the Clock in the forenoon then and there

Imp: To See what method they propose to pay their Schoolmasters Salary for this present year.

2^{ly} To See whether the proprietors will allow the Com^{ttee} of lands to fix the Bounds of the farm Granted to the Revd Mr James Macgregore by the Gover^{t}—the lines of it being partly unknown

3^{ly} To Choose a Com^{ttee} to take an Envoice of the poles & Estates in town for this present year, and any other thing that may be thought needfull and this Shall be your warrant Given under our Hands this 27th of June 1732

James Lindsay
Allen Anderson
John Archibald
John Wallace
James Reid
Select men

To Mr Thomas Stiel & m^{r} Thomas Bogle Town Constables

At a meeting of the Inhabitants & freeholders of Londonderry Conven'd at their meeting House on munday the tenth of July 1732.

voted for moderator Robert Boyes

Imp: The first and prior artickle Deferd

2^{ly} The Second artickle Defer'd untill a fuller proprietors meeting

3^{ly} voted that Willm Gregg and Willm Moore Shall take the Invoice of the poles & Estates of this town for this present year, and that they Shall Have the Same Wages that they had last year which was three pounds

You are hereby Required to Warn the proprietors & freeholders of Londonderry Legaly Qualified to Conven at their meetinghouse on Munday the 28th Currant by Eight of the Clock before fore noon then & there

Imp: To Chuse a fitt person to Represent our town at the next Genera^{ll} assembly to be Held at portsmouth teusday the 29th Instant

2^{ly} That the proprietors Chuse fitt persons to fill up the Com^{ttee} of meadows

3^{ly} To See whether the proprietors will Reconsider the Supplication presented to them last meeting by Jane and Margaret Macgregore and anything Else necessary and this Shall be y^{r} warrant Given under our Hands this 12th Day of agust 1732

James Lindsay
John Archibald
Allen Anderson
John Wallace
James Reid
Select men

To Thomas Bogle town Constable

At A meeting of the proprietors & freeholders of Londonderry Legally Qualified Conven'd at their meetinghouse upon munday ye 28th of agust 1732

voted for Moderator James Mackeen Esqr

voted for Representitive John MacMurphy

The 2^{ed} & 3^{d} artikles Defer'^{d} at this meeting

You are hereby Required to Warn the freeholders & Inhabitants of London-Derry to assemble themselves at their meetinghouse upon friday the third Day of november next by nine of the Clock in the forenoon then & there

Imp: To lay down Some probale method in order to the Calling and transporting of Such aminister from Ireland as they Shall agree upon and to propose what Encouragement Such minister Shall have to Setle among us

2^{ly} To See what method they will take to Defray the part of their School-master's Salary above w^t is Setle'd on them by law

3^{ly} To See whether the proprietors will Contribute any thing towards Robert Kenady's Cost at Law, in defence of his place against Richard Hazzen and any other thing or things needfull, and this Shall be your warrant

Given under our Hands this 23^d of october 1732

James Lindsay
Allen Anderson
John Archibald
James Reid
Select men

To Messures Thomas Stiel and Thomas Bogle Town Constables

At ameeting of the Freeholders & Inhabitants of Londonderry assembl'd at their meetinghouse upon friday the third of Nov^{br} 1732

voted for Moderator Robert Wear

The moderator by & with the Consent of the Freeholders and Inhabitants of our town of Londonderry has adjurn'd the S^d meeting untill friday the tenth Instant at nine of the Clock before noon

Meet according to adjurnment

voted that the Revd Mr Macbride of Belemony in the Kingdom of Ireland and Mr Robert Boyes of our town are Chosen if they will please to accept of it as Commissioners, in order to prefer our Call or Calls for aminister to this our Congregation and James Mac Keen Esqr Patrick Douglas & John Macmurphy be a Committee to treat w^t the $afores^d$ Robert Boyes and to aggree w^t him if possible to be our Commissioner upon the afores^d affair and Bussines, and if in Case our Commissioners acept and they obtain aminister for us, it is also voted and hereby to be understood that we have Concluded to pay yearly or p^r annum one Hundred and fourty pounds Salary besides transporting s^d minister from Ireland to newengland, and it is also voted and Concluded upon by our town that they will purchase Hugh Craigs Half lot, and bestow the Home lot of S^d Half lot and one Hundred acres of out lands to our first Settle'd minister for this Congregation and to his Heirs for Ever Still Giveing aliberty to our Commissioners to act and do as they think best for the Good of our Congregation

the 2^ed and 3^d artickle Defer'd at present

You are Hereby Required to Warn the Freeholders and Inhabitants of London-Derry to assemble themselves at their meetinghouse on Munday the 15th Currant by nine of the Clock in the Forenoon then and there

Imp: To See whether they will allow the Select men to applot Such Sum's of money as Shall be thought necessary for the Transportation of a Minister from Ireland for this Congregation

2^ly To See whether they will Chuse a Com^ttee to Sell or Buy lands as Shall be thought Expedient for the Setlement of a minister

3^ly To See whether or not the Proprietors will vote that Such proprietors lands as Have not Complied with the Condition of the town Charter, are not now in the power of the Resident proprietors and Henceforth to be disposs'd of as the said proprietors Shall think fitt, and any thing Else that Shall be thought needfull and this Shall be your warrant Given under our Hands at Londonderry aforesaid this 3^d day of January 1732/3

James Reid
John Archibald
James Lindsay
John Wallace
Allen Anderson
Selectmen

To Mr Thomas Stiel and m^r Thomas Bogle Town Constables

At ameeting of the Freeholders & Inhabitants of Londonderry at their Meeting House upon Munday y[e] 15th of January 1732/3

voted for Moderator Robert Wear

voted that our Select men Shall Have power to applott and raise Such Sum or Sums of money upon the Proprietors Freeholders and Inhabitants of our town as Shall be needfull to pay and Supply our Commissioners Charges in prosecuting our Call or Calls for the abtaining a Second minister for this Congregation and for transporting of the minister that they may or Shall obtain from Ireland to this Congregration

voted that M[r] Robert Boyes of our town be our Commissioner in order to prosecute and prefer our Call or Calls for the obtaining aSecond minister for this Congregation, and Have by this vote Impowr'd Said M[r] Boyes to Chuse an assistant with him for the Ends aforesaid in and at any Presbetrey or Synod in the Kingdom of Scotland or in the Kingdom of Ireland as he shall think meet and Convenient for the Ends aforesaid for the promoting and Continuing the Gospel in this part of God's vineyard.

the other artikles in the aforesaid Warrant Deffer'd at this time

You are Hereby Required to Warn the Freeholders proprietors and Inhabitants of Londonderry within your Severall Precincts to assemble them Selves at their meetinghouse on Munday the fifth day of March next precisely at Eight of the Clock Before noon then and there to Choose thir town officers for the year Enshewing, and in So doing this Shall be your Warrant Given under our hands this 13th day of February 1732/3

John Archibald
John Wallace
Allen Anderson
James Reid
James Lindsay
Select men

To M[r] Thomas Steell and M[r] Thomas Bogle Constables

At a Generall town Meeting of the Freeholders proprietors and Inhabitants of Londonderry assembled at their Meeting-house upon Munday the Fifth Day of March 1732/3

voted for moderator Robert Wear

voted that their Shall be five men Chosen to Serve as Select men for the Enshewing year, the men that are Chosen and voted as Select men is as followeth James Reid John Archibald Andrew Todd James Rodgers James Gregg

voted for town Clerk.................John MacMurphy

voted that their Shall be two Constables Chosen to Serve as Such for the Enshewing year, and that Beaver brook Shall be the divideing lines Betwen s[d] Constables, and that they Shall have for their Service five pounds, the Constable that Serves in y[e] westerly Side of Said Beaver Brook Shall have for his wages as Such of the aforesaid five pounds fourty five shi[lls] and the Constable that Serves in the Easterly Side of Beaver Brook shall have fifty five Shi[lls] of S[d] five pounds, the names of the Constables Chosen is John Moore and Robert Clerk

voted for Sirvayers of High Ways John Moore James Reid James nesmith James Cochran John Wallace John Woodburn James Rodgers John Tagart Thomas Horner Jesse Cristey George Duncan Esq[r]

voted for Tithing men Will[m] Humphra & Tho[s] Willson

voted for Howard James Boyes & Daniel Anderson

voted for Fence veiwers and prizers John Barnart Jun[r] and James Lindsay

voted as a Com[ttee] for Searching the towns accounts John Blair James Nesmith and John MacMurphy

voted that their Shall be two Schoollmasters in this town for the Enshewing year and that Said Schooll masters Shall be paid by the town as they were paid last year

You are hereby Required to Warn the proprietors of Londonderry to meet at their Meetinghouse on Munday the fifth day of March next at one of the Clock in the afternoon then and there

Imp: To See how they will Defray the Charges of the Lott bought for the encouragement of the first minister

2ly To See whether they will vote that the lands of the non Resident proprietors are forefited according to the Condition of our town Charter

3ly To See if they will aggree upon aCertain part in this township where they may be a fourth Division of Land laid out and whether they will allow the Same to be laid out and to Chuse a Comttee for the Same

4ly To See whether they will Confirm the Meadows Design'd by the then Comittee to Govr Shute and the Heirs of Govr Wentworth

5ly To See whether they will perform their first Grant to Benjn Willson in Reference to his mill

6ly To fill up the Comttee for the divisions of meadows and any thing Else that may Concern the propriety and this shall be your warrant Given under our hands this 13th day of February 1732/3

Allen Anderson
James Lindsay
John Wallace
James Reid
John Archibald
Select men.

To Mr Thomas Stiel and Thos Bogle Constable's

At ameeting of the proprietors of the town of Londonderry upon munday ye fith day of March 1732/3

The proprietors Chuse for Moderator Capt James Gregg

The aforesaid moderator at the Request of the proprietors and by & with the Consent of the Same has adjurn'd Sd meeting untill thursday ye 22 of this Instant March at ten of the Clock in the forenoon

The aforesd meeting meet acording to adjurnment.

The first artickle Deffer'd at present

voted that Willm Humphra be aperson appointed and authorized by the proprietors of our Town to take Care and Inspection of the wood and Timber that Grows upon our ministerall Home lott, and the Half lott lying by the meetinghouse that was bought in order to be Confer'd and Given to our first Settled minister, and in case that any person or persons Shall be found Cutting timber or wood on the aforesaid lands, that then in that Case, the Said Willm Humphra Shall and is hereby Impowr'd to prosecute any Such Transgressor as the law directs, and it is hereby to be understood that said Humphra Shall have only one days wages allow'd him for S^{d} Service and no more, Except what he Shall recover from Such as Trespass upon the aforesaid Lands by Law

2^{ly} voted that the proprietors will not forefit James Nickels lott, nor none of the rest of the non Resident proprietors lott, at this time

3^{ly} voted that their Shall be afourth division of lands laid out in this town in the westerly part thereof, and that their Shall be nine proprietors Chosen to project a method to lay out the aforesaid fourth Divisions and to Conclude how many acres Shall be laid out to Each proprietors Share, the names of the aforesaid Com^{ttee} is John MacMurphy, Capt James Gregg, Lev^{t} Andrew Todd, James Rodgers, John Goffe Junr, Jo^{n} Archibald, John Wallace, Sam^{ll} Graves, Thos Steil, and that the Said fourth Divisions Shall be laid out Quantity & Quality Considred and w^{n} all laid out Shall be Lotted for and the method that the aforesaid Com^{ttee} Shall Conclude upon, Shall be the rule that the Lott layers Shall go by, as also the method that S^{d} Com^{ttee} Shall Conclude upon in laying out the Said fourth Divisions Shall be put upon record with this vote and shall be authentick and valid for the Ends aforesaid

The names of the Lottlayers for S^{d} fourth Divisions is Jo^{n} Macneall John Barnatt Junr Sam^{ll} Barr

4^{ly} voted that the meadow laid out to Govr Shute is Defer'd at present, and the meadow that was laid out to Govr Wentworth above Leverts Bridge is confirm'd to S^{d} Govr Wentworths Heirs for Ever

5^{ly} voted that the proprietors will Confirm their first

Grant to Benjn Willson in reference to his mill in purchasing Mr Toyes meadow formerly Ro^{t} Doaks meadow for the Equivolent of it of meadow provideing there Can be Comon meadow found Convenient in our town

6^{ly} Their being a Coram of the Com^{ttee} of meadows at present it is Defer'd

voted that Mr John Willson Shall be Schoollmaster in the Easterly Side of Beaver Brook for the Enshewing year

The Severall returns Hereafter mentioned was by the Lottlayers of our town brought in read and approv'd of to the owners thereof and their Heirs for Ever (viz) one to Benjamin Kidders Right one to Andrew Todd, one to Willm Cochran one to Sam^{ll} Penhallow one to Capt Cargill Servt Willm nutt one for m^{r} mac Gregor's Servt one for Sam^{ll} Moore

You are hereby Required to Warn the proprietors Freeholders and Inhabitants of Londonderry to meet at their meetinghouse upon Thursday the Seventh Day of June next by nine of the Clock before noon then & there.

First to See what method they will Conclude upon to pay for the half Lott of land latley purchas'd in order to be Confer'd on a minister.

2^{ly} To fill up the Committee for meadows.

3^{ly} To Chuse a Com^{ttee} to Enter & Defend Law Shuts against Incroachers on the town bounds.

4^{ly} To Chuse a Com^{ttee} to take a Deed of James Moore for the land he had from Alex^{r} Walker at Cobats pond and to give him a Deed of that land he now lives upon, or any other thing needfull and this Shall be your Warrant Given under our Hands this 22^{ed} Day of may 1733.

James Gregg
James Rodgers
John Archibald
Andrew Todd
James Reid
Select men

To Messures John Moore and Robert Clerk Constables.

At ameeting of the proprietors Freeholders & Inhabitants of Londonderry meet at their meeting house upon Thursday the Seventh Day of June 1733.

They Chuse for Moderator James Mac Keen........Esqr

voted that the Hundred and Sixty acres of land Laid out by the proprietors Southerly of Sam^{ll} moor's mendment land beyond Cannada Second Divisions Shall be Sold to the Highest Bidder, and that the prise that Shall be gott for Said land Shall be a propriated So farr as it Shall go, for the paying of Lands bought by the proprietors from Hugh Craig near our first meetinghouse, to be Confer'd upon our first Setled minister that Shall Setle at Said meetinghouse for his Encouragement and that James Clerk, John Archibald John Wallace James Rodgers and Willm Humphra Shall be a Comittee authorized and Impowered by the proprietors afores^{d} to Sell and dispose of the aforesaid one hundred and Sixty acres, for the Ends and uses aforesaid which is the true Intent and meaning of Said vote.

2^{ly} voted that Allen Anderson John Mitchell and John Bell formerly apart of the Com^{ttee} for veiwing and laying out meadows, Shall now be the whole Com^{ttee} for laying out what meadows is wanting to the Severall persons or proprietors that they Judge that wants of their Equal Share, and to give transcripts of Said meadows as also to give Transcripts of meadows allready laid out to Such as have not yet got them; but are hereby forbid and Discharg'd to veiw no meadows formerly veiwed laid out and recorded in order to allow them any mendments without particular order from the proprietors for that End and purpose.

voted that the proprietors remaining and Continuing as proprietors and hearers and owners of our first meetinghouse Shall have full power and authority to use and dispose of the afterdaughts of our ministeriall lott, for religious uses and Ends and are hereby authorized and Impowered to lay out or Cause to be laid out another ministeriall lot in the South part of our town if needfull

also voted that the Congregation or parish that is to be

made up at Cannada Shall have full power to dispose of the one half of aministerall lott laid out at Cannada Consisting of one Hundred and twenty acres for Religious uses and Ends, particularly for the Encouragement of their minister that Shall Setle there, and the other half of Said ministeriall lott in Quantity & Quality to remain and Continue for aministeriall for Ever for the Benefit will and use of the aforesaid Congregation that is to be at Cannada aforesaid.

You are hereby Required to Warn the proprietors of Londonderry to Conven at their meetinghouse on Thursday the 13th of Sep^{tr} next by nine of the Clock before noon then and there.

Imp: To hear their accounts Read.

2^{ly} To See what Sums of money they will vote on Each propriety to be aploted for Defraying the Charges of the Current year.

3^{ly} To Chuse a Com^{ttee} to Regulate the mistakes that are in the Schedule annexed to our town Charter.

4^{ly} To Chuse a Com^{ttee} to give John & Thos Mac Clerg and James Moore Deeds of their lands and to receive a Deed from James Moore of the land he first had.

5^{ly} To See whether the proprietors will Chuse $Will^{m}$ Moore and $Will^{m}$ Gregg to take the Invoice of the poles & Estates of this town for the present year.

6^{ly} To approve of the transcripts that Shall be read before the proprietors and this Shall be your Warrant. Given under our hands this 28th of august 1733.

James Gregg
James Rodgers
John Archibald
James Reid
Select men

To Messures John Moore & Robert Clerk Constables for Said Londonderry

At ameeting of the Proprietors of Londonderry upon Thursday ye 13th of Sep^{tr} anno Dom: 1733. the proprietors Chuse for moderator James nesmith voted that Constable Willm Humphra and Constable Willm Gregg's lists of payments is received and approv'd of, James Leslie's account or Charge Excepted.

voted that the Select men Shall raise and applot twenty Five Shi^{lls} upon Each propriety Right for this present year to Defray the Contingent Charges.

voted that James MacKeen Esqr Capt Gregg John Blair James Clerk John Wallace John Bell and John MacMurphy Shall be a proprietors Com^{ttee} with as full power and authority as we the proprietors Can give them, to regulate, if they can, any mistakes or Ground or foundation for after Disturbance or Law Shuts that might happen afterwards or arise, or that appears to them might Cause any uneasiness among the proprietors or Law Shuts afterwards whether in the Schedule of our Charter or in any Entries that may appear in our Records to be the ground or Cause of what is before mentioned in S^{d} vote whether in lands or meadows, and all and whatsoever the aforesaid Com^{ttee} Shall act and do in the aforesaid affair Shall be authentick and as binding on us the proprietors as if we were all personally present.

Voted that the proprietors Chosen and appointed to Sell the hundred and Sixty acres acres Joying to Sam^{ll} Moore's mendment and lying beyond Cannada Second Divisions (viz) James Clerk John Archibald John Wallace James Rodgers and Willm Humphra Shall and is hereby authorized and Impowered to Execute and Give John & Thos MacClerg a Good Quite Claim Deed of the aforesaid land and Shall be good and authentick for the Ends aforesaid to the aforesaid purchasers and the proprietors, after haveing heard the Com^{ttee} for Laying out Lands Return Read of S^{d} land they have approv'd of the Same and have order'd the Same to be put upon Record.

voted That Willm Moore and Willm Gregg take the Invoice of the poles and Estates of this town for the present year and Shall be paid for their Service three pounds ten Shi^{lls} in Bils of Credit.

voted That the return of the Lottlayers for Willm Humphra's land and Jon^{tn} Taylors land was Read & approv'd of to the aforesaid persons and their heirs for Ever.

You are hereby Required to Warn the Severall proprietors freeholders and Inhabitants of Londonderry with in your severall districts to assemble themselves at their meeting-house on Tewsday the 30th Currant by nine of the Clock before noon then & there.

1st To Chuse a Com^{ttee} to acount with Robert Boyes for the money Expended on their Behalf when in Ireland, as also to Chuse a Com^{ttee} to Confirm the land Bought for our first minister, to the Revd Mr Thomas Thomson and See what method they will take to applot Mr Thomson's Stipends and the money Expended.

2^{ly} To See how they will dispose of James Callderwood

3^{ly} To See whether or not they will proceed against the Delinquent proprietors

4^{ly} To See whether the proprietors will Condescend to Sell any tract of Land for Defraying Some part of the aforesaid Charge

5^{ly} To See how they will dispose of the Schools till the 5th of March.

6^{ly} To hear and approve of transcripts of land laid out by the Com^{ttee} and this Shall be your Warrant Given under our hands this 16th Day of october 1733.

James Gregg.
John Archibald.
James Rodgers
Andrew Todd.
James Reeid.
Select men

To Messures John Moor and Robert Clerk Town Constables

At a meeting of the proprietors Freeholders and Inhabitants of the Town of Londonderry assembled upon Tewsday ye 30th Day of october 1733.

Voted and Chose for moderator Robert Boyes.

1st voted that James Mac Keen Esqr Capt James Gregg Levt Andrew Todd John Blair and John Macmurphy Shall be a Comttee authorized and Impowered, to Count with Robt Boyes for what money he Expended on the behalf of the town of Londonderry in Ireland in Calling and ordaining The Revd Mr Thomas Thomson*................Also voted that the Half Lott bought from Hugh Craig by the proprietors Shall be Convey'd and a Deed Given of the Same To the Revd Mr Thomas Thomson and his heirs for Ever, and the Comttee Chosen and appointed to Execute Sd Deed is James mac Keen Esqr John Moore James Reid Robert Wear and Willm Humphra and said deed or Conveyance Shall be as Good and authentick to all Intents & purposes as if the whole proprietors had sign'd the Same, Provided nevertheless and it is the true Intent and meaning of this vote any thing to the Contrary not withstanding, that the aforesaid Mr Thomson Shall Give a Good and Sufficient Instrument under his hand & Seal that if he Sho'd remove & Depart from this Congregation Either by his own desire or by arule of presbetry any time within ten years from the date hereof he Shall pay the town or Congregation aforesaid one Hundred pounds Bils of Credit and the aforesd Comttee is ordered and Impowered to take Said Instrument in the name of the proprietors town or Congregation as well as in their own names. Otherwise their Deed or Conveyance Shall not be authentick.

*Rev. Thomas Thompson, who had been ordained a colleague of Rev. Matthew Clark in 1733, was a native of Ireland, born in 1704, and had married before coming to this country a Miss Cummings, who seems to have been a most estimable woman. He had been ordained by the presbytery of Tyronne. He died September 22, 1738, leaving a widow and one child. Parker in his history of Londonderry says: "Though his ministry was short, it was highly acceptable to the people, and attended with the divine blessing, the church being very considerably increased during the period of his connection with it." The sincere affection felt for him is shown by the generous action of the town in voting so liberally towards the education of his infant son.—EDITOR.

voted that our minister or minister's Salary together with the Charges that have arisen in Calling ordaining and transporting Mr Thomson our minister Shall be asses'd applotted and rais'd upon the town in Generall according to Law,

The 2^ed artikle Concerning James Callerwood is left to the Select men.

The Third artickle is Defer'd at this time

The Fourth is past in the negative

The Fifth articckle is left to the Select men

the Sixth past in the negative

You are hereby Required to Warn the proprietors Freeholders & Inhabitants of Londonderry within your Severall Districts to Conven at their meetinghouse on munday the 26th Currant by nine of the Clock before noon then & there.

Imp: To See how they will applot and levey the money dew to Mr Robert Boyse which he Expended on their Behalf when in Ireland, as also how they will applot Mr Thos Thomson's Stipend.

2^ly To See whether the proprietors will dispose of the Seats in the meetinghouse that have been a lotted to Such proprietors as have not paid their proportion in Building and finishing of the meetinghouse.

3^ly To See whether they will vote to be forfitted and make Sale of the lands of Such proprietors as have not fulfill'd the Condition of the Charter and Chuse a Committee for that End.

4^ly To See whether the proprietors will vote that the four Seats in the South Side of the meetinghouse be Converted into an alley.

5^ly To See whether the proprietors will vote that the High way to Heverhill be in Some part of Sixteen acres of land once Supposed to be Alex^r Nickels but now found by the Com^ttee for lands to belong to the proprietors and to See how they will dispose of the Said Sixteen acres of land.

6^ly To See if they will vote that Some Certain Sum of money be allowed to the Grand Juriour or Juriour's to bear their Expence to the sessions from year to year.

7^{ly} To See how the proprietors will deal with Such persons as are dissatisfied with the rates put on their Seats by the Com^{ttee} for Seats, and this Shall be your warrant, Given under our hands this 12th Day of nov^{br} 1733.

James Rodgers
John Archibald
James Reid
James Gregg
Select men

To Messures John Moore and Robt Clerk Constables for Londondery

At a meeting of the proprietors Freeholders and Inhabitants of Londonderry legaly warn'd, to meet upon Munday the 26th Day of nov^{br} 1733.

voted and Chosen for moderator James Clerk.

1st voted that the money that Mr Robert Boyes Expended in behalf of our town when in Ireland after our minister Mr Thomson with the Charges that have arisen on that account with the advance upon the same Shall be rais'd upon the poles and Estates of our town together with M^{r}. Thomson's transportation money, as also voted that Mr Thomson's Salary or Stipends Shall be rais'd upon our Seats in the meetinghouse according to the rule prescrib'd by the Com^{ttee} that valou'd the aforesaid Seats in the year 1729.

2^{ly} voted that $Will^{m}$ Gregg and Sam^{ll} Barr be a Committee authorized and Impowr'd to See how many Seats in our Meetinghouse have not been paid up by the proprietors thereof their Equall Share, and to Demand the Same from Such as have not paid up their proportion of Building & finishing Said meetinghouse, and upon their non payment of the aforesaid Charge the Said Com^{ttee} is to Sell & Dispose of the Said Seats.

3^{ly} voted that $Will^{m}$ Humphra Sam^{ll} Barr and John Morison Junr Shall be a Com^{ttee} to Dispose of the Delinquent or non resident proprietors lotts,

The fourth fifth & Sixth and Seventh artickles in Said Warrant pass'd in the negative

You are hereby required to Warn the proprietors, freeholders, and Inhabitants of Londonderry to Conven at their Meeting House on friday the 28th Currant by ten of the Clock before noon then & there.

Imprimus To Chuse a fitt person to Represent them at the Generall assembly to be Conven'd at Portsmouth on January ye 1st next Enshewing:

2^{ly} To Indemnify Robert Boyes of the Bonds Given on their behalf when in Ireland:

3^{ly} To Confirm the Stipend yearly to be Conferred on a minister Expressed in Robert Boysess Commission to Ireland, to the Revd Mr Thos Thomson.

4^{ly} To Choose a Com^{ttee} to Dispose of the vacant room in the meetinghouse.

5^{ly} To approve of transcripts and this Shall be your warrant,

Given under our hands this 13th Day of no^{br} 1733

James Gregg.
James Rodgers.
James Reid.
John Archibald.
Select men

To Mr John Moore and, Robert Clerk Town Constables.

At a meeting of the proprietors Freeholders & Inhabitants of Londonderry Conven'd at their meetinghouse upon Friday the 28th of Dec^{br} 1733

1st voted for moderator..................John Blair.

2^{ly} Voted for Representitive Robert Boyse.

3^{ly} voted that the proprietors freeholders & Inhabitants of Londonderry Doth Confirm to the Revd Mr Thomas Thomson our present minister the yearly Sallary of one Hundred & fourty pounds p^{r} annum, which was the Sum our Commissioner Robert Boyse oblig'd himself by Bond to the aforesaid Mr Thomson when in Ireland.

4^{ly} voted that the vacant room in the meetinghouse is to be Dispos'd of and the Com^{ttee} appointed for the Sale of Said vacant room is James Clerk, William Gregg & Sam^{ll} Barr.

5^{ly} The Severall transcripts was approv'd of after Reading (viz) one to David Craig for his right & an half one for James Anderson, Capt David Cargill for Willm Nutt, one for Hendrey Green Capt David Cargill for Willm nutt, one for Elizabeth Willson & Capt Cargill in behalf of his Servants, and one for Capt David Cargill in behalf of his Servants

Willm Humphra Enters his Decent against the approving of the foregoing transcripts

You are hereby Required to Warn the proprietors freeholders and Inhabitants of Londonderry to Conven at their meetinghouse on Tewsday the fifth day of march next by ten of the Clock before noon then and there.

1st To Chuse all the town officers for the Enshewing year

2^{ly} To Confirm the one hundred and fourty pounds yearly to Mr Thomas Thomson being Stipend voted by the town to be Confer'd on aminister, and Included in Mr Robert Boyes Comission to Ireland when sent to procure aminister of the Gospell.

3^{ly} To Chuse a Committee to Confirm the half lott of land bought for aminister to the Said Mr Thomson.

4^{ly} To See whether the proprietors will make any adition to, or Change for Somepart of the Farm Bequeathed by the late Rev'd Mr Mac Gregore to his Doaghter's Jane and Margaret by way of Gift or otherwise.*

5^{ly} To See whether or not the proprietors will make a Division of their lands lying on the river Merrimack and what method they will take to prevent Setlements by people from other towns or this town thereon.

6^{ly} To See what answer they will Send to m^{r} Achimutey's letter

7^{ly} To See whether the town will allow Robert and Sam^{ll} Mac Keen and Hugh Bolton James Cochran and Daniel An-

*Rev. Robert McGregor died March 5, 1729, in his fifty-second year. He was a man of talent, excellent judgment and valuable in civil affairs as well as in ministering to the spiritual welfare of the infant colony. He was succeeded by Rev. Matthew Clark, a native of Ireland.—EDITOR.

derson Highways from their houses to the Highways Contigious to them allready laid out.

8^{ly} To Chuse a Committee to Regulate the bounds of the pond Sold to Sam^{ll} Graves &c and to fix the bounds of it.

9^{ly} To hear transcripts read and approven and this Shall be your warrant, Given under our Hands this 13th of February 1733/4

James Gregg.
John Archibald.
James Reid.
Andrew Todd.
Select men

To Messures John Moore and Robert Clerk Town Constables

At a Generall town meeting of the proprietors freeholders and Inhabitants of Londonderry March ye 5th 1733/4 assembl'd at their meeting on said Day, voted For Moderator Robert Boyes.

voted that their Shall be five men Chosen to Serve as Selett men for the Enshewing year, the men that are Chosen to Serve as Such is Patrick Douglas. John Morison Junr Andrew Todd. James Gregg. James Rodgers.

voted For town Clerk for the Enshewing year. John Macmurphy,

voted that their Shall be two Constables Chosen to Serve as town Constables for the Enshewing year and Beaver brook Shall be the Divideing line for S^{d} Constables to Collect rates and taxes and Said Constables Shall be paid by by the town for their Service five pounds Bils of Credit, the Constable that Serves in the Easterly Side of Beavër Brook Shall have of Said Sum fifty five Shi^{lls} and the Constable that Serves in the westerly Side of Beaver Brook Shall have fourty five Shi^{lls} of the aforesaid five pounds, the names of the men Chosen for Constables for the Enshewing year is. James Callwell & Arch^{d} Clendinen

voted that Samuel Barr Shall also be a Constable for the

Enshewing year to Serve Such writts and warrants as Shall be Committed to his Care and trust and Shall be paid for his Service as Such, by those persons only that Employes him but is not oblig'd to Collect no rates nor taxes that are to be rais'd or Collected in our town for the Enshewing year he being formerly town Constable, and now being Chosen voluntary and of his own free will and accord.

Voted for Sirvayers of High ways John Archibald. James Reid. James Morison. James Cochran. Willm Eayers Junr Willm Cochran. John Bell. John Taggart. Alex^{r} Macneall. Daniel Mac Duffi. James Gillmore. Francis Smilley. George Duncan. Esqr

voted For tithing men Robert Wear. Samuel Houston.

voted for Howards Randle Alexander John Houi,

voted for fence veiwers and prizers James Lindsay. Samuel Allison.

voted for Searching the towns accounts John Blair. James Nesmith. John Macmurphy.

2^{ly} voted that the yearly Salary of one Hundred and fourty pounds that Robert Boyes Engaged in behalf of the town, and was Included in his Comission when he went to Ireland to procure aminister for us, is hereby Confirmed to the Revd Mr Thomas Thomson dureing his ministeriall Services in this town.

3^{ly} voted that James Mac Keen Esqr James Reid, John Moore, William Humphra, and Robert Wear Shall be aCommittee to Execute a Deed in behalf of the town to the Revd Mr Thomas Thomson of the Half lott of land that the proprietors purchased from Hugh Craig.

4^{ly} & 5^{ly} the fourth and fifth artickles Defer'd untill our next proprietors meeting

6^{ly} voted that the answer to Mr Achimutey's letter is Defer'd untill another meeting.

7^{ly} voted that the town will not purchase Roads to Robert & Sam^{ll} MacKeen James Cochran and Daniel Anderson from their Houses to the High ways Contigous to them allready laid out.

8^{ly} voted that this artickle be Deffer'd untill the next proprietors meeting

9^{ly} The Severall returns or transcripts hereafter mentioned was by the lott layers brought in read and approv'd of by the proprietors to the owners Thereof and their heirs for Ever (viz) one to Abell merrils right of his mendment land and one of said Merrills addition land one to Sam^{ll} Penhallows of his adition land and to Jo^{n} Clerk half right of the mendment & adition belonging to it, one to James & Jo^{n} Doaks right belong to the mendment laid out to S^{d} right in Taylor's Grove, one to Sam^{ll} Allison of his Second Division & one of want of home lot beyond Leverts Bridge, one of Jo^{n} Woodburns Second Division, one to John Macmurphy being part of his mendment land one to John Macneall of his mendment adition want of home lot & High way land, one to Robert Willson & $Will^{m}$ Gillmore, one to Richard Waldron's Right of his mendment & adition land, one to the ministeriall lott, one to the original lott of John Gray, of his adition land, one to Robert Doaks originall lot for what mendment it wanted adition land high way land & want of home lot one to Jo^{n} Anderson for Six acres of Good land his right wanted

Reasons of the Discent and protestation of the under named Subscribers, Proprietors of the town of Londonderry and province of newhampshire against the acts & doings of John Wallace John Archibald & James Rodgers who was Chosen Lott layers by the Proprietors of Said town (viz) to lay out the amendments to the home lotts and the twenty acres of Aditionall land.

1st Because they the Said lottlayers acted Contrary their orders or power in laying out to a Second Division originally belonging to Mr James Macgregore Seventy acres of the towns land in lew of six acres of wood leave, Wheras they had no power to Intermedl with any Second Division formerly laid out.

2^{ly} Because they have laid out land to themselves and their Relations which is Contrary to law.

Jo^{n} Barnat Junr
William Humphra
John Stewart
Arch^{d} Clendinen
Robt Wear
John Anderson
John Blair

You are hereby Required to Warn the Proprietors Freeholders and Inhabitants of London-Derry to Conven at their Meeting house upon Thursday the fourth Day of April next at nine of the Cloak before noon.

Imprimus To See what method they will take to Dispose of the Publick School or Schoole's

2^{ly} At the Desire of ten men to See whether they will vote that the Com^{ttee} for accounts take in no note but what the particulars Shall be made appear.

3^{ly} To Converse about the most proper method to help m^{r} Thomson Forward with this Building & Improvements.

4^{ly} To See if they will Chuse a new Com^{ttee} for Defending the town lines or Comons otherwise to Strengthen the hands of the present Committee.

5^{ly} To See if the proprietors will Confer a Small Gratuity of land on the late Revd Mr Mac Gregore's Doughters (viz) Jane and margaret bounding on the farm granted him by the Government

6^{ly} To See what method the proprietors will take about the land on the River.

7^{ly} To See if they will dispose of that tract of land granted to Osgood.

8^{ly} To See if the proprietors will Exchange Deeds with James Moore for the land he had at Cobats pond by Deed from Alex^{r} Walker, and the land he now lives on.

9^{ly} To Chuse men to take the Invoice of the poles & Estates in this town for this Currant year and this Shall be your Warrant, Given under our hands this 15th of march 1733/4

James Gregg.
Patrick Douglas.
John Morison Junr
Andrew Todd.
Select men

To Messures Archibald Clendinen and James Callwell Constables

At ameeting of the Proprietors Freeholders and Inhabitants of Londonderry Conven'd at their Meetinghouse on thursday the fourth Day of april 1734 at nine of the Coack in the forenoon, voted for Moderator Robert Boyes

1st voted that their Shall be two Schools Kept in this town for the Enshewing year, and that the Inhabitants of the westerly Side of Beaver Brook Shall have one of the aforesaid Schoolmasters as the formerly had, and paid as formerly.

2ly voted that the Comttee for the towns accounts Shall receive no notes from the Select men or Constables but what the particulars for Said notes Shall be made plainly appear to Said Comttee

The third artickle is pass'd

4ly Voted that the Comttee for the Defence of the town is now rechosen with all the power's and Strenth that the proprietors Invested Said Comttee with, at a Generall town meeting held at Londonderry March ye 6th 1731/2 the names of Said Comttee is as followeth Robt Boyes. John MacMurphy. John Morison Junr John Archibald. James Clerk.

5ly voted that the proprietors will Bestow as a Gratuity or Gift to Mr Macgregores two Doughters (viz) Jane and Margaret thirty acres of land by measure, Joyning to the Farm Granted and laid out to the late Revd Mr Mac Gregore Deceas'd which thirty acres is to be laid betwen Said Farm and Cobats pond.

6ly voted that the proprietors will take the most properest method that they Can think of to lay out a fourth Division upon the river and that their is a Com^{ttee} or lotlayers Chosen to lay out Said fourth Division (viz) Sam^{ll} Graves John Barnat Junr Sam^{ll} Barr

and in order to Effect the most properest method the proprietors have Chosen four men to project a Scheme for the forming and laying out Said fourth Division (viz) Robert Boyes. John Archibald. John MacMurphy. William Gregg.

7^{ly} voted that the proprietors will not, at this time Sel the land granted to osgood

8^{ly} Voted that John Morison Junr John Senter and James Reid Shall be a Com^{ttee} to Exchange Deeds with James Moore of the land that he bought from Alex^{r} Walker at Cobats pond and give the Said Moore a Deed of the land he now lives upon.

9^{ly} voted that William Moore and William Gregg Shall take an Invoice of the poles & Estates of this town for the present year, and Shall be allowed for their Service four pounds Bils of Credit.

We the under Subscribers protest agains the vote pass'd to give any land to any person as a Gift, untill we have our land made up Equall with other proprietors.

Willm Humphra
Robert Wear
John Stewart

We the under Subscribers protest against that vote of Exchangeing Deeds w^{t} James Moore

John Blair.
Willm Humphra.
Robt Wear.
Archibald Clendinen.

You are hereby Required to Warn the Freeholders Proprietors and Inhabitants of London-Derry to Conven at their meetinghouse on Thursday the fourth Day of July next by nine o' the Cloack before noon then and there.

Imp. To See what Proprietors ministers & town rates they Shall assess for the year Runing and what Sums for Each of them.

2^{ly} To See what method the Proprietors will take to make up a Second Division laid out to James and John Morison which wants Sixteen acres of the measure Incerted in the transcript of it.

3^{ly} To See if they will allow the Grand Jury men from year to year money to Defray Some part of their Charge.

4^{ly} To See whether they will vote that Every freeholder & Proprietor pay in proportion to the number of Good acres laid out to them, in all rates assessed on them for Defence of law Shutes

5^{ly} To See whether they will allow Robert Duncan Intrest for the want of the full money he Expended for them in Ireland.

6^{ly} To See if they will take any method to Extricate those men that are presented to the Quarter Sessions for narrow high Ways.

7^{ly} To See whether they will allow James Leslie the twenty Shi^{lls} he formerly had for makeing fires for the minister.

8^{ly} To See how the Severall Quarters of the town will dispose of the Publick School untill the fifth of march next.

9^{ly} To See if the Proprietors will help James Adams in his present trouble by the people of Haverhill. and this Shall be your Warrant

Given under our hands this 18th of June 1734.

James Gregg.
Patrick Douglas.
John Morison. Junr
James Rodgers.
Andrew Todd.
Select men

At ameeting of the Freeholders, Proprietors and Inhabitants of London-Derry Conven'd at their meetinghouse upon Thursday the fourth Day of July 1734

Voted for Moderator Robert Boyes

Imp: voted their Shall be twenty five Shi^{lls} apploted upon Each full proprietor, for the Defence of the propriety for the

Enshewing year, and to Defray their present Debts and also voted that Mr Clerks Salary for the runing year Shall be fourty pounds according to the vote pass'd in Dec^{br} ye 3^{d} 1729. and also voted that Mr Thomson's Salary Shall be apploted by the Select men according to what was Setled upon him March ye 5th 1733/4 for the runing year. and also voted that the Select men is to applot the town rate for the runing year according to their Discretionary Judgement as they understand the Debts of the town require

2^{ly} voted by the proprietors that the Com^{ttee} that lay'd out James and John Morison's Second Division Shall Judge whether they realy want of their Second Division, and if So, they the Said Com^{ttee} are to do them Justice if not, they are to let it Stand as it is.

3^{ly} voted that the Grand Jury man or Grand Jury men that is oblig'd to attend the Severall Courts & Sessions in this province yearly, Shall have from the town as Such for the aforesaid Service paid them five pounds yearly in bils of Credit.

4^{ly} voted that the artickle Concering the freeholders & proprietors paying their proportion or rates according to what Good land laid out to them is pass'd in the negative for this present year.

5^{ly} voted that Robert Duncan Shall be paid lawfull Intrest for the want of his money that he Expended in Ireland for the time he lay out of it.

6^{ly} voted that the town will not Extricate those men that are presented to the Quarter Sessions for narrow high ways.

7^{ly} voted that James Leslie Shall be allow'd twenty Shi^{lls} for makeing fires for the minister for this present year.

8^{ly} voted that the town will not at present Intermedle with the Publick Schooll

9^{ly} voted that their Shall be twenty pounds added to the town rate and Given to James Adams of our town as a Gift to help him to defray his Lawshuts Commenc'd against him by Haverhill Claiming his land.

You are hereby Required to Warn the Severall Freeholders of Londonderry legally Qualified within your Severall Precincts to Conven at their meeting house on Saturnday the 5th day of october next by four o' the Cloack in the afternoon then and there to Chose one fitt person to Represent the Said freeholders in Generall assembly to be Conven'd at the Court house in Portsmouth on tuesday the Eight Day of october next, and for so doing this Shall be your warrant. Given under our hands this nineteenth Day of Sep^{tr} 1734

2^{ly} To See whether they will Clear Mr Thomson's Board for the runing year

and this Shall be your Warrant as before

James Gregg
Patrick Douglas
Andrew Todd
James Rodgers
Select men

To Messures Archibald Clendinen and James Callwell Town Constables

At a Meeting of the Freeholders of Londonderry Conven'd at their meetinghouse on Saturnday the fifth Day of october 1734. voted for Moderator John Goffe Esqr

1st voted for Representitive Robert Boyes

2^{ly} voted that the town will pay Mr Thomson's Board, from the time he Came to this town for one full year. as a Gift to him the Said Mr Thomson

You are hereby Required to Warn the Proprietors Freeholders & Inhabitants of Londonderry to Conven at their meetinghouse upon Friday the twenty fourth of this Instant January at ten of the Clock in the forenoon then & there

1st To See if the town will allow the Selectmen to pay the Schoolmaster in the westerly side of Beaver brook according to their vote last pass'd for that End.

2^{ly} To See if the town will let William Nickels have a litle land that he has made Improvement upon it being upon the Comons at areasonable price it being done throu amistake which artickle was Entred at the Request of ten men.

3^{ly} To See if the town will Refound John Bell his

Charges that he Expended when he was Sitted to last Sep[tr] Sessions to Serve as Grand-Jury-man

4[ly] To See if the town will Choose men to take the Invoice of the poles & Estates of this town, for this year.

5[ly] To See what method the town will take to Discharge M[rs] Cargill of the money to be paid by her to the town, which was left by Archibald Macpheadris Esq[r] Deceas'd, as a Gift for the use of our Meetinghouse.*

6[ly] To hear transcripts read.

and this Shall be your Warrant

Given under our hands this Eight Day of January 1734/5

7[ly] To See if the town will allow the Select men to applot money to maintain this part of the presbiterian Intrest.

and this Shall be your Warrant as before.

James Gregg.
Patrick Douglas.
Andrew Todd.
James Rodgers.
Select men

To Messures James Callwell and Archibald Clendinen Town Constables

At a meeting of the Proprietors Freeholders & Inhabitants of Londonderry Conven'd at their meeting house upon Fri-

*Archibald MacPheadris, Esq., settled in Portsmouth previous to the settlement of Londonderry, and his standing is shown by the fact that he built a house in 1719-23 which cost six thousand pounds. This mansion has since become known as the Warner house, and it is claimed has the distinction of having been the first house in New Hampshire to have lightning rods, put on under the personal instruction of Dr. Benjamin Franklin. Captain MacPheadris was of Scotch ancestry, and was a pioneer in the manufacture of ironworks in this country, beginning his first operations upon the Lamprey river. He married Sarah, one of the sixteen children of Lieut.-Governor John Wentworth, and his daughter married Hon. Jonathan Warner. Captain MacPheadris died in 1729. He was greatly interested in church work, and left several bequests for the benefit of the Presbyterian church. There seems to have been a strong friendship between him and Captain Cargill, and possibly a relationship.—EDITOR.

day the twenty fourth of January at ten o' the Clock before noon 1734/5

The town Chose for moderator John Blair

1st Voted that the town do adhere to their former vote, with respect of paying their Schoolmaster's, particularly the vote pass'd the fourth of april last pass'd which was in the year 1734.

2^{ly} voted that the land incerted in the Second artickle is Defered at present to be given to William Nickels and that William Humphra's return or transcript of the aforesaid land Shall also be Deffer'd and not approv'd of nor put upon Record untill the proprietors take it to further Consideration.

3^{ly} voted that John Bell Shall have fourty Shi^{lls} and no more Refounded him for his Charges, as he was Sited to last Sep^{tr} Sessions to Serve as a Grand Jury man, he haveing paid his fine to the Sessions as the law Directs

4^{ly} voted that William moore & $Will^{m}$ Gregg Shall take the Invoice of the poles & Estates of this town for this year, and that they Shall be paid for their Service as Such fourty Shi^{lls} Each of them.

5^{ly} voted that John Macmurphy Shall Discharge Mrs Cargill of the money that is due by Capt Cargills Heirs, to the Heirs of Archibald Macpheadris Esqr Deceas'd when he Shall receive Said money which is twenty Eight pounds which money is to be appropriated for the use of our meetinghouse according to Archibald Macpheadris Esqr Deceas'd his orders, and the Said John Macmurphy is to Keep Said money in his Custody untill the town Call for Said money and discharge the Said Macmurphy of Said money.

6^{ly} voted that the Severall returns or transcripts hereafter mentioned was by the lott layers brought in read & approv'd of by the proprietors to the owners thereof and their heirs for Ever (viz) one to Capt David Cargill, Daniel Mac Duffi John Richey $Will^{m}$ Thomson & Robert morison, one to Jenat and Margaret Macgregore being a Gratuity or Gift given to them by the proprietors upon the fourth of april last past as by their vote of that date may now plainly appear

Consisting of thirty acres one to Robert morison, one to Capt Cargill for his Servant Willm Nutt to Allen Anderson James Gillmore & Daniel macduffi, one to Sam^{ll} Moor's right, one to Willm Gillmore, one to Alex^{r} Macneall, two to James Mac Keen, one to James Mac Laughlin, one to James mac Laughlin & Willm Gregg, one to Dan^{ll} Mac Duffi

7^{ly} The Said artickle pass'd in the negative.

You are hereby Required to Warn the Proprietors Freeholders & Inhabitants of Londonderry to Conveen at their meetinghouse upon wensday the fifth day of March at nine o' the Clock in the forenoon then & there

Imp^{rs} To Chuse all their town officers for the Enshewing year as the law directs

2^{ly} To See what the town will do about a Schooll or Schools for the Enshewing year

3^{ly} To See if the town will Chuse a Com^{ttee} to give a Deed to Jean & Margaret Macgregore of the thirty acres of land the proprietors Bestow'd upon them the fourth Day of april last past

4^{ly} To See if the town will Chuse one of the NonCommoners to Sitt with the Com^{ttee} that takes the towns accounts

5^{ly} To See if the town will grant and give full power to the Com^{ttee} of accoumpts that they Shall receive no notes of no man but Such as they have a town vote for according to the laws of the province.

and this Shall be your warrant

Given under our hands this fourteenth day of February 1734/5

James Gregg
Patrick Douglas
John Morison Junr
James Rodgers,
Select men

To Messures James Callwell and Archibald Clendinen town Constable

At a Generall town meeting of the propretors Freeholders and Inhabitants of Londonderry Conveend at their meetinghouse upon Wensday the fifth day of March 1734/5 at nine o' the Clock in the foreenoon

voted for Moderator Robert Boyes

voted that their Shall be five men Chosen to Serve as Selectmen for the Enshewing year, the names of the men that are Chosen to Serve as Such is as followeth James Clerk. Robert Boyes. John Gregg. Thomas Willson north James Aiken.

voted for Town Clerk for the Enshewing year John Macmurphy

voted that their Shall be two Constables in this town to Serve as Such for the Enshewing year, and that Beaver Brook Shall be the Divideing line betwen the Said two Constables and that they Shall be allow'd for their Service as Such five pounds by the town, that is to Say the Constable that Serves in the Easterly Side of Beaver Brook Shall have for his Service fifty five Shi^{lls} and the Constable that Serves in the westerly Side of Said Beaver Brook Shall have for his Service as Constable fourty five Shi^{lls} the names of the Constables Chosen is John Stewart & Abraham Holms.

and Whereas the Said John Stewart after being Chosen have hired another person to Serve for him and in his room & Stead as Constable for the Enshewing year it is hereby to be understood that S^{d} person is accepted of and voted as Constable in the room of John Stewart and is Intitled to the wages allow'd by the town to S^{d} Stewart the person's name is as follows Sam^{ll} Barr.

voted for Sirvayers of Highways for the Enshewing year Alexander Renkine. William Adams. John Mitchell. James Anderson. Hugh Willson. Gabriel Barr. Willm Macmaster.

Rev. Matthew Clark died January 25, 1735, in his seventy-fifth year. While somewhat eccentric in his manners, he was a man of ability, who had received a military training in his early life, having distinguished himself in the siege of Old Londonderry in 1688-9. He was, at his own request, borne to his grave by his former companions in arms, several of whom were then living in his congregation.—EDITOR.

Willm Gillmore. James Moor. Thomas Cochran. Jo^{n} Wallace. William Holms. James Murray.

voted for Titheing men for the Enshewing year Allex^{r} Macneall. John Crumey.

voted for Howards for the Enshewing year. John Wallace. John Mac Conehey.

voted for fence veiwers and prizers James Morison. William Eayers Junr

voted that their Shall be four men Chosen for this Enshewing year as a Com^{ttee} for Searching the towns accounts, and that S^{d} Comm^{ttee} Shall not receive no notes from the Clerk of the Select men, nor from any Constable but what they Shall Judge right Equitable and Just for the town to pay the names of the Said Comm^{ttee} is as followeth John Blair. James Nesmith. John MacMurphy. Robert Clerk.

2^{ly} voted that their Shall be three Schools Keep in this town for the Enshewing year and that their Shall be fifty pounds rais'd upon the whole town as publick money for the paying of the Schoolmaster's that Shall be aggreed with for the Keeping Said Schools, and that one of Said Schools Shall be furnis'd with a Gramer School master, and that that third part of the town that will take up with Gramer School Shall be allow'd ten pounds of S^{d} fifty pounds & their Equall Share of the remaing fourty pounds provided that they Continue S^{d} Gramer Schoolmaster the whole year but if otherwise then to have no more of Said fifty pounds than an Equall Share or proportion and when Said Gramer Schoolmaster moves to any of the other two thirds of the town, then the Schoolmaster that teaches their to move to where the Gramer Schoolmaster Came from and their to Continue untill he move again, and then the English Schoolmaster to return from whence he was mov'd which is to be Quarterly, the town is to be diveded in three Equall Shares by the pole as near as possible by a Com^{ttee} of three men Chosen & appointed for that End which is John Blair Jo^{n} Archibald and John MacMurphy and the aforesaid three Schoolmaster's is to take a list of the Schoolers they teach which list is to be

Given to the Select men in order the overplus money over and above the fifty pounds may be laid upon the parents or masters of S^{d} Schoolars or upon those Schoolars that are of age if any Such their be, and the Select men Shall rate them according to their Equall proportion and Shall be Colected by the Constable's as other town rates are. and it is further aggreed upon that their Shall be a Com^{ttee} nominated Chosen and voted to Each third of the town with full power & authority to hire and aggree with a Schoolmaster for the third that they Belong too, the Com^{ttee} Chosen for the westerly Side of Beaver Brook for the Ends aforesaid is John Blair John Wallace & John Duncan, the Com^{ttee} Chosen for the Southery Side of the Easterly Side of Beaver Brook is James Reid John Archibald John Barnat Junr the Com^{ttee} Chosen for the Easterly Side of the town upon the Easterly Side of Beaver Brook is Willm Moore John Greeg & John Mac Murphy.

voted that their Shall be a Com^{ttee} Chosen and appointed by the proprietors to give a Deed to Jean Macgregore & Margaret Macgregore of their thirty acres of Land that the proprietors Bestow'd them as a Gratuity & Gift, the names of the Com^{ttee} is John Blair John Bell and James Nesmith.

We the under Subscribers do protest against the Chuseing of a Com^{ttee} to Convey away any of our land which is Contrary to the Intent of our Charter

Willm Humphra.
Archibald Clendinen,
Robt Wear.
John Stewart.
John Barnat Junr.

Londonderry Aprill ye 14th 1735

You are hereby required to Warn the Freeholders and Inhabitants duely Qualified in law to meet at their meeting-house upon tewsday the twenty ninth Instant at nine of the Clo'k in the forenoon then & there.

1st To Ellect & Choose one fitt person duely Qualif'd in the law to represent the town in Generall Assembley appointed to be Conveen'd and held at the Court house in portsmouth on wendsay the thirtieeth day of april Instant at ten of the Clo'k in the forenoon.

2ly To See if the town will make a Publick pound and where they will appoint it to be

and this Shall be your warrant given under our hands this fourteenth day of april at Londonderry 1735.

Robert Boyes.
Thomas Willson.
John Gregg.
James Aiken.
James Clerk.
Select men

To the Constables of Londonderry or Either of them (viz) Abraham Holms & Samll Barr

Att a Meeting of the Freeholders & Inhabitants of Londonderry Conveen'd at their Meetinghouse upon Tewsday ye 29th of April 1735.

votted for Moderator Robert Given

1st votted For Representitive Robert Boyes.

2ly voted that their Shall be apound built at the Expence of the town by the Select men and that Said pound Shall be Sett near our first meetinghouse

Londonderry Septr ye 1st 1735

You are hereby Required to warn the freeholders and Inhabitants of Londonderry to meet at their meetinghouse on thursday ye 18th Instant at ten of the Clo'k in the foreenoon then and there.

1st To See what or how much money they will vote to be assessed upon the town for this Enshewing year.

2ly To See if the town will Impower a Comttee to Sue the Constables of this town that neglect to make up their accoumpts and this Shall be your warrant Given under our hands this 1st day of Septr 1735.

Robert Boyes.
James Clerk.
Thomas Willson.
John Gregg.
James Aiken.
Select men

To Samll Barr Town Constable

Londonderry Sept ye 18th 1735.

Att ameeting of the freeholders & Inhabitants of Londonderry Conven'd at their Meetinghouse on thursday ye 18th of Septr 1735

voted for Moderator John Blair

voted by & with the Consent of the aforesaid Freeholders & Inhabitants that the Moderator has adjurn'd Said meeting untill Thursday ye 2ed Day of october next at ten of the Clo'k in the forenoon.

Meett according to adjurnment &

1st voted that their Shall be three Hundred pounds Bils of Credit rais'd upon the town for defraying the town & province Chargess for the Enshewing year, Besides what the Schoolers is liable to pay according to the vote pass'd in March ye 5th 1734/5 and that the Select men Shall make an Equall assesment of Said Money.

2ly voted that their Shall be three men Chosen by the town for Shewing the Constables that have not Clear'd up their lists or assesments Committed to them the names of the men that is Chosen is as followeth. William Humphra. Robert Clerk. Robert Wear.

Londonderry Septr ye 1st 1735

You are hereby Required to Warn the proprietors of this town to meet at their meeting house upon thursday ye 18th Instant at three of the Clo'k in the afternoon then & there.

1st To See what or how much money they will allow to be rais'd for defraying the proprietory Charges for the Enshewing year.

2ly At the desire of ten men we Insert this artickle to See if the town will Confirm to Mr Mathew Morton that Gratuity of land promis'd to him by Severall proprietors.

3ly To Hear transcripts read in order to approveing

4ly To See if the town will Confirm to William Nutt as Successor to Capt David Cargill the land flow'd by the Fulling mill according to Covenant and this Shall be your Warrant Given under our hands this 1st day of Sep^{tr} 1735.

Robert Boyes.
Thos Willson.
James Clerk.
John Gregg.
James Aiken.
Select men

To Sam^{ll} Barr Town Constable.

At a meeting of the Proprietors of Londonderry at their meetinghouse upon Thursday ye 18th of Sep^{tr} 1735

voted for Moderator John Blair

The aforesaid meeting by the Consent of the proprietors was adjurn'd by the moderator to thursday ye 2^{ed} day of october next at ten of the Clo'k in the forenoon

Meett according to adjurnment.

1st voted their Shall be twenty Shi^{lls} in Bils of Credit asses'd and rais'd upon Each propriety to defray their Chargess this present year.

2^{ly} The 2^{ed} artickle pass'd in the negative.

3^{ly} The Severall transcripts brought in read & approv'd of to their owners & their Heirs for Ever one to Elias Keyies of his Second Division, one to William Nickles of his home lott, one to Jo^{n} Peter & Andrew Cochran, one to Arch^{d} Macpheatres Esqr one to Stephen Peirce, one to Robt Boyes, one to Alex^{r} Nickels, one to Jo^{n} Grays right.

John Morison Junr Enters his descent against Elias Keyies Second Division being approv'd of in order to be put upon record.

4^{ly} voted that the affair of will^{m}Nutt's is Deffer'd to a larger propriety meeting.

You are hereby Required to Warn the proprietors Freeholders and Inhabitants of Londonderry according to law in your precincts to meet at the old meetinghouse on munday the first Day of December next at ten o' the Clock in the forenoon then & there.

To See how much of the Westerly Side of Londonderry they will Sett of for a precinct towards the maintainance of a Gospell minister in that part of Londonderry, or what other method they will take for the peace of the town, and this Shall be your Warrant Given under our hands at Londonderry this 11th Day of Nov[br] 1735.

John Gregg.
Thomas Willson.
James Aiken.
James Clerk.
Select men

To Abraham Holms of Londonderry Town Constable

At a Meeting of the proprietors Freeholders & Inhabitants of London-Derry at their old meetinghouse on Munday the first Day of Dec[br] 1735

voted For Moderator John Blair.

Whereas at the aforesaid meeting after Severall arguments and overtures made by the proprietors Freeholders & Inhabitants where they wo'd have the aforesaid line made for a new-precinct in the westerly Side of this town in order to maintain a Gospel ministery in that part of Londonderry, the moderator Desired all those that were Qualified to draw or form themselves up before the South Side of the meetinghouse in two parties, those that was for haveing a line Determin'd to be in one place, and those that was not for haveing a line made to be in another place, upon which those that was willing and Consenting to have a line Determined formed themselves together in order to be numbr'd and the town Clerk (viz) John MacMurphy reskn'd or Counted them one Hundred and twenty for haveing a line Determin'd for anew precinct, upon which the Moderator desir'd all those that was not for S[d] line to form themselves also, but they wo'd not, and upon their refusall the moderator desir'd them to repair into the meetinghouse & Either to Bring in written votes or to put themselves in form So as they might be Reckn'd or Counted, it was answer'd it was not worth while for that a Great many was gone away, and none Spoke to the Contrary which line is voted as followeth, that the Southerly line of our town upon the westerly Side of Beaver Brook Shall be the line upon that Side and from Said line and by Beaver Brook upon the westerly Side untill it Come to the Road that leads towards ammasceegg Begining near the old Saw mill upon the Southerly Side of Willm Cochran's Lott, thence runing as Said Road or High way leads to the Foord way upon the Brook Known by the name of the twelve acre Brook, and from Said foord way upon a north line untill it Come to Chester town line, and from Said Chester line to the Southerly line first mentioned.

Province of Newhampshire

At a Town meeting in Londonderry Dec^{br} ye 1st 1735.

We the Subscribers freeholders and Inhabitants of the town aforesaid do protest against any Division in this town at this time for the reasons herein given.

1st That our meetinghouse is Sufficient to Contain us all and so no need of another.

2^{ly} That part of the town never petitioned the town for to be set of in time.

3^{ly} The Eregular measures that they have taken or part of them in with drawing themselves without leave of the Generall Court or any other authority Either Eilesiasticall or Sivel known to us.

4^{ly} The vote was not legall

Given under our hands as above.

Robert Boyes,
Hugh Rogers,
Joseph Cochran,
David Hopkine
Hugh Willson.

Province of newhampshire

At a Town Meeting in Londonderry Dec^{br} ye 1st 1735.

We the Subscribers Freeholders and Inhabitants of the westerly part of this town do protest against our being Sett off or Disanex'd from under the Revd Mr Thomson's Ministrey or being Erected into atown parish or precinct any other wise than we are now

Given under our hands.

Andrew Todd,
John Wallace,
Abraham Holms,
David Bogle,
John Dunham,
John Willson,
John MacClurg,
John MacClery,
John Craig,
Alex[r] Mac Collum,
Peter Cochran,
James Cochran,
Christopher Eayres.
Robert Given,
Samuel Morison,
David Morison,
Thomas Bogle,
William Holms,
Sam[ll] Todd
Benj[n] Willson,
Tho[s] MacClery,
Sam[ll] Morison,
Ninian Cochran,
John Holms,
Alex Craig

Londonderry February y[e] 13th 1735/6

You are hereby Required to Warn the proprietors Freeholders & Inhabitants of Londonderry to meet at their old meetinghouse on friday y[e] fifth day of march next at ten o' the Clock in the forenoon then and there.

1st To Chuse their town officers as the law directs

2[ly] To See what method the town will take about the Schools

3[ly] To See if the town will Chuse two fitt men to take the Invoice

Thomas Willson.
John Gregg.
James Clerk.
James Aiken.
Select men

To Abrahan Holms & Sam[ll] Barr Town Constables

At a meeting of the proprietors Freeholders & Inhabitants of Londonderry meet at their old meetinghouse upon Friday y[e] fifth day of March 1735/6

voted for moderator John Blair by one Hundred and twenty three votes and no Contrary

voted that their shall be five Sutable persons Chosen to Serveas Selectmen for the Enshewing year the first person Chosen is Samuel Barr by 100 votes and no Contrary

and ye 2^{ed} is John Gregg by 100 votes and no Contrary
ye 3^{d} is James Blair by 81 votes and no Contrary
ye 4th is James Aiken by 78 votes and no Contrary
ye 5th is James Clerk by 68 votes & no Contrary

voted for Town Clerk John MacMurphy by 98 votes and no Contrary

voted that their Shall be two Constables Chosen for the Enshewing year and Shall be paid by the town as formerly the first Constable Chosen for the Easterly Side of Beaver Brook is Robert Boyes by 59 votes and no Contrary

2^{edly} voted for the westerly Side of Beaver Brook by 33 votes and no Contrary Patrick Douglas as Constable and Whereas Said Patrick Douglas let the town understand that he was not Capable to Serve, and that he had hired another to Serve in his room namely Sam^{ll} Renkine the town accepted of Said Renkine in the room of Patrick Douglas

Voted for Sirvayers of Highways Robert Morison Robt Clerk. James Dunlop Randle Alexander John Moore Gabriel Barr James Willson Robert Cochran Dan^{ll} Macduffi Willm Moore Sam^{ll} Gregg John Blair John Holms Joseph Bell

voted for Tithing men Hugh Muntgomery and Robert Mackeen

voted for Howards Alex^{r} Walker & Willm Eayers Junr

voted for Fence veiwers & prizers Willm Macneall & Sam^{ll} Alison

voted for Searching the towns as formerly John Blair James Nesmith Robt Clerk & Jo^{n} MacMurphy

voted that Sam^{ll} Barr Shall be a particular Constable for Serveing of writs & warrants as he was last year

voted that Robert Boyes Shall be appointed to Joyn Ebenezar Steeven of Kingstown Esqr to Petition the Gen^{ll} assembley at Boston in behalf of the Grivances that Kingstown and this town Suffer by the massachusets province on the account of Lawshuits and that they appear by the 16th Instant but in Case of Said Robert Boyes refusall the Select men are Impowered to Send another fitt person in his room for the End aforesaid.

voted that the aforesaid meeting be adjurn'd by the Consent of the people present to ye 2^{ed} Tewsday in april next at ten o' the Clock in the forenoon being the 13th Day,

Tewsday April ye 13th 1736 meet according to adjurnment.

The Moderator adjurn'd the Said meeting to Munday ye 19th Currant at three o' the Clock in the afternoon

Londonderry April ye 13th 1736 We the under Subscribers all Freeholders of the aforesaid Londonderry doth protest againstall the actings of our March meeting this being part of it by adjurnment for (these reasons) that the said meeting was not legal in it Self, neither was it legalee Carried on, for a great maney of them that was voters in it was not Qualified according as the law directs, & also that a gratt meny of the votters was only trangent persons and paid no rates in this town besides maney other reasons given under our hands the day and year above

Robert Boyes.
Willm Humphra.
John Moore.
Hugh Willson.
Archibald Clendinen.

Munday April ye 19th 1736

Meet according to adjurnment.

voted that their Shall be three Schools Kept in this town for the present year according to the same method that they were Kept last year and the Select men Shall aggree with Said Schoolmasters

voted for field Drivers John Senter & Sam^{ll} Morison Junr

april ye 19th 1736 Andrew Todd, Abraham, Holms John Mitchell, Sam^{ll} Morison, James Morison, Jo^{n} Stewart, John Morison, Robert Wear, David Morison, Robert Given, Daniel Anderson, Enters their descent against Said meeting

Province of newhampshire

To Samuel Renkine Constable

You are hereby Required to Warn the Proprietors of London Derry to meet at their old meetinghouse in Londonderry aforesaid upon Friday the ninth day of april next Enshewing the date hereof at ten o' the Clock in the forenoon then and there.

First To See what answer they will give to the Honble Robert Achimutey who promises to be personally at Said Meeting.

2^{edly} At the Desire of ten men who Desired us to Insert the Following artickle in the first proprietors warrant for a meeting (viz) To See if the proprietors will Confirm to William Nutt the land of the Fulling mill dam that Capt Cargill Sold S^{d} William Nutt.

3dly To See what transcripts the proprietors will approve of after reading them and this Shall be your warrant Given under our hands this 22 day of march 1735/6

James Aiken.
James Clerk.
James Blair.
John Gregg
Sam^{ll} Barr.
Select men

At a Proprietors meeting held at Londonderry old meetinghuse upon Friday ye ninth day of April 1736.

voted for Moderator John Blair.

1st voted that the Com^{ttee} now in being to lay out lands are ordered to lay out a peace of land to the valow of what money the Honble Robert Achimutey paid for James Wallace Joyning to his own Claim which Sum was one hundred & Eighteen pounds being the answer Return'd to ye Honour^{ble} Robert Achimuteys letter.

2^{ly} voted that Willm Nutts affair is Defer'd at this present time.

3^{ly} The Transcripts Deffer'd at present. &

Province of newhampshire

To Sam^{ll} Renkine Constable

You are hereby Required to Warn the Freeholders of Londonderry duely Qualified to assemble themselves at their old meetinghouse in Londonderry afores^{d} on Munday ye nineteenth day of this Instant april at two o' the Clock in the afternoon then & there.

To Elect one fitt person Qualified in law to represent the above said town in a Generall Assembley appointed to be Conven'd & held at the Courthouse at Portsmouth on Wendensday the twenty first day of this Instant april at ten o' the Clock beforenoon. and this Shall be your warrant Given under our hands this third day of april 1736.

James Clerk.
John Gregg.
Sam^ll^ Barr.
Select men

At a meeting of the Freeholders of Londonderry on munday the nineteenth day of april 1736.

voted For Moderator John Blair

voted For Representitive James Gregg

Province of newhampshire

To Samuel Renkine Constable

you are hereby Required to Warn the proprietors of Londonderry to meet at their old meetinghouse in Londonderry afores^d^ upon friday the fourth day of June next at one o' the Clock in the afternoon then and there.

1st To See what method the proprietors afores^d^ will take to Defend themselves from law Shuts, and if they Chuse aCom^ttee^ for that End to Invest them with Such power as is needfull.

2^ly^ To See what method the proprietors will take to make up the meadows that Some of the proprietors wants or that ly in debateable places

3^ly^ To See if the proprietors will Satisfue Mr Robert Achimutey in the Cost & Charge that he laid out for Willm Hogg as they did in James Wallac's affair.

and this Shall be your Warrant, Given under our hands this 15th of may 1736 at Londonderry

James Aiken.
James Clerk.
James Blair.
John Gregg.
Sam^ll^ Barr.
Select men

At a meeting of the Proprietors of Londonderry at their old meetinghouse upon Friday the fourth day of June 1736.

voted for Moderator John Blair.

Whereas there was but a Small number of proprietors present at Said meeting it was Concluded upon by & with the Consent of the proprietors then present, that the moderator adjurn S^{d} meeting to Thursday ye 24th Instant at 11 o' the Clock in the forenoon accordingly the moderator adjurn'd S^{d} meeting to ye day and hour aforesaid.

June ye 24th 1736 the proprietors meet according to adjurnment.

1st voted that their Shall be a Committee Chosen and appointed for the defence of the proprietors which Com^{ttee} Shall Consist of three Sutable men all proprietors for ye Ends aforesaid and that the Said Com^{ttee} now Chosen Shall be Cloathed and Invested with all the powers and authorities that the former Committee For that End had of what Kind and nature So ever the names of S^{d} Com^{ttee} is Robert Wear Jams Rodgers Sam^{ll} Barr.

2^{ly} voted their Shall be a Com^{ttee} of three men to Inspect into the wants of those proprietors that Complain of not haveing had their just & Equall Shares of the meadows according to their propriety and Said Com^{ttee} is to take a list of these persons names that they think and Judge have Just reason to Complain of their wants and Carry in their report to the proprietors at their next meeting, but that nothing of their oppinion or report be put upon Record untill it be brought before the proprietors. The names of S^{d} Com^{ttee} is John Blair Jam^{s} Nesmith John MacMurphy

3^{ly} voted that Willm Hoggs affair be deffer'd untill next proprietors meeting

We the under Subscribers do protest against the Chuseing any Com^{ttee} to Levey any more of the proprietors to Defend any particular mans Estate in law as they formerly have done.

Propriety meeting June ye 24th 1736

Willm Humphra.
Robt MacKeen.
Randle Alexander.

Province of newhampshire.

To Sam^{ll} Renkine Constable.

You are hereby Required to Warn the proprietors Freeholders & Inhabitants of Londonderry to meet at their old meetinghouse in Londonderry aforesaid upon wednesday the twenty fourth day of November at ten o' the Clock in the forenoon then & there.

1st To hear their accounts Read.

2ly To See if the town will Either Chuse or hire aConstable to Serve this year on the Easterly Side of Beaver Brook, and if they do Either of these to Invest him with Such power as is needfull

3ly To See what money the town will allow to be aploted or asses'd on the Inhabitants of this town to defray the present debt and Continging Charges and this Shall be your warrant Given under our hands at Londonderry this Eight Day of Novbr in the year 1736.

James Aiken.
James Blair.
James Clerk,
John Gregg.
Samll Barr.
Select Men

Province of newhampshire

Londonderry novbr ye 24th 1736

By virtue of the foregoing warrant I have notified the proprietors Freeholders & Inhabitants in the usuall manner.

Samll Renkine Constable.

At a meeting of the proprietors Freeholders and Inhabitants of Londonderry assembled at their old meetinghouse upon wednesday the twenty fourth day of novbr 1736.

voted for Moderator Robert Boyse and after being desir'd to take his place he said it was his opinion that the warning for Sd meeting was not legall and that Samll Renkine was not Impower'd as Constable to warn that part of the town upon the Easterly Side of Beaver Brook and further South that as his own Cause was to Come before him he did not think fitt to Sitt as moderator.

For which reasons the town proceeded to a new Choise and

voted for Modertor Robert Wear.

The Said moderator by the Consent of the people adjurn'd Said meeting to Wednesday the first day of Dec[br] presizely at ten c' the Clock in the forenoon

Meet according to adjurnment

voted that the reading the towns accounts be deferr'd at this time.

voted that Robert Cochran Shall Serve as Constable for the Easterly Side of Beaver Brook for this present year and that he Shall be for Ever Excluded from the office of Constable in this town afterwards, and that his wages as Such Shall be twenty Shi[lls] over & above the usuall Salary that the former Constables have had.

voted that their Shall be three Hundred and thirty pounds Collected and rais'd for defraying the town & province rates for the present year besides ten Shi[lls] by Each proprietor for his proprietors Rates.

Province of newhampshire

To Robert Cochran Constable in the Easterly Side of Beaver Brook in Londonderry

You are hereby Required to warn all the Proprietors freeholders and Inhabitants on the Easterly Side of Beaver Brook in Londonderry aforesaid Duly Qualified in Law to meet at the old meetinghouse in Londonderry aforesaid upon Saturday the fifth day of March next Enshewing the date hereof at ten o' the Clock in the forenoon then & there, with those on the westerly Side of Beaver Brook who have the like Qualification.

First to Chuse a town officers for the year Enshewing.

2[dly] To See what the town will do Concerning a Highway in Debeate Leading from Cannada to the town Subscribed by ten men.

3[dly] To See what the proprietors will do with M[r] Achimutey who desires Some land that was Granted to him by the proprietors Changed or laid out in Some other place.

4[ly] To See if the proprietors will Chuse fitt persons to Perambulate the town lines—and this Shall be your warrant

Given under our hands at Londonderry this tenth day of February in the year 1736/7

James Clerk,
John Gregg,
James Aiken.
James Blair
Sam^{ll} Barr.
Select men

I have posted up this Warrant according to the usuall manner three days Witness my hand.

Robert Cochran Constable.

Province of newhampshire

To Samuel Renkine Constable on the westerly Side of Beaver Brook in Londonderry.

You are hereby Required to warne all the proprietors freeholders and Inhabitants on the westerly Side of Beaver Brook in Londonderry aforesaid Duly Qualified in law to meet at the old meetinghouse in Londonderry aforesaid upon Saturday the fifth day of March next Enshewing the date hereof at ten o' the Clock in the forenoon then & there with those on the Easterly Side of Beaver Brook with the like Qualifications

First To Choose town officers for the year Enshewing.

2dly To See what the town will do Concerning a High Way in debeat leading Cannada to the town Subscribed by ten men.

3^{ly} To See what the proprietors will do with Mr Achimutey who desires to have Some land that was Granted to him by the proprietors Exchanged or laid out in Some other place.

4^{ly} To See if the proprietors will Choose Some fitt persons to perambulate the town lines and this Shall be your Warrant Given under our hands at Londonderry this tenth day of February in the year 1736/7

James Clerk.
John Gregg.
James Aiken
James Blair.
Sam^{ll} Barr.
Select men

I have posted up this warrant according to the usuall manner three days witness my hand

Sam^ll^ Renkine Constable

At a Generall town Meeting held at Londonderry by the proprietors Freeholders & Inhabitants of Said town Dully Qualified in law upon Saturday the Fifth day of March 1736/7 according to the afores^d^ Warrants.

voted for Moderator John Blair.

Voted for Town Clerk John Macmurphy,

voted that their Shall be five men Chosen to Serveas Selectmen for the Enshewing year James Lindsay. John Bell. Sam^ll^ Barr. James Clerk. James Nesmith.

Voted that their Shall be two Constables Chosen for the Enshewing year and that they Shall be allowed for their Service as Such five pounds and paid as formerly the Constable for the Easterly Side of Beaver Brook is Daniel Mac Duffi and the Constable for the westerly Side of Beaver Brook is John Craige that lives Betwen William Eayers and John Woodburn's.

voted Sirvayers for High ways John Richey. Willm Adams. Jo^n^ Mackeen. Dan^ll^ anderson. John Archibald. Jam^s^ Thomson. Jam^s^ MacCurdy. Thos Horner. Jam^s^ Gillmore. Jam^s^ Moore. Thos Willson. John Anderson. Thos Hogg. Willm Aiken.

voted Tithing men James Morison & Willm Macneall.

voted Howards Francis Smiley & Randle Alexander.

voted Fence veiwers & prizers Jam^s^ Anderson & James Leslie

Voted For Searching the town accounts John Blair James Nesmith Robert Clerk & John Macmurphy,

The Moderator for Said meeting by & with the Consent of the Qualified voters have adjurned Said meeting to the last Monday of this Instant march at ten o' the Clock in the forenoon.

Province of newhampshire

To Samuel Renkine Constable in Londonderry,

You are hereby Required in his Maj^tes^ name to Warn all

the freeholders in your presinct Qualified in law to assemble themselves at the old meetinghouse in Londonderry aforesaid upon Monday the Seventh day of March next Enshewing the date hereof at nine o' the Clock in the forenoon and then and their with those on the Easterly Side of Beaver Brook in Londonderry aforesaid who who have the like qualifications Joyntly to Elect one fitt person qualified in the law to represent the Said town in Generall assembly appointed to be Convin'd and held at the Court House in portsmouth on tewsday the Eight day of March next at two of the Clock in the afternoon and this Shall be your warrant Given under our hands at Londonderry this nineteenth day of February 1736/7

James Clerk.
John Gregg.
Sam[ll] Barr.
Select men

Londonderry March y[e] 7th 1736/7
I have posted this warrant three days according as the law directs

Samuel Renkine Constable.

Province of newhampshire
To Daniel Macduffi Constable in Londonderry
By virtue of a Precept to us Directed from the Sherif of said province Requiring us to Cause the Freeholders and other Inhabitants of Londonderry aforesaid Duly Qualified in the law to assemble themselves at Such time and place as we Shall see Cause to appoint, there to Elect and Chuse one fitt person to represent them in the Generall assembley of our Said province now Sitting at portsmouth in Said province the Said precept Bearing date March the tenth 1736, By virtue which you are hereby Required in his Maj[tes] name to warn all the freeholders & other Inhabitants of Londonderry aforesaid Duly Qualified in the law to assemble themselves at the old meeting house in Londonderry aforesaid upon Monday the fourteenth day of March Currant at Eight of the Clock in the forenoon then and there to Elect or Chuse one fitt person to represent them in Generall assembly now

Sitting at portsmouth in Said province and the person so Chosen by the major part of the voters then present as afores[d] is Required by the S[d] precept to appear at the place above mentioned on the aforesaid 14th Day of March Currant and in so doing this Shall be your warrant Given under hands at Londonderry this 11th day of march in the year 1736/7

James Lindsay.
James Nesmith.
James Clerk.
Sam[ll] Barr.
Select men

Province of newhampshire
Londonderry March y[e] 14th 1736/7
By virtue of the within warrant I have posted up S[d] warrant as usuall and went to as many of the freeholders Houses as I Could in the time and notified them.

Daniel Macduffi Constable

Province of newhampshire
Londonderry March y[e] 14th 1736/7
By virtue of the aforesaid warrant, The freeholders & other Inhabitants of Londonderry Duly Qualified assembl'd themselves at the old meetinghouse upon Monday the 14th Day of March 1736/ and did then and there.
vote for Moderator Robert Wear
also voted for Representitive Robert Boyes

Anne Regui Regis Gorgii secundi deeime
Pro: of N--hamp[r] ss
In the House of Representatives
March 30th 1737
The Within Petition Read and Voted that the last parragraph in the Petition as to having another Town meeting be granted and that the Freeholders and other Inhabitants qualifyed meet at the old meeting Hous in Londonderry on the third tuesday of April next to make Choice of town officers for the year Ensuing as the law directs and that Nathaniel Weare Esq[r] be a Moderator to Govern said meeting and

that a Copy of this vote be set up by the Constables on both the Meeting Houses in the town two Sabbathe days before the day of meeting and all Persons Concern'd are to Conform themselves accordingly

James Jeffry Cler: assem[l]

Eodm die

In the House of Represen:

Upon Reconsidering the above vote Voted the House adheres to their former vote with the addition that one of the Honoerabl the Council be added with M[r] Weare

James Jeffry Clar: Assm[l]

In Council April 1: 1737

Read and Concurr'd and Richard Waldren Esq[r] is appointed to Joyn with Nathaniel Weare Esq[r] to transact the above mentioned affare

Rich[d] Waldron Sec[y]

Same day I assent to the above votes

J Belcher

Copy Rich[d] Waldron Sec[y]

Whereas there is no hour appointed in the above order of the General Court for holding the town meeting above mentioned......We the Comittee have tho't proper to order and do hereby dereit that the said meeting shall begin at nine o' Clock before noon. as Witness our hands the 2[d] of april 1737

Rich[d] Waldron for y[e] Com[ttee]

Anno Regui Regis Georgii secundi decime

Pro: of N: Hamp[r] ss

In the House of Representives March 30th 1737

The Within Petition Read and voted that the last Parragraph in the Petition as to having another town meeting be granted and that the freeholders and other Inhabitants qualifyed meet at the old meeting house in Londonderry on the third tuesday of april next

To make Choice of town officers for the the year Ensuing as the law directs and that Nathaniel Weare Esq[r] be a moderator to Govern said meeting and that a Copy of this Vote be set up by the Constables on both the meeting Houses in the town two Sabbathe days before the day of meeting and all Persons Concern'd are to Conform themselves accordingly

James Jeffry Cler. Assm[l]

Eod[m] die

In the House of Represen.

Upon Reconsidering the above vote voted the House adheres to their former vote with this addition that one of the Honorable the Council be added with Mr Weare

James Jeffry Cle[r] Assem[l]

In Council April 1: 1737

Read and Concurr'd and Richard Waldron Esq[r] is appointed to Joyn with Nathaniel Weare Esq[r] to transact the above mentioned affair

Rich[d] Waldron Sec[y]

same day I Assent to the above votes

J Belcher

Whereas there is no hour appointed in the above order of the General Court for holding the town meeting above mentioned We the Com[tee] have thot proper to order and do hereby dirict that the said meeting shall begin at nine o'Clock before noon as Witness our hands the 2[d] of April 1737

Rich[d] Waldron for the Committee.

Londonderry April 18th 1737

I have posted up this order with the other two Sabbathe days Samuell Ren Ken Constable

By vertow of the fore Going order the freeholders and other Inhabitants of Londonderry Meet April 19th 1737 for the Choice of town offesirs for the Enshewing year

voted there shall be five Select men for the Enshewing year the Names of the men is

Robert Boyes
Robert Weare
Andrew Todd
Thomas Willson
Hugh Willson

Select men

voted for town Clerk John Wallace.

voted that their shall be two Constables for the Enshewing year and they shall be allowed Equall in the allowances that the town makes to the Constables for their Service: the Constable for the Easterly Side of Beaver Brook is Matthew Taylor the Constable for the Westerly side is James Aiken

voted for Sirvayers their Names is Alexander Renken James Callwell Moses Barnat Dan^{ll} Anderson John Archbald Sam^{ll} Morison Sam^{ll} Mitchell Thos Horner Jesse Cresty James Taggart Thos Cochran John Taggart John Duncan Willm Aiken voted for tithing men their is Willm M^{tt} Nell John Moreson tithing men

voted for Howards their names is Francis Smiley Willm Nickels Howards

voted for fence veiwers their Names is John Crumey Willm Humphry fence veiwers

voted for a Com^{ttee} to Search the towns aCompts their Names is John Wallace. Senr Moses Barnat Robert Clark Com^{ttee}

Londonderry May 16th 1737

You are hearby Required to Warn the Inhabetanes Propriators and free holders of this town to meet at their old meetinghouse upon thursday the second day of Jun nixt at ten of the Clok before noon then and there

1:ly to see what method the town will tak about schools for this year and Act there on

2:ly to Call the trusttees that wer Chosn by the town to agree for the Reparing and finishing the old meeting house and whether it be don or not

3:ly to see what is become of the money that hes ben sesed upon the town and Propriators these years past

4:ly to see what method the Propriators of the old meeting hous will tak for the Repairing of it and what is become of the money that was aloted for it

5:ly to see if the town will Chouse aCommittee to perambulat or Run the town lins

6:ly to see if the town will alow Mr Achmuty to Chouse his land in another part of the town where he sees Caus

7:ly to see if the town will Chouse men to tak the Invoice this year: and this Shall be your Warant Given under our hand the day and year above mentioned

To Mr. Mathow Tylor Constabl for the Easterly Sid of Bever Brook in Londonderry

Robart Wear
Robart Boys
Thomas Willson
Hugh Willson
Andrew Todd
Select men

I have posted the within Warning agreeable to the a proved Custom at the place of publick worship two Lordsday

Atest pr

Mathow Tylor Constabl

[This warrant is given in the same words to James Aiken Constable for the westerly side of Beaver brook.—Ed.]

By vertow of the fore Going Warant the free holders and Inhabitants of Londonderry meet at their old meeting house June 2th 1737

and voted for Moderator Ro^t Wear

1:ly voted that the schools shall be keep as formerly these years past and also voted that Each Quarter shall Chouse aCommitee to agree with their own Master the Com^tee for the westerly side of Bever Brook is Willm Nute John Moore Senr John Duncan Com^tee

The Com^tee for the sou: Easterly side of Bever Brook is James Reid John Archbald Moses Barnat Com^tee

and the select men is to be a Com^tee for the third Quarter

2:ly voted that the trustees is to bring in their Articls the nixt town meeting

3:ly voted that the Com^tee for serching the towns a Compts shall have time till the nixt town meeting to bring in their a Compts

4:ly voted that the old meeting house shall be Repared and the select men for the time being shall hire Workemen to do the same

5:ly voted that the town lins shall be perambulated and also voted that three men shall be a Com^{tee} to do the sam and s^{d} Com^{tee} shall be men from a nother town not Intrested in Lo: derry and also voted that Robart Boys and John Archbald and Robart Wear shall hire s^{d} Com^{tee} and also voted that the proprietors shall pay s^{d} Com^{tee}

6:ly voted that Mr Achmuty shall have leberty to Change his Cleame and tak it in any place of the undevided lands

7:ly voted y^{t} their shall be two men to tak the Invoice for this year of the pole and Estats of this town and the men voted for taking the same is Robart Cochran Samuell Bar

and also voted their wages shall be four pounds and ten shillings for the above s^{d} Serves (viz) for taking the aforesaid Invoice of the pols and Estates of this town

Province of New hamr

You are hereby Required to warn the freehoulders of Londonderry in said province duly Qualified in Law to meet at the old meetting hous in Londonderry aforesaid on tusday the 23 of Augst Corrent at ten of the Cloak in the fore noon then and there

1stly to Chouse one fitt person Qualified in law to Represent them in Gennaral assimbly

2:ly to Chous a Com^{tee} if they see Caus to take Carr if needbe to any thing Relating to the province lind

3:ly to see if the Condition of fencing the Grave yeard be fullfiled or not and to act any thing there on

and this shall be your Warran given under our hands at Londonderry August the 13th 1737

Robert Wear
Thomas Willson
Robert Boys
Select men

To Matthow Tayler Constable

Londonderry August the 28th/1737

pursuant to the within presept I have posted the said Warran as uesuall,

Matthew Tayler Constable

[A copy of this warrant is given to James Aiken, Constable, followed by his affidavit, recorded on page 102 of Vol. 2, Early Records of Londonderry.—Ed.]

By vertow of the fore going Warnings the free holders of Londonderry meet at their old meeting house on August the 23th/1737

and voted for moderator, Robart Wear

1st ly voted for Representitive Robart Boys Esqr

2:ly voted there shall be a Comtee Chosen to wait upon the Contee that is to Run the province line now setting at Hamptown, and the men voted for is Robart Boys Andrew Todd Hugh Willson Comtee

3:ly voted that the select men shall Call for the Articls of the Greve yeard and see if they be full fild or not

Provance of New hampsr

Londonderry August 29th 1737

You are hereby Required to warn the propriators freeholders and Inhabitans of this town to meet at their old meeting house on wensday the twenty first day of September next at nine of the Clock in the fore noon then and there

1st to Call the select men and Constables to an a Ccount what or how the Town's propriators money is desposed of these four years by past and if they will not give the town and propriators an account to their acceptance of all and Every pairt of their money then for the town and propriators to Chuse a Comtee to shew the money out of their hands and the Comtee that have been Chosen to sarch the town's accounts are desired to give in their accounts that they have to the said meeting on the afore said day

2 ly to see how much of the debts given in to the select men the town will alow to be apploted for this year & also what the propriators will alow to be apploted for the propriaty this year

3ly to see if the town will alow the select men to gett that money that was Lodged in John mtt murphy's hand for Reparing the meeting house and this shall be your waran and make due return of this warran to us before the time of meeting on said day given under our hands the day and year above written

Robert Boys
Robert Wear
Thomas Willson
Hugh Willson
Andrew Todd
Select men

To James Aiken Constable

I have posted the within warning three several publick meeting day's upon the house of publick worship
Attest P James Aiken Constable

[This warrant was given in duplicate to Matthew Taylor, Constable, and recorded on page 104 of Vol. 2. Early Records of Londonderry.—Ed.]

At a meeting of the propriators and freeholders of Londonderry at their old meeting House on wensday Sept^{br} the 21th 1737

voted for moderator Robart Wear

voted to adjourn said meeting to Oct^{br} the 18: 1737 and the Reason of said adjournment is that the Constabals and Com^{tee} of accounts did not meet according to warning to make up their accounts with the town accordingly the Moderator adjourned the said meeting to Oct^{br} the 18th 1737 at 9: of the Clock before noon

Londonderry Oct^{br} the 18th 1737

Meet according to adjournment

and voted James Moore shall have no pay for that part of his fence that takes off no part of his land nor no man Else for any such fence the money for said fence is £1=04=0

2:ly voted that the town will not pay that Charge Conserning prosicuting Robert Boyes to be Constable for the year 1736 the Charg is £14=13=09

3:ly voted that the town will not pay that Charge brought in by Samuell Barr for petitionning the Geannarall Court for apresept and makeing return of the same the said Charge is £6=06=08

4:ly voted that Robart Wear John Morison and Willm Humphry shall be a Com^{tee} to shew the Constabls at the law that have not pay'd up the sums of money that were Returned to them in their lists by the select men

5:ly voted that all the debts given in to the select men perticulerly that Conserning the march meeting is to be apploted on the town

6:ly voted that the town shall pay the twenty one yeards of Cloath given to afreind for the towns Benifite brought in, in the select mens list of Charge

7:ly voted that the select men shall Call for that money that the town lodged in Jo^{n} m^{tt} murphy's hand (viz) that money that Capt m^{tt} feturks gave to the bulding and repearing the meeting House and The select men shall take the said money and lay it out in reparing of the old meeting House and the select men shall discharge the said m^{tt}murphy in behalf of the town for said money

Province of Newhampshir

Londonderry Oct^{br} the 22th 1737

You are here by Required to warn the propriators of this town to meet at their old meeting House upon tuesday the Eight day of Nov^{br} at ten of the Clock before noon then and there

1stly to see if the propriators will sell a pis of land or lay down som other method to pay Mr John Goff Junr his money

2ly to see if the propriators will answer John Goff's Junr letter and this shall be your warrant given under our hands the day and year above mentioned

Robert Boyes
Robert Wear
Thomas Willson
Hugh Willson
Select men

to James Aiken town Constable

[A duplicate of this warrant was given to Matthew Taylor, Constable and so recorded on page 106, Vol. 2, Early Records of Londonderry.—Ed.]

By vertow of the fore going Warrant the propriators of

Londonderry meet at their old meeting House Nov^{br} the Eight day 1737 and voted for moderator William Humphry

1stly Voted that the propriators will sell a peace or peaceses of land to pay John Goff Junr his money the pro^{ters} ose him upon an Exicusion.

2ly voted that the Com^{tee} for laying out of mendements (viz) John Archibald James Rodgers and John Wallace shall go and vew som Common land for the pro^{ters} Bennifite and make a Return of the same to the propr^{tors} in order that it may be sold to pay the above said money to the above said Goff

3ly voted that Robert Wear John Archibald and moses Barnat shall be a Com^{tee} to sell the above said lands and give a deed or deeds of the same in behalf of the pro^{tors} as well as their own

voted that this meeting shall be adjorned to the 22 day of this Instant at ten of the Clock before noon

Londonderry Nov^{br} 22th 1737

meet according to adjornment Nov^{br} 22th, 1737, and voted that the giving an answer to John Goff Jun^{rs} letter is defer'd to the nixt propriators meeting

Province of Newhampshire

Londonderry Feb^{ry} the 9th 1737/8

You are hereby Required to warn the proprietors Inhabitans and freeholders duly Qualifi'd within your Respective Bounds to meet at the old meeting house upon the fifth day of March by the order of the Charter but it being the Sabbath or Lords day you are to Warn them to meet upon Munday the sixth of march at nine of the Clock before noon then & there

1st ly to Choose all their town officers for the Enshewing year

2:ly to see what meathod the town will take about schools for the Enshewing year

3:ly to see if the town will lay down any meathod to Rise some money to help to Deffray the Charges of the province line

4:ly to see if the town will Choose two men to take an

Invoice of the pols and Esteats of this town for this Enshewing year

5:ly Entered at the Requist of ten men to see if the town will aprove the old or New Record of that highway betwixt John Duncan's and the town that was presented to the Quarter sessions and they the s^{d} sessions ordered the select men to lay it out upon good Ground

6:ly to see if the town will alow Nathan m^{tt}farland his Reats the year past for the troble he heas had with his Brother, and this shall be your Warrant Given under our hands the day and year above mentioned

Robert Wear
Thomas Willson
Andrew Todd
Select men

To Mr. Matthew Taylor Constable for the Easterly Side of Beaver Brook

I have posted the within Warning as usewall at Londonderry March the 6th 1737/8

as wittness my hand

his
Matthew :m : Taylor
mark
Constable

[A duplicate of this warrant was given to James Aiken, constable, and recorded on pages 107-108, Vol. 2, Early Records of Londonderry.—Ed.]

By virtue of the for going Warrant the free holders and Inhabitans meet at their old Meeting House March the sixth 1737/8 and

voted for moderator Liv^{t} Andrew Todd

voted that their shall be five select men for this Ensuing year and they are Robert Wear Hugh Willson Liv^{t} Andrew Todd Thos Willson Moses Barnat Select men

voted for town Clerk John Wallace town Clerk

voted that their shall be two Constables for this Ensuing year and

voted for Constable on the Easterly side of Beaver Brook John Humphra—and

Where as John Humphra Being Chosen Constable for the Easterly side of Beaver Brook it is

voted that William Humphra by his own Consent shall serve as Constable in the Rume of the said John Humphra on the Easterly side of Beaver Brook

voted for Constable on the Westerly side of Beaver Brook James Tagart—and

voted that the said William Humphra and James Tagart shall have five pounds in money from this town for serveing as Constables this Ensuing year

voted for leather sealer Hugh Bolton

voted for sirvayers for high ways for this Ensuing year their Names on the Easterly side of Beaver Brook is

Hugh Montgomre
Ezek^{l} Morison
Hugh Rodgers
John Moore
James Thomson
Samuell Miller
Allex^{r} Kellsy
Willm Chambers

their Names on the Westerly side of Beaver Brook is

John Craig
Thos Willson
Willm Holms
John Barnat
John Bell
Robert Cark

voted for tithing men Willm Robertson Willm Humphra tithingmen

voted for Howards Allex^{r} m^{cc} Neall Willm Gamble Thos Hoaig Howards

voted for fence viewers and prizers Sam^{ll} Alleson Thos Cochran

voted for a Com^{tee} to serch the town's accounts Hugh Ramsey Robert Clark Jo^{n} Wallace Com^{tee}

voted that the Second artical in the Warrant is Deffear'd to the aDjornment of the afore s^{d} meeting

voted that the town will Raise some money to healp to Deffray the Charg of the Province line for the Benefite of this town and

voted that the said money is to be Raised by subscriptions off the proprietors of this town and an account kept of Each mans subscription that if the Publick shall hereafter pay the

Charges Each pson may and shall Recive his money again or some other ample sattisfaction

also voted that two men on Each side of Beaver Brook (viz) proprietors shall Recive the money at the hand of Each pson so subscribing, and that the said men shall be accountable for the money, and ye mens Names is James Bleair Willm Humphra Hugh Willson Thos Cochran

Also voted that Robert Cochran Thos Horner Robt Clark and Thos Willson, shall Recive the subscriptions at the hands of Each none Comoner in this town for the End afore s^d and shall be accountable for the s^d money that Each person shall subscribe

voted that Robert Cochran and Thos Campble shall take an Invoice of the pols and Estats of this town for this Ensuing year, and make return of the same to the select men of this town—and

also voted that the town will allow the said Robt Cochran and Thos Campble five pounds of money for taking the said Invoice

voted that the afore said meeting is adjorn'd to the first tusday in april nixt at ten o Clock before noon

Londonderry April the 4th 1738

Meet according to adjornment and......

voted that there shall be but one publick school master for this Ensuing year, and said master shall be ordered by a Com^tee to go from one Quarter of the town to another as said Com^tee shall order from time to time and......

voted that the schoolmaster shall be ordered by a Com^tee to Keep school at seven particular placeses or Houses in this town for this Ensuing year (viz) two mounths in the South Range, two monnths in the Doble Range, two mounths in the Backe Range or near James Gillmors in the paik, two mounths in the English Range, two mounths in the Aiken's Range, one mounth in the Most Conviniant place in the paik for them that has had but litle benefite of the schools hitherto, one mounth in Cannady in the most Conviniant place for them that has had but litle benefite hitherto, which is to be desided by lot where it shall begine by said Com^{tee}—and

voted for a Com^{tee} to order the schoolmaster to the particular Quarters or School Houses in this town for this Ensuing year, their Names is Hugh Willson Jo^{n} Moore plain Jo^{n} Wallace sen^{r} Jo^{n} Anderson Moses Barnat James Rodger Com^{tee}

voted that the town acquiesses with the Courts orders Conserning that High way that was presented at the Quarter Sessions (viz) that High way from John Bells to Cannady

voted that the select men is to alow Nathan m^{cc}farland his Reats for the year past for the trobl he has had with his Brother

Province of Newhampshire

Londonderry may ye 15th 1738

You are hereby Required to Warn the proprietors within your Respective bounds to meet at their old meeting House upon thursday the first of June nixt at ten of the Clock before noon then & there

1 ly to see if the proprietors will Chous a Com^{tee} to give Deeds of the lands that they Choos a Com^{tee} to sell to Defray the Charg of Jo^{n} Goffe' Jun$^{r's}$ action

2ly to hear transcripts of lands Red and to aprove or Disaprove them

3 ly to see if the proprietors will alow Matthew Reid a transcript of a second Devision that was laid out to that land that he purchased, that he Cannot find any Record of

4 ly to see whither the proprietors will treat with John Goffe Junr Conserning apeace of land that he is looking after from them

5 ly to see whither the town will lay down any method to the select men to lay out High ways to sundrey persons that are wanting them, and this shall be your warrant

Given under our hands the Day and year above mentioned

Robt Wear
Thos Willson
Hugh Willson
Moses Barnat
Andrew Todd
Select men

To Mr James Taggart Constable for the westerly side of Beaver Brook

Province of New hampshire

Londonderry June ye 1th 1738

In obediance to ye within presept I have posted it upon ye meeting House three Publick days

P James Taggart Constable

[A duplicate of this warrant was given to William Humphrey, constable for the easterly side of Beaver Brook.—Ed.]

By vertue of the fore Going Warrant the proprietors of Londonderry meet at their old meeting House June the 1th day 1738 and

voted for moderator Li^t^ Andrew Todd

voted that the former Com^tee^ (viz) Robt Wear John Archibald and Moses Barnat shall be Continnowed as a Com^tee^ to Give Deeds of these peaces of lands that they the Com^tee^ (viz) Robt Wear Jo^n^ Archibld and Moses Barnat hath sold to pay John Goffe Junr his money y^t^ the proprietors ow'd him upon an Exicusion

voted that the severall transcripts Read at said meeting is to be put on Record in the town Book and s^d^ transcripts is approv'd of by the proprietors of the aforesaid Londonderry to there perticuler owners Benefite (viz) one for Robert Armstrong one to Mark Hunkens one to James m^tt^ Neall two to Abraham Holms one to John Given one to Samuell Greves one to Joseph Simmonds one to Hendrey Green also eleven to the proprietors one to James Clark and the proprietors one to Hugh Mountgomrey one to Andrew Spalding,

Londonderry June 1th 1738

We do protest against the vot past y^t^ I William Humphra shall not have the priviledge of our towns vots nor in Entering his Claim Conserning to his land that he wants or in selling of any Comon lands against the law of Justis for one proprietor to sell an others lands

voted that Willm Humphra's transcript of part of his second Division is not to be put on Record unless he will alow land in s^d^ Return for a high way through that land he bought from Allex^r^ Neckell's voted that Andrew Spaldings transcript is to be put on Record

voted y^t the third Article is Deferd to ye nixt proprietors meeting

voted that Robt Wear James Nesmith & Samuel Barr shall be a Com^{tee} to agree with Jo^n Goffe Junr a bout a peace of land he is a luking after from them, and s^d Com^{tee} is to order s^d Goffe to have it laid out according as s^d Com^{tee} and Goffe may agree about s^d land

the fift article is Deferd

Province of $Newham^{sr}$

Londonderry August the 1th 1738

You are hereby Required to warn y^e proprietors within your Respective Bounds to meet at the old meeting House upon thursday the seventeen of this Instant August at ten o' the Clock before noon then and there

1st ly to see what the proprietors will do with Jo^n Goffe Junr about a pice of land that he is a looking after from them that Com^{tee} was Chosen to treat with him about it are Desired to Bring a Report to the proprietors meeting what they have Don with him about it

2 ly to see whither the proprietors has ordered the Com^{tee} of meadow's to take away any of Jo^n Creaigs and $Will^m$ Nutts or not

3 ly to see whither the proprietors will sell apice of land to $Will^m$ Nickels that he has Improven it being Comon and he did not know of it

4 ly to see if the proprietors will sell apice of land to Mr Thos Bacon

5 ly to hear transcripts Read and approv'd of or not, and this shall be your Warrant Given under our hands the Day and year above mentioned

Robert Wear
Thos Willson
Hugh Willson
Andrew Todd
Moses Barnet
Selectmen of Londonderry

To Mr James Tagart Constable for the Westerly side of Beaver Brook

[A duplicate of this warrant was given "to William Humphra constable for the easterly side of Beaver Brook" and is recorded on page 115, Vol. 2, Early Records of Londonderry. —ED.]

By vertue of the fore going Warrants the proprietors of Lo: Derry meet at their old meeting House August the 17th 1738, and voted for moderator...............Robert Wear

1st ly voted that the first article shall be Defeard to the 15th of Sep^{br} nixt Ensuing

2: ly voted that the proprietors did not order the Com^{tee} of meadows to take a way any of Jo^{n} Creaigs and Willm Nutts meadows from them that they the s^{d} Creaig or Nutt Can produce any Records or transcripts from under the s^{d} Com$^{tee's}$ hands

3:ly the third articl is Defear'd at this time

4:ly voted that the proprietors will not sell any land at this time

5ly voted that Willm Humphra's transcript of part of his second Division is aprov'd off by the proprietors for s^{d} Humphra's Benefit and his asigns for Ever

voted that this afore s^{d} meeting shall be adjorn'd to Sep^{br} next the 15th day at Eight o' the Clock before noon

the proprietors of Londonderry meet according to adjornment the 15th of Sep^{br} 1738

and voted by the proprietors afore said to adjorn the said meeting to the second wensday of oct^{br} nixt at ten o' the Clock before noon

the proprietors of Londonderry meet according to adjornment the second wensday of oct^{br} the 11th day 1738

it is voted and agreed upon by the proprietors of Londonderry that they agree and Confirm this agreement as followeth made with Jo^{n} Goffe Junr and the proprietors Com^{tee} of Londonderry Chosen for that End at ameeting of the proprietors held at the old meeting House June the 1th day 1738 (viz) Robert Wear James Nesmith and Sam^{ll} Barr about a full shear or propriety in s^d^ Londonderry and said agreement is as followeth (viz) that Jo^n^ Goffe Junr shall have sixty acres of land for a hom lot made Good as other hom lots are in said Londonderry Quantity and Quallity Considered with two acres of meadow laid out in the first Comon meadow that can be found in s^d^ Comons or land Equivelant to two acres of meadow as also twenty six pounds and Eight shillings in bills of Cridit pay'd to him the s^d^ Jo^n^ Goffe Junr by the proprietors of s^d^ Londonderry in full setisfaction for all the s^d^ Jo^n^ Goffe Junr'^s^ Right and title for lands and meadows that the s^d^ Jo^n^ Goffe Junr Can Claim Challainge or Demand from the proprietors of s^d^ Londonderry for Ever: by Reson of his Name being Entered in the schedule of Londonderry's Charter. and it is further to be known and understod that the s^d^ Jo^n^ Goffe Junr doth Confirm s^d^ agreement by his signing sealing and Delivering a Quitt Claim deed of all his Right and title in s^d^ Londonderry to s^d^ proprietors s^d^ Deed bearing date sep^tr^ the 15th 1738

the Returns of Jo^n^ Goffe Junr's^ land being Read to the proprietors of Londonderry is approven of by s^d^ proprietors for the Benefit of s^d^ Goffe and his assigns for Ever

two Returns being Read to the proprietors (viz) one to his Excellencey Sam^ll^ shute and one to Thos Westbrook was approven of by s^d^ proprietors for the Benefite of said shute and Westbrook and their assigns for Ever

P Jo^n^ Wallace town Clerk

Province of Newhamp^r^

Londonderry August 31th 1738

You are here by Required to warn the proprietors within your Respective bounds to meet at the old meeting House upon friday the fifteen day of sep^tr^ nixt at ten o' the Clock before noon then and there

1: ly to see what methoud the proprietors will take to Regulat some mistakes that are Entered in the town book Conserning the proprietory

2: ly to see if the proprietors will alow Jo^n^ and Thos m^t^ Cleary other land in the Comon for that land that was laid out to them. and Chouse a Com^{tee} to Give them Deeds of it

3:ly to see what answer the proprietors will Give to Jo^{n} Roby's pitition: and this shall be your warrant given under our hand the day and year above mentioned

Robert Wear
Thos Willson
Hugh Willson
Moses Barnet
Select men

to Mr James Taggart Constable for the westerly side of Beaver Brook

I have posted this warrant as usel two sabath days

P me James Taggart Constable

[A duplicate of this warrant was issued "to Willm Humphra, Constable for the Easterly side of Beaver Brook," and recorded on page 117, Vol. 2, Early Records of Londonderry. —Ed.]

By vertue of the foregoing Warrants the proprietors of Londonderry meet at their old meeting House afriday the 15th of sept^{r} 1738

and voted for Moderator............Robert Wear

voted that the third article in the warrant is deffer^{d} to the second wensday of oct^{br} nixt. after being Read

the second article being Read is voted to be Deffer'd

voted that the aforesaid meeting shall be adjorned to the second wensday of oct^{br} nixt Ensuing the Dat hereof: at ten o' the Clock before noon

the proprietors of Londonderry meet at their old meeting House oct^{r} the second wensday the 11th of s^{d} Instant at ten o' the Clock before noon according to adjornment

the third article in the warrant being Read and Considered it is voted that said article anent Giveing Sam^{ll} Roby an answer to his pitition is Deffer'd

the first article in the warrant being Read it is voted and agreed upon by the proprietors of Londonderry that there shall be a Com^{tee} of five men Chosen and appoynted by said proprietors to serch the town Books and feind out what fals

Records they Can in s^d Books and it is also agreed upon by said proprietors that the said Com^{tee} shall present a pitition to the first Gennerall Court that shall site at portsmouth to see of his Excellency and their Honnours will Grant us some order or power to Regulat all the fals Records that Can be found in s^d Books. and it is to be understood by s^d vote that the afore said proprietors is to bear all the Expance or Charges that shall arise Either in serching the Books or in the s^d $Com^{tee's}$ applying to the Gennerall Court upon the afore said account. and the Com^{tee} Chosen for the afore said End is Robert Wear Saml Greaves Jo^n Bleair sin^r James Clark and Jo^n Wallace sin^r.

Jo^n Wallace town Clerk

Province of Newhampshire

Londonderry $Nove^{br}$ the 6th 1738

by vertue of an Express in his $Maj.^{ts}$ Name from Mr Eleazer Russal head sherreff of this province to us

You are hereby Required fourthwith to warn the proprietors freeholders and Inhabitants of s^d Londonderry Duely Qualified by the law to Convine at the old meeting House upon tusday the seventh of this Instant at nine o' the Clock before noon then and there

1: ly to Chous one fit person Duely Qualified in law to Represent them in Jennarel Assembly now sitting in portsmouth in s^d province and this shall be your Warrant Given under our hands the Day and year above mentioned

Robert Wear
Thomas Willson
Hugh Willson
Moses Barnet
Andrew Todd
Select men of L: Derry

To James Taggart Constable for the Westerly side of Beaver Brook

Province of Newhampshire

Londonderry November the 7th 1738

By Viertue of this precept I have Warned the people to this town meeting as far as time would alow

P me James Taggart Constable

[A duplicate of this warrant was given to "Willm Humphra constable for the Easterly side of Beaver Brook" and recorded on page 119, Vol. 2, of Early Records of Londonderry. —ED.]

Province of Newhampshire

Londonderry November the 7th 1738

by Viertue of the aforesaid Warrant the propre^trs and other Inhabitants Duely Qualifed by law meete at the old meeting House upon tusday ye 7th of Nov^br 1738 and did then & there vote for moderator—Robert Wear

also voted for Representive—Hugh Willson

P Jo^n Wallace town Clerk

Province of Newhamp^r

Londonderry November ye 9th 1738

You are hereby Requiered to Warn the proprietors Inhabitants and freeholders of said Londonderry to Convine at the old meeting House in said town upon mounday the 27th day of this Instant november at ten o' the Clock before noon then & there

1: ly: to see if ye town will Receive ye seats in the old meeting House from those men y^t Joyns with ye other side of the town they Giveing them up under their hands

2: ly: to see if the town will vote y^t the ministers sallary be Raised this present year as these leat years past

3: ly to see if the town will vote that ye select men shall asses so much money as shall pay all the publick Debts that are Due upon the town

4: ly: to see how much money ye proprietors will Raise for to Defray the Charges of the propriety for this present year

5: ly: to see if the town will oblidge the Constables that was Chosen to serve for ye year 1737 to Reaise the money that was assed upon the Scoolers or their parrents for that present year or lay down some other Method how it shall be Reaised

6: ly: to see if the town will Give y^{t} Com^{tee} that was Chosen to sue the Delinkquant Constables of ^{sd} Londonderry full power to sue all the Delinkquant Constables of ^{sd} Londonderry

7: ly to see if the town will alow the m^{t} Clentos any thing for ye the Bridges that they have made betwixt and amasceage and this shall be your Warrant Given under our hands the day and year above mentioned

Thomas Willson
Moses Barnet
Andrew Todd
Select men

To Mr James Taggart Constable for the westerly side of Beaver Brook

Province of Newhampshire
Londonderry Nove^{br} ye 27th 1738

I Received this paper Derícted to me in form of atown Warrant but not signed by the select men I therefore supose it hath no authority, notewithstanding I have posted it according to former Custom

P me James Tagger Constable

[A duplicate of this warrant was given to "Mr Willm Humphra Constable of the Easterly side of Beaver Brook" signed by "Robert Wear Thos Willson Moses Barnet Andrew Todd select men," and recorded on page 121, Vol. 2, Early Records of Londonderry.—Ed.]

Province of New ^{sr}

By Veirtue of the fore Going Warrant being leaugally Call'd the proprietors freeholders and Inhabitants of Londonderry meet at their old meeting House November ye 27th 1738 and voted for moderator—Jo^{n} Morison

1: ly the first article in the fore going Warrant being Read and Considered by the freeholders & Inhabitants of Londonderry afore s^{d} it is voted and agreed upon that the select men of s^{d} Londonderry shall be a Com^{tee} to treat or agree with the people of M^{r} m^{t}Gregore's sosiety about their seats in the old Meeting House the pleace appoynted for said

Com^{tee} to meet is at the old meeting House December next Ensueing the 14th day: 1738

2: ly: the second article in the foregoing Warrant being Read & Considrd by the freeholders and Inhabitants of ^{sd} Londonderry it is voted and agreed upon by ^{sd} freeholders & Inhabitants of ^{sd} Londonderry that the ministers sallary of the old meeting House shall be Raised and assesed for this Runing Year as it has been these years by past (viz) assest upon the seats of the old meeting House of ^{sd} Londonderry according to their former agreement which may more fully appear in this book of Records for ^{sd} Londonderry

3: ly: the third article in the fore Going Warrant being Read & Considrd by ye freeholders & Inhabitants of ^{sd} Londonderry it is voted and agreed upon by ^{sd} freeholders & Inhabitants that the select men of ^{sd} Londonderry shall asses so much money upon ^{sd} Inhabitants as shall pay all the publick Debts Due upon the aforesaid Inhabit^{ts} which are given in into the ^{sd} select mens list of publick Debts for this present year 1738. abstract from the proprietors

4: ly: the forth article in the fore going Warrant being Read and Considered by ye proprietors of ^{sd} Londonderry, it is voted and agreed upon by ^{sd} proprietors that the select men of ^{sd} Londonderry shall asses ten shillings of publick bills of Creidet upon Each proprietor of ^{sd} Londonderry for this present year 1738 to Defray lawsuts and other Charges that may arise upon ye propriety

5: ly: the fift article in the fore Going Warrant being Read and Considered by ye freeholders & Inhabitants of ^{sd} Londonderry it is voted and agreed upon by ^{sd} freeholders and Inhabitants that they will oblidge the Constables of ^{sd} Londonderry (viz) James Aiken & Matthew Tailor that was Chosen to serve as Constables for the year 1737 to Colect the scoolmasters money as it is alridy assesed upon the parrants of the scoolers which may more fully appear by lists given to ^{sd} Constables for that End

6: ly: the six article in the fore Going Warrant being Read and Considered by the freeholders & Inhabitants of Lo^{n} Derry it is voted & agreed upon by said freeholders &

Inhabit^{ts} that the former Com^{tee} that was Chosen to sue Delinkquant Constables at the law (viz) Robert Wear Jo^{n} Morison & Willm Humphra is Rechosen with full Power & authorety from us the proprietors freeholders and Inhabitants of ^{sd} Londonderry to sue and to prossecute all and Every one of the Delinkquant Constables of ^{sd} Londonderry at the law with full power to substytute one or more aturnnys as ^{sd} Com^{tee} shall think fite. and it is further to be known by ^{sd} vote that the aforesaid proprietors and freeholders Doth promise and Ingage to bear and pay all Cost and Charges that shall or may arise in sueing or in prossecuting the afore ^{sd} Constables at any Court or Courts within this His Maj^{tes} province of newhampshire afore ^{sd}

7: ly the seventh article in the fore Going Warrant being Read & Considered by the freeholders and Inhabitants of ^{sd} Londonderry it is voted and agreed upon that Michall m^{t} Clinto & Willm m^{t} Clinto shall have twenty shillings P year pay'd to them by the Inhabitants of ^{sd} Londonderry for the space of ten years providing that they the ^{sd} m^{t} Clintos do keep up two Good sofisiant Bridges over Great Cohassat upon the high way or Road to amascage for the speace of ten years Commenceing the time from this present year 1738 &

Province of newhampshire.

Londonderry Jan^{ry} ye 19th 1738-9

You are hereby Required to warn the proprietors and Inhabitants of Londonderry afore said upon whom the Ministers sallary is assesed upon to meet at ye old meeting House upon tusday ye sixt Day of feb^{ry} next Ensuing at ten o' the Clock before noon then & there

1st ly to see how they will Dispose of ye Remaining part of ye sallary that is assesed upon them after they have paid ye surviving Widow of ye Revr^{d} Mr Thos Thomson our leat Deces^{d} minister What was Due to him. and this shall be your Warrant Geven under our hands ye Day & year above

Robt Wear
Thos Willson
Moses Barnet
Andrew Todd
Select men

To Willm Humphry Constable in ye Easterly side of Beaver Brook

I have posted this Warrant as useuall P me Willm Humphry Constable

[A duplicate of this warrant was given to "James Taggart Constable in ye Westerly side of Beaver Brook," and is recorded on page 124, Vol. 2, of Early Records of Londonderry. —ED.]

Province of Newhampshire.

By veirtue of ye fore Going Warrant being leaglly Call'd the proprietors & freeholders of Londonderry met at the old meeting House of ^{sd} Londonderry on tusday the sixth of feb^{ry} 1738-9 and

voted for moderator—Robert Boyes Esqr

the first article in ye fore Going Warrant being Read and Considered by ye proprietors & freeholders of ^{sd} Londonderry it is voted & agreed upon by ^{sd} proprietors & freeholders that the select men of ^{sd} Londonderry shall pay & Clear off what was Due of ye sallary of one hundred & forty pounds for the year 1738 to ye Revr^{d} Mr Thos Tomson leat Decesed minister of ^{sd} Londonderry and that y^{e} ^{sd} select men shall Give the Remaining part of y^{e} ^{sd} years sallary to Mrs Fra^{s} Thomson Widow to y^{e} ^{sd} Mr Thomson to ye support of mantaining her Child Allex^{r} Thomson

We the under subscribers protest against ye paying of any Ministers Rates assesed by ye select men of Londonderry for ye year 1738 as also ye actings of this present meeting feb^{ry} ye 6th 1738

1st Because a Great Number who are assesed in this Rate are paying yearly sallary to another setled minister

2^{ly} because ye meeting at which this Rate was voted was warrned by a paper signed only by mens Names in a private Capacity & not as select men. James Clark Jo^{n} Blair James Blair

Province of Newhampshire

Londonderry feb^{ry} ye 15th 1738-9

You are hereby Required to Warn ye proprietors freeholders & Inhabitants of this town Duly Quallifyd By law to meet at ye old meeting House upon monday ye fifth of march at nine o' the Clock before noon then and there

1st ly Chouse all their town officers for ye Ensuing year

2. ly to see what method they will take about school or schools for the Ensuing Year

3. ly to see if ye town will Chouse two men to take an Invoice of ye pols and Estats of this town for the Ensuing Year

4: ly to see what method ye town will take about Daniel mt Aferson Considering his scircomstance laying at Charges

5. ly to see if ye town will Chouse one two or three fitt men for to Record high ways and fences that ye town has paid for

and this shall be your Warrant Given under our hands the day and year above mentioned

Robt Wear
Thos Willson
Hugh Willson
Andrew Todd
Mos Barnat
Select men

to James Taggart Constable for ye westerly side of Beaver Brook

Province of Newhampshire

Londonderry march ye 5th 1738-9

I have posted this prescept according to former Custom

P me James Taggart Constable

[A duplicate of this warrant was given "to Willm Humphra Constable for ye Easterly side of Beaver Brook," and recorded on page 125, Vol. 2, Early Records of Londonderry.—Ed.]

By virtue of the fore Going Warrant being leagaly Call'd the proprietors freeholders & Inhabitant of Londonderry met at their old Meeting House on Monday ye fifth Day of March 1738-9. and.

Voted for moderator—Robt Boyes Esqr

the first article in the fore Going Warrant being Read and Consider'd by sd freeholders & Inhabitants and it is voted for select men for the Ensuing Year Liv^{t} Andrew Todd Thos Willson Hugh Willson Mo^{s} Barnat Allan Anderson Select men

voted for town Clerk Jo^{n} Wallace sin^{r} for ye year Ensuing

voted for a Constable on ye Easterly side of Beaver Brook for ye Ensuing Year Sam^{ll} Alleson

voted for a Constable on ye Westerly side of Beaver Brook for ye Ensuing Year Willm Adams.

Whereas Willm Adams being Chosen Constable for ye Westerly side of Beaver Brook for ye Ensuing Year it is voted and agreed upon by ^{sd} freeholders & Inhabitants that James Taggart (viz) by his own Consent shall serve as Constable in ye Rum of ^{sd} Willm Adams for ye Ensuing Year. and it's further to be Known that y^{e} ^{sd} Taggart serves as Constable at y^{e} ^{sd} Adams Charge

voted that y^{e} ^{sd} Constables shall have five pounds for Colecting all ye Rats that shall be assesed or apploted by ye select men of ^{sd} Londonderry for ye Ensuing Year

and it is also agreed upon by sd vote that Each Constable shall have his Equall share of ye afore ^{sd} five pounds according to ye Rats that they shall Colect on Each side of Beaver Brook for ye Ensuing Year

voted for lather sealer for ye Ensuing Year Hugh Bolton Sealer

voted for tithing men for ye Ensuing Year Willm Humphra Thos Cochran tithing men

voted for surviers for ye Easterly side of Beaver Brook for the Ensuing Year Jo^{n} Richey Jo^{n} Morison Daniel Anderson Thos Willson. Benj^{m} Thomson. James Willson Allex^{r} Kelsey David Hunter Thos Morison surviers

voted for surviers for ye Westerly side of Beaver Brook for ye Ensuing Year James Doak Jo^{n} Cromey Sam^{ll} Dickey Jo^{n} Barnat Wm Aiken Jo^{n} Hunter surviers

voted for Howards for ye Ensuing Year Sam^{ll} Boyd Jo^{n} Bleair Junr Allex^{r} Walker Willm Hogg Howards

voted for fence vewers & prizers for the Ensuing Year Archilbald Clendinin Robt Clark fence vewers voted for a Com^{tee} to serch the towns accounts for the Ensuing Year Hugh Ramsey Robt Clark Jo^{n} Wallace siner Com^{tee}

voted that Robt Cochran & Thos Campbel shall tak an Invoice of ye pols and Estats of ^{sd} Londonderry for this Ensuing year, and make areturn of ye same as soon as possable to the select men of ^{sd} Londonderry

voted that ye publick school shall Go from Each Quarter of ^{sd} L: Derry to ye other as it did in the year 1738 &

the forth article of ye fore Going Warrant Being Read and Considered by ye freeholders & Inhabitants of ^{sd} Londonderry it is voted and agreed by ^{sd} freeholders & Inhabitants that ye select men of ^{sd} L: Derry shall provide Irons at ye towns Coast to secure Daniel m^{t} Afarson from hurting or Desturbing any of ye Inhabitants of ^{sd} Lo: Derry. and it is further agreed upon by ^{sd} Inhabitants that ye select men of ^{sd} L: Derry shall not bear any more truble or Expences with the sd m^{t} Afarson then any other person or persons in ^{sd} town and it is hereby to be Known by ^{sd} vote that Each Inhabi^{nt} of ^{sd} town shall lodge and take Care of ^{sd} m^{t} Afarson for ye space of 24.hours and so to take him to his next Neighbour untill he shall Go through ye whole Inhabitants of ^{sd} town if need so Require. and if it shall so happen that any person shall Refuse and neglact and not lodge nor take Care of sd m^{t} Afarson as other persons in ^{sd} town Dos, that then By virtue of ^{sd} vote the select men are to asses ten shillings as they do other Rats and add ^{sd} ten shillings to Each mans Rats that so Refuses or neglact to take Care or lodge y^{e} ^{sd} m^{t} Afarson as other Inhabitants in ^{sd} town Dos

the fifth article in ye fore Going Warrant being Read and Considered by the free holders of ^{sd} town it is voted and agreed upon by said free holders that the select men of ^{sd} town shall agree With ye town Clerk to put all the Disburssments of the town Rats Espashally fences and high ways paid for by ^{sd} Inhabitants in abook provided by ye town for that End the fore Going Warrants and ye tranceations of ye aforesaid meeting

Recorded this 10th Day of march 1738-9

P. Jo^{n} Wallace town Clerk

Province of Newhampshire

Londonderry March ye 19th 1738-9

You are hereby Required to warn the proprietors of ^{sd} town Within your Respective Bounds to meet at ye old meeting House upon Wensday the fourth Day of aprile at nine o' the Clok Before noon then and there.

1st ly to see if ye proprietors will Chouse a Com^{tee} to search the town's accounts to see if ye town be Indebted to ye proprietors or ye proprietors to ye town

2. ly to see what Meathod ye proprietors will tak to pay their Debt

3. ly to see if ye proprietors will Chouse a new Com^{tee} to Commence or Defend Law suts against Incrochers on the bounds of the town or Continen ye old Com^{tee}

and this shall be your Warrant Given under our hands the Day and year above mentioned

Allan Anderson
Hugh Willson
Andrew Todd
Moses Barnet
Thos Willson
Select men

to Constable Jam^{s} Taggart in ye Westerly side of Beaver Brook

Province of New: sh^{r}

Londonderry aprile ye 4th 1739

I have Posted this precept according to former Custom

P. me Jam^{s} Taggart
Constable

[A duplicate of this warrant "to Sam^{ll} Alleson Constable for the Easterly side of Beaver Brook" and recorded on page 129 of Vol. 2, Early Records Londonderry.—Ed.]

Province of New. sh^{r}

By Virtue of the fore Going Warrant being legaly Cal'^{d} the proprietors of Londonderry met at ye old Meeting House april ye 4th 1739 and.

Voted for moderator.................. Jo^{n} Morison sin^{r}

the first article in ye fore Going Warrant being Read and Consider'd by ^{sd} proprietors it is voted not to Choose a Com^{tee} for the End mentioned in ye fore Going Warrant

the second article in ye fore Going Warrant being Read & Consider'd by sd proprietors it is voted and a Greed upon by ^{sd} proprietors that ye select men are hereby Impowered by ^{sd} vote to pay all the ^{sd} proprietors publick Debt so fare as they find money in any of ye Constables hand Either of town or proprietors money, and What Debt Remains, the ^{sd} Select men are to Make a Return to ^{sd} proprietors of ^{sd} Debts against ye next proprietors meeting in order to make a new assesment.

the third article in ye fore Going Warrant being Read and Consider'd by ^{sd} proprietors it is voted & agreed upon by ^{sd} proprietors that the former Com^{tee} (viz) Robert Wear James Rodgers & Sam^{ll} Barr is to Continow with all ye power that Ever they had as a Com^{tee} to Defend ye town S^{d} Londonderry from Incrochers from any town or towns Whatsoever Recorded P

Jo^{n} Wallace
town Clerk

Province of New-sh^{r}

Londonderry march ye 19th 1738-9

You are hereby Required to Warran the proprietors freeholders & Inhabitants of ^{sd} town Within your Respective bounds to meet at the old meeting House upon wensday the fourth Day of april at Eleven o' the Clok before noon then & there

1-ly to see if the town will Discharge all the Constables of the Desperat Debt that is in their lists that they may pay the Rest of the money

2. ly to see if ye town will Chouse a Com^{ttee} to Judge What are or how much Desperat money is in the Constables lists and make Return of ye same

3. ly to see if ye town will Chouse a Com^tee^ in the Diferant parts of the town to lay out ye high ways in ye town

4. ly to see if ye town Will Chouse and Impower a Com^tee^ to lift the money that was lodged in Jo^n^ m^t^ murphys hand to Repar the old meeting House & What Repairation they will make upon it.

5. ly to see if the town will Repair ye pond Bridge or alow the surviers that belongs to that presenct to Repair it.

and this shall be your Warrant Given under our hands ye Day and Year above Written

Hugh Willson
Thos Willson
Allan Anderson
Moses Barnet
Andrew Todd
Select men

To Constable James Taggart in the Westerly side of Beaver Brook

Province of New. sh^r^

Londonderry april ye 4th 1739

I have posted this precept according to former Custom P me James Taggart Constable

[A duplicate of this warrant was given "to Sam^ll^ Alleson Constable in the Easterly side of Beaver Brook," and Recorded on page 131, Vol. 2, Early Records of Londonderry.—Ed.]

Province of New. sh^r^

By virtue of the fore Going Warrants being legally Called ye proprietors freeholders & Inhabitants of Londonderry met at the old meeting House of ^sd^ Londonderry april ye 4th 1739. and.

voted for moderator.................... Jo^n^ Bleair sin^r^

the first article in ye fore Going Warrants being Read and Consider'd by ^sd^ freeholders & Inhabitants. it is voted and a Greed upon to Discharge all ye Constables of ^sd^ Londonderry of all the Desperat Debt that may be found in their lists, which lists is to be Judged by a Com^tee^ Choosen & appoynted for that End (viz) to Judge What is Desperat Debt or What is not. or what ^{sd} Constables May be Justly Charged with, or Discharged from and it is also to be Known by ^{sd} vote that if it shall so hapen at any time that any of ^{sd} Constables shall Receive any of the ^{sd} Debts that they shall make areturn of the same to the select men for ye time being for the use of s^{d} proprietors or Inhabitants of Londonderry

the second article in ye fore Going Warrants being Read and Consider'd by ^{sd} free holders & Inhabitants it is voted and A Greed upon by sd freeholders & Inhabitants that Liu^{t} Todd James Reid and Robert Clark shall be a Com^{tee} authrized and appoynted to Judge What is Despreat Debt in all the Constables lists of ^{sd} Londonderry, from the first Constable of ^{sd} town to this present Instant april ye 4th 1739 and it is to be further to be Known by ^{sd} vote. that ^{sd} Com^{tee} is to Discharge all y^{e} ^{sd} Constables of What they think is Desperat Debt in their lists

Liu^{t} Todd
James Reid
Robt Clark
Com^{tee}

the third article in the fore Going Warrants being Read & Consider'd it is voted and a Greed upon that ye select men is to lay out all the publick & privat High ways in ^{sd} town

the fourth article in the fore Going Warrants being Read & Consider'd by ^{sd} freeholders & Inhabitants it is voted and a Greed upon that Patrick Douglas and Allan Anderson & Liu^{t} Todd shall be a Com^{tee} authrized and appoynted by ^{sd} proprietors freeholders and Inhabitants to Receive that money that the town lodged in Jo^{n} Mt Murphy's hand by a vote at a town Meeting held at ye old meeting house of ^{sd} Londonderry Jan^{ry} ye 24th 1734-5 (viz)

that money that Capt m^{tt} Fetrick's Deceas'^{d} Gave as a Gift to the building of ye old meeting House of ^{sd} Londonderry, and ^{sd} Com^{tee} is hereby Impowr'd to Discharge the ye afore ^{sd} Jo^{n} m^{tt} Murphy for ^{sd} money. and it is further to be Known by ^{sd} vote. that if it shall so hapen that the said Jo^{n} m^{tt} Murphy shall Refuse to Deliver up ^{sd} money for the use afore sd. that y^e^ ^sd^ Com^tee^ (viz) Patrick Douglas Allan Anderson and Liu^t^ Todd is hereby Impowered to sue or prossecut for ye same at any of His Maj'^tes^ Courts of Judicattuer in ^sd^ province. and it is further to be Known by ^sd^ vote that ye proprietors of ye old meeting House of ^sd^ Londonderry is to bear all ye Coast and Charges that shall or may arise upon ye same (viz) those that are proprietors or adhears to the old meeting House afore ^sd^

Patrick Douglas
Allan Anderson
Liu^t^ And^w^ Todd
Com^tee^

the fifth article being Read and Consider'd it is Defear'^d^ Recorded

P. Jo^n^ Wallace
town Clerk

Province of New.shire

Londonderry June the 27th 1739

You are hearby Required to Warn the proprietor's freeholders and Inhabitants of ^sd^ Londonderry Within Your Respective bounds, to meet at the old meeting House upon thursday the twelth Day of July next Ensuing the Date hereof at ten o' the Clock before noon then & there

1st ly to see What method the town will take about those seats in ^sd^ old meeting House that is Returned to the select men to be sold

2: ly to see what meathod the town will take to pay their supliers

3: ly to see if the town will alow Rhods or High ways to Hugh Bolton Jo^n^ Durham and the Cokses, and Charls Stuart and Robert Gilmore that they may have some Corespondance with their neighbours as others in s^d^ town

4: ly to see what the town will Do With Patrick Douglas and James Callwell about a high way that the select men has laid out betwen them leading to Chaster, and has offered them the towns price for it and they will not take it but has stoped said high way till they be paid for it

5: ly to see what the town will Do with Hugh Willson that is trublsom to ^{sd} town and this shall be your Warrant Given under our hands ye Day and Year above mentioned

Thos Willson
Allan Anderson
Hugh Willson
Andrew Todd
Moses Barnet
Select men

To Mr James Taggart Constable in the Westerly side of Beaver Brook

Province of N. shire
Londonderry July ye 12 1739 I have posted precept according to former Custom

P James Taggart Constable

[A duplicate of this warrant addressed to "Mr Sam^{ll} Alleson Constable for ye Easterly side of beaver Brook" is recorded on pages 133-4, Vol. 2, Early Records Londonderry. —Ed.]

Province of Newhampshire
By virtue of the fore Going Warrants being leagally Called and Warned the proprietors freeholders and Inhabitants of Londonderry met at the old meeting House, July the 12th 1739, and voted for moderator

Jo^{n} Morison se^{r} mod^{tr}

1stly The first article in the fore Going Warrant being Read and Consider'^{d} by s^{d} proprietors freeholders & Inhabitants it is voted and agreed upon by s^{d} Inhabitants that there shall be a Com^{tee} Chosen Consisting of five men. to treat & agree with those men (viz) James Aiken and Matthew Taylor that is to make a Return of their seats or pews in ye old meeting House of s^{d} Londonderry to the select men of Londonderry afore^{sd} to be sold according to their Convenant or agreement With s^{d} sealect men......and it is further to be known by s^{d} vote that y^{e} ^{sd} Com^{tee} is to agree and buy s^{d} seats or pews at a Reasonable price. for the use and Benefit of ^{sd} Inhabitants the s[d] Com[tee's] Names are. Liut Andrew Todd Robert Boyes Esq[r] Will[m] Humphra Hugh Willson Jo[n] Wallace se[r] Com[tee]

2: ly The second article in the fore Going Warrant being Read and Consider'd by s[d] proprietors freeholders & Inhabitants, it is voted & agreed upon by s[d] Inhabitants that they will Raise and asses money upon s[d] Inhabitants according to law and Custom of s[d] province to pay their suppliers or preachers of the Gospel in the old meeting House of s[d] Londonderry

3: ly the third article in the fore Going Warrant being Read and Consider'd it is voted and agreed upon that the select men of s[d] town shall Regolat and lay out What high ways is needfull for s[d] Inhabitants

the forth and fift article being Read it was voted to Defare s[d] articles (viz) the 4: and 5 &

Province of New. shire

Londonderry Sept[br] y[e] 18th 1739

You are hereby Required to Warn the proprietors freeholders & Inhabitants Within your Respective Bounds to Meet at the old Meeting House upon saturday the sixth Day of oct[br] next at nine o' the Clock before noon then & there

1st ly to see what meathod the town will take to Call a Minister ofthe Gospel to Labour a mongst them & Chouse Commissioners to Prossecut the same

2: ly to see what presbyterien Minister preacher or probationer they will Call to Labour a mongst them

3: ly to see what Incuragment they will Give for the settelment of [sd] minister preacher or probationer when Call'd

4: ly to see how much yearly sallary they will propose to Give to such Minister preacher or probationer as they will Call

5: ly to see if the proprietors freeholdher & Inhabitants of L: Derry will vot that the money to be Raised for paying suppliers shall be Raised from the Inhabitants that attend the ordinances at the old meeting House only, or whether they will vot that the people that adhears to M[r] m[tt] Gregore shall pay or be Exempted Considering their Erregullar Building a Meeting House at James Aikens to the Great Disturbance of the peace of ^{sd} town

6: ly to see if the town will vot that the town Clerk shall Record a protest Given in at a town Meeting held ye 12th of July last past, by Mr Jo^{n} Bleair & others Considering the form that ^{sd} protest is Drod in

7: ly to see if the town will vot that the most Westerly Meeting House in the Westerly side of ^{sd} town shall be the place of publick Worship when set off by authority

8: ly to see how much money they will vot to be Raised to Defray The Charges of the town for this year

9: ly to see how much money the proprietors will vot to be Raised of the proprietors for to pay their Debts & Defray the Charges of s^{d} proprietors for this year

10: ly to see if the Inhabitants will vot that their be an Equall Division of high ways according to the Number of men in the town and that their be a Com^{tee} Chosen to Divied s^{d} highways in Equall shars to Each Quarter in s^{d} town

11: ly to hear our towns accounts Read that we may know how the towns money has been Disposed that has been Colected in the years 1738 & 1739.

and this shall be your warrant Given under our hands the Day & Year a bove mentioned

Allan Anderson
Hugh Willson
Thos Willson
Moses Barnet
Andrew Todd
Select men

To Mr Sam^{ll} Alleson Constable for the Easterly side of Beaver Brook

Province of New: shire

Londonderry oct^{br} ye 6th 1739

I have posted the within precept according to former Custom

P me

Sam^{ll} Alleson Constable

[A duplicate of this warrant was made out to "Mr James Taggart Constable for the Westerly side of Beaver Brook," and recorded upon page 136, Vol. 2, Early Records of Londonderry.—ED.]

Province of New: shire

By Virtue of the fore Going Warrants being legally Call'd &c. the proprietors freeholders and Inhabitants of Londonderry mett at the old meeting House oct^{br} ye 6th 1739. and

voted for Moderator..............Robt Boys Esqr mod^{tr}

1st ly the first article in the fore Going warrant being Read and Consider'd by the proprietors freeholders and inhabitants of s^{d} Londonderry, it is voted and a Greed upon by s^{d} Inhabitants that they will adhear & a Gree to the Rules of the presby^{tr} which is to held at Londonderry afore s^{d} the 10th Day of this Instant Currant, (viz) in the Choise of a minister of the Gospel to Labour a mongst them, it is also voted and a Greed upon by s^{d} Inhabitants that Robt Boys Esqr Lieu^{t} Andrew Todd and Moses Barnet shall be a Com^{tee} appoynted to Joyn with the sesion of s^{d} Londonderry to prossecut a Call at the aforc s^{d} presby^{tr} for Mr Willm Davidson probationer

2: ly the second article in the fore Going warrant being Read and Consider'd by the proprietors freeholders and Inhabitants of s^{d} Londonderry, it is voted and a Greed upon by s^{d} Inhabitants that Mr Willm Davidson preacher of the Gospel shall be their settled Minister of s^{d} Londonderry if he the s^{d} Mr Davidson see caus to tak up with the Proposels that may be made to him on that account

3: ly the third article in the fore Going warrant Being Read and Consider'd by the proprietors freeholders & Inhabitants of s^{d} Londonderry it is voted and a Greed upon by s^{d} Inhabitants that they will Give for Encuragment of Settlement to the s^{d} Mr Davidson one Hundred & sixty pounds of passable Bils of Credite, the one half to be paid this Year & the other half to be paid next Year following. the s^{d} money to be assesed on the s^{d} Inhabitants by the select men of s^{d} Londonderry, and to be Colectted by ye Constables

4: ly the fourth article in the fore Going warrant being Read and Considered by the proprietors freeholders & Inhab^{ints}, it is voted and a Greed upon that s^{d} Inhabitants will Give one Hundred & sixty pounds of passable Bils of Credite to the afore s^{d} Mr Davidson for yearly sallary During his aboade or preaching of the Gospel in s^{d} Londonderry*

5: ly the fifth article in the fore Going Warrant being Read and Considered by ye proprietors freeholders & Inhabitants of s^{d} Londonderry, it is voted & a Greed upon by s^{d} Inhabitants that they will pay their suppliers or preachers of the Gospel in the old meeting House according to the law a Custom of s^{d} province

6: ly the sixth article in the fore Going Warrant being Read and Considered by s^{d} Inhabitants, it is voted and a Greed upon by s^{d} Inhabitants that that protest mentioned in the sixth article of the fore Going Warrant shall not be put on Record in our town Book

*Rev. William Davidson, a native of Ireland, who married the widow of Mr. Thomson, succeeded that divine as pastor of the East Church in 1739, continuing in that capacity for fifty years, or until his death, February 15, 1791, in his eightieth year. His wife outlived him five years.

This year, 1739, the General Court invested sundry persons in the westerly part of the town with parish privileges, and it became known as the "West Parish." Rev. David MacGregor, son of Rev. James MacGregor, the first minister of the town, became the minister of this new society. Mr. MacGregor had been a pupil under Rev. Matthew Clark, his father's successor, and he was an eloquent preacher, much beloved by his parishioners. But religious dissensions had already crept in, which lasted for nearly forty years. Mr. Parker in speaking of this says:

"The site first selected by the West Parish and a house erected there was known as West Hill. But a number of families residing in the easterly part of the town being dissatisfied with Mr. Davidson's ministry, and particularly attached to Mr. MacGregor, as he was the son of their former pastor, and more evangelical in his doctrinal views, and a more talented preacher than Mr. Davidson, united with the newly formed parish, and thus occasioned a change in the location of their house of worship from the Hill, so called, to Aiken's Range." More than this it brought about an unhappy condition of society. This move caused about forty of the families of the West Parish to join the other, while as many families left the East Parish to become a part of the rival church. This unfortunate division not only severed friendly and social ties, but it awoke bitter animosities between the members of the two religious societies, causing even the pastors to ignore each other.—EDITOR.

7: ly the seventh article in the fore Going warrant being Read and Consider'd by s[d] Inhabitants it is voted and a Greed upon that the most westerly Meeting House in the westerly side of s[d] town shall be the place of publick worship for that parish when sett off by authority and Laws of s[d] province

8: ly the Eight article in the fore Going Warrant being Read & Considered by s[d] Inhabitants it is voted & a Greed upon by s[d] Inhabitants, that the select men of s[d] town shall asses so much money upon the poles & Estates of s[d] town as shall be sufficant to pay all the publick Debts, that s[d] select men has made a Return of at the afore s[d] meeting, together with what more Just Debts may be Returned to s[d] selectmen before the assesment of the afore s[d] money, y[e] 9th article passed in the Negative

10: ly the tenth article in the fore Going Warrant being Read and Considered by s[d] Inhabitants, it is voted and a Greed Upon to Divied the High ways in s[d] town according to the Number of poles in s[d] town, and also voted that their shall be five men Chosen as a Com[tee] to Divied s[d] High ways where there is Complents made. s[d] Com[tee] is Hugh Willson Allan Anderson Tho[s] Horner Tho[s] Bogles Tho[s] Willson

11: ly the 11th article being Read is Deffer'd at this time

Will[m] Gregg Jo[n] Gregg James Nesmith Jo[n] Bleair James Clark James Reid Sam[ll] Barr Daniel m[tt] Duffee Jo[n] M[tt] Murphy James Lindsay David Hunter James Anderson Do Deshent a Gainst the vote passed on the fifth article in the fore Going Warrant

Jo[n] m[tt] Murphy Jo[n] Jameson Enters their Deshent against the first five votes passed upon the fore Going articles and the vote passed upon the seventh article

James Nesmith & James Reid Enters their Deshent against the first five votes passed upon the fore Going articles and the vote passed upon the seventh article

James Reid
James Nesmith

We the subscribers Do Enter our protest & Deshent against

the first five articles and seventh article of the town warrant now Disscussed being ye 6th of oct^{br} 1739 Jo^{n} Anderson James Gregg James Adames James Lindsay Willm Adames Jo^{n} Gregg

Province of Newhampshire

Londonderry oct^{br} ye 6th 1739

By vertue of a precept Derected to us from Mr Russel shireff of sd province you are hereby Required to warn the proprietors freeholders and Inhabitants Within your Respective Bounds Duly Quallifyd by Law to meet at the old meeting House upon Mounday the 22th Day of sd Instant at nine o' the Clock before noon then and there

1stly to Elect one fit person Quallifyd in the law to Represent the sd town in assembly appointed to be Conveened and held at the Court House in ports mouth on Wensday the 24th Day of sd Instant

2: ly Entered at the Request of some none Commaners to see if the town will vote that the none Commaners shall be allow'd pay for their highs and fenceing as will as the proprietors or Els to free the none Commaners from paying the proprietors for their High ways and fenceing

and this shall be your warrant Given under our hands the Day and Year above mentioned

Allan Anderson
Hugh Willson
Thos Willson
Moses Barnet
Andrew Todd
Select men

To Mr James Taggart Constable for the Westerly side of beaver Brook

Province of Newhampshire

Londonderry oct^{br} 22th 1739

I have posted this precept according to former custom

P. me James Tagart Constable

[A duplicate of this warrant was given "To Mr. Sam^{ll} Alleson Constable for the Easterly side of Beaver Brook," and recorded upon page 140 of Vol. 2, of Early Records of Londonderry.—Ed.]

Province of New: shire

By vertue of the fore Going Warrants being legaly Call'd the proprietors freeholders and Inhabitants of Londonderry meet at the old meeting on mounday the 22th Day of oct^{br} 1739 and

Voted for moderator Livt Andrew Todd

the first article in the fore Going Warrant being Read it is voted that Robt Boys Esqr shall be their Representive of sd L: Derry

the 2d article being Read and Considered it is passed in the neagetive

Province of New....sr

Londonderry Febry ye 18th 1739/40

You are here by Required to Warn the proprietors free holders & Inhabitants of sd town duly Quallified in law, to meet at the old meeting House upon wensday the fifth Day of March, at nine o' the Clock, before noon, then and there

1.st ly to Chouse all their Town officers for the Ensuing Year

2. ly to see what meathod they will take a bout schoolor schools

3. ly to see if the Town will approve of the select men sending out Robt Cochran & James Adams, to take the Invoice for this present year, and if they will make some addition to their wadges

4: ly to see if they will Chuse two men to take ye Invoice for the Ensuing Year

5. ly to see what meathod the town will take to pay men for the land that the high ways takes of them where there is no land allow'd for highways

6. ly to see whether they will Vote that the pay for fenceing be as formerly or whether they will Vote no pay for the futter

7. ly to hear trancscripts Read and approven or disapproven of

8. ly to see what meathod they will take about some land that Alexr Nikels says that he is wronged of

and this shall be your Warrant Given under our hands the Day and the Year above mentioned

Moses Barnet
Allan Anderson
Andrew Todd
Hugh Willson
Tho[s] Willson
Select men

To Mr James Tagart Constable for the Westerly side of Beaver Brook

Province of New....sr

Londonderry March the fifth 1739/40

I have posted the within precept according to former Custom

P. me James Tagart Constable

[A duplicate of this warrant given "To Mr Samll Alleson Constable for the Easterly side of Beaver Brook," and recorded on page 142 of Vol. 2, Early Records of Londonderry. —Ed.]

Province of New....[sr]

By virtue of the fore Going Warrants being legally call'd the proprietors freeholders & Inhabitants of Londonderry and province afore sd, met at their old meeting House on wensday the fifth Day of March 1739-40. and,

Voted for a moderator, for sd meeting Jo[n] Morison sin[r]

Voted for select men for the year Ensuing Thos Willson Allan Anderson Andrew Todd Hugh Willson Moses Barnet select men

Voted for town Clerk, for the Year Ensuing, Jo[n] Wallace sin[r]

Voted for Constables, for the Year Ensuing, James Gillmore for the Easterly side of Beaver Brook, and James Smith for the Westerly side of Beaver Brook, and to be paid as formerly for their serving as such

Voted for leather sealers David Hopken, Jo[n] Cockes

Voted for tithing men, Willm Thomson fair Jon Cochran Willm Cockes tithing men

Voted for surviers for the Ensuing year, and for the Easterly side of Beaver Brook Andrew Clendenin Jam^{s} Dunlap Jo^{n} Cochran Jo^{n} Archibald Jo^{n} Stewart Junr James Willson miller Alex^{r} Kelso Piter Christy Sam^{ll} Moreson Hugh Muntgomry surviers

for the westerly side of Beaver Brook Willm Nutt James Blair Jo^{n} Tagart Thos Hoige Jo^{n} Bell Matthew Wright surviers

Voted for Houards for the Ensuing year Frances Smilly. Hugh Rodgers black James Willson Robt Thomson Robt Riddel Houards

voted fence vewers & prizers for the year Ensuing Jo^{n} m^{tt} Keen Jo^{n} Cromey fence vewers & prizers

voted for a Com^{tee} to search the selectmens or the towns accounts for the Ensuing Year James Aiken Jo^{n} Wallace sin^{r} Robt Clark Com^{tee}

2. ly the second article in the fore Going Warrant being Read and Considered by the afore s^{d} Inhabitants, it is voted that there shall be but one publick school in s^{d} town, for this Year Ensuing

3. ly the third article being Read of the fore Going warrant it's voted that the s^{d} town, approves of the select men's sending out Robt Cochran & James Adams to take an Invoice of the poles & Estats of s^{d} town, for the year Ensuing, and also that there shall be an adition made of ten shillings to their wages, for the s^{d} service

4. ly. voted on the fourth article, that the same men (viz) Robt Cochran & James Adams is to take an Invoice of the poles and Estats of s^{d} town, some time in the months of Jan^{ry} & Feb^{ry} or before the fifth Day of March next Ensuing the Date hereof, & make a Return of the same to the select men for the time being

5. ly Voted on the fifth article, that there shall be no pay alowed any person in s^{d} town, for high way land for the futter, Except where any highway gos the lenth of any person's

land or angls on a mans land, that then any such person, or persons, shall have Reasonable pay for what land such highways takes off their land

6. ly the sixth article in the fore Going warrant being Read and Considr'd by sd Inhabitants, it's voted that there shall be no pay alowed any person or persons, by the select men of sd town, for fenceing high ways for the futter

7. ly voted on the seventh article, that Alexr Nikels being a proprietor in sd town, shall be made Equall in one shear with other proprietors in sd town

8. ly the Eight article being Read & Considered by the proprietors it is voted, that the severall Returns or transcripts Read at sd meeting is to be put upon Record, and is approven of by sd proprietors (viz) one for Abram Holms, one for George & Thos Clark, one for Samll Morison & Stephen Perce & one for James Nikels

We the subscribers Being proprietors and Inhabitants of Londonderry Do by these presents Protest a Gainst the vote as it was acted by a majority of sd proprietors and Inhabitants of Londonderry, the fifth and sixth articles of the town warrant then voted upon it being Contrary to the laws of this province made and provided (viz) on the 5th Day of march 1739/40

James Morison
James Reid
Matthew Reid
David Vance
Jon Humphrey
Protests

Recorded this 15th of march 1739-40

P. Jon Wallace town Clerk

Province of Newhampshire

Londonderry July ye 5th 1740

You are hereby Required to Warn the proprietors Freeholders & Inhabitants Duly Qualified in Law to Meet at the old meeting House upon Monday the 21th Day of this Instant at ten o'Clock Before noon then & there

1. ly to Chouse one meet person Duly Qualified in Law to Represent them to sit in Genrall Assembly to meet at the Court House in Portsmouth on Wensday the 23th Day of this Instant Currant at ten o'Clock Before noon

And this shall be your Warrant Given under our hands the Day and Year above mentioned

Allan Anderson
Thos Willson
Andrew Todd
Selectmen

To James Gilmore Constable in the Easterly side of Beaver Brook

Province of Newhampshire

In obedince to the within precept I have posted this Warrant three publick days according to Custom

P. James Gilmore Constable

[A duplicate of this warrant was made "To James Smith Constable in the Westerly side of Beaver Brook," and recorded on page 145, Vol. 2, Records of Londonderry.—Ed.]

Province of New. sr

By Virtue of the fore Going Warrant Being legally Call'd the proprietors freeholders & Inhabitants of Londonderry met at the old Meeting House on Monday the 21st Day of July 1740. and

Voted for moderator, Hugh Willson

Voted for Representitive Robert Boyes Esqr

Recorded this 28th of July 1740.

P. Jon Wallace town Clerk

Province of New. shr

Londonderry Sepbr ye 1th 1740

You are hereby Required to Warn the proprietors free holders & Inhabitants Within your Respective Bounds to meet at ye old meeting upon tusday ye sixteen Day of this Instant at ten o' the Clock before noon then & there

1. ly to see how much town Reats they will vot to asses for this year

2. ly to see if ye town will Chouse & Impower a Comtee to

lift that money from Jo^{n} m^{c}Murphy that they put into his hand by a vot till they pleased to Call for ye same & Give Every parish their Equall share of ye same

3. ly to see if the town will tak som prudent meathod to lift the money from ye Constables that are Delinequant

4. ly to see if ye town will Repear ye pond Bridge at ye neck of ye pond upon ye publick Charge of ye town or not

5. ly to see if ye proprietors will vot to Rais any money to Defray the Charges of the propriety for this year

6. ly to hear transcripts Read & approven or not

And this shall be your Warrant Given under our hands the Day and year a bove mentioned

Allen Anderson
Hugh Willson
Thomas Willson
Andrew Todd
Moses Barnet
Select men

To James Gillmor Constable in ye Easterly side of Beaver Brook

P. N—^{sr}

Londonderry sep^{br} ye 16th 1740

In obidence to ye Within precept I have posted this Warrant two publick Days.

James Gillmore Constable

Recorded P. Jo^{n} Wallace town Clerk

[A duplicate of the above warrant, excepting that the word "House" was given immediately after "meeting" in the third line, was made out to "James Smith Constable in ye Westerly side of Beaver Brook," and recorded on page 145, Vol. 2, Records of Londonderry.—Ed.]

Province of New: shire

At a meeting of ye proprietors freeholders and Inhabitants of Londonderry and province afore said Sep^{br} ye 16th 1740. then voted for moderator

Thos Willson

The first article of ye fore going Warrant Being Read and Considered by s^{d} Inhabitants it is voted & agreed upon that ye select men of s^{d} Londonderry shall applot or asses all ye Publick Debts of s^{d} town. viz. all ye list of Debts Read at the afore s^{d} meeting ye total sum of s^{d} list amounting to fifty pounds

The second article of ye fore Going Warrant being Read and Consider^{d} it is voted and a Greed upon to Call for that money that the town lodged in Jo^{n} m^{t} Murphy's hand in the year 1734 the total sum of s^{d} money amounting to twenty Eight pounds viz. that money that was to Repare the meeting House and lay in the hands of the heirs of Capt Cargill Deceas'd, and it is also voted and agreed upon that Hugh Ramsey Samuell Barr & Jo^{n} Wallace sin^{r} shall be a Com^{tee} to Call for s^{d} money and it is hereby to be understood by s^{d} vot that if it shall so hapn that if ye s^{d} Jo^{n} mt Murphy Neglect or Refuse to Deliver up ye afore s^{d} money to ye afore s^{d} Com^{tee} that then we ye s^{d} Inhabitants Doth Authirise & appoynt ye s^{d} Com^{tee} they or Either of them then to sue and prossecute ye afore s^{d} Jo^{n} m^{t} Murphy Before any Judge or Judges Justice or Justices in any Court or Courts and shall act & do Every thing needful in ye procuring the afore s^{d} money with as full ample authority as if we ye whole Inhabitants of ye afore s^{d} Londonderry were all present and it shall be in ye power of s^{d} Com^{tee} or any of them to Constitute appoynt make & ordain & substitute one or more attorneys under them if they or any of them think meet and conveniant in ye afore s^{d} affair and that ye Cost & Charges thereof shall be at ye Expence of ye whole Inhabitants afore s^{d} and it is also to be known by s^{d} vot that the s^{d} Com^{tee} is to Discharge ye s^{d} m^{tt} Murphy for s^{d} money when Received also voted that ye above s^{d} money is to be Equally Devided amonge ye proprietors afore s^{d}. viz. y^{t} money ye town lodg'd in Jo^{n} m^{tt} Murphys hand in the year 1734 & was to Repair ye meeting House

The third article of ye fore going Warrant being Read it is voted and agreed upon to Chouse a Com^{tee} to sue all the Delinquant Constables of s^{d} Londonderry, & s^{d} Com^{tee} voted for is Hugh Ramsey Sam^{ll} Barr & Jo^{n} Wallace sen^{r} & it is hereby to be Known that we ye afore s^{d} Inhabitants do authorise & appoynt ye s^{d} Com^{tee} they or Either of them to sue & prossecute ye s^{d} Delinquant Constables them or any of them Before any Judge or Judges Justice or Justices in any Court or Courts & shall act & do Every thing needfull in that afear with as full ample authority as if we ye whole Inhabitants of ye afore s^{d} Londonderry were all present and it shall be in ye power of s^{d} Com^{tee} or any of them to Constitute appoynt make & ordain & substitute one or more attorneys under them if they or any of them think meet & Conveniant in the afore s^{d} affear, and that ye Cost & Charges thereof shall be at ye Expence of ye whole Inhabitants afore s^{d}

The afore s^{d} Meeting is adjorned to tusday ye 30th of s^{d} Instant at ten o' the Clock before noon

Liv^{t} Todd Willm Humphry & Robt Wallace Enters their protest against the adjornment of ye afore s^{d} Meeting

Tusday ye 30th of Sep^{br} 1740, then ye afore s^{d} Inhab^{ts} met according to adjornment, and voted to Build the pond Bridge at the charge of ye town

Robt Wallace Sam^{ll} Dickey James Tagart & Jo^{n} Wallace sen^{r} Enters their protest against a hand vote on ye fourth article of ye fore Going Warrant

The fifth article of ye fore Going Warrant being Read and Consider'd by the proprietors of s^{d} L: Derry, it is voted & agreed upon to asses or aplot six shillings on Each propriety for this present Year and to be assesed by ye select men of s^{d} L: Derry

The Sixth article being Read, the following ttrancrepts or Returns was approven of one to James Nickels Deceas'd one to Benjn Keeder one to ye Hon^{ll} Robt Achmuty of one hundred & fifty acres which is full setisfection for one Hundred & Eighteen pounds he paid for ye proprietors upon James Wallace Deceas'd Case two to Robert Weir, one to Jo^{n} Given one to Sam^{ll} Greaves and to their assigns for Ever

Province of Newhampshire

Londonderry Jan^{ry} 26th 1740-1

You are hereby Required to warn the proprietors freeholders & Inhabitants in Your Respective Bounds Duly Qualli-fied in law in s^{d} town to meet at the old meeting House upon tusday the tenth day of fe^{br} next at ten o' the Clock Before noon then & there

1^{s} ly To Chouse one meet Pson Duly Quallified in law to Represent them to the Genrall Court that is to meet at ports-mouth upon thursday the twelth of fe^{br} at ten o' the Clock Before noon at the Court House in portsmouth

2. ly To see what ye town will do with some orders that is in the Constables hands for money that was Given them by the select men to pay ye towns Debts that the Com^{tee} of ac-counts wont Receive from them

and this shall be your Warrant Given under our hands the day and year above mentioned

Hugh Willson
Andrew Todd
Allen Anderson
Thos Willson
Moses Barnet
Select men

to Mr Ja^{s} Gilmor Constable for the Easterly side of Beaver Brook

province of Newhampshire
Londonderry fe^{br} the tenth 1740/41
this warrant has ben posted two publick days according to the Custom
Ja^{s} Gillmor Constable

[A duplicate of this warrant, given to "Mr Ja^{s} Smith Con-stable for the Westerly side of Beaver Brook," is recorded on page 149, Vol. 2, Records of Londonderry.—Ed.]

Province of Newhampshire
By virtue of the fore Going Warrants Being legaly Cal'd the proprietor freeholders and Inhabitants of L: Derry met at the old meeting House on tusday the tenth day of fe^{br} 1740/41. and
voted for Moderator Jo^{n} Bleair
the first article in the fore Going Warrant Being Read it

is voted that Sam^{ll} Barr shall Represent the s^{d} town of Londonderry at the Jenerall Court which is to be holden at portsmouth the twelth day of s^{d} Instant

The second article in the fore Going Warrant Being Read it is voted that Thos Steel & Thos Bogle shall be a low'd ten shillings Each for Extrordenery Wages for serving as Constables in the year 1732. and also

voted that James Callwell shall be Descharged for that order that lay in his hand, that the Com^{tee} of towns accounts wod not receive from him, the total sum of s^{d} order amounting to fifteen pounds

Recorded P. Jo^{n} Wallace town Clerk

Province of Newhampshire

Londonderry Jan^{ry} 26th 1740/41

You are hereby Required to Warn the proprietors within your Respective Bounds to meet at the old meeting House upon tusday the tenth of fe^{br} at one of the Clock in the after noon then & there

1^{s} ly to see what meathod they will take with the Delinquant proprietors that dos not pay their proprietory Reats

2. ly to hear transcripts Read and approven or Disapproven

and this shall be your Warrant Given under our hands the day and Year above mentioned

Thos Willson
Hugh Willson
Andrew Todd
Allan Anderson
Moses Barnet
select men

To James Smith Constable in the Westerly side of Beaver Brook

[A duplicate of this warrant was given to "Mr Ja^{s} Gillmore Constable for the Easterly side of Beaver Brook," and recorded on page 150, Vol. 2, of Records of Londonderry. —Ed.]

Province of Newhampshire

By virtue of the fore Going Warrants being legally Call'd the proprietors of Londonderry met at the old meeting House on tusday the tenth day of fe^{br} 1740/41 and

voted for moderator Ja^{s} Rodgers

The fifth article of the fore Going Warrant Being Read and Consider'd it is voted & agreed upon to prefear a supplication to the Generall Court which is to set at portsmouth the twelth day of fe^{br} Corrant, in order to procure a law to Dispose of so much of the Delinquant proprietors lands as may be suffisant to pay up their propritory Reats Equall with other proprietors of s^{d} Londonderry according to the Claws of the Charter of the afore s^{d} Londerry and also voted that James Reid James Nesmith and Jo^{n} Wallace shall be a Com^{tee} authorised and Impowered by s^{d} proprietors to prefear the afore s^{d} supplycation to the s^{d} Generall Court

The second article being Read of the fore Going warrant the Hon^{ll} Robt Achmuty had a transcript of his amendment and adition lands Read and approven of by s^{d} proprietors for the Benefit of the s^{d} Achmutty and his assigns for Ever

and to prevent mistacks Conserning the afore s^{d} transcript it is hereby noted that there is six acres of mendment land laid out on said transcript more than What is Return'd in the list of mendment there being a wrong Return made in the s^{d} list..........viz. (11 acres) whereas there should have ben 17 acres

Province of Newhampshire

Londonderry February ye 17th 1740/41

You are hereby Required to Warn the freeholders proprietors and Inhabitants Duely Quallified in Law within your Respective Bounds to meet at the old meeting House upon thursday the fifth Day of March at ten of the Clock before noon then & there

1. ly to Chous all their town & old parish officers for the Ensuing Year

2. ly to Chouse two men to take the towns Invoice for the Ensuing Year

3. ly to see if they will vote to move the faire from the old Meeting House it Being a very Great Deterement to some Psons and Conclude upon some Convenieant place to hold it where ye Inhabitants may suffer least Damage by it

4. ly to hear the accounts of the Dispursments of the money assesed upon the town these three or four Years last past, which accounts is in the hands of the Comtee Chosen by the town to Count with ye select men

and this shall be your Warrant Given under our hands the Day & Year above mentioned.

To James Smith Constable in the Westerly side of Beaver Brook

Hugh Willson
Thos Willson
Moses Barnet
Allan Anderson
Andrew Todd
select men

Londonderry march the 1th
I have made a due Return according to Law
James Smith Constable

[A duplicate of this warrant was given "To Mr Jas Gillmore Constable Eastrely side of Beaver Brook," and recorded on page 152, Vol. 2, Records of Londonderry.—Ed.]

Provence of New....shire
Londonderry ye 5th 1740/41
in obidance to the within Warrant I have posted sd Warrant according to the formore Custom P. me
James Gillmore Constable

Provence of New....shire
By virtue of the fore Going warrant Being legally Call'd the proprietors freeholders and Inhabitants of Londonderry met at the old meeting House upon thursday the fifth day of march 1740/41

And the Major part of the Electors present voted for Moderr Lieut Andrew Todd

the first article in the fore Going Warrant being Read and Considered, the town and parish offecers was Choosen and voted for as followeth for the Ensuing Year

voted for select men Jo^{n} Barnet David Vance Robt Cochran Th^{s} Cochran Robt m^{tt}Cordey selectmen for ye year Ensuing

also voted for town old parish & proprietors

Clerk Jo^{n} Wallace sen^{r}

voted for tithing men Willm Humphry and Willm Eayers

voted for Constables Hendrey Campble & Willm Mordough to serve as such for the town & old parish and also voted that s^{d} Constables shall be alow^{d} five pounds by ye town for serveing as Constables for the s^{d} town and old parish and also that Each Constable shall be alow'd Equally of s^{d} five pounds according to the severall sums they Colect for the town and old parish, and it is further to be Known by s^{d} vote that the old parish is to alow or pay their Equall share of s^{d} five pounds according to their particular sum, that may be Colected by s^{d} Constables

also voted for surviers for the Ensuing Year for the Easterly side of Beaver Brook David Hopken Willm Thomson Nathaneall Hamphill Ja^{s} Campble Gabrall Barr Jo^{n} Archibald Ja^{s} Willson Willm Hogge Archibald Miller Ja^{s} Gillmor pollece pond

for the Westerly side of s^{d} Brook for s^{d} Offece Sam^{ll} Greaham Hugh Ramsey Archibald m^{t} Cormick Sam^{ll} Thomson Willm Duncan Jo^{n} Wallace Matthew Wright

also voted for leather sealer Jo^{n} Jameson

also voted for Howerds Willm Kelsy James Dunlapt

and Jo^{n} Allexander Willm Robertson & Ja^{s} Morrow

also voted for fence Vewers & prizers Jo^{n} Stewart and Willm Aiken

also voted for a Com^{tee} to serch the Towns & select mens accounts for ye Ensuing Year Ja^{s} Aiken Robert Clark & Jo^{n} Wallace also voted to take an Invoice of the pols & Esteats of s^{d} town for the Ensuing Year Robert Cochran & Ja^{s} Adams Junr

and also that s^{d} Cochran & Adams shall have three pounds & ten shillings Each for serving as such and makeing a true

Return of s^d pols and Esteats to the select men for the time Being

The Third article being Read it is voted to hold the fear at the Meeting House

The afore s^d meeting is adjorn'd to tusday the 24th Instant at ten o' the Clock Before noon

Londonderry March the 24th 1740/41

The proprietors freeholders & Inhabitants met according to adj^{nt}

the fourth article in the Warrant Being Read the following accounts was Read at s^d meeting. Viz. Matthew Taylors $Will^m$ Humphry's & James Tagarts, and there was no objectons made against any of s^d accounts

voted that Jo^n Humphry & James Callwell is to take Care of the fear that they be not Destroy'd for the Year Ensuing

Province of Newhampshire

Londonderry July the 1th 1741

You are hereby Required to warn the proprietors free Holders & Inhabitants Within your Respective Bounds to meet at the old Meeting House upon friday y^e seventeenth of this Instant July at four o' the Clock After noon then & there

1: ly to see What money the town will allow to be aploted to Defray the Depending Charges this Year

2: ly to see if the town will strenthen that $Com^{tee's}$ power. viz. Hugh Ramsey Jo^n Wallace & Samuell Barr that was to Call for that Money that the town lodged in Jo^n m^t Murphy's hand in the year 1734. viz. that money that was Given to Repair the Meeting House, by Archibald m^t Fetrece Esqr Deceas'd

and this shall be your Warrant Given under our hands the Day & Year above mentioned

Jo^n Barnet
Thos Cochran
Robt Cochran
David Vance
Robt m^c Curdy
select men.

To Mr Willm Murdough Constable for the Westerly side of Beaver Brook

July 17. 1741 In obediance to ye within precept I have posted up this warant according to usewall Custom

W: Murdough

[A duplicate of this warrant was given "To Mr Hendrey Camble Constable for the Easterly side of Beaver Brook," and recorded on page 155, Vol. 2, Records of Londonderry. —Ed.]

Province of Newhampshire

By Virtue of the fore Going Warrants being legally Call'd the proprietors freeholders and Inhabitants of Londonderry met at their old Meeting House upon friday the 17th of July 1741

and voted for Moderator Mr Thos Cochran

the first article in the Warrant being Read & Consider'd it is voted & agreed upon that the select men of s^{d} town shall applote and asses three Hundred and fourty seven pounds upon the poles & Esteats of s^{d} Londonderry for this Year in order to Defray the Depending Charges

The second article of the fore Going Warrant being Read. viz. to see if the town will strenthen that Com$^{ttee's}$ power. viz. Hugh Ramsey Jo^{n} Wallace & Sam^{ll} Barr that was to Call for that money that the town lodged in Jo^{n} m^{t} Murphy's hand in the year 1734. viz. that money that Archibald m^{t} Pheadris Esqr Deceas'd gave as Gift to the Building of the old meeting House

The fore Going articl being Considr'd by the afore s^{d} Proprietors freeholders & Inhabitants it is voted & agreed upon that Hugh Ramsey Jo^{n} Wallace & Sam^{ll} Barr Shall be a Com^{tee} to Demand & Receive s^{d} money of s^{d} Jo^{n} m^{t} Murphy & if it shall so hapn that if the s^{d} Jo^{n} m^{t} Murphy neglact or Refuse to Deliver up the afore s^{d} money to the afore s^{d} Com^{tee} that when we the s^{d} proprietors freeholders & Inhabitants Do hereby Authirise & appoynt the s^{d} Com^{tee} they or any or Either of them to be our agant or agants attorney or attorneys to sue & prossecute the s^{d} Jo^{n} m^{t} Murphy Before any Judge or Judges Justice or Justices in any Court or

Courts & shall act & do Every thing needfull in the Name of the s^d^ proprietors freeholders & Inhabitants for the Recovering the afore s^d^ money with as full ample Authority as if we the whole Proprietors freeholders & Inhabitants of the afore s^d^ Londonderry were all present

and it shall be in the power of s^d^ Agents or Attorneys or any or Either of them to Constitute appoynt make & ordain & substitute one or more Attorneys under them if they or any of them think meet & Conveniant in the afore s^d^ affair and that the Cost & Charges thereof shall be at the expence of the proprietors freeholders & Inhabitants afore s^d^ and it is also to Known by s^d^ vot y^t^ ye s^d^ Com^tee^ is to Discharge the s^d^ m^t^ Murphy for s^d^ money when Receiv'd

Province of New Hampshire Londonderry Dec^br^ 21th 1741

You are hereby Required in His Maj^tes^ Name to warn all the freeholders in your Respective Bounds Duly Qualified in law to Assemble at the old Meeting House upon wensday the sixth Day of Jan^ry^ next at ten o' the clock Before noon then & there

1. ly. To Chouse one Meet Pson Duly Qualified in law to Represent the town at the jenerall Court that is to be Convin'd at the Court House in ports mouth upon wensday the thirteenth of Jan^ry^ at ten o' the Clock Before noon

and this shall be your warrant Given under our hands the Day and Year above mentioned

Jo^n^ Barnet
Thos Cochran
Robt Cochran
David Vance
Robt m^t^ Curdy
Select men

To Mr William Murdough Constable for the westerly side of Bever Brook

Province of Newhampshire

Londonderry Jan^ry^ the 6th 1741-2

In obidiance to the within precept I have posted up this warrant three publick Days as usuewall in this Place

P. me Willm Murdough Constable

[A duplicate of this warrant was given "To Mr Henrey Campble Constable for the Easterly side of Beaver Brook," and recorded on page 157, Vol. 2, Records of Londonderry. —ED.]

Province of Newhampshire

By Virtue of the a fore Going warrants being legally Cal'd, the freeholders of Londonderry Qualified in law met at the old meeting House upon Wensday the 6th Day of Jan^{ry} 1741-2

And voted for Moderator Moses Barnet

The fore Going Warrant Being Read & Consider'd, the s^{d} freeholders, voted that Liu^{t} Andrew Todd shall Represent them at the Generall Court that is to Meet at the Court House in ports mouth upon wensday the thirteen of this Instant at ten o' the Clock Before noon

Province Newhampshire Londonderry feb^{ry} 12th 1741-2

You are hear by Required in His Maj^{tes} Name to Warn all the freeholders proprietors and In habitants in your Respective Bounds to assemble and Meet at the old Meeting House upon friday the fifth Day of March Next Ensuing at ten of the Clock before noon then and there

1. To Chouse all the town & old parish officers for the Year Ensuing

2: ly To hear the towns accounts Read and this shall be your Warrant Given under our hands the Day and Year above Mentioned

Jo^{n} Barnet
David Vance
Robt McCurdy
Robt Cochran
Thos Cochran
select men

To Henry Campble Constable for the Easterly side of Beaver Brook

These Have been proclaimed as formerly by me

Henrey Campbell Constable of the Easterly side of Beaver Brook Londonderry

[A duplicate of this warrant was given "To Mr Willm Murdough Constable for the Easterly side of Beaver Brook," and recorded on page 158, Vol. 2, Records of Londonderry.—ED.]

Province of Newhampshire

By virtue of the fore Going Warrants legally Cal'd the freeholders proprietors and Inhabitants of Londonderry Met at the old Meeting House on friday the fifth of March 1741/2

and after Reading s^{d} Warrant, Voted for Moderator Hugh Willson for s^{d} meeting

the fore Going Warrants Being Read and Consider'd voted for Selectmen for the Year Ensuing Jo^{n} Barnet Robt Cochran Robt m^{t} Curdy Thos Cochran David Vance Select men

Voted for town. proprietors & old parish Clerk for the Ensuing Year Jo^{n} Wallace

Voted for tithing men for the Ensuing Year Hugh Ramsey for the Westerly side of Beaver B^{r} Charls Stuert for ye Easterly side of Beaver Brook

voted for Constables for the Ensuing Year for the town and old parish........Jo^{n} Mitchel Junr for the Easterly side of Beaver Brook........Jo^{n} Creaig for the Westerly side of Beaver Brook, and

also voted that s^{d} Constables shall have five pounds from the town for serving as such and that s^{d} money shall be Divided betwen s^{d} Psons as it was last Year according to the sums Each Constables Colects, and that the old parish shall pay their Equall share of s^{d} five pounds according to their sums that Each Constable Colects within sd Year

Voted for Surviers for the Ensuing Year Jo^{n} m^{t} Keen Willm Willson Ja^{s} Anderson Gabrall Barr Hugh Willson Matthew Reid William Hogg Archibald Miller surviers for the Easterly side

Jo^{n} Duncan Jo^{n} Willson Ja^{s} Callwell Thos Bogel Jo^{n} Bleair sen^{r} Sam^{ll} Morison sen^{r} Sam^{ll} Dickey surviers for the Westerly side

voted for leather sealer for the Year Ensuing David Hopken

voted for Hourds for the Ensuing Year Willm Kelso Thos Camplel George Knox Hourds for the Easterly side

Willm Eayrs Ja^{s} Morrow Hourds for the Westerly side

voted for fence viewers for the Ensuing Year Sam^{ll} Barr & Thos Willson north

voted for a Com^{tee} to search the towns accounts Robt Clark Sam^{ll} Barr Jo^{n} Wallace

voted that Robt Cochran & James Adams shall take an Invoice of the poles & Eastcats of s^{d} town for the Year Ensuing and their Wages for the same to be as last Year

voted that Jo^{n} Humphry & James Ramsey shall take Care of the Dear that they be not Kil'd unsasonably for the Year Ensuing

the aforesaid Meeting is Adjorned to the 15^{tt} of this Instant march at 12m o' the Clock

Londonderry March the 15th 1741/2

Then Met according to the aforesaid Adjornment and according to the second articl of the fore Going Warrant the towns accounts was Read so far as the Constables. viz. Henry Campbel & Willm Murdough had accounted with the select men and the Com^{tee} of the towns accounts for the Year 1741. and no objctions was made at s^{d} meeting in Respect of s^{d} accounts

Province of Newhampshire

Londonderry August 16th 1742

You are hereby Required to warn the freeholders & Inhabitants within Your Respective Bounds to Meet at the old meeting House upon tusday the thirty first Day of this Instant August at three o' the Clock after noon then and there

1: to see what Money the town will alow to be apploted to Defray the Depending Charges this Year

and this shall be your Warrant Given under our hands the Day & Year above mentioned

Jo^{n} Barnet
Thos Cochran
David Vance
Robert m^{tt} Curdy
Robert Cochran
Select men

To Mr Jo^{n} Mitchell Constable for the Easterly side of Beaver Brook

Province of Newhampshire

Londonderry August 31th 1742

In Obidence to the within Warrant I have posted it two publick days

P. me Jo^{n} Mitchell Constable

[A duplicate of this warrant was given "To Mr Jo^{n} Creaig Constable for Westerly side of Bever Brook," and recorded on page 161, Vol. 2, Early Records of Londonderry.—Ed.]

Province of Newhampshire

By Virtue of the foregoing Warrants Being legally Cal'd the freeholders and Inhabitants of Londonderry met August the thirty first 1742, and voted Jo^{n} Bell moderator for s^{d} Meeting

The foregoing Warrants Being Read and Considered it is voted and agreed upon that the select men for the time being shall asses and applot all the publick Debts which the s^{d} town are in at present, which a mounts sixty nine pound four shillings, together with so much money as will clear Jo^{n} Bleair for one Jurny to the Bank when the march meeting was overture'd. viz. in the year 1736

By virtue of the fore Going Warrants* being legaly Cal'd the proprietors free holders & Inhabitants of Londonderry met at the old Meeting House March the 5th 1742-3 and after Reading the warrants for s^{d} meeting, they voted for moderator for s^{d} meeting, Hugh Willson

voted that their shall be five select men for the Year Ensuing, and their Names is as foloweth. viz. Jo^{n} Barnet Robt Cochran David Vance Robt m^{t} Curdy Jo^{n} Ramsey select men

voted for town and old parish Clerk, Moses Barnet Clerk

voted for tithing men......Hugh Ramsey & Jo^{n} Weir tithing men

voted for Constable for the Easterly side of Beaver Brook for the Ensuing Year......Willm Nickels Constable

*A blank page was left to record the warrants for this meeting, but for some reason they were not recorded.—Ed.

voted for Constable for the westerly side of Beaver Brook for the Ensuing Year....James Boys Constable

voted for surviers for the Ensuing year, for the Easterly side of Beaver Brook....Jon mt Keen Robt Morison Junr James Anderson Willm Humphry Hugh Willson Matthew Reid Thos Horner Thos Cristy surviers

for the westerly side of Beaver Brook James Moor Hugh Moor Jon Blair Samll Renkin John Holms Samll Thomson John Duglas & sd Douglas is to Come with His High way work to the cross Road at the long Hill so Cal'd & Robert Anderson Joseph Bell John Bell Willm Adams surviers

voted for leather sealer for the Ensuing Year David Hopken leather sealer

voted for Hourds for the Ensuing Year Michall Gordon George Knox Jon Cromey Daniel mt Keeny Hourds

voted for fence veiwer & prizers for the Ensuing Year Samll Barr Thos Willson fence veiwers

A memorandum. viz. that James Boys was Chosen Constable at the afore sd for the Ensuing Year, and sd Boys apper'd at sd meeting & absolutly Refused to serve as Constable and paid his fine as the law Derects in that Case made & provided, to the moderator of sd meeting

voted for Constable for the westerly side of Beaver Brook for the Year Ensuing....Jon Hunter Constable

voted for a Comtee to serch the towns accounts with the sellect men & Constables for the Year Ensuing Robert Clerk Samll Barr Robt Wallace Comtee of accounts

voted that Robert Cochran & James Adams shall take an Invoice of the poles & Estates of sd town for the Year Ensuing & make a Return of the same to the select men for the time being, and their wages to be the same they had last Year

voted that the Constables wages or the five pounds Yearly paid them is to be Divided according to the severall Sums Each of them leavies off the Inhabitants of sd town

voted that Jon Humphry & Thos mt Cleary shall take Care of the Deear that they be not Kil'd out of seson as the Law Directs in that Case made & provided the afore s^{d} meeting is Adjorn'd to the 22th day of this Instant March at ten o' the Clock be fore noon

Londonderry March the 22th 1742-3

Then met according to the afore s^{d} Adjornment the towns account Being Read so fare as the Com^{tee} had a Counted with the Constables, was approven off by s^{d} meeting. viz. Willm Murdough Jo^{n} Creaig & Jo^{n} Mitchel Constables

Provance of Newhampshir

Londonderry May ye 30th 1743

You are hearby Requiered to Warn the freeholders and Inhabitance in your Respective bounds to asembel and Meet at the old Meetinghous upon tusday the fourteenth day of June Next at two of the Clooke after Noon then and there

1 To See What thy Will dow about that highway Leading to Chaster betwen Patrick Dugless and James Callwells Whither they Will give up the poient and let the Way go by James Callwells house or let the Commitee now appointed by the jenerall Court Come and Judge of said Way

2 ly To see if thy Will Pass avot that the select men for the time being shall be acommitee to sew all former Cunstabels that is Indebt to the town and Invest them With power accordingly

3 ly To see if thy Will alow the select Men to buy a Book to Enter the towns acounts in and Choose some meete person for that End purpose or alow the select Men to agree With such person and to Consider Whither all the s^{d} acounts shall be entred or only some particular part of them

and this Shall be your Warant given under our hands the day and year above Mantioned

John Baranett
David Vance
Rob^{tt} m^{t}Curdy
John Ramsey
Rob^{tt} Cochran
select Men

To Mr William Nickell Constable for the Easterly sid of Beaver Brook

Note the other Warant for said Meeting Was Exemind and found Word for Word and so not needfull to be put on Record

Attast P Moses Barnett town Clerk

Londonderry June the fourtenth 1743

In obedience to the Within Warant I have posted up the Within two publick Days as usuall

William Nickell Constable

Provance of Newhampshir

Londonderry June the 14th 1743

by vartu of the forgoing Warants bing legely Caled the freholdrs and Inhabitance of Londonderry mete on said Day and Chus for Moderater for sd Meeting Thos Cochran

the first artickel of the Warant being Rede and Considered it is voted that the high Way is to stand betwixt Patrick Dugless and William Adams Whear it is Now Recorded

the second artickel of the Warant being Rede and Considered it is voted that the Select Men for this year is a acomtee Chosen and Impoured to sue all the Delinkued Counstables and Make them pay up What thy ow to the town

the third artickel of the Warant being Rede and Considered it is voted that the select Men is to buy abook for the towns vse to Enter the towns acounts in and ye book is to Contain in its vollm six quier of peeper in it and Robart Cochran is Chousen by the forsd Vot to Enter the acounts in the Book

Voted that When the select Men hath Goten the Book to Enter the acounts in that the Counters (Viz) James Nesmith John Bleer Robt Clark John Wallace or any others that has Been Counters for the town shall give sd Cochran all the acounts Begining at the first and so in order to the last to be by him Entered and the Counters is to keep a Regester of all Sd acounts and When the aounts is Entered Sd Cochran is to Deliver all the Peepers Back to the Counters Who is to Compare the Book and the Counts together

Provance of Newhampshir

Londonderry Octr the 10th 1743

You are hearby Requaired to Warn all the freeholders and Inhabitance in your Respective Bounds to assembel and Meet at the old Meeting hous upon tusday the twinty fifth of this Instant at one of the Clock after Noon then and their

1 to see What Money thy will allow to Defray the Depending Charges this year

2ly to see What Metthod they Will take about taking care of the pam Cloath

and this shall be your Warant given under our hands the Day and Year above mentioned

David Vance
Robart m^{c} Cordy
Jo^{n} Ramsey
Robt Cochran
John Barnett
Selectmen

To William Nickells Constable for the Easterly side of Bever Brook

Londonderry Octr 25th 1743

In obedience to the Within Warant I have posted up the Within Warant two Days as usuall

Pr Me William Nickels Counstable

Note the other Warant for said Meeting Was Exemened and found Word for Word and so not Needfull to be put upon Record

Attast Pr Moses Barnett town Clerk

Provance of Newhampshir

Londonderry Octr the 25th 1743

by Vertue of the foregoing Warants being Legely Caled the free holders and Inhabetance of Londonderry Mett on said Day and Chous for Moderater for s^{d} meeting John m^{c} Murphy Esqr

the first artickl of the Warant being Red and Considered it is voted for the selectmen to asses two houndred and ten pounds old tener to Defray the town and provance Debts for this year

2 the second artickel of the Warant being Rede and Considered it is Voted that Moses Barnett shall Keep the pam Cloth and Impowered to Let it out in the town for five shillings for Each funerel that Imploys it and When it gos out of the town thy Must pay ten shillings and S^d^ Barnett is to acount With the select Men wonst in the year for all the money that is Receved for s^d^ Cloth

Provance of Newhampshir

Londonderry feb^ery^. ye 17th 1743/4

You are hearby Required to Warn all the freeholders and Inhabetance in your Respective Bounds to asemble and Meet at the old Meetinghous upon Monday the fifth Day of March next at ten of the Clock before Noon then and their

1 to Choose all the town and old parresh officers for the year Ensuing

2ly to see Whither thy Will pay for aRhoad from Dainell m^c^Duffies Corner next to James Adams Land and so betwen M^r^ m^c^ Gregors Land and Esqr Boys land to the publick Rhod in the Back Rang for the Convanincy of the peck people and others

3ly to hear the towns acounts Read and aprovd or not aproved of

4ly to see what thy Will allow Robt Cochran for Entring all the Counstables acounts from the first settlement of the town to the present year

and this shall be your Warant Given under our hands the Day and year above Mantioned

John Barnett
David Vance
Robart Mc Cordy
Robart Cochran
John Ramsey
Select men

to William Nickels Counstable for the Easterly side of Beaver Brook

Londonderry march the fifth 1743/4

In obedance to the Within Warant I have posted as usuell

P Willm Nickels Counstable

Note the other Warant for S[d] Meeting Was Exemend and found Word for Word and so not Needfull to be put upon Record

attest Pr Moses Barnett town Clark

Provance of Newhampshir

Londonderry March the fifth 1743/4

by vertu of the forgoing Warant being Legely Cald the propriators freeholders and Inhabtence of Londonderry Mete at the old Meetinghous and after Reeding the Warant for said Meeting thy Voted for Moderator for s[d] meeting Hugh Willson

Voted that there shall be five select men for the year Insuing and there Naims is as followeth (viz) Robert Cochran David Vance Robart M[c]Cordy Robart Wallace John Moor selectmen

Voted for town and old parish Clerk Moses Barnett Clark

Voted for tithingmen John M[c]Keen John Wallace tithingmen

Voted for Counstable for the Easterly sid of Bever Brook for the Insuing year Benjmen Thomson

Voted for the Westerly side Counstable for the Insuing year David M[c]Calester Counstabls

Voted for survairs for the Insuing year on the Easterly sid of Bever Brook for the Insuing year John Wiar Alex[dr] M[c]Neel Samuel Miller James Cochran Hugh Willson Will[m] Clindinin William Caledy Peeter Cristy survairs

Voted for surviers for the Westerly side of Bever Brook for the Insuing year Tho[s] Gregg Tho[s] Bogel John Bleer Will[m] Cox John Mack Sam[l] Dicky Archbald m[c] Murphy Rob[t] Anderson Gorg Dounken John Wallace Will[m] Adams surviers

Voted for Lather sealer for the Ensuing year John Cox

Voted for Hog Hourds for the Insuing year Tho[s] Horner Gorg Nox Will[m] Eairs Tho[s] Hogg Hogg Reves

Voted for fence voueers and praysers for this Insuing year James Reede Tho[s] Cochran fence viewers

Voted for towns Counters for this Insuing year John Wallace Hugh Willson Moses Barnett Counters

Voted for Invoice Men for the Insuing year and there wages is to be four pound Each Rob[t] Cochran James Adams Invice men

Voted for the tacking care of Weights and Mishers being Right for the Insuing year

John Moreson John Bleer tacking care of Mishers

Voted for the tacking care of the Deer for the Ensuing year Tho[s] Gregg Joseph Senter Will[m] Clindinin John Dugless tacking care of the Deer

the second artickel of the Warant being Red and Considered it—is voted that the select men is to treet With thes Men for there Land and agree with them for aRoad at a Resenable Lay (?)

the third artickel of the Warant being Red and Considered it is Defared untill the next Meeting

the forth artickel of the Warant being Rede and Considered it is voted that Robart Cochran is to Enter all the towns acounts in abook from the first setelmen of this town and s[d] Cochran is to have ten shillings for Each Counstables acount Entering

and Dismised s[d] Meeting

Advirtizement

taken up by James M[tt] Keen of Londonderry a Redish bay Stalyeon Judged to be Coming three Years old he is but small of his age he hath a black main and tail the two hind feet somthing white with a black noas som white hairs in his forehead and som white under his belly without any artifishall mark that can be found

Londonderry feb[r] 9th 1737/8
James M[t] Keen

Recorded this 9th day of feb[e] 1737/8
P John Wallace town Clerk

taken up by John Senter of Londonderry an old brown meer branded on the near sholder with the figer of four, also branded on the off bottoke with the letters E S

may the 6th 1738
Jo[n] Senter

Recorded this 6th of may 1738
P John Wallace town Clerk

Londonderry 9^{br} the 24 1738

then taken up by David Gregg and stray'd a small Brindled heifer Coming in three years old with some White on the back and taill without any artifisiall marks or brand. With upright horns

David Gregg

Recorded this 27th of Nov^{br} 1738

P John Wallace town Clerk

taken up by Andrew Clendinin of Londonderry a Reed heffer Coming in three years old with a peace Cut out of the off Ear and the loer End of her tale white with no other marks which Can be known & he that owns s^{d} heffer may come to the aforesaid Clendinin & pay all Due Demands and he may have s^{d} haffer

oct^{br} 15th 1738

Adrew Clendinin

Londonderry Sep^{br} 29th 1739

Then taken up by David m^{tt} Collestar of S^{d} Londonderry a black Mear about four year's old, with a star in her forrat and the near hind foot white, with no other mark's which can be known

David m^{tt} Callester

Londonderry oct^{br} 27th 1739

then taken up by Randle $Allex^{r}$ a light brindled heffer Coming in 3 Years old white belle'd white horns & a short taill no artificel marke Discovered

Randle $Allex^{r}$

$Lond^{ry}$ Nov^{br} y^{e} 3^{d} 1755

Taken up in Damage sepret in Inclosher by John Tagart abrindled stere Coming four years old with the form of the leter P. upon his off horn with hooked horns and some white upon his tale Nigh his Rumpe and some White upon his belley. s^{d} steer is Now Impounded and put through the Law

John tagart

Recorded this 3^{d} of Nob^{r} 1755

Pr Mo^{s} Barnett town Clerk

An account of the Severall proprietors that have apropprety in the old Meeting House the number of Seats or pews and the prise or Salary Sett upon it by the Com^{ttee} appointed by the town for that End. &c

	£	s	d
James Nesmith N°. 1 Sallary	1	8	00
Jo[n] Shields & James Callderwood No 2 Sallary	1	10	00
Arch[d] Clendinen N°. 3 Sallary	1	10	00
Jesse Cristey N° 4 Sallary	1	10	00
Will[m] Aiken N° 5 Sallary	1	9	00
Joseph Simons N° 6 Sallary	1	8	00
James Clerk & Jams Willson No 7 Sallary	00	19	00
Jo[n] Bell N° 8 Sallary	1	2	00
Gov[r] Shute N° 9 Sallary	00	19	00
Jo[n] Barr N° 10 Sallary	00	18	00
Sam[ll] Moore N° 11 Sallary	00	15	00
Benj[n] & Jo[n] Willson N° 12 Sallary	00	13	00
Abell Merrell N° 13 Sallary	00	13	00
Arch[d] Wear N° 14 Sallary	00	15	00
Jams Mackeen N° 15 Sallary	00	18	00
allen Anderson N° 16 Sallary	00	19	00
Robert Moreson N° 17 Sallary	1	2	00
George Monk N° 18 Sallary	00	19	00
Rob[t] Macgregore & Hugh Craig N° 19 Sallary	1	8	00
Randle Alexander N° 20 Sallary	1	9	00
Andrew Todd N° 21 Sallary	1	10	00
Mrs Macgregore & Sons N° 22: 23 Sallary	3	00	00
Hugh Ramsey N° 24 Sallary	1	8	00
David Morison N° 25 Sallary	1	10	00
Will[m] Cochran N° 26 Sallary	1	10	00
Rob[t] Cochran N° 27 Sallary	1	10	00
Jams Rodgers N° 28 Sallary	1	10	00
Will[m] Gregg N° 29 Sallary	1	9	00
Benine wentworth N° 30 Sallary	1	7	00
Rob[t] Willson N° 31 Sallary	1	5	00
Will[m] Eayers N° 128 Sallary	1	6	00
Richard walldron No 32 Sallary	1	8	00
Jo[n] Crumey N° 33 Sallary	1	5	00
Hugh Muntgomry N° 34 Sallary	1	8	00
Jo[n] Barnatt Sen[r] N° 35 Sallary	1	8	00
Jo[n] Archibald & Alex[r] Renkine N° 36 Sallary	1	8	00

	£	s	d
Sam[ll] & Gab[ll] Barr N° 37 Sallary	1	8	00
Jam[s] Gregg N° 38 Sallary	00	19	00
Jo[n] MacClurg N° 39 Sallary	1	2	00
Jo[n] Mac Conechey No 40 Sallary	00	18	00
James Gillmore No 41 Sallary	00	17	00
Joseph Kidder No 42 Sallary	00	14	00
James Wallace & James Liggett No 43 Sallary	00	12	00
Jo[n] Barnat Jun[r] 44 Sallary	00	11	00
Sam[ll] Graves 45 Sallary	00	13	00
Jam[s] Anderson 46 Sallary	00	19	00
Jo[n] Macneall 47 Sallary	0	1	00
Jo[n] Wheelwright N° 48 Sallary	1	3	00
Jam[s] & Mathew Reed 49 Sallary	1	7	00
Jo[n] Gregg 50 Sallary	1	7	00
Will[m] Thomson 51 Sallary	1	8	00
Jon Richey & Will[m] Willson 85 Sallary	1	10	00
Allex[r] Walker 53 Sallary	1	10	00
Ministeriall Seat 52 Sallary	1	10	00
Allex[r] Macneall 54 Sallary	1	10	00
James Adams 55 Sallary	1	9	00
D: Craig & Will[m] Gillmore 56 Sallary	1	7	00
Will[m] Nickels 57 Sallary	1	5	00
Jam[es] MacNorthey & David Gregg 58 Sallary	1	8	00
Jo[n] & Dan[ll] Anderson 59 Sallary	1	5	00
Jo[n] Stewart 60 Sallary	1	8	00
David Craig 61 Sallary	1	8	00
James Nickels 62 Sallary	1	8	00
Sam[ll] & Jo[n] Mackeen 63 Sallary	1	8	00
Jo[n] Moore 64 Sallary	00	19	00
Alex[r] Nickels 65 Sallary	1	00	00
John Morison 66 Sallary	00	18	00
John y[e] Man Cochran 67 Sallary	00	17	00
Mathew Clerk 68 Sallary	00	14	00
John Mitchell 69 Sallary	00	12	00
Tho[s] Steell 70 Sallary	00	11	00
James Morison 71 Sallary	00	16	00

	£	s	d
John Goffe Esq[r] 72 Sallary	00	19	00
Ninian Cochran & partners 73 Sallary	1	1	00
M[r] Foye N[o] 74 Sallary	1	5	00
Arch[d] Stark & Tho[s] Clerk 75 Sallary	1	7	00
James Aiken 76 Sallary	1	7	00
M[r] Phillips 77 Sallary	1	8	00
John Macmurphy & Will[m] Chambers 78 Sallary	1	10	00
David Cargill Jun[r] 79 Sallary	00	17	6
James Leslie 80 Sallary	00	11	6
John Macmurphy 83 Sallary	00	11	6
Edward Aiken 84 Sallary	00	17	6
John Blair 87 Sallary	00	7	6
Sam[ll] Houston 88 Sallary	00	8	6
James Blair 89 Sallary	00	8	6
Gov[r] Wentworth 90 Sallary	00	17	6
James Clerk 91 Sallary	1	10	00
Jo[n] Senter 92 Sallary	1	10	00
David & Tho[s] Bogle 93 Sallary	00	17	6
Robert Mackeen 94 Sallary	00	11	6
Andrew Spalding 95 Sallary	00	7	6
Dan[ll] McDuffi & Sterrat 96 Sallary	00	7	6
Cap[t] Bowers 97 Sallary	00	11	6
Sam[ll] Allison 98 Sallary	00	17	6
Cap[t] Cargill 99 Sallary	1	10	00
Jo[n] Woodburn 100 Sallary	1	10	00
Cap[t] Macpheadris 101 Sallary	00	17	6
David Dickey & Mathew Taylor 102 Sallary	00	11	6
Kidder & Callwell 103 Sallary	00	7	6
Sam[ll] Renkine 104 Sallary	00	6	6
Patrick Douglas N[o] 105 Sallary	00	17	6
James Hunter N[o] 106 Sallary	00	11	6
Saw mill lott N[o] 108 Sallary	00	7	6
Cap[t] Wiberd N[o] 109 Sallary	00	8	6
Abraham Holms N[o] 110 Sallary	1	10	00
Jam[s] MacCurdy & Rob[t] Gillmore N[o] 111 Sallary	1	10	00

	£	s	d
Andrew walker & Robert miller 112 Sallary	00	17	6
James Lindsay 113 Sallary	00	8	6
Jo^{n} Craig & will^{m} Nutt 114 Sallary	00	7	6
Jo^{n} Archibald 115 Sallary	00	11	6
Robert Wear 116 Sallary	00	17	6
James Alex^{r} 117 Sallary	1	10	00
Jo^{n} Anderson 118 Sallary	1	10	00
Robert armstrong 119 Sallary	00	17	6
Robert Boyes 120 Sallary	00	11	6
Alex^{r} Macmurphy 121 Sallary	00	7	6
Jo^{n} Wallace 122 Sallary	00	7	6
Mr Achimutey 123 Sallary	00	11	6
Mr Philips & Willm Adams 124 Sallary	00	17	6
Sam^{ll} Morison 125 Sallary	1	10	00
John Miller & Hugh Riddell 126 Sallary	00	6	6
William Humphra 127 Sallary	1	6	00

Wheras at the first Setlement of our town of Londonderry their was the priviledg of the Stream Called Beaver Brook above Beaver pond Granted to Capt David Cargill to raise a Grist mill upon, and by the Consent and with the Good will of Sam^{ll} Houston of our town of Londonderry aforesaid and he Giveing liberty thereunto the S^{d} Capt David Cargill & David Cargill Junr Erected Sett up & rais'd and aGrist mill upon s^{d} Brook the House of s^{d} mill Standing upon the land of s^{d} Houston, & their s^{d} mill has been occupi'd and Improv'd for these nine or ten years last past without any molestation or Disturbance Whatsoever, and the owners of s^{d} mill and others pass'd and repass'd peaceably & quitely to & from S^{d} mill without any let or Hinderance from the High way to the s^{d} mill w^{c} is about five Rhods, but the owners of s^{d} mill finding their mill Decay'd thought fitt to pull down their mill and rebuild and raise her up in the same place again, but the said Sam^{ll} Houston Giveing the owner's trouble and fenceing in s^{d} mill place & Road and Declareing that they sho'd have no liberty or priviledge to sett their mill upon his land again nor a Road thereunto the owner or owners

Desireing and Requesting us the Subscribers to meet upon the s^d^ place, and if we See'd Cause to Lay out a Road for the Conveniency of s^d^ mill and prize the land at S^d^ Road requir'd if we pleas'd Double the valoue of w^t^ any land was Ever Sold for in our town, we Seeing a necessity for S^d^ Road to the afores^d^ mill and by virtue of a power that the Law Gives us.

We have laid out a Road for the Conveniency to s^d^ mill Begining at the High way at the westerly End of the Bridge upon Beaver Brook Below s^d^ mill thence runing up by the side of s^d^ Brook two Rhods wide to the back of the Dam of s^d^ mill w^c^ is in or about five Rhods in lenth, and have valou'd the land of s^d^ road to Double the valoue that we Judge it to be worth, or Damage that the s^d^ Houston receives by said road to our Judgement, and have made a tender of the prise of S^d^ Road to s^d^ Houston which is Sixteen Shi^lls^ S^d^ land being valou'd by us at ten pounds an acre but Refus'd to take it

Given under our Hands this Ninteen of Sep^tr^ 1732.

James Lindsay
Allen Anderson
John Wallace
James Reid
John Archibald
Select men

[NOTE.—Vol. 2 of Records of Londonderry, pages 175 to 231, inclusive, are filled with records of highways, vital records and advertisement, which are omitted here in order to continue the political records unbroken.—ED.]

Provence of Newhampshir

Londonderry May 28th 1744

You are hearby Requaired to Warn all freeholds and Inhabitance in your Respective Bounds to assembel and Meet at the old meeting hous upon tuesday the 12th of June Next at two of the Clock after Noon then and their

1 to see What Money thy Will alow to be Reased in order to purchase astock of powder and Bullets for the towns use

2-ly to see if thy Will allow sume Money to be Reaised

to suport the poor of the town and this Shall be your Warant Given under our hands the Day and Year above Mentioned

John Moore
Robt Wallace
Robt McCurdy
Robt Cochran
Men select

To Benjamin Thomson Counstable for the Easterly side of Beaver Brook

Londonderry June the 12th 1744

in obedence to the Within Warant I have posted it two Days as uswell by Me

Benjemen Thompson Counstable

the other Warant for s^{d} Meeting Was Exemened and found Word for Word so not Needfull to be put upon Record

atest Pr Moses Barnett town Clerk

Provence of Newhampsher

by vertue of the forgoing Warant being legelly Called the freeholders and inhabitance of Lond^{ry} Mete at the old Meetinghous on said Day and after Reeding the Warant for s^{d} Meeting thy Voted for moderator to the afors^{d} meeting Lift^{n} Hugh Willson

the first artickel of the Warant being Rede and Considered it is Voted that the Select men is to purchas astore of amonition for the town at the town's Charg and the Quantity Voted for is one Barall of powder and Bullets and flints Equellant there unto and it is Leckwis voted to Lodg the afor^{sd} amonition When Bought the one half With Capt James Gregg and the other half With Insign John Wiar and the select men is to tack these mens Note for the afors^{d} amonition on the the vellow of the saime for the towns use when Called for

the second artickel of the Warant is passed in the Negitif

Province of Newhamp[r]

Londonderry Sept[r] the 3th 1744

You are hereby Required to Warn all the freeholders and Inhabitance Within your Respective bounds to assemble and Meet at the old Meetinghous teusday the Eighteenth of this Instant at two of the Clock after Noon then and there

1 To See What Money the town Will allow to be apploted to Defray the Depending Charges this year

2 ly to see if thy Will allow asmall Gift to be given to aspeciall frend to the town

And this shall be your Warant Given under our hands the Day and yeare above Mentioned

John Moore
David Vance
Rob[t] M[c]Curdy
Rob[t] Wallace
Rob[t] Cochran
Select Men

To Benjamin Thompson Counstable for the Easterly side of Beaver Brook

Provance of Newhampshir

Londonderry sub[t] the 18th 1744

in obedence to the Within Warant I have posted it two Days as usewell by Me

Benjemen Thompson Counstable

the other Warant for said Meeting Twas Exemened and found Word for Word and so not Needfull to be put upon Record

Atest P[r] Moses Barnett town Clark

Londonderry sub[tr] the 18th 1744

then Mete acording to the apointment of the forgoing Warant being Legelly Called and Chus for Moderater for s[d] Meeting James Nesmith

The first artickell of the forgoing Warant being Rede and Considered it is Voted to asses and Rese one houndred and thirty pound old tener to Defray the town Debts for this year the second artickel of the Warant being Rede and Considrd it is voted that the select Men is to purches one houndred weight of butter at the towns Charge to give to the afors^{d} Speael frend

Provance of Newhampsher

Londonderry Jan^{ry} 7th 1744/5

Pursuant to apresipt or writ to us Directed from Thos packer high shireff of the provance afores^{d} for to Choose a Representative for this town afforesai^{d} In order that the said person so Chosen May Give his atendance the Next sessions of Generall asembley to be holden at portsmouth the twenty fourth of this Instant by tene of the Clock befor Noon

You are hereby Requiered in his maj^{ess} name to warn all the freeholders in your Respective Bounds Duly Qualified by Law to Elect Representatives that thy Meet at the old Meetinghous on tusday the twinty second Day of this Instant Jan^{ry} at one of the Clock after Noon then and their

1 to Choose or Elect one person Qualified by Law to Represent the said town in Generiall assembly

2 ly to see wither they Will alow Capt Todd somthing of apresent for his Good servese Done to the town these three years past

and this shall be your warant given under our hands the Day and yeare above mentioned

John Moore
David Vance
Robt Wallace
Robt Cochran
Men Select

to Benjamin Thompson Constable for the Easterly side of Beaver Brook

Provance of Newhampsher

Lond^{ry} Jan^{ry} 22th 1744/5

In obedance to the Within Warant I have posted it too Days as yousuell by me

Benj^{h} Thompson Counstable of Lond^{ry}

the other Warants for said Meeting Was Compar^{d} and found Word for Word so not Needfull to be put upon Record

Attest Pr

Moses Barnett town Clerk

Provance of Newhampsher

by vartue of the forgoing Warant being legelly Call^{d} the freeholders of Lond^{ry} and Windham Qualified in law mete at the old Meetinghous upon tusday the 22th Day of Jen^{ry} 1744/5 and voted for Moderater Lif^{t} Hugh Willson the forgoing warant being Rede and Considered the said freeholders voted that John Wallace Ju^{r} shall Represent them at the Generell Court that is to meet at the Courthous in ports mouth upon thursday the 24th of this Instant at ten of the Clock befor Noon

it is Voted to pass the second artickell of the Warant

Provance of Newhampsher

Londonderry feberuary 18th 1744/5

You are hereby Requaired to Warn all the freeholders and Inhabitance in your Respective Bounds to assemble and Meet at the old Meetinghous upon tuesday the fifth Day of March Next at ten of the Clock before Noon then and there

1 to Choose all the town and old parish officers for the year Ensuing

2 ly to hear the towns acounts Read and aproven or Not aproven of

And this shall be your Warant Given under our hands the Day above Mentioned

John Moore
David Vance
Robt Wallace
Robt McCurdy
Robt Cochran

Men Select

to David McCalaster Counstable for the Westerly sid of Bever Brook

Londonderry March the 5th 1744/5

In obediance to theis Warant I have Posted it up two Publick Days

Pr David McCallester Counstable

Note the other Warant for sd meeting Was Exemd and found Word for Word so not Needfull to be put upon Record

Atests Pr Moses Barnett town Clerk

Provance of Newhampshir

Londonderry March 5th 1744/5

by Vertu of the forgoing warant being legelly Called the freeholders and Inhabetance of Londonderry Meet at the old Meetinghous on sd Day Efter Reeding the Warant for sd meeting thy voted for Moderator Liftn Hugh Willson

voted that there shall be five select Men for Insuing year and there names is as followeth Liftn Hugh Willson Robt Wallace Andrew Clendinin Thos horner Thos Cochran

Voted for town Clerk for the Insuing year Moses Barnett

Voted for tithing Men for the Insuing year John Moreson Jur John Cromey James Willson south

Voted for Counstabl for the Esterly sid of Baver Brook Samuell Alleson Jur

voted for Counstable for the West sid of Baver Brook Joseph Bell But sd Bell hairing Samll Dicky Was Excpted of in his Room Samuell Dickey

voted for old parish Couststals Thos Willson Nathenell Martian

Voted for survairs for surviers for the Esterly side of Baver Brook Moses Barnett Alexdr McNeel Samuell Miller Liftn Robt Cochran Liftn Hugh Willson Dr. John Cochran Robt Gillmor Willm Kelliey (?)

Voted for survaiers for the Westerly sid of Baver Brook Nathenall Hollms John Bleer Samll Greems Willm Cox Thos Wallace the 2 Samuell Senter James Willson John Carr Junr John Barnett James Moore Alexdr McCollm Willm Adams

voted for fence Vers and praisers John Archbald John Wallace voted for lather seler for the Insuing year John Cox

voted for Hoge hourds for the In[s] year for the Esterly sid of Beaver Brook Alexd[r] Cellsey Joseph Scobey

voted for Hoge hourds for the Westerly sid of Baver Brook for In[s]. year Will[m] Robartson Black James Willson

Voted for Counters with the select Men for the Insuing year John Bleer John Wallace Moses Barnett

voted for Invoice Men for the Insuing year. Lif[t] Rob[t] Cochran James Adams

voted for tacking Care of Weights and Mishers John Bleer John Moreson sen[r]

voted for the tacking Care of the Deer for the Insuing year James Willson Tho[s] Wallace the 3 Rob[t] Moore Insin William Bleer

this Meeting is ajorn[d] untill Wedensday the 20th of this Instant at ten of the Clock befor Noon

Provance of Newhampshir

Londonderry march the 20th 1744/5

then meet acording to the ajornment on s[d] Day and the towns acounts was Rede and aproven of (viz) John Hounters Will[m] Nickells Benjmen Thomptsons and David M[c]Callasters

then dismis[d] said meeting

Provance of Newhampshir

Londonderry March the 5th 1744/5

You are hereby Requiered to Warn all the freeholders and Inhabatance in your Respective Bounds to assemble and Meet at the old Meetinghous upon Wensday the twinty Day of this Instant at teen of the Clock before Noon then and thier

1 To see what Incorigment the town Will Give to the Volenteers of this town that Intends for the Expediton by this Gournment

2ly to see if the town Will Execpt of James Boyses fine fine as if he had served Counstable and this shall be your

Warant given under our hands the Day and year above Mentioned

Rob[t] Wallace
Tho[s] Horner
Tho[s] Cochran
Andrew Clendinin
Hugh Willson
Men select

to Joseph Bell Counstable for the Westerly side of Baver Brook

Provance of Newhampshir

Londonderry March the 20th 1744/5

I have posted up this Warant two publick Days as usuel

Pr Joseph Bell Counstable

the other Warant for said Meeting was Exemend and found Word for word so not Needfull to be put upon Record

Attests Pr Moses Barnett town Clerk

Provance of Newhampshir

Londonderry March the 20th 1744/5

then mete on said Day acording to the apointment of the warant and Chous for Moderator for s[d] meeting John Bleer

the first artickel of the warant being Considred it is Voted as the men Was not sent for and the town understood that the fleet was gon to pas this artickell at the present*

*This vote has reference to the Louisburg expedition. The first troops from New Hampshire, that started several days before the Massachusetts men left Boston, sailed from Portsmouth March 23d O. S., or April 4th N. S., 1745. This regiment of over five hundred men was under command of Col. Samuel Moore of Portsmouth. Dr. Matthew Thornton of Londonderry accompanied this body of soldiers as surgeon. The attack of the New England troops, in conjunction with the British seamen, was made upon June 17 of the same year, and upon June 20th the following men enlisted from Londonderry, serving during the rest of the campaign among the reinforcements sent to aid the first troops, all doing duty under Colonel Moore: John Adams, John Carter, Robert Cunningham, Andrew Logan, John McLaughlin, James McLaughlin, Samuel Miller, John Miller, Adam Gault, Patrick Gault, privates; Robert Kennedy, sergeant; Hugh Montgomery, ensign; Daniel McGregor, captain. It is possible others went from Londonderry, for there is no complete record to show the facts.—EDITOR.

2ly the second artick being Rede and Considered it is voted to Enter Down James Boys he serving as Counstalle for his fine

Provance of Newhampshir

Londonderry May 20th 1745

Pursuant to a presept or writ to us Directed from Thos Packer high shirif of the provonce of forsd for to Chose a Representative for this town aforsd in order that the said person so Chosen may Give his attandance the next sessions of Jenerall Assembly to be holden at portsmouth on the fifth Day of June next at ten of the Clock in the fore Noon you are hearby Requiered in his Majts Name to Warn the freeholders in your Respective bounds Duly Qualified by law to Elect Representative that thyMeet at the old meetinghous on Munday the third Day of June nixt at one of the Clock in the after Noon then and their

1 to Chouse or Elect one person Qualified by Law to Represent the said town In Generall assesembly and this shall be your Warant Given under our hands the Day and year above Mentioned

Thos Horner
Thos Cochran
Andrew Clendinin
Hugh Willson
Robt Wallace
Selectmen

to Samuel Dickey Counstable for the Westerly side of Beaver Brook

Londonderry June the 3: 1745

In obedeince to the Within Warant I have posted it two publick Days as usuall

Pr. me

Samuell Dickey Constable

the other Warant for said Meeting was Exemened and found word for word and so not Needfull to be put upon Record

attests P Moses Barnett
town Clerk

Provance of Newhampshir

Londonderry June the 3th 1745

then Mete the freeholders and Inhabitance of said Londry Qallified by Law the Meeting being legelly Called and Chus for Moderater for said Meeting Lift Hugh Willson

1 the first artickle of the Warant being Rede and Considered it is voted by the Eleetors then present that John MacMurphy Esqr shall Represent them in Jenerall asembly to be holden at portsmouth the fifth Day of this Instant at ten of the Clock in the fore Noon

Provance of Newhampshere

Londonderry September 2th 1745

You are hereby Requiered to Warn all the freeholders and Inhabitance in your Respective Bounds to assemble and mee at the old Meetinghous upon Munday the sixteen Day of September Instant at two of the Clok in the after Noon then and their

1 ly to see What sume of Money the town will allow to be Ressed for to Defray the Debts or Charges of this town for this present year

2ly to see wither the town will Repair the fence of the greave yeard at the old Meetinghous and fence the greav yeard at the hill Meetinghous

and this shall be your warant given under our hands the Day and year above Mentioned

Robt Wallace
Thos Horner
Andrew Clendinin
Hugh Willson
Select Men

to Samuell Dickey Counstable for the Westerly sid of Beaver Brook

Londonderry September 16th 1745

In obedence to the within warant I have posted it two publick Day

Pr Samuell Dickey Counstable

the other warant for s^{d} Meeting was Exemn^{d} and found word for word so not Needfull to be put upon Record

attests Pr Moses Barnett
town Clerk

Provance of Newhampshir

Londonderry Supt^{r} the 16th 1745

the freeholders and Inhabitance of Lond^{ry} Meete on S^{d} Day acording to the apointment of the warant it being legilly Called and voted for Moderator for S^{d} meeting John Bleer

1 ^{ly} the first artickle of the forgoing warant being Rede and Considered by the afor^{sd} Inhabitance itis voted that the select men is to bay two Barals of gunpouder for atown stock and said pouder when bought is to be Louged the one half in the old meetinghous and the other half in the new and it is further voted that the select men is to buld Close apartments in the Roofs of Said meetinghouses to secure S^{d} pouder

2 ^{ly} voted that the select men is to Reas and and asses two houndred pounds old tenner to Defray the town Debts for this year it is voted that the select men is to get the two grave yards fenced and the one at the old meetinghous fenc'd with Rocks and bords*

*The financial problem at this period was even more difficult of adjustment than at the present time. Mediums of exchange were scare, and the paper money issued by the courts of Massachusetts and New Hampshire depreciated in value very rapidly, and in 1741 the government was able to pay only one fourth of the face value of the "Bills of Credit," as they were known. Government undertook to remedy this evil by issuing in 1742 new bills, giving the year and value according to the old and new rates. These became known as "New Tenor," while previous issues were styled "Old Tenor." In order to meet the expense of the Louisburg expedition another emission was made in 1745, which created further confusion in the money market. Parliament then undertook to stop the colonial courts from issuing further paper money. Circumstances compelled them to make three issues during the French and Indian War, known as "New Tenor or Crown Point Bills." Fifteen shillings of this paper were equal to one dollar in specie. These bills soon depreciated, and finally sterling money became the standard in value, paper passing as currency regulated in its valuation by the price of silver.—ED.

Provance of Newhampshir

Londonderry febr^{ry} the 10th 1745/6

You are hereby Requiered to Warn all the freeholders and Inhabitance in your Respective bounds to asemble and meet at the old Meetinghous upon Wensday the fifth Day of March Next at Nine of the Clock in the fore Noon then and there

1 ^{ly} to Choose all the town and old parish officeres for the year Insuing

2 ^{ly} to see if the town will approue of the selectmens greement With Insin John Wiar for Nine Rhods and one half Rhode of Land for stragting of the graveyard fence

3 ^{ly} to see if the town Will alow Thos Campbell any allowence for fenceing of the grave yard at the old Meetinghous for he sayes that he is at agrete Loose by it

4 ^{ly} to see if the town Will Chuse aCommite to Clear the graveyarde and sow it With Heay seed

5 ^{ly} to see What the town Will do With the Mor Cloth and the Money that is goten for it

6 ^{ly} to hear the towns acounts Rede and aproven or not aproven of

and this shall be Warant given under our hands

Hugh Willson
Thos Cochran
Thos Horner
Robt Wallace
select men

to Samuell Dickey Counst^{bl} for the Westerly sid of Baver Brook

Londonderry march the 5th 1745/6

In obedence to the within Warant I have posted it up two publick Days

Pr Samuell Dickey Counstable

Note the other Warant for s^{d} meeting was Exemnd and found word for word so not Needfull to be put upon Record

attests P Moses Barnett town Clerk

Provance of Newhampshir

Londonderry March the 5th 1745/6

by vartu of the forgoing warant being legelly $Calle^{d}$ the freeholders and Inhabitance of Londondery Mete at the old Meetinghous on s^{d} Day and after Reeding the warant for s^{d} Meeting thy Chuse for Moderater for s^{d} meeting Lif^{tn} Hugh Willson

voted for five selectmen for the Insuing year and thy are as followeth Lif^{t} Hugh Willson Thos Horner Andrew Clendinin John Crumey James Wallace

voted for town Clerk for the Insuing year Moses Barnett

voted for tayithingmen of the Insuing year Janes m^{c}Keen Ju^{r} Samuell Boyd

voted for Counstable for the Esterly side of Baver Brook $Will^{m}$ Clendinin

Counstable for the Westerly side $Will^{m}$ Ears

voted for old parish Counstables John Wallace Samuell Miller

voted for survayers for the Esterly sid of Baver Brook Capt Mitchell Hugh Mungoumbrey Thos Campbell Lif^{t} Cochran Lif^{t} Willson David Hopkens Peeter Cristey arther Boyd

voted for survayers for the Westerly side of Baver Brook $Nalh^{ll}$ Holms James Tagart John Bleer Samuell Renken John Anderson Ju^{r} Samuell Senter John Pinkertown Robt Anderson Thos Hogg James Moor $Alex^{dr}$ McCollm John Hunter

Lather seler of the Insuing year voted Samuell Boyd

voted for Hoghourds for the Insuing year Samuell Peterson Joseph Scobay Gorg Clark James Willson Black

voted fence vawers and praysers James Moreson Thos Cochran

voted for Counters with the select men and Constables Sam^{ll} Barr John Bleer Moses Barnett

voted for tacking the Invoice $Alex^{dr}$ McNeell John Crombey Ju^{r}

voted to Inspect into Killing of Deer out of seson $Will^{m}$ Pirim Thos Wallace the third Joseph Moreson John Cromey Ju^{r}

the second artickell of the warant being Red and Considered it is voted to aprove of the select mens agreement With Insin John Wiar in paying for the Land tacken in to Mack the grave yard fence streght

this Meeting is ajorined untill tusday the Eight day of aprill Next at Eight of the Clock befor Noon

Londonderry aprill the 8th 1746

then Meete acording to the ajornment of the afor^sd Meeting and Voted upon the third artickell of the warant to allow Thomas Campbell fifteen pounds old tenner for ahelp to his former wages for fenceing the Grave yard at the Meetinghous becaus he Complen^d that he had two Little Wages by his bargain

it is voted upon the fourth artickel of the forgoing warant to pay for the palm Cloth as formerly and it is to be Contained in its Lodging where it Was and Moses Barnett is to have the fifth Shilling of what is got for s^d Cloth for his troble in tacking Care of it

voted that Robt Alex^dr is to Cleare the grave yarde of all Logs Reals and Brosh withen the saim at orbefore the first of augst Next and S^d Alexdr is to have fifteen shillings old tener for his trobl

voted upon the fifth artickle of the forgoing warant to aprove of the town acounts (viz) Samuell Allesons and Samuell Dickeys

the sixth artickell of the warant being Considred it is Voted by the Mager part of the Inhabetance being present to Lodg the one half of the towns store of amonition in old Capt Gregg and the other half of said store in Capt Barrs

Provance of Newhampshir

Londonderry June ye 16th 1746

Your are hereby Requiered to Warn all the freeholders and inhabitance in your Respective bounds to assemble and meet at the old Meetinghous upon Monday the thireyeth Instant at one of the Clock after Noon then and their

1 to see What Incorigment the town Will give to those

volenteers that have or May InList in this town for the present Expedition by this government

2 ly to see What sume of Money the town will vote to be assesed for the Defraying thier Charges for this present year

and this shall be your warant given under our hands the Day and year above Mentioned

Thos Horner
John Cromey
Andrew Clendinin
James Wallace
Hugh Willson
Select Men

to Mr William Clendinin town Counstable
posted two poblick Days acording to Costom
P Willm Clendinin Constable

Londonderry the 30th 1746

Then Mete acording to the apointment of the forgoing Warant it being legelly Called and Chuse for Moderater for sd Meeting John Bleer

the first artickell of the forgoing Warant being Red and Considered it is voted to Com to avote to Now wither the town Will give any Incoridgment or Not to vollunteers that gos out of the town to the present Expedition

it is voted to pass this first artickell untill the town be More Ripe to give avote upon that purtickeler

2 ly the second artickell being Red and Considered it is voted that the Select Men is to assess one houndred and forty pounds old tenner for to Defray the town Debts for this present year

Note the other Warant for sd Meeting was Red and Compard and found word for word and Not Needfull to be put upon Record

attests Pr Moses Barnett
town Clerk

Provance of Newhampshir

Londonderry January the 19th 1746/7

You are hearby Requiered to warn all the freeholders In

your Respective bounds to assemble and meet at the old meeting hous upon Monday the second Day of feb^{ry} next at ten of the Clock in the fore noon then and their

1 To see What the town will do with sum Lawsuts that are Leake to arise in their afers

2 ^{ly} to see What the town will do with Insine John Ramsey about apeace of ahighway that is Recorded in his feld Not for the benifit of any But the people Wants ahighway in that End of the town

3 ^{ly} to see what the town will do with Charls Stueart about ahigh way to go to to Meeting and Mill

and this shall be your Warant given under our hands the Day and year above Mentioned

Hugh Willson
John Cromey
Thos Horner
Andrew Clendinin
James Wallace
Select Men

To Willm Clendinin town Counstable

Provance of Newhampsher

Londonderry feb^{ry} the 2th 1746/7

In obedance to the within warant I have posted it up two Days acording to former Custom

P Willm Clendinin Counstable

the other warant for S^{d} Meeting was Rede and found word for word so not Needfull to be put upon Record

attests P Moses Barnett town Clerk

Provance of Newhampshir

Londonderry feb^{ry} the 2th 1746/7

Then Mette acording to the apointment of the forgoing warnt it being Legelly Called and Chuse for Moderater for said Meeting John Bleer

the first artickell of the forgoing warant being Read and Considered it is voted that the select men is to acte in this artickell acording to what advice Capt Sam^{ll} Barr Brings from the Bank the other two artickells of said warant being Read and Considred it is voted to pass them Both in the Negitve

Provance of Newhampshir

Londonderry febry the 10th 1746/7

You are hearby Requiered to warn all the freeholders and Inhabitance in your Respective Bounds to assemble and Meet at the old Meetinghous upon thorsday the fifth Day of March Next at Nine of the Clock in the for Noon then and their

1 To Choose all the town and old parish officers for the Year Insuing

2 ly to heare the towns acounts Rede and approven or not approven of

3 ly to see What the town Will Do with the Mor Cloth and the Money that is Gotten for it

and this shall be your warant Given under our hands the Day and Year above Mentioned

Hugh Willson
Thos Horner
Andrew Clendinin
James Wallace
John Cromey
select men

To Mr William Eayrs Town Counstable

Provance of Newhampsher

Londonderry March the 5th 1746/7

In obedence to the within warant I have posted it three publick Days

Pr me
William Earse Counstable

Note the other Warant for the aforsd Meeting was Rede and Exemened and found word for word so not Needfull to be put upon Record

attests P Moses Barnett Town Clerk

Provance of Newhampshir

Londonderry March the 5th 1746/7

By vertu of the forgoing warant it being legaly Called the

Inhabatence and freeholders of Lond[ry] Mete at their old Meetinghous on s[d] Day and after Reding the warant for s[d] Meeting thy Chuse for Moderator for s[d] Meeting Lif[t] Hugh Willson

voted by the afor[sd] freeholders and Inhabetance that there shall be five select Men for the Insuing year and there Names is as followeth Lift Hugh Willson Tho[s] Horner Andrew Clendinin John Cromey James Wallace

voted for assesers or Doomers for the Insuing year John Bleer Sam[ll] Barr Moses Barnett

voted for Town Clerk for the Insuing year Moses Barnett

voted for tayithingmen for the Insuing year Charls Cox Rob[t] Moreson Ju[n]

voted for town Counstables for the Insuing year Arther Boyd James Moore

Voted for Counstables for the old Parish for the Insuing year James Moreson John Brown James Moreson Jun[r]

James Moreson geting his son James Willing to serve for him was Exep[t'd] of by the town for the Insuing year

Voted for surviers for the Esterly side of Beaver Brook for the Insuing year Cap[t] John Mitchell Rob[t] Boys Esq[r] Rob[t] Mungombrey Lift Rob[t] Cochran Lift Hugh Willson Tho[s] Dunshee Arther Boyd Will[m] Clendinin

Voted for survairs for the Westerly side of Baver Brook for the Insuing year Peeter Cochran John Clark John Bleer Mathaw Ramsey Rob[t] Wallace Sam[ll] Dickey Archbald M[t] Murphy Sam[ll] Anderson Tho[s] Hogg James Moore Alex[dr] M[t] Collom Mathew Wright

Voted for Lather sealler for the Insuing year Samuell Boyd

Voted for Hogg Reves for for the Insuing year Sam[ll] Peterson John Karr Ju[r] Will[m] Adams Will[m] Dunken

voted for Counters with the select men and Counstables for the Insuing year Rob[t] Cochran Sam[ll] Barr Moses Barnett

voted for Invice Men for the Insuing year Alex[dr] M[t] Neell John Cromey Ju[r]

voted for Inspecters into the Killing of Deer for the Insuing year James Nesmith Ju[r] James Anderson Ju[r] James Moore Ju[r] Rob[t] Moor North

This Meeting is ajorn[d] untill Thorsday the Ninteenth Day of this Instant at twelf of the Clok

Provance of Newhampsher

Londonderry March the 19th 1746/7

then the freehoders and Inhabteants mete acording to the ajorinment of the afor[sd] Meeting and the second artickell of the afor[sd] Warant being Red and Considred it is voted by S[d] Meeting to aprove of the towns acounts thy being Red

the third artickell of the forgoing Warant being Red and Considred it is voted to Lodg the Mor Cloth in James Nesmeths for this Insuing year and S[d] Nesmeth is to Recive for the saim as formerly and it is voted S[d] Meeting that the select Men is to Count with Moses Barnett and Recive the Money that he has got for S[d] Cloth and hair as Much Money at the towns Cost to put along with the Money got from s[d] Barnett as Will bay aCloth which will be small for young Childer and it is to go at two Shillings and six pence to Each Corps

Provance of Newhampshir

Londonderry oct[br] the 12th 1747

You are hereby Requiered to warn all the freeholders and inhabitance in your Respective Bounds to assemble and meet at the old Meetinghous upon Monday the twinty sixth Day of this Instant at one of the Clock in the after noon then and their

1 to see What money the town will allow to be Reased to Defray the Debts or Charges for this present year

2ly to see what the town will do with that Bridg at Benj[mn] Willsons Mill it being in debet with windham

and this shall be your warant given under our hands the Day and year above

Hugh willson
John Cromey
James Wallace
Tho[s] Horner
select men

To m[r] Arther Boy[d] Town Constable

Provance of Newhampsher

Londonderry oct^{br} the 26th 1747

In obedance to the within warant I have posted it up two publick Days acording to Custon

P^{r} mee Arther Boyd Counstable

the other warant for S^{d} meeting being Red and Exemened and found Word for word so not Needfull to be put upon Recod

attests P Moses Barnett town Clerk

Lond^{ry} Oct^{br} the 26th 1747

In obedance to the within warant the freeholders and Inhabitence of S^{d} Lond^{ry} met on S^{d} Day the warant being legelly Called and Made Choice of Robt Boys Esqr for moderater for said meeting

the first artickell of the forgoing warant being Red and Considered it is voted that the select men shall asses or aplot theree houndred pounds old tenner upon the polls and Estats of the Inhabitence of Lond^{ry} for this present year for the payment of town and provance Reats

voted upon the second artickle of the forgoing warant by S^{d} Inhabitance as followeth that the Surviers belonging to the Bridg at Benjamen Willsons Mill is Left to alter it at their own plishour them Not Bringing any Charge upon the town for S^{d} Bridg

Provance of Newhampshir

Londonderry feb^{ry} the 1th 1747/8

You are hereby Required to warn all the freeholders and Inhabitance in your Respective Bounds to assemble and Meet at the old Meetinghous upon Monday the fiftenth Day of this Instant at ten of the Clock before Noon then and their

1 to see what the town will Do about apitition that windham have put in to the Jenerall Court to have this towns land lying in their town to pay Reats to them though Not setelled

and this shall be your warant Given under our hands the Day and Year above Mentioned

Hugh Willson
Andrew Clendinin
James Wallace
Select Men

To Mr Arther Boyd town Counstable

Provance of Newhampsher

Lond^{ry} feb^{ry} the 15th 1747/8

In obediance to the above warant I have posted it up two publick Days as usuell

Pr me Arther Boyd Counstable

the other warant for S^{d} Meeting was Red and Compar^{d} so Not Needfull to be put upon Record

attests Pr Moses Barnett town Clerk

Provance of Newhampshir

Londondery feb^{ry} the 15th 1747/8

In obedance to the within warant it being Legelly Called the freeholders and Inhabitance of S^{d} Lond^{ry} mete on s^{d} Day acording to the apointment of the forgoing warant and after Reeding the warant thy Made Choyse of Capt Andrew Todd for Moderter for S^{d} Meeting the warant being Rede and Considered it is voted by the afor^{sd} free holders and Inhabitance as followeth (viz) to Defend the pitition that is put into the Jenerall Court by the Inhabitance of windham to have our Common Lands Reated it is voted Leckwise by the afor^{sd} freeholders and Inhabitance to Chouse two Men to go S^{d} Court and Defend the Rights of S^{d} Lond^{ry} with full pow^{r} and outheraty as if the wholl Inhabitance were all personelly present and the mens Names that is Chosen to go to S^{d} Court by S^{d} Inhabitance is Capt Andrew Todd and Capt Sam^{ll} Barr

Provance of Newhampshir

Londonderry febe^{ry} the 10th 1747/8

You are hereby Requaired to warn all the freeholde and Inhabitance in your Respective Pounds to assemble and meet at the old Meetinghous upon Saterday the fifth Day of March Next a Nine of the Clock before Noon then and their

1 to Chuse all the town and old parish officers for the year Insuing

2ly to Heare the towns acounts Rede and aproven or Not aproven

and this Shall be your warant Given under our hands the Day and year above Mentioned

Hugh willson
Tho[s] Horner
John Cromey
James Wallace
Select Men

To M[r] Arther Boyd town Counstable

Provance of Newhampsher

Lond[ry] March the 5th 1747/8

In obedence to the forgoing warant I Have posted it up three publick Days acording to former Custom

P me Arther Boyd town Counstable

the other warant for S[d] Meeting was Red and Compar[d] and found Word for word so Not Needfull to be put upon Record

attests P Mo[s] Barnett town Clerk

Provance of Newhampshir

Lond[ry] March the 5th 1747/8

by vertue of the foregoing warant it being legely Called the free holders and Inhabitance of S[d] Lond[ry] Met acording to the apointment of the forgoing warant and after Reeding the warant for S[d] Meeting thy Made Choyse of Lif[t] Hugh willson for their Moderater to S[d] Meeting

voted to Chuse five select men for the Insuing year & thier Names is as followeth John Cromey James Wallace Tho[s] Horner Lif[t] John Humphra John Mitchell Ju[r]

voted for town Clerk for the Insuing year Mo[s] Barnett

Counstable for the Easterly sid of Baver Brook Chused S[d] office by Consent Arther Boyd

Counstable for the westerly side James Doage the town hes Excepted of James Doages son Rob[t] Doge to Serve Counstable in his fathers place for this Insuing year Rob[t] Doage voted for old parish Constables for the Insuing year John Alex[dr] Nineon Cochran

Voted for tithing Men for the Insuing year Rob[t] Clark Rob[t] Clendinin

Voted for Sirvayers for the Easterly sid of Baver Brook for the Insuing year Cap[t] John Mithell James Rodger Joseph Steell Lif[t] Rob[t] Cochran Halbart Moreson John Hopkens James Willson Gorge Moore Will[m] Hogg

Chosen Sirvairs for the westerly side of S[d] Brook for the Insuing yeare Peeter Cochran John Clark Tho[s] Willson David Dickey John Mack Rob[t] M[t]Clure Corly James Willson* Tho[s] Boyd Will[m] Smith John Barnett James Nesmeth Jun[r] John Scobey James Callwell

Chosen Lather sealer for the Insuing year Samuell Boyd

Voted for hogg Reves for the Insuing yeare John Stinson John wallace Ingles Range

fence vewers & praysers for the Insuing year John Stwart John Bleere

Chosen to tack Care of the select men and Counstables acounts Sam[ll] Barr Mo[s] Barnett Rob[t] Cochran

Chosen to tack the Invoice for the Insuing year Alex[dr] M[t]-Nell John Cromey

Chosen to Inspect into the Cilling of Deere for the Insuing yeare James Moore Canada John Anderson Jun[r] Sam[ll] Archbald Archbald M[t] Murphy

the towns acounts being Rede (viz) James Morrows and arther Boyds this Meeting is ajorned untill the second tusday of June Next at nine of the Clock before Noon at the old Meetinghous

Lond[ry] June the 14th 1748

Then Mete acording to the ajorenment of S[d] Meeting and Voted as followeth by the propri[ts] and Inhabitance of S[d] Lond[ry] to Chuse two propri[ts] and two non-Commenrs to pro-

*There being two James Wilsons they were distinguished by the designations of "Black Jim" and "Curly Jim," from the characteristics of their hair.—ED.

portion that twinty four pounds that was Spent at the Court by Cap[t] Todd and Cap[t] Barr to over torn the pition preferd to S[d] Court By Windham people the Mens Names is as followeth John Bleer John Moreson Rob[t] Clark Rob[t] Wallace all the Rest of the acounts is aproven of

Provance of Newhampshir

Londonderry March the 15th 1747/8

You are hereby Requiered to warn all the freeholders and Inhabitance in your Respa[t] bounds to assemble and meet at the old Meetinghous in Lond[ry] afor[sd] upon tusday the twinty Ninth of this Instant at ten of the Clock before Noon

To see what thy will allow of bounty to the Men that shall Inlist in this town in the provance servese above the provance Wajess

and this shall be your warrant given under our hands the Day and year above Mentioned

John Humphrey
John Cromey
James Wallace
select men

To M[r] Arther boyd Town Constable

Provance of Newhampsher

Lo: Derry March the 29th 1748

In obedince to the within warant I have posted it acording to Costom

P[r] Me Arther boyd town Counstable

The other warant for S[d] Meeting was Red[e] and found word for word so not needfull to be put upon Recod

attests Pr Moses Barnet town Clerk

Provance of Newhampshir

Lond[ry] March the 29th 1748

In obedance to the within warant it being legelly Cal[d] the free holders and Inhabitance of Lo: Derry Mete on sd Day acording to the apointment of the forgoing warant and Made Choice of John Macmurphy Esq[r] for their Moderater for S[d] Meeting the warant being Rede and Considered it is voted by S[d] freeholders and Inhabitance to allow abounty to the noumber of forteen men that Inlists in the provance servise out of S^d^ Lo: Derry and serves for S^d^ Derrys Cotto of provance service for this year of S^d^ nomber Voted by s^d^ freeholders & Inhabitance to give Eight pounds old tenner to Each of the afos^ad^ Nomber of Men that Serves in S^d^ service for this year

Lond^ry^ March the 29th 1748

John Bleer Enters his Desent against the acttings of the afor^sd^ Meeting

Provance of Newhampsher

Londonderry September ye 15th 1748

You are hereby Requiered to warn all the freeholders and Inhabitance in your Respective Bounds to assemble and Meet at the old Meetinghous in Lond^ry^ upon wansday the twinty Eight of this Instant at ten of the Clock before Noon then and their

1 To see what money the town will allow to be assesed for to Defray Charges that is in the town and will be in the town this present year

2^ly^ To See if the town will Com to En Equallent or Division of the high ways in Each Destrick in the town

3^ly^ To see if the town will Chuse aproper and fite person or persons to survay and Inspect the linens and hollands made in this town for seal that so the Credete of our Manefectars may be keept up and the bayers and purshers of our linens may Not be Imposed upon with foraign and outlandish Linens in the name of ours or any other Mathod that may be thought proper and necerey for that End as may be agrreed upon

and this shall be your warant Given under our hands the Day and Year above Mentioned

John Cromey
James Wallace
Thos Horner
John Mitchell
John Humphry
select men

To Mr Arther Boyd town Counst for the Easterly side of Baver Brook

Provance of Newhampshir
In obideance of the within warant I have posted it acording to Costom

P me Arther Boyd Couns^{t}

The other warant for S^{d} meeting was Rede and Compard and found word for word so not Needfull to be put upon Record

attests P Mo^{s} Barnett town Clerk

Provance of Newhampshir

Lond^{ry} Sep^{tr} the 28th 1748

In obidence to the within warant it being Legelly Call^{d} the freeholders and Inhabitance of S^{d} Lond^{ry} mate on S^{d} Day and made Choys of John Mt Murphy Esqr for thier Moderater for S^{d} Meeting

the first artickell of the warant being Rede and Considered it is voted by S^{d} freeholders and Inhabitance that the select men of S^{d} Lond^{ry} is to aplot or asses four houndred and twinty pounds old tenner to Defray the town Debts for this present year

2^{ly} the second artickell of the forgoing warant is voted to be past for this time

3^{ly} The third artickel of the forgoing warant being Rede and considered by S^{d} Inhabitance thy voted that the select men of S^{d} Lond^{ry} is to portchis seals to seal all the Linens that is made in S^{d} Lond^{ry} and it is voted by said propri^{ts} that John Macmurphy Esqr and John Wallace yoman shall be Sealers and Inspecters of all the Hollands and Linens that are made or to be made in our town whither brown white spackled stript or chak^{d}

That are to be Exposed to seal untill our anuall Meeting in March next for the Choise of town officers and that thy shall be upon oath to the faithfull Discharge of their trust and that the s^{d} sealers and Inspecters shall seal any of the afor^{sd} Linens with astamp in Each End of the peace of Cloth with the words (Londonderry in Newhampshire and Give a Certificate to the persons that are owners of the Cloth of their so doing for which stamp Inspection and sertificate thy shall Recive from the owners of S[d] Linens sixpence old tenner for Each peace and when the said sealers and Inspecters shall suspect any Linens Brought to be Marked not Made and Manafactered in this town thy shall be Invested with power to have the oath or oathes of any Suspected person or persons Conserning the same and also that there shall be one or more sutable persons Chosen by the town to Pitition the Gen[ll] assembley of this provance when siting to have aspeciall act of Gov[t] for the Good purposses afor[sd]

and if the Gen[ll] Court find that the town in thier vote have not Gaurded sufficeently against any fraud that Might be purpetrated in the afor[sd] affair or any other thing nesecery for the Intended Good purposses that thy wo[d] please to add in s[d] act any and Everything that might be Needfull for the Ends afor[sd]*

*The first settlers of Londonderry, as well as introducing the cultivation of the potato in this country, were the pioneer manufacturers of linen cloth, which for many years was a leading source of profit in New England. Mills were erected within two years of the coming of these sturdy builders of a new town. In this enterprise, however, they met with difficulties from unscrupulous parties and were forced to seek the courts for redress and protection, as witness the following action:

In the House &c May 7th 1721.

Whereas there are great frauds and deceipt practised by p'sons travelling in this Province by selling of Foreign Linens, under pretence they were made at Londonderry in this Province, which tends to the Damage of those who realy make and sell the Linen in Londonderry, and to evade the Act made by this Goverm[t] agt Hakwing & Pedling, &c.; For prevention of which, & for encouraging the manufacturing Linnen in said Town,

Voted, That an Act be drawn up authorizing the said Town to make choice of a suitable p'son to Seal all such Linen as shall be made in the said Town, and to have a seale with the name of the Town engraved on it, & authority to such sealer (if Suspect y[t] 'twas not made in the Town) to adm[r] an oath to the p'sons that brings Linen to be sealed, that it was bona fide made in said Town.—Ed.

Provance of Newhampsher

Londonderry Dec^{br} ye 17th 1748

You are hearby Requiered in his Maj^{tes} Name to warn all the free holders and Inhabitance in your Respective bounds that are Quallifed in Law for Voters to assemble and Meet at the old Meeting hous in Lon^{d} afor^{sd} upon Monday the Second Day of Jan^{ry} next at ten of the Clock in the fore Noon then and their

To Elect on parson Quallifid by Law to Represent the s^{d} town In Gen^{rl} assembley to be Convined and holden at porsmouth on the third Day of Jan^{ry} Next at ten of the Clock in the for Noon

John Cromey
Thos Horner
James Wallace
John Mitchell Junr
John Humphry
select Men

To Mr Arther Boyd Cons^{bl} for the Easterly sid of Baver Brook

Lond^{ry} Jan^{ry} the 2th 1748/9

In obedence to the within warant I have posted it acord^{n} to former Costom

P Arther Boyd Constable

The other warant for s^{d} Meeting Exemened and found word for word so not Needfull to be put upon Record

attests P Mo^{s} Barnett
town Clerk

Provance of Newhampsher

Lond^{ry} Jan^{ry} the 2^{d} 1748/9

In obidence to the forgoing warant it being Legelly Called the freeholders and Inhabitance of Lond^{ry} and windham assembled and Meete on s^{d} Day and after Reeding s^{d} warant thy Made Choice of Capt And^{w} Todd for Moderater for s^{d} Meeting the artickle of the forgoing warant being Rede and Considered the Electors of Lond^{ry} and Windham Made Choice of John Macmurphy Esqr to Represent them In Generall assembley and So Dismised

Provance of Newhampshir

Londonderry feberry ye 16th 1748/9

You are hearby Requiered to warn all the freeholders and Inhabitance in your Respective Bounds to assemble and Meet at the old Meetinghous on Monday the sixth Day of March Next at nine of the Clock before Noon then and thier

1^t^ To Choose all the town and old parish officers for the Insuing year

2^ly^ To see if the town will mack an acte for the term of time that the Law allows of in Every town of the provance and that is to mack or put a fine on all such persons that Do Not Make aRetorn of the Names of such persons that Coms into the town as borders or as trangent persons Coming in to the town and such persons that Entertans Such and Do Not Mack aRetorn of such persons Names to the select Men for time being may be thought Gilty of Damage to the town

3^ly^ To see if the town will Com to an Equallent of the high ways in the town in proportion of the Surviers in S^d^ town

4^ly^ To here the towns acounts Rede and approven or Not approven of

and this shall be your warant Given under our hands

Jo^n^ Cromey
Thos Horner
John Mitchell Ju^r^
John Humphry
James Wallace
select Men

To Mr Arther Boyd Couns^tl^ on the Easter^y^ sid of Baver Brook

Provance of Newhampshir

Lond^ry^ March the 6th 1748/9

In obideance to the within prrespt I have posted it acording to Costom

P^r^ me Aarther Boy^d^ town Counstable

the other warant for Sd Meeting was Rede and Exemen^d^

and found word for word so Not Needfull to be put upon Record

attests P Mo^{s} Barnett town Clerk

Provance of Newhampshir

Lond^{ry} March the 6th 1748/9

By vartu of the forgoing warant it being Legelly Called the Inhabitance and freeholders of Sd Lond^{ry} Mate at the first Meetinghous of s^{d} Lond^{ry} on S^{d} Day and after Reeding the warant for S^{d} Meeting thy voted for Moderater for S^{d} Meeting Robt Boys Esqr

Voted for five select Men for the Insuing Year thier Names is as followeth John Cromey John Humphry John Mitchell Ju^{r} James Morrow Peeter Cristey

Voted for town Clerk for the Insuing year Mo^{s} Barnett

Voted for town Counstables for the Insuing year David Anderson Jo^{n} Anderson Ju^{r}

Voted for old parish Counstabls for the Insuing year Halbart Moreson John Moore

Taything Men Chouson for the Insuing year Robt Clark Willm Gregg

Survayrs Choson for the Insuing year on the Easterly side of Baver Brook In^{s} Jo^{n} Wiar Hugh Ramsey Robt Alexd^{r} Ju^{r} Banjamen Thomptson Thos Davidson John Cochran Ju^{r} John Mitchell Ju^{r} Robt Ridell John Carr

Survayers Chosen for the Insuing year on the westerly sid of s^{d} Brook Charls Mt Clorge Robt Boyd Sam^{ll} Boyd Sam^{ll} Renken Robt Wallace Willm White Willm Betey John Stell Joseph Boys Joseph Bell James Moore John Wallace James Callwell

Chose for Lather Sealer for the Insuing year David Hopkens

Chose for Hog Reavis for the Insuing year Hugh Ramsey Nath^{ll} Aken

Chose for fence vers and praysers for the Insuing year John Bleer John Stwart

Chose for Countes with the select men and Counstables for the Insuing year Sam^{ll} Barr Robt Cochran Moses Barnett

Chose for Inspecting into the Killing of Dear for the Insuing year Sam[ll] Archbald Tho[s] Willson Cannad Arther Nesmeth Daniell Lesley

Chose for the Sealers of Linen for the Insuing year Rob[t] Boys Esq[r] John Wallace

The second artickell of the forgoing warant being Rede and Considered it is voted to ajorn it untill further Consideration

the 3 artickell of the forgoing warant being Considered it is past

the forth artickell being Considered it is voted to approve of all the towns acounts that was Rede (viz) Lif[t] John Humphrys Arther Boyds and Rob[t] Dooaks as far as thy had Discounted

Joseph Boys John Hillands and David Baverlend Enters thier Desent against having two surviers of high ways in their part of the town where thy usuelly had But one

Provance of Newhampshir

Londonderry April y[e] 13th 1749

You are hereby Requiered to warn all freeholders and Inhabitance in your Respective bounds to assemble at the old Meetinghous upon friday the fifth Day of May Next at two of the Clock in the after Noon then and thier

1 [ly] to see if the town will approve or Note approve of agramer school in the town for the present year for som of the Inhabitance of the town have Charged us the select Men of the town for to provide aGramer school Master in the town and if Not thy will take the benifite of the law: and we have Provided a Gant[l] Man for that End and if the town thinks it Not fiting to have one for the present yeare and pass avote to Clear the Select Men of the fine that the law Exacts upon them for Not keeping of one and if the town vots to have None then we will pay the Gant[l] Man for the time by past

2 [ly] To see if the town will allow pay to the select Men for Laying out of high ways in the town and any other thing that the town Shall think Nessecery for the benifite of the town

and this be your warant Given under our hands the and year above

Jo^{n} Cromey
Jo^{n} Mitchell Ju^{r}
Peeter Cristy
Jo^{n} Humphry
select men

To Mr David Anderson Town Counstable for the Easterly side of baver Brook

Provance of Newhampshir

Lond^{ry} May the 5th 1749

I have posted this warant acording to former Costom

P me David Anderson Counstale

The other warant for s^{d} Meeting was Rede and Comperd and found word for word so Not Needfull to be pute upon Record

attests P Mo^{s} Barnett Town Clerk

Lond^{ry} May the 5th 1749

In obidance to the forgoing warant the freeholders and Inhabitance of S^{d} Lond^{ry} Mete on s^{d} Day and after Reeding the warant for s^{d} meeting thy made Choys of Mr John Bleer for their Moderater

the first artickle of the forgoing warant being Rede and Considred it is voted by S^{d} Inhabitance wheras the Inhabitance of S^{d} town thinks thy are More Benefited by their schools as thy have them in all parts of the town than thy Can be by agramer school and Nobodey appeering to Insist for one and it is voted to pass this artickell and Chuse aCommishener to Go to the Quarter Seshens to see if we Can be Relivd of the same and the select men is to Chuse and send s^{d} Commishener and if thier be any ill Minded person that will Complean upon the select men for want s^{d} scholl that then the town is to pay all the Charges that will increw to the select Men

The second artickell of the forgoing warant being Rede and Considered it is voted by sd Inhabitance Note to allow the select Men any pay for Laying out highways and so Dismis^{d}

Provance of Newhampsher

Lond^{ry} Sep^{tr} ye 13th 1749

You are hereby Requiered to warn all the freeholders and Inhabitance in your Respective Bounds to Meet at the old Meetinghouse upon wadenday the twinty seventh Day of this Instant at three of the Clock after Noon then and thier

1 To see what money the town will allow to be assesed for Defreying of Charges for the present and allso for to have the towns acounts Rede and approven or Not approven

2 ^{ly} To see if the town will Run En Equall Chance with those men that Give Bounds for Capt Mitchells Inlargment since we all beleve in aJudgment of Chaety that he is Clear of the Charge laid against him and whatsoever Ellse may be thought Needfull on that affear and to acte there on

and this shall your warant Given under our hands the Day and year above Mentioned

Peeter Cristey
Jo^{n} Mitchell Ju^{r}
John Humphry
men select

To Mr David Anderson Counstable in the Easterly side of Baver Brook

Lond^{ry} Sep^{tr} the 27th 1749

In obidance to the forgoing warant I have posted it two publick Days acording to Costom

P David anderson Counstable

the other warant for Sd Meeting was Rede and Exemen^{d} and found word for word so note Needfull to be put upon Record

attests P mos Ba^{t} town Clerk

Provance of Newhampsher

Lond^{ry} Sep^{tr} the 27th 1749

In obedance to the for going warant it being Legellay Called the freeholders and Inhabitance of S^{d} Lond^{ry} mete ons^{d} Day and after Reding the warant for s^{d} meeting s^{d} freehorders and Inhabitance made Choys of Lif^{t} Hugh willson for their moderater for s^{d} Meeting

The first artickle of S^{d} warant being Rede and Considered it is voted to approve of the towns acounts that was Rede

Voted Leckwise by S^{d} freeholders and Inhabitance that the select men of s^{d} town is to applote or assess the Sume of three houndred pounds old tenner for this present year (viz) in order to pay the Houndred and forty pounds that was expended upon Capt John Mitchells being Confined and the Ren^{d} to pay the towns Debts*

The second artickell of the forgoing warant being Rede and Considered it is voted by the for^{sd} freehord^{rs} and Inhabitance that thy will pay equally their proportion of what Damage will Com upon John Macmurphy Robt Boys Andrew Todd Sam^{ll} Barr Mo^{s} Barnett and John Mitchell Ju^{r} Relating to abond that the afor^{sd} Gentl^{men} Give to the high Shirive

*This act of the town relates to a difficulty that one of her most respected citizens had encountered. In 1749 Jotham Odiorne, of Portsmouth, a wealthy man and a man of considerable political prominence, incurred the enmity of parties unknown to him. These men sent him several threatening letters, and finally declared that unless he deposited three hundred pounds "at the westerly end of the long bridge, which is between Kingston and Chestar," within two days his buildings would be burned and his life jeopardized. Hoping to discover the identity of the writer the money was deposited as directed and three men stationed near by to watch for the other.

Before these men appeared to get the concealed money John Mitchell, on his way to Portsmouth, reached the place, and, stopping his horse, dismounted near the spot where the money had been deposited. Thinking they had discovered the culprit, the men employed by Mr. Odiorne arrested Mr. Mitchell, and, in spite of his protestation or ignorance in regard to the affair, bore him to Portsmouth, where he was placed in jail to await his trial. Public sentiment was against him, and even the lawyers refused to defend him. In this dilemma Rev. Mr. David MacGregor, pastor of the West Parish church, and third son of Rev. James MacGregor, convinced of the innocence of his parishioner, volunteered to aid him. If lacking a lawyer's legal tact to look after the interests of his client, Mr. MacGregor made an ingenious and able defence in behalf of the prisoner. Still he was unable to clear him, and he was convicted and sentenced to one thousand pounds and cost. Not being able to pay this, he was kept in prison. Still the faithful Mr. MacGregor did not desert him, and through his efforts largely he was finally released on a bond. This had to be renewed frequently, and caused much trouble and expense before Mr. Mitchell was at last honorably acquitted, though there is nothing to show that he was ever able to obtain any redress for the wrong done him.—ED.

of S^{d} provance for Capt John Mitchell Inlargment or for any further Inlargment that thy Can procure for S^{d} Mitchell to Get him out of confinment we the afor^{sd} freeholders and Inhabitance of s^{d} Lond^{ry} Clearing all Damages that may Increw upon them for sodoing

Province of Newhampshier

Londonderry feber^{y} 9th 1749/50

Yow are heirby Required to warn all the freeholders and Inhabitents in your Respective bounds to assemble at the old Mettinghouse upon Monday the fifth day of March nixt at nine of the Clock before Noon then and there

1 To Chose all the town & old parish officers for the present year

2^{ly} to See if the town will allow of agrammar Schooll in the toun for Som persons are Calling for one.

3^{ly} To See if the toun will Chuse three or five or Seven or Nine Meet persons for to Judge and determin all Causes that is brought before them in S^{d} toune and to act theron as the toune sees Cause.

4^{ly} To See whither the toune will allowe aroad across Justice Boyces and to Evade the greate hill above Willm McMasters going to heaver hill or let it goe where S^{d} Mc Master Avrs and to act theron

5 ^{ly} To See if the toune will abate James M^{c} keen being ratted by windham for his Cattell that he keeps one the heay that he mowes on his land in S^{d} windham

6^{ly} To hear the touns aCounts read and aprove or not approve.

and this shall be your warrant given under our hands the day & year above

John Cromey
Petter Cristey
John humphry
John Mitchell Junr
Select Men

To David Anderson Constable in the Easterly side of beaver brook

Londonderry March 5th 1749/50

In obedience to this warrant I have posted the Same acording to law

David Anderson Constable

Provance of Newhampshier

Londonderry March 5th 1749/50

By vertow of the foregoing warrant it being Legaly Caled the Inhabitents and freeholders of Sd londy Meet at the old Metting house on Sd day and after reading the warrand for Sd Meeting they voated for Modrator for Sd Meeting Lievt Hugh willson

Voated for five selectmen for the Insuing year their Names are. John Cromey Samll Morison Lievt Robt Cochran Alex: Celso John Barnit

Voated for toun Clark for the ensug yar James Nesmith

Voated for Constable for the Eastrly Side James Stell

Voated for Constable for the west side of beaver brook Willm Cox

Voated for old parish Constables or Colectors Alex: McCollom Ranald Alexander

Voated for taithing men for the ensuing Year James Callwall John Morison Junr Jas Son Willm White

Voated for Surviors for the Easterly Side of beaver brook John Morison Robert Morison Junr Samll Miller Lievt Robert Cochran Robert fairservice Lieut Hugh Willson Nathanll Mertin Alex: Mc Neall Robt Mc Curdey

Voated for Serviers for the westerly Side of beaver brook Livet Samll Gregg James tagart Thoms Willson James Ramsey John Tagart Peter Petterson John Pinkerton Samll Anderson Neall Tagart Willm Duncan Samll Boice Willm Adams James aken

Voated for leather Sealer for this Ensuing year David Hopkin

Voated for hoghouards for the Enshuing year David Mountgumrey Robert Craige George Moore

Voated for fence veors for the Ensing year John Barnit John Stewart voated for Counters with the Select men and Constabls for the Ensuing year Captn Samll Barr Luiett Hugh Wilson Capn Moses Barnit

voated for taking the Invoice for the Ensuing year Alex: Mc Neall John Cromey Junr

voated for Inspecting into the killing of Deer for the ensuing year Joseph Senter James Nesmith Junr

Voated for Sealling of Linning for the Euseuing year Robert Boice Esqr John Wallace

Voated on the Second article as followeth to pass this article for this time

voated on the third article as foloueth to pass it

Voated on the fourth of Sd warrant to Chuse five men aComtee to Joyn the Sellectmen to vew the Roads that Goes throw Esqr Boice farm and the Commties Names is Capt John Mitchell Capt Andrew todd Thos wilson James Clark James Nesmith and they are to be Sworn to the faithfull Discharge of their office.

then this mitting is ajorned untill Munday the 26 Day of this instant at two a Clock. after Noon

Londonderry March 26th 1750

Then the freeholders & Inhabitents of Londonderry Meet acording to ajurnment and voated on the fifth article of Sd warran as followeth, that James Mckeen is to be Exempted of the money that he payes to windham Constable for this year.

The Sixt article of the warrant being Considred it is voated to aprove of all the touns acounts that was then read

Province of Newhampshire

Londonderry Septr 5th 1750

Yow are heirby Required to warn all the freeholders and Inhabitents in your Respective bounds that they Meet at the old Meettinghouse upon teusday the eightenth Day of this Instant at one of the Clock afternoon then and there

1 To See what money they will allow to be Raised to Defray the touns Charges this year

2ly To see what they will do with the touns Stock of Pouder

And this Shall be your Warrant Given under our hands the day and year above Mentioned

John Barnit
Alex: Kelsey
John Cromey
Sam^{ll} Morison
Lev^{t} Robt Cochran
Commti^{e}

to James Stell toun Constable

Londonderry Sepb^{r} 18th 1750

In obedience to the within warrant I have posted up S^{d} warrant as usewall

p^{r} me James Stell Constb

By verteow of the foregoing warrant it being legaly Called the the Inhabetents & freeholders of S^{d} Londerry Meet and after Reading the warrant for S^{d} Meetting they Chuse for moderator Lewt^{t} Hugh willson

The first article of S^{d} warrant being Read and Considred it is voated that the Select men is to Rise two hundred pounds old tennor for defraying the touns Debts for the present year

The Second Article being Considred it was thought proper to pass it over for the present

Province of Newhapshire

Londonderry feber^{y} 15th 1750/1

Yow are herby Required to warn all th freeholders and Inhabitents in your Respective bounds to assemble and Meet at the old Meettinghouse upon Tusday the fifth Day of March Nixt at ten of the Clock before Noon then and there.

1 To Choose all the toun and old parish officers for the year Enshuing

2^{ly} To See if the toun will Chose a Commtie to make an Equall Devison of the highways and poals in this toun

3^{ly} To hear the towns acounts read and aprove or not aprove the Same

4^{ly} To See if the towne will allow Ensign John Ramsey any pay for his Extraordnary truble with widow Shiels

And this Shall be your warrant given under our hands the day and year above Mentioned

John Barnitt
Alex: Kelsey
Sam[ll] Morison
Liev[t] Robert Cochran
Selectmemm

To M[r] James Stell town Constable

London[y] March 5th 1750/51

In obedience to the within warrant I have posted it up as usewall

James Stell Constable

Londonderry March 5th 1750/51

By Vertue of the foregoing warrant it being Legaly Caled The Inhabitents and freeholders of S[d] Lond[y] Mett at the old Mittinghouse on S[d] Day and after Reading the warrant for S[d] Mitting they voted for Modrature Live[t] Hugh willson

Voted for 5 Select Men for this Enceuing year their Names is Leiv[t] Rob[t] Cochran Alex: Kelsey John Holms, Sam[ll] Morison Joseph Scobey

Voted for toun Clark James Nesmith.

Voated for Constables Daniell M[c]Dufie Nathaniell Aekin M[c]Dufie Refusing to serve voated for Cons[ble] John Hopkin he refus[d] to serve voated for Consta[le] James Willson

Voated for old parish Constabls Robert M[c] Curdey James Willson

Voated for tything Men John Stewart Joseph Cochran Piter peterson David Hunter

Voated for Surveirs for the Easterly Side of Beaver brook Cap[t] Moses Barnitt James M[c]Gregor Cap[t] John Gregg Liv[t] Hugh Willson Joseph Morison Liev[t] Robert Cochran Will[m] Karr Tho[s] Cristey Will[m] Kelsey Halbert Morison

Voated for Surviers for the westerly Side of beaver brook Joseph Cochran John Clark Tho[s] Willson Sam[ll] Renkin Rob[t] Walace Piter peterson will[m] Beetty John Stell Tho[s] M[c] Cleary John Duncan James Moore Will[m] Adams James Evins

Voated for Leather Sealer David Hopkin

Voated for Howards for this year John Gillmor Hugh Moore Archebald Cunigham

Voated for fencever for this year Willm Eiers John Stewart

Voated for Searching the towns acounts Cap^n^ Sam^ll^ Barr Lieu^t^ Hugh Willson Cap^n^ Moses barnitt

Voated for taking the Envoice John M^c^keen John Cromie

Voated for Inspecting ovor the dears Joseph Senter James Nesmith Junr

This Miting is ajurned untill the 27 day of this instant at teen of the Clock,

Met on the abovs^d^ day of ajurnment and

2 voated on the Second article of the foregoing warran and paSed it in the Negitive

3 Voated on the third article that the acounts of the year 1750 is Not to be aproved of untill they be paid up by the Constables

4 voated on the fourth article that the Selectmen is to goe to Mr John Ramseys and Compair John Ramseys acount with the bond that is in Mr John Blairs hand and Make a-return at the Nixt Mitting to the toune

Province of Newhampshire

Londonderry March 9th 1750/51

Yow are herby Required to warn all the freeholders and Inhabitents in your Respective bounds to assemble and Meet at the old Mitting house upon wensday the twinty Seventh day of this Instant at ten of the Clock before Noon then and there

To See what Method they will take to Defend there Charter right and act thereon

And this Shall be your warrant Given under our hands the Day and year above Mentioned

Sam^ll^ Morison
Joseph Scobey
Robt Cochran
Seleetmen

To Mr Nathanill Aekin Toun Constable

Londonderry March 27th 1751

In obedience to the within warrant I have posted it up as usewall

Nathaniell Aekin toun Constable

Londonderry March 27th 1751

By vertue of the foregoing warant it being legaly Caled the freeholders and Inhabetents Mett at the old Metting house on Sd day and after the reading of Sd warrant for Sd Metting they voated for Moderator Robert Boice Esqr

Voated upon the article of Sd warrant to leave it for further advice, and Desmist Sd Metting

Province of Newhampshire

Londonderry Agust 12th 1751

Yow are heirby Required to warn all the freeholders and Inhabitants in your Respective bounds to assemble and Meet at the old Meettinghouse upon Wensday the twinty Eight day of this Instant at ten of the Clock before Noone then and there

1 To See how Much Money they will allow to be Raised this year to defray the touns Charges

2ly To See what they will do in Regard of apition presented by Thos George and one Merrill with others for to have aStrip of off the side of this toun to Make anew parish at or Near amuskeage

3 ly To See how Many taverns they will allow to be in toun and where Sittuated and lay down some Method to prevent amultiplicity of tavrns in this toun

4 ly to See what they will do in Regard of Danied Mc-Duffie and John Hopkin being Chosen Constables and would Not Serve

5 ly to hear the touns acounts Read and aprove or Not aprove of the Same

And this Shall be your Warrant Given under our hands the day and year above Mentioned

Alex: Kelsey
Joseph Scobey
Samll Morison
Robt Cochran
Seleetmen

To Mr James Willson toun Constable

Londonderry Agust 27 1751

In obedience to the within Warrant I have posted it up as usewall

p[r] Me James Willson Constable.

In obedience to the foregoing warrant the free-holders and Inhabetents of S[d] Londe[y] Meet and after reading of S[d] warrant they Chuse for Moderator Cap[n] Sam[ll] Barr

1 Voated on the first article of S[d] warrant that the Selectmen is to raise on hundred & fifty pounds old tennor to Defray the touns Charges

2[ly] Voated to grand the prayer of the petition of Tho[s] George, and one Merrill & others this farr (viz) begining at the pine tree N[o] 134 and run South half amile into Derry tounship and then awest line or point to Derry toun line providing that they of the New parish or toun, to be Incorprated Shall Not Reate our land till Setteled also that John M[c] Murphey Esq[r] is to apear at Court to See that the thing May be don acording to this Voat*

3[ly] Voated that the third article is passed in the Negative

4[ly] Voated that the Reasons that Daniell M[c]Duffie & John Hopkin his given for there Not Serving Constables is suficant and so Clears them.

5[ly] Voated on the fifth article that the touns a Counts is aproven of as farr as they were read

Province of Newhampshire

Londonderry feber[y] 18th 1751/2

Yow are hereby Required to warn all the freeholders and Initents in your Respective bounds to assemble And Meet at the old Meetinghouse upon Thursday the fifth day of March Nixt at ten of the Clock before Noon then and there

1 To Choose all the toune and old parish officers for the present year

2[ly] to hear the touns acounts Read and aprove or not aprove of the Same

*The reader is referred to "Early Records of Derryfield, Vol. 1, pages 17 to 20, for the charter to this territory, and the action of the inhabitants of the new township.—Ed.

3[ly] to See whither the toun will allow Ensign John Ramsey what the Sellectmen Judge was his dew in regard of his troubell about Widow Sheells or whither they will allow him Some More or Not

And this Shall be your Warrant Given under our hands the day and year above Mentioned

Samwell Morison
John Holms
Joseph Scobey
Alex: Kelsey
Robert Cochran
Select Men of Londonderry

To M[r] Nathaniell ackin toun Constable

Londonderry March 5th 1751/2

The within warrant have been posted acording to the Common Custom by Me

Nathaniell Ackin toun Constable

The other Warrant bing Compair[d] and found Word for word thought it Not Needfull to be put upon record

attests James Nesmith toun Clark

Londonderry March 5th 1751/2

By Vertue of the foregoing warrant it being legaly Called the Inhabitences and freeholders Meet at the old Meeting house on S[d] Day and after Reading the warrant for S[d] Meeting they Chuse for Moderatur Liev[t] Hugh Willson

1 article Voted that the toun will have 5 Select Men for this year there Names are Cap[n] John Mitchell Alex: Kelsey John Wallace Sin[r] Sam[ll] Alison Jun[r] Joseph Scobie

Voted for toun Clark James Nesmith

Voted for Constable for the East Side of beaver brook Will[m] Kelsy

Voted for Constable for the Westerly Side of bever brook John Steell

Voted that the toun Excpted of John Clark to Serve as Constable in the room of John Stell

Voted for Colectors for the old parich Alex: Walker Robert Craige

Voted for tithing Men for the present year Hugh Ramsey Joseph Boice Tho[s] Wallace Jun[r]

Voted for Sirviers for the Easterly Side of beaver brook James M[c]keen Liev[t] Hugh Mountgomry James Anderson Gabriell barr John Hopkin Will[m] Clendinin Pitter Cristy Archebald Cunigham Tho[s] Davison

Voted for Surviers for the westerly Side of baver brook Nathaniell Holms James Tagart Daniell Lasly Sam[ll] Renkin Sam[ll] fisher Sam[ll] Dickey John pinkerton Sam[ll] Smith Will[m] Hogg Daniell M[c]Mullan James Nismith Jun[r] Robert Moor Sam[ll] Miller John Scobey

Voted for Lather Sealler for this year Tho[s] M[c]Clirey at the ajurnment they Choose David Hopkins in Stead of Tho[s] M[c]Clirey

Voted for Hewards for the present year James Miller Daniell Ellet Robert Alexander

Voted for fence veuers for this year Cap[n] Samuell Barr Robert Wallace

Voted for Searching the touns acounts Cap[n] Sam[ll] Barr Cap[n] Moses Barnit Liev[t] Hugh Willson

Voted for taking the Envoice John Crumey Daniell Lesly

2 voted on the Secont article of the warrant that the toun aproved of the Select Mens acounts for the year 1750

Then ajurned this Metting untill the Second teusday of May at ten of the Clock in the fore Noon

Londonderry May 12th 1752

3 Then the freeholders and Inhabitents Meet acording to ajurnment and voted upon the third article of the foregoing Warrant that they would Not allow John Ramsey any thing of the acount that he brought against Jean Shields

Province of Newhampshire

Londonderry Agust 22th 1752

In pursuance of his Maj[ts] writ to us by the Shirf of the province aforeS[d] Yow are heireby Required to warn all the freeholders belonging to the toun of Londonderry that they Meet at there first Metinghouse upon the first Monday of Sep^{br} Nixt at Seven of the Clock before Noon then and there to Elect or Chuse arepresentive for the S^{d} toun

and this Shall be your warrant Given under our hands the day and year above Mentioned

John Mitchell
John Wallace
Sam^{ll} Alison
Sellect-Men

To Mr Willm Kelsey Constable in the toun aforeS^{d}

Province of Newhampshire
Londonderry Se^{br} first Munday 1752

In obedince to the within Comand I have posted it as useuall by Me

Willm Kelsey Constable

The other warrant being read and found word for word thought it Not Needfull to be put on record

attests Ja^{s} Nesmith toun Clark

Londonderry Sep^{br} first Munday 1752

By Vertue of the fore going warrant it being legaly caled the freeholders meet and after reading the warrant of S^{d} Meeting they Chuse for Moderator Cap^{n} Andrew Todd

The first and only article being read and Concidered the freeholders Made Choice of John McMurphey Esqr for there Representative or assembly Man

Province of Newhampshire
Londonderry Novem^{r} 7th 1752

Yow are hereby Required to Warn all the freeholders and Inhabitents belonging to your presinck in the toun afore S^{d} that they Meett at their first Meeting house upon tuSday the 21th of this Instant at ten of the Clock in the fore Noon then and there

first to See how Much Money they will allow to be Raised for to Defray toun Charges for this year

2 To See if the toun will Chuse acom^{tie} to Preamble there toun line

3 to See what the toun will allow to be done with the Money that hath been Recived for the palm Cloath and Chuse a Com^{tie} to Call the trusties to acount and to apoint the Money to Some Vse

4 to See What Method the toun will take to prevent the inhabitents from Cutting and Carring away timber off the Highways

5 to heire the touns aCompts read and aprove or Not aprove of them

And this Shall be your warrant Given under our hands the day and year above Mentioned

John Mitchell
John Wallace
Alex: Kelsey
Sam^{ll} Allison Junr
Sellect Men

To Mr Willm Kelsey Constable

Nove^{br} 21th 1752

In obedience to the within warrant I have posted up this warrant as Usewall

p^{r} Me Willm Kelsey Constable

The other Warrant being read and found word for word thought it Not Needfull to be put on Record

attests James Nesmith toun Clark

Then the free holders and Inhabitents Meett acording to this Warrant and Chus for Moderator James Clark

1 Voted on the first article that the Sellect Men is to assess £ 300—0—0 to Defray the Expence of the Toun for this present year

2 Article Voted that the toun line is to be preambled Excpting the line betwixt us and Chester and they have Chosen three Men as aCom^{tie} for that End there Names is Cap^{n} Sam^{ll} Barr Liv^{t} Robt Cochran and John Mitchell and they are to have for there wages 1—5—0 p^{r} Day and they

have voted 50 — 0 — 0 to bear the Expence of preambeling S^d line

3 Article they Voted two Men as aCom^tie to See What Money is in the hands of the trusties of the Mortcloath and take part of S^d Money to Repaire the Mortcloath that Now is and to purchas asmall Cloath with the Remainder of S^d Money if there be So Much the Mens Names is John Wallace & Robert Clark

Then the Moderator ajurned S^d Meeting untill tusday the 5th day of Dec^br Nixt at one of the Clock in the after Noon

Then the freeholders and Inhabitents Meet aCording to ajurnment and voted on the 5 article of the foregoing Warrant and aproved of the Sellectmens aCounts as farr as the Com^tie aCounted with them and No further

Province of Newhampshire

Londonderry feber^y 12th 1753

Yow are hereby Required to warn all the freeholders and Inhabitents Bellonging to your Respectie bounds that they Meett at there first Metting house upon Monday the fifth of March Nixt at Nine of the Clock in the fore Noon then and there

1^ly To Chose all their toun and old parish officers

2^ly to See if the toun will Make any allowance to John Mc Murphey Esqr as there Representitave he having No wages for that Service Since June 1748 which service his been attended with great Expence

3^ly To hear the touns aCompts read and aprove or Not approve of them

And this Shall be your warrant given under our hands the day and year above Mentioned

John Wallace
Joseph Scobey
Alex: Kelsey
Sam^ll Allicon Junr
Sellect Men

To Mr William Kelsey toun Constable

Province of Newhampshire

Londonderry March 5th 1753

This warrant his been posted as Usewall by Me.

Willm Kelsey toun Constable.

The other Warrant being Compaired and found word for word therefore thought Not Needfull to be put on Record

Attests James Nesmith toun Clark

Londonderry March 5th 1753

Then the freeholders and Inhabetents Meet being legaly Called acording to this warrant and after reading of Sd warrant Chuse for Moderator Capn John Mitchell

1 Voted upon the first article of the above warrant that three Men Shall Serve as Sellect Men for the Enswing year there Names are Capn Andrew Todd James Rodgers Capn Moses barnett

Voted for toun Clark for the Enswing year James Nesmith

Voted for Constable for the Easterly side of baver brook for the Ensuing year James Cochran

Voted for Constable for the Westerly Side of beaver brook for the Enswing year James Petterson

Voted for Collector for the Easterly side of beaver brook for the Enswing year Robert Gillmor

Voted for Collector for the Westerly Side of beaver brook Willm Cochran

voted for thitheng Man for the Easterly Side of beaver brook Gabriell Barr

for the Westerly Side of beaver brook Robert Campble

Voted for Surviers for the Easterly Side of beaver brook Robt Boice Esqr Andrew Clendening Deacon John Alexander Levt Robert Cochran John Cochran Willm Clendining John Gilmor Archebald Cunigham Mathew tylor

William Kelsey Enters his Desent against Archebald Cunighams Serving as Survier for the present year

Voted for Surviers for the Westerly Side of beaver brook Robert Parkicon William boide James Ramsey John Crumiey James Wallace William Dickey Alex: Petterson Samuell

Anderson Thos McCleary John Barnett Samuell Boice Samuell Calwell Abraham Holms John Wallace

Voted for leather Sealler William Wallace

Voted for Heuard Robert Riddall Thos Walker Samuell Boice Robert Petterson

voted for fence vewers and priesers James Adams John Blair

voted for aCounting with the Clark of the Sellect men and Constables Capt Sam^{ll} Barr Robert Clark Sam^{ll} Alison Junr voted to Serve in the rume of Cap^{n} barr James Nesmith

voted for taking the Envoice Daniell Leslie Isace Cochran

Then the Moderator ajurned S^{d} Meeting untill the Second tusday of Apriell at ten of the Clock in the fore Noon

Then the freeholders and Inhabitents Neet acording to ajurnment on Said day and the three Men that was Chosen to Serve as Sellect Men Refused to Serve therefor Voted three other Men to Serve as Sellect Men for this present year there Names are Liev^{t} John Humphrey Cap^{n} Sam^{ll} Barr Sam^{ll} Alison Junr

Then the Moderator thought fitt to ajurn Said Meetting untill the tenth day of May Nixt at tuelve of the Clock then the Moderator forgot the day and S^{d} Meeting dropt throw

Province of Newhamp^{s}

Londonderry June ye 22 1753

Yow are herby Required in his Maj^{es} Name to Warn all the Inhabitents in your Recipective bounds to Meett at the old Meeting house on teusday the third day of July Nixt at ten of the Clock in the fore Noon then and there

1 ^{ly} to See What Money the toun Will allow to be raised for to Defray toun Charges for the present year

2 ^{ly} to Chuse toun officers in the Rume of those thare are Remved' by Death the Said persons being Chosen last March Meeting

3 ^{ly} to See what the toun will doe about that book that the touns aCompts was Entred in that Liv^{t} Robert Cochran had

4 ^{ly} To see what the toun will do about that Road petioned for by John Mc Murphey and Robert Boice Esq^{rs} and others and have Cost the toun Concidrable and is like to fall throw by the Neglect of Some persons and a Ctt thereon

5 ^{ly} to See what the toun will do in Regard of a Constable for the Easterly Side of the toun

6 ^{ly} to See what the toun Will do about the touns Stock of pouder that Will be Spoiled by long keeping if Not taken of

7 ^{ly} for to hear the touns aCompts Read and aproven or Not aproven

And this Shall be your Warrant Given under our hands the day and year above S^{d}

Cap^{n} Sam^{ll} Barr
Liev^{t} John Humphrey
Sam^{ll} Alison Junr
Sellect Men

To Mr James Peterson toun Constable

Londonderry July* ye 23 1753

In obedience of the Within Warrant I have posted it aCording to Custom by Me

James Petterson toun Constable

The other Warrant being read and Considered and found word for word thought not meedfull to be put on Record

Attests James Nesmith toun Clark

Province of Newhampsh ^{re}

Londonderry July 3th 1753

The Inhabetents Meet aCording to the foregoing Warrant and Chuse for Moderator James Clark

1 ^{ly} Voted upon the first article of the foregoing warrant to Raise two hundred pounds old tennor for Defraying the touns debts for the presente year

2 ^{ly} voted for Sirvier in the place of Liev^{t} Robert Cochran Deses^{d} Leiv^{t} John Humphrey and in the prace of Abraham Holms Samuell Miller

*Intended to be June.—Ed.

voted for fence veur and prieser in the place of John blair decs[d] Tho[s] Willson

3 [ly] voted on the third article that Cap[n] Samuell Barr and Liev[t] John Humphrey is Chosen as aCom[tie] to Recive the book that is lodged with Lev[t] Robert Cochran Deses[d] and all the pepers belonging to both parishes and Liev[t] Humphrey is to keep S[d] book and to Enter the touns aCompts in it

4 [ly] voted that Cap[n] Sam[ll] Barr is to take Care to geet the order of the Sesions Relating to ahighway that Robert Boice and John M[c]Murphey Esq[rs] petioned for

5 [ly] Voted that the Sellect Men is prosecute or Make up with James Cochran as they thinke Most proper

6 [ly] voted and Chuse two Men as aCom[tie] to Despose of the touns pouder that is lodged in Cap[n] barrs Gerison and to provid More as fare as the money will goe in aNew Stock there Names are Cap[n] Sam[ll] Barr and Lev[t] John Humphrey also for Cap[n] Greggs Gerison Cap[n] John Gregg and Joseph Cochran to doe the Same

7 [ly] voted that the touns aCompts for the year 1752 is Not aproven of

Province of Newhampsh[r]

Londonderry Sept[r] y[e] 14th 1753

Yow are hereby Required in his Maj[tes] Name to Warn all the Inhabetents in your Respective bounds to Meet at the old Meeting house on thursday the twinty Seventh of this Instant at two of the Clock in the after Noon then and there

1[ly] to Chuse a Constable for the Easterly Side of beaver brook in the place of James Cochran Sinor that will Not Serve

2[ly] to See what the toun will allou to apettey Jury Man from one Coart to another

3 [ly] to See if the toun will past avote that No persons Shall Cutt No turf in the old grave yeard for to Cover graves With

And this Shall be your Warrant given under our hands the day and year above said

Cap^{n} Sam^{ll} Barr
Sam^{ll} Allison
Liev^{t} John Humphrey
Select Men

To Mr James Petterson toun Constable

Londonderry Sepb^{r} ye 27th 1753

In obedience of the within warrant I have posted it aCording to Coustom

p^{r} Me James Petterson Constable

The other warrant being Read and Considred and found Word for word thought Not Needfull to be Recorded

Attests James Nesmith toun Clark

Londonderry Sepb^{r} 27th 1753

Then the Inhabitents Meet in obedience to this warrant and after reading Said warrant they Chuse for Moderator Capt Moses Barnett

1 Voted on the first article and Chuse for Constable Robe^{t} Mountgumerey to Serve in the Stead of James Cochran

2 Voted on the Second article that the toun allloueth Every Jury Man that Serveth at the Supiror Court as Petty Jury Man throughout the whole of the Court thirty pounds old Tennor

3 voted on the third article that No person Shall Cut any turf within the Grave yeard hereafter

Then the moderator thought fitt to ajurn S^{d} Meeting untill the fiftenth day of Ocb^{r} Nixt at three of the Clock in the after Noon

Then the Inhabetents Meet aCording to ajurnment on S^{d} day and Axcpted of Arthur Boide to serve as Constable in Stead of Robert Mountgumrey for this present year

Provance of Newhampshir

Londonderry febe^ry^ ye 15th 1754

You are herby Required in his Maj^tes^ Name to warn all the Inhabitance in your Resp^te^ bounds To meet at the old meetinghouse on tusday the fifth Day of March Next at Nin of the Clock before Noon then and teheir

first to Chose all the town and old parish officers for the Insuing year

2^ly^ To See if the town allow the Selectmen to ansure apitition that thy were Served with by m^r^ Spalding and others

3^ly^ To See if the town will Give Insine John Ramsey any allowence for the Extrordnery Charges that he was at in Regarde of wedow Shelds in their Low Sircomstance the S^d^ artickle being Sined by ten Inhabitance of the town

4^ly^ To See what the town will Do in Regard of the Money y^t^ was Gote for the towns Stock of powder that was Disposed of by the Com^tee^ Chosen for that End

5^ly^ To See what the town will Do or allow to be Don in Regard of anote that was Lodged with Robt Boys Esqr to Save the town harmless from Damage by Johanna Brousters Childs Menteanance

6^ly^ To See if the town will order ahighway to be laid out upon the line betwen Danill M^c^Duffies land and the Estat of David Cochran Dec^d^ and as streght to the highway that leads from M^r^ M^c^Gregors to widow m^c^Nealls as the Good Ground will allow the S^d^ artickell being Signed by ten Inhabitance of the town

7^ly^ To see what the town will Do with these Counstabls that have Not Cleared of their lists Som of them Near twinty years Standing

8^ly^ To Here the towns acoumpts Rade and approven or Not approven

and this Shall be your warant Given under our hands the Day and year above

Samuell Barr
Sam^ll^ Aleson Junr
John Humphrey
Selectmen

To Mr Arther Boyd Town Constable

Provance of Newhampshir

Lond^{ry} March ye 5th 1754

In obidence to the forgoing warant I have posted it acording to Costom

p^{r} me arther Boyd town Constabls

The other warant for S^{d} meeting being Rade and Compered and found word for word so not needfull to be upon Record

attests Pr Mo^{s} Barnett town Clerk

Lond^{ry} March ye 5th 1754

Then the freeholders and Inhabitance of S^{d} town being legelly Called mate acording to the forgoing warant on S^{d} Day and after Reeding S^{d} warant thy Chuse for to Moderate S^{d} Meeting James Clark

voted on the first artickel of the forgoing warant and Chuse for town Clerk for the Insuing year Mo^{s} Barnett

voted that three men Shall Serve as Selectmen for the Insuing year their Names is as followeth Capt Sam^{ll} Barr Lif^{t} Jo^{n} Humphry Sam^{ll} Aleson Junr

voted for Counstable for the Easterly Side of Baver Brook Gorge Moore

voted for Counstable for the westerly side of Baver Brook Robt Wallace

S^{d} wallace appering in S^{d} meeting and told the moderater that he wold Not Serve

Collecters for the old parish for the westerly Side of Baver Brook John Barnett

for the Easterly Side of Baver Brook Mathew Reid

voted for taythingmen for the Insuing year Hugh Ramsey Samu^{ll} Boyes Robt Moore North

voted for Survers for the Easterly Sid of Baver Brook for the Insuing year Joseph Scobey Mo^{s} Barnett Capt John Gregg Sam^{ll} Moreson Ephram Marsh James Willson Sam^{ll} Peterson Robt Wallace Thos Davidson

Voted for Surveirs for the westerly Side of Baver Brook for Insuing year Joseph Cochran James Anderson Junr

James Ramsey Jon Wallace James McCormick Joseph Willson Samll Dickey willm Beetey Andrew Thomptson Willm Smith James Boyes Samll Miller Alexdr mcCollam John Dunken Robt Clark

Voted for Lather Sealer for the Insuing year Willm Wallace

Voted for Hoge hourds for the Insuing year Jon Stevins Hugh Thompson Black James Willson Willm Aris

Voted for fence vers and prisers for the Insuing year Samuell Renken Jon McKeen

voted for Counters with the Select Men and Counstabls for the Insuing year Robt Clark Mos Barnett Jon mcKeen

voted for town Counstable for westerly Side of Baver Brok in the Roome of Robt wallace that Denays to Serve Charls Coox

voted for two men for tacking the Invice John mcKeen John Cromey Junr for the Insuing yere and thier wages is to be fifteen pounds ten Shillings old tener

The Second artickell of the forgoing warant being Rade and Considered it is voted by Sd freeholders and Inhabitance that Capt Samll Barr is to Go to the Jenerall Cort upon the towns Cost to ansore to that pitition put in by Spalding and others

Gorge Moore hairing Arther Boyd to Serve Counstable for this Insuing year in his Roome the town hes excepted of Sd Boyd in that stacion

Voted on the third artickell of the forgoing warant as foll to Give Insine John Ramsey twinty five pounds old tener for his troble Conserning widow Shelds Decd

this meeting is ajorned untill the first tusday of aprill next at ten of the Clock before Noon

Londry Aprill ye 2d 1754

Then the aforsd freeholders and Inhabitance Mate acording to the Ajornment and after Considering the forth artickell of the forgoing warant it is voted on Sd Artickell as followeth

to lay out the Money that wase Gote for the towns Stock of powder for anew Stock or Store as Soon as May be and Capt Samll Barr is appointed to purtches Sd Stock

The fifth artickell of the forgoing warant is past in the Neg^{t}
voted on the Sixth artickell of the forgoing warant by S^{d} freeholders and Inhabitance that thy will Not purtchess away from Dainell McDuffies to the back Range
voted on the Seventh artickell as followeth that the towns Select men is Impowered by S^{d} vote to prosecute the delink-quid Counstabls at the towns Charge
voted on the Eight Artickell to approve of the acounts that was Rad (viz) Ja^{s} pattersons Arther Boyds and Lif^{t} Jo^{n} Humphrys
then apperred Charls Cox and Disiered the moderator of the afor^{sd} Meeting to See if the town wold Recive his brother william to Serve Counstable in his place for this year and the town asented to it in the Rome of Robt wallace that was Chosen on the first Day of the meeting and wold Not Serve being aComition offecer

Provance of Newhampshir

Londonderry June ye 4th 1754

You are hereby Required in his Maj^{tes} Name to Warn all the Inhabitance in your Resptv bounds to Meete at the old Meetinghouse on Monday the Sevinteenth of this Instant at twelve of the Clock in the Day then and their

first To See what Money the town will allowe to be ap-ploted for to Defraye town Charges for the Corant year

2 ly To See what the town will allow the Select men to Do in Respact of the Division of higways the lemitishion of Divison being past before the Selectmen Knowed of Such En act of Law in in Regard of Devision of highways

3 ly To See if the town will Chuse aCom^{tee} to Clear the town Common of all Incumbrance about the old Meeting-house and tack Care of the Grave yard and this Shall be your warant Given under our hands the Day and year above

Sam^{ll} Barr
Sam^{ll} Alison
John Humphry
Select Men

To Mr Willm Cox Town Counstable

Provance of Newhampshir

Lond[ry] June y[e] 17th 1754

In obediance of the within presept I have posted it acording to Costom

P[r] Me William Cox town Constable

The other Warant for S[d] meeting was Rade and and Compared and found word for word So Not thought Needfull to be put upon Record

P[r] Mo[s] Barnett town Clerk

Lond[ry] June the 17th 1754

The freeholders and Inhabitance of S[d] town Mate acording to the appointment of the forgoing warant it being Legelly Called and after Reeding the forgoing warant for S[d] Meeting thy Chuse Will[m] Humphra for Moderater

the first artickell of the forgoing warant being Rade and Considered thy voted to work and mend there highways and ways acording to their former Costom

Voted on the Second Artickell as followeth that the Selectmen is to applote or assess two houndred and fifty pounds old tener to Defray the town Debts for the present year

Voted on the third artickell of the forgoing warant by the afor[sd] freeholders and Inhabitance that the Select men is Impowered as aCom[tee] to Clear of all the Incoumbrances that is on the Commons at the old Meetinghouse or order it to be Don and to tacke Care of the Grave yard by S[d] Commons

Provance of Newhampshir

Londonderry feb[ry] y[e] 18th 1755

You are bereby Requiered in his Maj[tes] Name to warn all the Inhabitance in your Respective bounds to Meete at the old Meetinghouse on Wadensday the fifth of March Next at Nine of the Clock before Noon then and their

1 ly To Chuse all the town and old parish ofecers of the Corant year

2 ly To See if the town will allowe the Survers of S[d] town to worke on the highways as formly the Costom was in S[d] town

3 ly Lond^{ry} feb^{ry} ye 1st 1755 we the under Subcribers Disiers that the Selectmen of Lond^{ry} to put this artickell in the first town warant thy make to See if thy will vote that Every Man that atroue Invoice is taken of Should pay the first assesed after the Invoice tacken

4 ly To hear the towns acounts Rade and approven or Not approven

and this Shall be your warant Given under our hands

Sam^{ll} Barr
Sam^{ll} Alison Ju^{r}
John Humphry
Select Men

To Mr Arther Boyd town Counstable

Provance of Newhampsher

Lond^{ry} March ye 5th 1755

In obidence to the within warant I have posted it Acording to former Costom

Pr Arther Boyd Counstable for the Easterly Side of Baver Brook

The other warant for S^{d} Meeting was Rade and Exemnd and found word for word so Not Needfull to be put upon Record

attest Pr Mo^{s} Barnett Town Clerk

Londonderry March ye 5th 1755

In obidance to the forgoing warant it being legelly Call^{d} the Inhabitance of the afor^{sd} town Mate acording to the afor^{sd} appointment and Chuse for Moderater to S^{d} Meeting Capt Sam^{ll} Barr and after Reeding the warants for S^{d} Meeting these under Named ofecers was Chosen by Vote by those that was Quallify^{d} to vote for to Serve in their Stations for this Corant year

town Clerk Mo^{s} Barnett

their is five Select Men Chosen for the present year their Names as followeth Capt Sam^{ll} Barr Sam^{ll} Alison Junr Mo^{s} Barnett James Ramsey John Hounter

Chosen for town Counstabls John M^{tt} Keen James Evens and S^{d} M^{tt}Keen told the Moderater he wold Not Serve old parish Colecters Andrew Clendinin Willm White

Chosen for taythingmen Mathew Taylor John Stoel Junr Hugh Mountgombrey Ju^{r}

Chosen for Survers of the High ways for ye present year on the Easterly Side Robt Boyes Esqr James M^{tt} Keen Junr James Clark Willm Humphra John Hopken Joseph Morison Thos Cristy Archabld Coningham Robt ferservice

Chosen for the westerly Side of Said town James Gregg Junr James Anderson Junr Willm Renkin Thos Willson Willm Wallace David Huston James Ares Alexd^{r} Peterson Robt Anderson Willm Hogg James Moore David Moreson John Scobey Gorge Dunken Mathew Wright

Chosen for Lather Sealer Willm Wallace

Chosen for Houerds for this year John Stinson Willm Humphra James Morrow Robt peterson

Chosen for fence vers and prisers John Mitchell Junr John wallace ye Second

Chosen for Counters with the Selectmen and Constables Robt Clark John Mitchell Junr James Nesmeth

Chosen for Invice Men for the Insuing year John M^{tt} Keen John Cromey Junr and their wages is to be Sixteen pounds old tener

Voted on the Second artickell of the warant on the afor^{sd} Day that the Survers of highways Shall work on the Rods this Insuing year acording to their former Costom

this Meeting is Ajorned untill tusday the first Day of aprill Next at one of the Clock after Noon

Lond^{ry} aprill ye 1S^{d} 1755

the Inhabitance of ye afor^{sd} town Mate on S^{d} Day acording to the Ajornment of S^{d} Meeting and Voted to Recive James Campbell Junr and Except of him to Serve town Constable for this Insuing year for James Ivens S^{d} Service ansuring for S^{d} Ivens but not for Campbell

The third artickell of the forgoing warant being Rade and Considered it was Voted to pass it in the Negitive

voted to ajorn this Meeting untill untill tusday the 22^{d} of this Instant at one of ye Clock after Noon

Lond^{ry} Aprill ye 22^{d} 1755

Then Mate acording to the ajornment of the forgoing Meeting and after the Inhabitance had Considered the Case of John Mt Keen being latly aColecter for the west parish thy past avote that he shold Not Serve as town Constable for this year and by vote of S^{d} Inhabitance thy Chuse Archibald Cuningham to Serve as town Counstable for the Easterly Side of Baver Brook for the present year

Provance of Newhampsher

Lond^{ry} March ye 12th 1755

You are herby Requiered to Warn all the Inhabitance in your Respective bounds to meete at the old Meetinghouse in S^{d} town upon tusday the first Day of aprill Next at three of the Clock after Noon then & there

first to See if thy will Chuse aCom^{tee} and Impower them to proscut any parson or persons that Maks any Incrotchments upon the Minesterell lote or hes alredy Don

2ly To See if thy will Chuse aCom^{tee} to Reglate the acounts that was Not approvd of when Robt Cochran Dec^{d} was Clerk to the Select men

and this Shall be your warant Given under our hands the Day and year above

Sam^{ll} Barr
John Hunter
James Ramsey
Sam^{ll} Alison
Mo^{s} Barnett
Selectmen

To Mr Willm Cox town Constable

Provance of Newhampsher

Lond^{ry} Aprill ye 1^{d} 1755

This warant hes been posted acording to former Costom
Pr Willm Cox Constable

Lond^{ry} Aprill ye 1^{d} 1755

In obedence to the forgoing warant it being legelly Cal^{d} the free holders and Inhabitance of S^{d} town Mate acording to apointment and after Reeding the warnt for S^{d} Meeting thy made Choice of Capt Sam^{ll} Barr for their Moderater

voted that three Men Shall be Chosen as aCom^{tee} to proscute all Incrotchers that Incrotches upon Either land or timber Standing or lying within the boundres of the minesterell hom Lote belonging to this town to finell End and Determenation as if the whole town where personelly present at S^{d} towns Charge the mens Names is as followeth Thos willson North Willm Humphra Capt Sam^{ll} Barr

The Second Artickell of the forgoing warant being Rade and Considered it is voted to Chuse aCom^{tee} to Sertch or Regelate the acounts that was Not approven of when Robt Cochran Dec^{d} was Select Clerk the Com^{tee} is Capt Sam^{ll} Barr Lif^{t} John Humphry Mo^{s} Barnett

Provance of Newhampsher

Londonderry Agust ye 27th 1755

Youare hereby Requiered to warn all the freeholders and Inhabitance in your Respective Bounds to assemble and Meete at at their first Meetinghouse upon tusday the Ninth Day of Sep^{tr} Next at two of the Clock after Noon then and their

first To See how Much Money thy will allow to be aploted to Defray the town Debts for the present year

2 ly To See what the town will Dow in Regard of aRode that James Morrow was Going to present and was advised to Lay before the town

and this Shall be your warant Given under hands the Day and year above

Sam^{ll} Barr
Sam^{ll} Alleson Junr
Mo^{s} Barnett
Select Men

To Mr James Campbell Junr town Constable

provance of Newhampshier

Lond^{ry} Sep^{tr} ye 9th 1755

I have posted this warant two Days

Pr Me James Campbell Constable

the other warant for S[d] Meeting was Rade and Comper[d] So Not Needfull to be put upon Record for it was found word for word

attest P[r] Mo[s] Barnett town Clerk

Lond[ry] Sep[tr] y[e] 9th 1755

The freeholders and Inhabitance of Lond[ry] afor[sd] Mate on S[d] Day acording to the appointment of the forgoing warant and after Reeding the warant for S[d] Meeting thy Chuse by vote to Modreat S[d] Meeting James Campbell

the first artickell of the forgoing warant being Rade and Considered it is voted by S[d] meeting that the Select Men is to asses or applote two houndred and fifty pounds old tener to Defray the towns Debts this present year

the Second artickell of S[d] warant being Rede and Considered it is voted to be past in the Negitive

Provance of Newhampshir

Londonderry Sep[tr] the 9th 1755

You are hereby Required to warn all the freeholders and Inhabitance in your Respective bounds to assemble and meet at the old Meetinghouse in S[d] Lond[ry] upon Monday the twinty second Day of this Instant at ten of the Clock before Noon then and their

first To Chuse a Counstable to Serve the Easterly Side of S[d] town this present year in the place of Archibald Coningham Dec[d]

2ly To See what the town will Do with the man that thy Imployed to Gete atowns Stocke of powder and hes Not Don it also to See what Mathode thy will take to Gate the Money out their Hands that hes Sold the old Stocke and what Mathode thy will take to purtches anew one

3ly To heve the towns acounts Rade and approven or Not

4ly To See what Incoridgment thy will Give to those men that will Inlist to the asistance of the Reinforcement against Crown point and this Shall be your warant Given under our hands the Day and yeare above

Sa^{ll} Barr
James Ramsey
John Hunter
Sam^{ll} Alison Junr
Mo^{s} Barnett
Select Men

To Mr James Campbell Junr town Constable

Lond^{ry} Sep^{tr} the 22th 1755

this warrant hes been posted two publick Days acording to former Costom

P^{r} Me
James Campbell Dep^{d} Constable

the other warant for S^{d} Meeting was Rade and Comper^{d} and found word for word so Not Needfull to be pute up on Record

Pr Mo^{s} Barnett town Clerk

Provance of Newhampsher

Londonderry Sep^{tr} ye 22th 1755

Then the freeholders and Inhabitance of S^{d} town Mate on S^{d} Day acording to the appountment of the forgoing warant it be Legelly Call^{d} and After Reeding S^{d} warants thy Made Chys of James Clark to Moderat in S^{d} Meeting

the first artickell of S^{d} warant being Rade and Considered it is Voted that Sam^{ll} Clark Shall Serve as town Constable for the Eastwardly Side of Baver Brook for this present year

voted on the Second artickell by the S^{d} Inhabitence as followeth that the Selectmen is to Lift the Money out of Capt John Grggs hand that was Gote for the old Stock of poder in order to purtches anew one

Voted to pass the third artickell in the Negitive

voted by S^{d} freeholders and Inhabitance on the forth artickell of the forgoing warant as followeth that Each Solder that Inlists out of this town of S^{d} Lond^{ry} or any part of the two perishes therof upon the acounte of the present Express now Sent to the Miletry of wers of S^{d} town And Joynes the armey Now at leck Gorge in order to the Redouction of Crown point Shall have thirty pounds old tener pay^{d} as abounty by S^{d} town for their Incoridgment to S^{d} Cotto of men Inlisted by the Cap^{ts} out of S^{d} town

Provance of Newhampshir

To Sam^{ll} Clark one of the Constables in Londonderry in S^{d} provance Greeting

By vertue of the Shirifs writte of S^{d} provance to us Deerected You are hereby in his Maj^{tis} Name Requiered to warn all the freeholders and Inhabitance in your Respective Bounds in S^{d} town Quallify^{d} by Law to meet at the old meetinghouse in S^{d} Lond^{ry} upon tusday the twinty first Day of oct^{br} Corant at one of the Clock in the after Noon then and their

To Elect one person Quallify^{d} by Law to Represent the S^{d} town In Jenerall assembley to be Convend and holden at Portsmouth on the twinty third Day of oct^{br} Corant at ten of the Clock in the fore Noon and S^{d} De Die in Diem During their Seshon or Seshons and Make Retorn of this warant and of your Doings to us the Subscribers at or before the S^{d} twinty first Day of oct^{br} and this Shall your warant Given under our hands this Seventh Day of oct^{br} in thy year 1755

Mo^{s} Barnett
Sam^{ll} Barr
John hounter
Sam^{ll} Aleson Junr
James Ramsey
Select Men

Provance of Newhampsher

Londonderry oct^{br} ye 21^{d} 1755

In obidence to the within Command I have posted this warant as uswell

P^{r} Me

Sam^{ll} Clark Constable

Provance of Newhampshir

Lond^{ry} oct^{br} ye 21^{d} 1755

In obidence to the forgoing warant the freeholders and Inhabitance of S^{d} town and Windham mate on S^{d} Day acording to the apointment of the warning it being legelly Call^{d} and after Reading the warants for S^{d} meeting thy Made Choys of Robt Boyes Esqr for to modrate S^{d} meeting by the maj^{er} part of the Legell Voters the artickell for S^{d} meeting being Rade and Considered it is Younanemusely voted by the Qualleyfy^{d} Electers that Robart Clark is to Serve in the Jenerell assembley as a Representive for S^{d} town and windham*

Note the other warant for S^{d} Meeting was Rade and Comper^{d} and found word for word so Not Needfull to be put upon Record

attest P^{r}

Mo^{s} Barnett town Clerk

Provance of Newhampshir

Londonderry Dec^{br} ye 2^{d} 1755

You are hereby Requiered to warn all the freeholders and Inhabitance in your Respective Bounds to Meet at the old Meetinghouse in S^{d} town upon tusday the Sixteen Day of this Instant at one of the Clock after Noon then and their

first to Scc if the town will Chuse a Com^{tee} to Defend that Case Conserning the Rode that James Morrow has presented the town for and to pitition the Janarell Cort in Rela-

*The reason for this election was the vacancy in the office of representative caused by the sudden death of Squire John McMurphy while attending to his duties in that capacity. The following entry upon page 350, Records of Londonderry, Vol. 2, gives further official facts:

John MacMurphy Esqr Justice of the Quoram Departed this life September the 21st 1755 on Sabath Day about twelve o;Clock on Said Day at Portsmouth and was Carried to London Derry upon Teusday and was Buired upon Wednesday the 24th Instant about four of the Clock in the afternoone at the old Burieng Place in this town.With an Exterordinary Compenay; Aged about Sevinty three years.

Squire John McMurphy, as he was known, was one of the most active and influential members of the little band of pioneers breaking the wilderness of Londonderry and laying the foundations of the new government. A ready writer, he was clerk of the town for eleven years. He received the appointment of justice about 1721, holding the office until his decease. He was elected selectman in 1722, and he was the first representative to the general court, holding that office for eleven years, dying, as we have seen, while serving in that honorable, capacity.—EDITOR.

tion of the Same and this Shall be your warant Given under our hands

Subcribed at Lond^{ry} the Day and year above

Sam^{ll} Barr
John Hunter
James Ramsey
Sam^{ll} Aleson Junr
Mo^{s} Barnett
Select Men

To Mr Sam^{ll} Clark town Constable

Provance of Newhampsher

Lond^{ry} Dec^{br} ye 16th 1755

In obedence to the forgoing warant I have posted it two publick Days acording to former Costom

P^{r} Me Sam^{ll} Clark town Constable

The other warant for S^{d} Meeting was Rade and Comper^{d} and found word for word so Not Needfull to be put upon Record

attest Pr Mo^{s} Barnett town Clerk

Lond^{ry} Decb^{r} ye 16th 1755

In obedence to the forgoing warant the freeholders and Inhabitce of S^{d} town Mate on S^{d} Day thy being Legelly Call^{d} and after Reeding the warant for S^{d} Meeting thy Made Choys of Coll^{n} Sam^{ll} Barr to be Moderater for S^{d} Meeting

then the Artickell of the forgoing warant being Considered by S^{d} freeholders and Inhabitance thy voted to Chuse aCom^{tee} to Defend the present men Given in by James Morrow to our Quarter Seshons in Regard of the Rode and to pitition the Jenerall Corte in order to Disanull S^{d} Rode and it is allso voted by S^{d} Inhabnc that the Select men for the time being is to be aCom^{tee} for the afor^{sd} End with full power and autherity as if S^{d} town were persenally present S^{d} Com-^{tees} nams is as followeth Sam^{ll} Barr John Hunter James Ramsey Sam^{ll} Aleson Junr Mo^{s} Barnett Select Men

I the Subcriber Do Enter My Desent against the proceedings of the for^{sd} Meeting

James Morrow

Provance of Newhampsher

Lond^{ry} Feb^{ry} ye 18th 1756

You are hereby Requiered to warn all the freeholders and Inhabitance Quallified by law in your Respective bounds to Meet at their first Meetinghouse in S^{d} Lond^{ry} upon friday the fifth Day of March Next at ten of the Clock before Noon then and their

first to Chuse all thier town and old parish oficers for the Insuing year

2ly To See if thy will Chuse aCom^{tee} to Gete the Grave-yard fence at the old Meetinghouse Reper^{d}

3ly at the Disier of aNumber of Subcribers to Inserte an Artickell to See what the town will Do in Relation to tranjen persons that is harbert in S^{d} town and May become atroble to the Same

4ly To here the towns acounts Rade and approven or Not approven

and this Shall be your warant Given under our hands the Day and year above

Sam^{ll} Barr
John Hunter
James Ramsey
Sam^{ll} Aleson Ju^{r}
Mo^{s} Barnett
Select men

To Mr Sam^{ll} Clark town Constable

Provance of Newhampsher

Lond^{ry} March the 5th 1756

In obidance to the forgoing warant I have posted it acording to former Costom

Pr Sam^{ll} Clark Constable

The other warant for S^{d} Meeting was Rade and Comper^{d} and found word for word so Not Needfull to be put upon Record

attest Pr Mo^{s} Barnett town Clerk

Provance of Newhampshir

Lond^{ry} March ye 5th 1756

In obidance to the forgoing warant it being Legelly Call^{d} the freeholders and Inhabitance of S^{d} Lond^{ry} Mate acording to the appointment of S^{d} warants and after Reeding the warants for S^{d} Meeting thy Made Choice of James Clark for their Moderater

there after the moderater had Rade the warrants the Electers Made Choice of the town oficers for the Insuing year as followeth

Chosen for town Clerk Mo^{s} Barnett

ye vote Cared for five Select men thier Names is as followeth Coll^{n} Sam^{ll} Barr Mo^{s} Barnett Dani^{ll} Leslay Thos willson Sam^{ll} Aleson Junr

then Emedently after the Select Men was Chosen Mo^{s} Barnett Decle^{d} that he wold Not Serve and thy mad Choice in his place Coll^{n} Andrew Todd

Chosen for Constables on the Easterly Side of Baver Brook Robt Alexd^{r}

for ye westerly Side John Dock

Chosen for Colecters for ye old parish Joseph Cochran John Cochran South

Chosen for taything men Hugh younge John Hogg Mathew wright

Chosen Survuers of highways for the Easterly Side of Baver Brook Joseph Scobey John Moreson Junr John Paton John Tayler John Hopkens John Stell Gorge Moore Robt Mt Curdy Robt ferservice

Chosen Surveris for ye westerly Side of Baver Brook Lif^{t} Sam^{ll} Gregg Adward Aken Willm Ares Capt Ja^{s} Bleer Thos wallace Ins^{n} John Senter Willm Edeson James willson Corley Sam^{ll} Anderson John Aken James Nesmeth Junr Sam^{ll} Miller Alex^{dr} Mt Collm Willm Dunken John Moore

Chosen lather Sealer for the Insuing year Willm Wallace

Chosen for hog Howards for the Insuing year Arther Boyd Sam^{ll} Boyes Willm Cox Thos Mt Glaughlen

Chosen for fence vewers and prysers James Campbell John Mt Keen

Chosen for Counters will the Select Men and Constabls James Ramsey James Nesmeth Mo[s] Barnett

Chosen for Invoice Men John M[t] Keen John Cromey Jun[r]

the Second artickell of the warant being Rade and Considered it Voted that the Select Men is to Gete the fences of the two Grave Yards Repe[rd] at the towns Cost

Voted to Ajorn this Meeting untill the first wadensday of Aprill Next at nine of the Clock before Noon

Lond[ry] Aprill y[e] 7th 1756

Then Mate according to the ajornment of S[d] Meeting and voted on the third artickell of the forgoing warant as followeth that the Select Men is to Gete appition Drawn and Send it with our Representitive to the Janarall Corte In order to See if the town Can be Relev[d] from those trangent parsons that Coms in to our town Every fall or at other tims

voted to ajorn this Meeting untill the 27th of May Next at three of the Clock after Noon

Lond[ry] May y[e] 27 1756

Then the freeholders and Inhabitance of S[d] town Mate according to the ajorenment and ajorened S[d] meeting untill the 12th Day of July Next at three of the Clock after Noon

Lond[ry] July y[e] 12th 1756

Then Mate according to S[d] Ajorenment and voted upon the forth artickell of the forgoing warant to approve of Sam[ll] Clarks and Ja[s] Campbell acounts as far as thy were Rade and Leckwise approve of Moses Barnetts acount being Clerk to y[e] Select Men

Provance of Newhampshir

Londonderry Febr[y] y[e] 10th 1757

You are hereby Requiered to warn all the freeholders and Inhabitance Belonging to your Respective bounds to Meet at their old Meetinghouse upon Saterday the fifth of March Next Insuing at ten of the Clock in the fore Noon then and their

I[t] to Chuse all their town and old parish oficers for the Insuing Year

2ly To here the town accoumpts Rade and approven or Not approven

3 ly To See if the town will Chuse aCom^{tee} to Devide the Huhhways and Give Every Survier their Equall part

4ly To See what the town will allow to be Done to the Grave Yards Stocks and pound

5ly To Se if the town will Chuse afite person to tacke that Book that was left with Capt John Humphrey and Enter the towns accounts that is Not Entered this four Years past

6ly To See if the town will Chuse aCom^{tee} to Defend the Minesterell against the traspases or Incrotchments of any persons

7ly To See howmuch the town will allow the petey Jurer for Serving the Superer Court through out for this present year

8ly To See what the town will allow the Constables this year for their Extrordnery troble

and this Shall be your warant Given under our hands the Day and year above

Thos Willson
Andrew Todd
Sam^{ll} Barr
Sam^{ll} Aleson Junr
Select Men

To Mr Robart Alex^{dr} town Constable

Provance of New Hampshir

Lond^{ry} March ye 5th 1757

In obideance to the forgoing warant I have posted it according to former Costom

Pr Robt Alex^{dr} Constable

Note the other warant for S^{d} Meeting was Rade and Compar^{d} with the forgoing and found word for word so Not Needfull to be put upon Record

attest Pr Mo^{s} Barnett town Clerk

Provance of Newhampshir

Londonderry March ye 5th 1757

In obidance to the forgoing warants thy Being Legelly Call^{d} the freeholders and Inhabitance of Lond^{ry} afor^{sd} Mate according to the appointment of the afor^{sd} warning and after Reeding the warants for S^{d} meeting thy Made Choys of Coll^{n} Andrew Todd for their Moderater

Then after Considering S^{d} warants thy Made Choys by the Majorety of their Legell Voters of their town officers as followeth for the Insuing Year

Chosen town Clerk Mo^{s} Barnett

Chosen for Select Men 5 Coll^{n} Andrew Todd Coll^{n} Sam^{ll} Barr Thos Willson Sam^{ll} Aleson Junr Dainell Lesley

Chosen for Constables for the Insuing year Robart Moor North Thomas willson Junr

Colecters for the old parish Joseph Boyes Robart Gillman

Taything men Chosen Samuell Huston Junr James Anderson Junr David Stell

Surviers for the Easterly Side of Baver Brook Ins^{n} James Mt Greger Capt John Mitchell David Anderson Gabrell Barr Willm Fisher Mathew Reid Thos Cristey David Doge David Morison

Survuers for the westerly Side of Baver Brook James Gregg Junr Sam^{ll} Grahims will^{m} Renken John Cromey Junr Sam^{ll} Fisher Sam^{ll} Senter Sam^{ll} Dickey John Pinkertown Sam^{ll} Mt Keen Willm Smith will^{m} Roger John Mungombrey James Jones (?) John Hilands John readall

Deer Keepers Insin James Mt Greger Lif^{t} will^{m} Dunken

Lather Sealers David Hopkens will^{m} wallace

Howards John patton John Barnett Hugh Thompson Gorge Clark

Fence vers and praysers John Hunter John Mt Keen

Counters with the Select men and Constabls James Nesmeth James Ramsey Mo^{s} Barnett

Invice Men John M^{tt} Keen John Cromey Junr

Voted upon the Second artickell of the forgoing warant as followeth to approve of the towns acounts as fare as Rade

Voted to pass the third artickell of the forgoing warant for this year and it may be Enter^{d} Nixt anwell meeting if thy plese

this meeting is Ajorne^{d} untill tusday the 29th Day of this Instant at ten of the Clock before Noon by avote of S^{d} meeting

Londonderry March ye 29th 1757

Then the freeholders and Inhabitance of S^{d} town Mate According to S^{d} Ajorinment of the afor^{sd} Meeting and after Reeding the warant for the afor^{sd} meeting thy voted upon the forth artickell of the forgoing warant as followeth

to Chuse Lif^{t} John wiar Insi^{n} James wallace and Moses Barnett as aCom^{tee} to Gate the Grave Yards fences Stoks and pound Reper^{d} At the towns Cost and Charges as Soon as may be

voted upon the fifth artickell of S^{d} warant that Lif^{t} John wiar is to Enter the towns acounts in that town book that is in Capt Humprhas hand and the Select Men is to Gate S^{d} book and Carey it to S^{d} wiar

voted upon the Sixth artickell to Chuse aCom^{tee} to prosecute any Incrotchers or traspassers upon the towns Minesterell lote with full power and outherity as if all S^{d} town were to Defend the Same S^{d} Com^{tee} is Thos willson North Sam^{ll} Aleson Junr Robt Moreson

Voted upon the Seventh artickell of the forgoing warant as followeth that Each man that is Sumn^{d} by the high Shirif and Serves the Superer Court through out as apette Jurer belonging to this town for this present year Shall have ten pounds old tener but S^{d} Jurer or Jurers Shall have no priviledg of any former vote of S^{d} town that is past in that Cass

voted upon the Eight artickell of S^{d} warant that the two years Constables of Lond^{ry} past and this present year is to have fifty Shillings old tener adidd to their wages

Provance of Newhampshir

Londonderry Feber^{ry} ye 15th 1758

You are hereby Requiered to warn All the freeholders and Inhabitance belonging to your Respective bounds to Meete at their first Meeting House upon Monday the Dixth Day of March Next Insuing at ten of the Clock in the fore Noon then and their

1 st To Chuse all their town and old parish officers for the Insuing year

2ly To Hear the towns acounts Rede and approve of them and this Shall be your warant Given under our hands the Day and year above

To Mr Thos willson Town Constable

Andrew Todd
Thos Willson
Sam^ll^ Barr
Sam^ll^ Aleson Junr
Select Men

Provance of Newhampsher

Lond^ry^ March ye 6th 1758

I have posted the above warant according to former Costom

P^r^ me Thos willson Constable

the other warant for S^d^ meeting was Rade and Exemen^d^ and found word for word So not needfull to be put upon Record

attest Pr Mo^s^ Barnett town Clerk

Provance of Newhampshir

Londonderry March ye 6th 1758

In Obidance to the forgoing warants thy being Legilley Called the freeholders and Inhabitance of Lond^ry^ afor^sd^ Mate according to the appointment of S^d^ warants and after Reeding the warants for S^d^ meeting thy made Choyse of Coll^n^ Andrew Todd to moderate S^d^ meeting and after Reeding the warants for S^d^ meeting thy made Choice of their town and old parish officers as followeth for the Insuing year

Chosen for Town Clerk Moses Barnett

Chosen five Selectmen as followeth Thos wallace Sam^ll^ Alleson Junr Joseph Cochran Ins^n^ James Mt Greger John Aken

Chosen for Constables David Craige will^{m} Dunkerr Junr

Chosen for old parish Colecters James Miller James Cochran Cannada

Chosen for Surveirs for the Easterly Side of Baver Brook Mo^{s} Barnett James Wallace Capt John Humphra John Hopken David Hopken John Gillmor David Doge Willm Taylor Capt John Moore

Surviers for the westerly Side of Baver Brook John Clark Willm Ears John wallace John Hollms Sam^{ll} Dickey John Pinkertown Robart Alexd^{r} John Aken Junr James Boyes Sam^{ll} miller John wallace Joseph Hogg Joseph Bell Alex^{dr} MacMurphy Willm Wallace James Paterson

Chosen for taything men Lif^{t} Thos Craige Robt Cochran Gorge Clark North Sam^{ll} fisher Correct Sam^{ll} Moreson in the Room of Robt Cochran

Chosen for Lather Sealers David Hopkens Willm Wallace Robt Mt Nell

Chosen for Howerds Willm Adams James Willson Thos Mt Glaughlin Willm Rodger in the Room of will^{m} Adams

Chosen for fence vewers and prisers John Mt Keen James Ramsey

Chosen for Invoice men John Mt Keen Jôhn Cromey Junr

Chosen to take Care that the Deer Dear be not Kill^{d} out of seson James Nesmeth Junr Jonathan Adams Lif^{t} will^{m} Dunken Ins^{n} James M^{t}Greger

This meeting is ajorned untill the Second tusday of Aprill Nixt at on of the Clock after Noon at the afor^{sd} Meeting-house

Lond^{ry} Aprill ye 11th 1758

Then the freeholders and Inhabitance of S^{d} town Mate according to ajornment and after Reeding the warants for S^{d} Meeting thy Chuse officers in place of those that was Not Quallify^{d}

voted to approve of the towns acounts that was Rade (viz) James Campbells John Doaks and Robt Alexdrs

Provance of Newhampshir

Lond^ry^ Aprill ye 15th 1758

By order of Cort to me Directed You are hereby in his Maj^tes^ Name Requiered to warn all the freeholders and Inhabitence in your Respective bounds Duly Quallify^d^ by Law to meet at their first Meetinghouse upon friday the twinty Eight Day of this Instant at one of the Clock after Noon In order to Chuse one Good and Lawfull man to Serve as Grand Jurer at his Maj^tes^ Superer Cort of Judicature to be held at Portsmouth in and for S^d^ provance on the third tusday of May Next and this Shall be your warant Given under my hand the Day and year above

Mo^s^ Barnett town Clerk

To Mr William Dunken town Constable

Provance of Newhampshir

Lond^ry^ Aprill ye 28th 1758

I have posted the within warant as usuell

P^r^ Me Willm Dunken Constable

the other warant for S^d^ meeting was Rade and Compar^d^ and found word for word So not Needfull to be put upon Record

attest Pr Mo^s^ Barnett town Clerk

Provance of Newhampshir

Londonderry Aprill ye 28th 1758

In Obedence to the foregoing warants thy Being legelly Call^d^ the freeholders and Inhabitance of S^d^ Lond^ry^ Mate according to the appointment of S^d^ warants and Made Choys of Mr James willson to Moderat S^d^ Meeting and after Reeding the warants for S^d^ meeting and Considering the Same thy Chuse Mr William Humphry by the Majoraty of Voters to Serve as a Grand Jurer for S^d^ Lond^ry^ at his Maj^tes^ Superer Court of Judicature to be held at portsmouth in and for S^d^ provance on the third tusday of May Next and S^d^ Humphry hes been warn^d^ accordingly by the Constable

Provance of Newhampshir

Londonderry Aprill ye 15th 1758

By order of Cort to me Dericted You are hereby in his Maj^{tes} Name Requiered to warn all the freeholders and Inhabitance in your Respective bounds Duly Quallify^{d} by Law to Meete at their first Meetinghouse upon friday the twinty Eight Day of this Instant at two of the Clock after Noon in order to appoint one person Duly Quallify^{d} to Serve as a Petit Juror at his Maj^{tes} Superer Corte of Judicature to be held at portsmouth in and for S^{d} provance on the third tusday of May Next and this Shall Be your warant Given under My hand

Pr Mo^{s} Barnett town Clerk

To Mr David Craige town Constable

Provance of Newhampshir

Lond^{ry} aprill ye 28th 1758

I have posted the forgoing warant according to former Costom

P^{r} me David Craige Constable

Note the other warant for S^{d} Meeting was Rade and Compar^{d} and found word for word So Not Needfull to be put upon Record

attest Pr Mo^{s} Barnett Clerk

Provance of Newhampshir

Lond^{ry} Aprill ye 28th 1758

The freeholders and Inhabitance of S^{d} Lond^{ry} Mate according to appointment and after Reeding the warants for S^{d} meeting thy Chuse James Willson for thier moderater

Then after the acte of Law was Rade for the Chusing of Petit Jurors the Select men of S^{d} town Give abox to the town Clerk which was lock^{d} with agreat Maney Names of persons according to the Direction of S^{d} acte and the S^{d} Clark Shak^{d} S^{d} Box and onlock^{d} it and Drew out James Ramseys Name out of S^{d} Box to Serve as petit Juror at our Supperer Corte of Judicature to be holden at portsmouth afor^{sd} the third tusday of may Next and S^{d} Ramsey hes been warnd accordingly and the S[d] Clerk write upon the back Side of the peper that S[d] Ramseys name was on the time he was Chosen and put it in to S[d] box again and lock[t] the box

Provance of Newhampshir

Londonderry July the 29th 1758

By order of Court to Me Directed You are hereby Requiered to warn all the freeholders and Inhabitance in Your Respective Bounds Quallify[d] by law to Meet at their first Meetinghouse upon friday the Eleventh Day of augst Next Insuing the Deate hereof at two of the Clock after Noon in order to apointe two men Duly Quallify[d] as the law Directs to Serve as petit Jurors at his Maj[tes] Inferer Court of Common plees to be holden at portsmouth in S[d] provance on the first tusday of Sept[r] Next and the Court of Janerall Quarter Seshons the next tusday following

and this Shall be your warant Given under my hand the Day and year above

P[r] Mo[s] Barnett town Clerk

To M[r] David Craig town Constable

Provance of Newhampshir

Londonderry augst y[e] 11th 1758

I have posted the forgoing warant two publick Day according to former Costom

P[r] David Craige town Constable

and the other warant for S[d] meeting was Retorn[d] and Rade and found word for word so not Needfull to be put upon Record

attest

P[r] Mo[s] Barnett town Clerk

Provance of Newhampshir

Lond[ry] Augst y[e] 11th 1758

the freeholders and Inhabitance of S[d] town Mate according to the apointment of the forgoing warant and after Reeding the warants for S[d] meeting thy made Choys of John Wallace to Modrat S[d] Meeting then the town Clerk after

Shacking the box of Names for the Inferer Court unlockt it and Drue out Robart Parkesons Name and Thomas Boyd to Serve as pette Jurers at our Next Inferer Court of Common pllis to be holden at portsmouth on the first tusday of Sep^{tr} Next and Court of Generall Seshons of the peace to be holden at portsmouth on the Second tusday of the Same Mounth

Provance of Newhampshir

Londonderry Sep^{tr} the 23^{d} 1758

You are hereby Requiered in his Maj^{tis} Name to warn the freeholders and Inhabitance belonging to your Respective bounds to meete or assemble at their first meetinghous upon thorsday the fifth Day of Oct^{br} Next at one of the Clock in the after noon then and their

To See if the town be Satisfied with alate acte of the Generall Court with Respecte to the Regulation of Taverns and Retalers in S^{d} town and this Shall be your warant Given under our hands the Day and year above

Joseph Cochran
James McGregor
John Aiken
Sam^{ll} Aleson Ju^{r}
Select Men

To Mr Willm Dunken town Counstable

Provance of Newhampshir

Lond^{ry} Oct^{br} ye 5th 1758

I have posted the forgoing warant according to former Costom

Pr Willm Dunken town Constable

the other warant for S^{d} meeting was Rade and found word for word So not Needfull to be put upon Record

Attest Pr Mo^{s} Barnett town Clerk

Provance of Newhampshir

Lond^{ry} Oct^{br} ye 5th 1758

The freeholders and Inhabitance of the afor^{sd} town Mate according the the appointment of the forgoing warant and made Choys of Robt Boyes Esqr for to Moderate S^{d} Meeting and after Reeding the warant for S^{d} meeting and Considering the Same the Moderater asked the mimbers of S^{d} meeting if thy wold have the vote upon the artickell of the forgoing warant by hand or by writing and thy voted to Give them in in writing and accordingly thy Give in their vots and there was Seventy vots Content with the Janerall Courts act and thirty Eight Came in not Content

Provance of Newhampshir

Lond^{ry} Septr ye 18th 1758

You are herby Requiered to warn all the freeholders and Inhabitence belonging to Your Respective bounds to meet at their first meetinghouse upon thorsday y^{t} fifth Day of Octb^{r} Next at one of the Clock in the after Noon in order that a Noumber who have pititioned us for S^{d} meeting may Lay their Greviences about highways before S^{d} meeting

and this Shall be your warant Given under our hands the Day and year above

Joseph Cochran
James M^{t}Greger
Thos wallace
John Aiken
Sam^{ll} Aleson Junr
Select Men

To Mr David Craige town Constable

Provance of Newhampshir

Londonderry Oct^{br} ye 5th 1758

I have posted the within warant according to former Costom

Pr Me David Craige Town Constable

the other warant for S^{d} meeting was Rade and found word for word So Not Needfull to be put upon Record

attest Pr Mo^{s} Barnett town Clerk

Provance of Newhampshir

Lond^{ry} Oct^{br} ye 5th 1758

In obedence to the forgoing warant the freeholders and Inhabitance of S^{d} town Mate according to appointment and after Reeding the warant for S^{d} meeting thy made Choys of Robt Boyes Esqr for their Moderater and after Due Consideration of the forgoing warant it was Concluded to be left with the present Select men

Provance of Newhampshir

Lond^{ry} Sep^{tr} ye 5th 1758

By order of Court to me Directed You are hereby in his Maj^{tis} Name Requiered to warn all the freeholders and Inhabitance in your Respective bounds Duly Quallify^{d} by Law to meete at their first meetinghouse upon thorsday the fifth Day of Oct^{br} Next at ten of the Clock Before Noon in order to Chuse on fite person Quallify^{d} by Law to Serve as agrand Jurer at his Maj^{tis} Superiour Court of Judicature to be held at portsmouth in and for S^{d} provance on the Second tusday of Nou^{br} Next

and this Shall be your warant Given under my hand the Day and year above

Pr Mo^{s} Barnett town Clerk

To Mr David Craige Town Counstable

Provance of Newhampshir

Lond^{ry} Oct^{br} ye 5th 1758

I have posted the within warant acording to former Costom

P^{r} Me David Craige town Constable

the other warant for S^{d} meeting was Rade and found word for word So not needfull to be put upon Record

attest P Mo^{s} Barnett town Clerk

Provance of Newhampshir

Lond^{ry} Oct^{br} ye 5th 1758

In obideance to the forgoing warant the freeholders and Inhabitance of S^{d} town Mate on S^{d} Day and Chuse for moderater John wallace and after Reeding the warant for S^{d}

meeting thy made Choys of James willson South to Serve as Grand Jurer at our next Superer Court of Judicature to be held at portsmouth in and for S^{d} provance upon the Second tusday of nou^{br} next and he was Notify^{d} accordingly

Provance of Newhampshir

Lond^{ry} Sep^{tr} ye 25th 1758

By order of Court to me Directed You are hereby In his Maj^{tis} Name Requiered to warn all the freeholders and Inhabitance in your Respective Bounds Duly Quallify^{d} By Law to Meete at their first meetinghouse upon thorsday the fifth of Oct^{br} Next at twelve of the Clock In order to Chuse or Dravft out one fite person Quallify^{d} as the late acte of Law Directs to Serve as petit Jurer as his Maj^{tis} Superiour Court of Judicature to be held at portsmouth in and for S^{d} provance on the Second tusday of Nou^{br} Next and this Shall be your warant Given under my hand the Day and year above

Pr Mo^{s} Barnett town Clerk

To Mr David Craige town Counstable

Provance of Newhampshir

Lond^{ry} Oct^{br} ye 5th 1758

I have posted the forgoing warant according to former Costom

P^{r} Me David Craig town Conbl

the other warant for S^{d} meeting was Rade and found word for word So Not Needfull to be put upon Record

attest Pr Mo^{s} Barnett town Clerk

Provance of Newhampshir

Lond^{ry} Oct^{br} ye 5th 1758

In Obedance to the forgoing warant the freeholders and Inhabitance of S^{d} town Mate on S^{d} Day and Made Choys of John wallace for their Moderater then after the forgoing warant was Rade the town Clerk took the box of Names for the Supereour Court and Shaked it and unlocked it and Drad out John Nesmeth to Serve as petit Jurer at our Next Superour Court to be held at portsmouth in and for S^{d} provance upon the second tusday of Nou^{br} Next

Provance of Newhampshir

Londonderry Oct^{br} ye 25th 1758

In Pursuance of his Maj^{tes} write to us Derected under the Seal of the Provance afor^{sd} You are hereby in his Maj^{tes} Name Requiered to warn all the freeholders Qualilfy^{d} by Law in your Respective bounds to meet at the old meetinghouse in Lond^{ry} upon friday the tenth Day of Nou^{br} Next at ten of the Clock in the fore Noon then and their to Electe one person Quallify^{d} by Law to Represent the S^{d} town in Jenerall assembley in the provance afor^{sd}

and this Shall be your warant Given under our hands the Day and year above

James Mt Gregore
John Aken
Sam^{ll} Alleson Junr
Select Men

To Mr Willm Duncan town Counstable

Provance of Newhampshir

Londonderry Nou^{br} ye 10th 1758

I have posted the forgoing warant according to former Costom

Pr Mee Willm Duncan town Counstable

the other warant for S^{d} Meeting was Exemen^{d} and found word for word So Not Needfull to be put upon Record

attest Pr Mo^{s} Barnett town Clerk

Provance of Newhampshir

Lond^{ry} Nou^{br} ye 10th 1758

In Obedence to the forgoing warant the freeholders and Inhabitance of S^{d} town & windham mate on S^{d} Day according to the appointment of the warants for S^{d} meeting and thy made Choys of Capt John Mitchell to moderate S^{d} meeting younanamously by all the Legell Voters

then the warants for S^{d} meeting was Rade and Considered it is voted by the majority of the Quallify^{d} Electers that Mathew Thorntown Esqr is to Serve in the Janerell Assembly as Representative for S^{d} town and windham

Provance of Newhampshir

Londonderry Febr^{ry} ye 14th 1759

You are hereby Requaired to warn all the freeholders and Inhabitance belonging to your Presink that thy meete at the old Meetinghouse upon Monday the fifth Day of March Next at ten of the Clock in the fore Noon then and their

First to Chuse all the town and old parish oficers for the present year

2ly to here the towns accounts Read and approven or Not approve of them

and this Shall be your warant Given under our Hands the Day and year above

James Mc Gregore
Thos Wallace
John Aiken
Sam^{ll} Aleson Junr
Select Men

To Mr David Craige Town Constable

Provance of Newhampshir

Lond^{ry} March ye 5th 1759

I have posted the forgoing warant according to former Costom

P^{r} Me David Craige Counstable

The other warant for S^{d} meeting was Rade and Compar^{d} and found word for word So Not Needfull to be pute upon Record

attest Pr Mo^{s} Barnett town Clerk

Provance of Newhampshir

Londonderry March ye 5th 1759

In Obidance to the forgoing warants thy being Legelly Call^{d} the freeholders and Inhabitance of S^{d} lond^{ry} Quallify^{d} as the law Directs Mate according to the appointment of the S^{d} warants and after Reeding the warants for said meeting thy made Choys by the Majority of vots of Coll^{n} Andrew Todd to Moderate S^{d} meeting then after Reeding the warants for the afor^{sd} Meeting thy prosided and Chuse the Town and old parish oficers as followeth

Chosen for town Clerk for ye present year Mo^{s} Barnett

Voted to Chuse five Select Men for the Insuing year and their names is as followeth Thos Moreson Coll^{n} Sam^{ll} Barr John Cromey Junr John Clark Sam^{ll} Dickey

Chosen for Counstables for the Insuing year Isaac Cochran John Mack

Chosen for old parish Colecters for the Insuing year Arther Archibald Joseph Cochran

Chosen for taything Men for the Insuing year Capt John Moore David Hopken Willm Aers Junr James Morrow

Chosen for Surviers of the highways for the Insuing year on the Easterly Side of Baverbrook Robt Clendinin John Paton Sam^{ll} Moreson John Cochran James willson Gorge More will^{m} Kalso Mathew Taylor Junr Capt John Moore

Sirveyers Chosen for the westerly side of Baver Brook for the Insuing year James Anderson will^{m} Renken John Cromey Ins^{n} James wallace Adward Aiken Sam^{ll} Alls Sam^{ll} Anderson Thos Mt Clerey Isaac Page Ja^{s} Nesmeth Junr John Mountgoumbrey John Scobey will^{m} Dunken Junr Lif^{t} will^{m} Dunken John Hunter Ninen Cochran Joseph willson

Chosen for to take the Invoice on the Easterly sid of Baver Brook Jo^{n} Mt Keen

Chosen to take the Invoice for the Insuing year on the westerly side of Baver Brook John Cromey Junr

Chosen for Lather Sealrs for the present year David Hopken Willm Wallace

Chosen for Hogg Revis for the present year Willm Rodger at ye pond Joseph Bell Hugh Thomson Willm allete

Chosen for fence vewers and praysers for the present year John Mt Keen James Ramsey

Chosen for Counters with the select men and Constables for the Insuing year Robt Clerk James Nesmeth Mo^{s} Barnett

Chosen to tack Care that the Deer Be Not Killed out of Seson James Nesmeth Ju^{r} Jonathan adams will^{m} Renken James Mt Grager this meeting is Ajorned untill the third tusday of Aprill Next at ten of the Clock before Noon

Londonderry Aprill ye 17th 1759

The freeholders and Inhabitance of S^{d} town Mate on S^{d} Day according to ajorinment and after Reeding the warants for S^{d} Meeting it was ajorned untill the twinty second Day of may next at two of the Clock after Noon

Lond^{ry} May ye 22^{d} 1759

The freeholders and Inhabitance of S^{d} town Mate according to ajornment and after Reeding the warant for S^{d} meeting the Moderater Inquiered at the Select Men if the town officers were all Quallify^{d} and it it was Ansured that there was one taything Man awanting for which David Anderson was Chosen

then the towns accounts was Rade (viz) Sam^{ll} Allesons Junr David Craigs and will^{m} Dunkens for ye years 1758 and thy voted Not to approve of them

Provance of Newhampshir

Londonderry Aprill ye 25th 1759

By order of Court to me Directed you are hereby in his Maj^{tis} Name Requiered to warn all the freeholders and Inhabitance in Your Respective Bounds Duly Quallify^{d} by law to meet at their first Meetinghouse upon Monday the Seventh Day of May Next at three of the Clock after Noon in order to Chuse or Dravft out one fitt person Quallify^{d} as the late acte of Law Directs to Serve as Petit Jurer at his Maj^{tis} Superour Court of Judicature to be held at Portsmouth in and for S^{d} provance on the third tusday in May Next and Make Return of this warant personally of your Self at the afor^{sd} Meeting and this Shall be your warant Given under my hand the Day and year above

Pr Mo^{s} Barnett town Clerk

To Mr Isaac Cochran town Constable

Provance of Newhampshir

Londonderry May ye 7th 1759

In obidence to the forgoing warant I have posted it according to former Costom

P^{r} Me Isaac Couchran Constable

The other warant for S^{d} meeting was Rade and Comper^{d} and found word for word So Not Needfull to be put upon Record

attest Pr Mo^{s} Barnett town Clk

Provance of Newhampshir

Lond^{ry} May ye 7th 1759

In obidence to the forgoing warant the freeholders and Inhabitane of S^{d} town mate on S^{d} Day and after Reeding the warant for S^{d} meeting thy made Choys of Thos Campbell for their Moderater then the town Clark tuck the box for the Supererer Court and unlocked it and Drew out abilit for apetit Juroer which was James willson of S^{d} town and he was warned to attend at the afor^{sd} term

Provance of Newhampshir

Lond^{ry} Aprill ye 29th 1759

By order of Court to me Directed You are hereby Requiered to warn all the freeholders and Inhabitance in your Respective bounds Duly Quallify^{d} by Law to Meet at their first meetinghouse upon Monday the Seventh Day of May Next at four of the Clock after Noon in order to Chuse one fite person Quallify^{d} as the Law Directs to Serve as Grand Juror at his Maj^{tis} Superer Court of Judicature to be held at portsmouth in and for S^{d} provance on the third tusday of May Next

and this Shall be Your warant Given under My hand the Day and year above

Pr Mo^{s} Barnett town Clerk

To Mr John Mack town Constable

Provance of Newhampshir

Lond^{ry} May the 7th 1759

In obedence to the forgoing presepte I have posted it according to former Costom

P^{r} me John Mack Constable

the other warant for for S^{d} meeting was Rade and found word for word so Not Needfull to be put upon Record

attest Pr Mo^{s} Barnett town Clrk

Provance of Newhampshir

Lond^{ry} May the 7th 1759

In obedence to the forgoing warant the freeholders and Inhabitance Mate on S^{d} Day according to apointment and after Reeding the warant for S^{d} meeting thy made Choys of Thos Campbell for their Moderater then after Reeding for S^{d} meeting thy made Choys of Capt John Gregg to Serve Grand Juror at our Next Superer Court of Judicature to be holden at portsmouth the third tusday of this Instant and he was Notify^{d} accordingly

Provance of Newhampshir

Lond^{ry} May ye 7th 1759

By order of Court to Me Dericted You are hereby Requiered in his Maj^{tis} Name to warn all the freeholders and Inhabitance in your Respective bounds to meete at their first Meetinghouse upon monday the twinty first Day of this Instant at two of the Clock after Noon Quallify^{d} as the law Directs in order to Dravft out one Good and Lawfull Man of S^{d} town to Serve on the petit Jury at the Next Inferer Court of Common pllees to be holden at portsmouth on the first tusday of June Next and Court of Generall Seshons of the peace to be holden at portsm on the Second tusday of the Same mounth and this Shall be Your Warant Given under my hand the day and year above

Pr Mo^{s} Barnett town Clerk

To Mr Isaac Cochran town Counstable

Provance of Newhampshir

Lond^{ry} May the 21^{d} 1759

In obedence to the forgoing presept I have posted it according to former Costom

Pr Mee Isaac Cochran town Constable

the other warant for S^d meeting was Rade and Exemened and found word for word So Not Needfull to be put upon Record

attest Pr Mo^s Barnett town Clerk

Provance of Newhampshir

$Lond^{ry}$ may the 7th 1759

In obedence to the forgoing warant the freeholders and Inhabitance of S^d town Mate on S^d Day according to appointment and Chuse Joseph Cochran for their Moderater then the town Clerk unlocked the Box for the Inferer Court and Seshons and Drew out abilit which was John Dunham of S^d town to Serve as petit Jurer and he was $Notify^d$ accordingly

Provance of Newhampshir

$Lond^{ry}$ August y^e 1^d 1759

By order of Court to Me Directed you are hereby in his Maj^{tis} Requiered to warn all The freeholders and Inhabitanc in your Respective Bounds Duly $Quallify^d$ by law to meet at their first meetinghouse upon wadensday y^e 15th Day of this Instant at three of the Clock after Noon in order to Chuse one fite person $Quallify^d$ as the law Directs to Serve as Grand Juror at the Next Court of Jenerall Seshons of the peace to be holden at portsmouth on the Second tusday of Sep^{tr} Next and this Shall be your warant Given under my hand the Day and year above

Pr Mo^s Barnett Clk

To Mr John Mack town Constable

Provance of Newhampshir

$Lond^{ry}$ August y^e 15th 1759

In obedence to the forgoing warant I have posted it according to former Costom

P^r Me John Mack town Constabl

Londonderry August y^e 15th 1759

In obedance to the forgoing warant the freeholders and Inhabitance of S^d town Mate on the $afor^{sd}$ Day and after Reeding the warnts for S^d meeting thy made Choys of David Hopken to moderat S^d meeting and after Reeding and Considering the artickell of S^d warants thy made Choys of

James Juings of S^{d} town to Serve as Grand Juror at the next Jenerall Sashons of y^{e} peace to be holden at portsmouth upon the Second tusday of Sep^{tr} Next Insuing

the other warant for S^{d} meeting was Exemn^{d} and found word for word So Not needfull to be put upon Decord

attest Pr Mo^{s} Barnett town Clk

Provance of Newhampshir

To Mr Isace Cochran Constable for the Easterly Side of Baverbrook in Lond^{ry} in S^{d} provance You are hereby Requiered to warn all the free holders and Inhabitance in your Respective bounds to Meet at the old Meetinghouse in Said Lond^{ry} upon thursday the Sixt Day of Sep^{tr} Next at two of the Clock after Noon then and their

first to See what Money the town will allow to be Raised to Defray the Charges of the present year

2ly To See what the town will Do in Regarde of the Peramblaition of the line betwen Londonderry and Litchfield as there has been Assays made by the Select Men of Lond^{ry} heretofore and to acte their on

3ly at the Requiest of a noumber of Subscribers to See if the town will Chuse aCom^{tee} to inquier at the towns ajasant if thy in Conjunction with Lond^{ry} will Pitition to have an act made in Regard of the fishing at amuskegg So that Every Man May Inioy his Natrell Right

4^{ly} at the Requiest of anoumber of Subscribers to See where the town will have their taverans placed for this year Lackwise to See if the town will pitition for to have Some more taverans as our Noumber is tow few and to have Retalers as in other towns in this and the Nighbering Goverments

and this Shall be your warant Given under our hands

Deated at Lond^{ry} august ye 23^{d} 1759

Sam^{ll} Barr
Sam^{ll} Dickey
John Clark
John Crombie Junr
Thos Morison
Select Men

Provance of Newhampshir

Lond^{ry} Sep^{tr} ye 6th 1759

In obideance to the forgoing warant I have Posted it as uswell

Pr Isaac Cochran town Constable

Note the other warant for S^{d} Meeting was Rade and Compared and found word for word So Not Needfull to be put upon Record

attest Pr Mo^{s} Barnett town Clerk

Provance of Newhampshir

Londonderry Sep^{tr} ye 6th 1759

In obidence to the forgoing warants the freeholders and Inhabitance of S^{d} town Mate on S^{d} Day and after Reeding the warants for S^{d} Meeting thy made Choys of Coll^{n} Andrew Todd for their Moderater and after Reeding and Considering the first artickell of the forgoing warant thy Voted to Rase Seven houndred pounds old tener to Defray the towns Debts for the present year

Voted on the Second artickell of the warant as followeth that the Select Men of S^{d} town Shall Call Letchfield Select men to Perambuelate the line betwixt the two towns and prosecute them of Litchfield if thy Refuse

Voted on the third artickell of the forgoing warant to Chuse aCom^{tee} to Inquier at the towns ajasant to See if thy will Joyn with Lond^{ry} to pitition the Janerall Court to have an acte of Law Made upon the account of the fishery at amasgigg So that Every Man may Injoy their Rights as also to have the brooks Clear that the fish may have their Runs to the heads theirof S^{d} Com^{tee} is as followeth Coll^{n} And^{w} Todd Coll^{n} Sam^{ll} Barr and Mathew Thorntown Esqr and S^{d} Com^{tee} is outherised by S^{d} vote if the ajasant towns Joyn in S^{d} affair to Draw or to assist S^{d} towns to Draw apitition and prefaire it to finell Judgment

Voted on the forth artickell of S^{d} warant that the Select Men is to place the taverns and Retalers according to the acte made for that Ende also voted that the town is to pitition the Jenerall Court for an aditionell acte to have three taverns More and Retalers as other towns have

Samuell Alleson Sam^{ll} Alleson Junr Lif^{t} John Wiar and Moses Barnett Enters their Desent against the Vote past upon the last artickell of the forgoing warant against piti-tishining for any more taverens

Provance of Newhampshir

Lond^{ry} Oct^{br} ye 10th 1759

By order of Court to me Directed You are hereby Re-quiered to warn all the freeholders and Inhabitance in your Respective bounds Duly Quallify^{d} by law to meet at their first Meetinghouse upon thursday the twinty fifth Day of this Instant at one of the Clock after Noon in order to Chuse or Dravft one person Quallify^{d} as the late acte of Law Directs to Serve as apetit Jurer as his Maj^{tes} Superour Court of Judicature to be held at Portsmouth in and for S^{d} provance on the Second tusday in Nou^{br} Next and this Shall be your warant Given under My hand the Day and year above

Pr Mo^{s} Barnett town Clk

To Mr John Mack town Constable

Provance of Newhampshir

Lond^{ry} Oct^{br} ye 25th 1759

In obedence to the forgoing presept I have posted it ac-cording to former Costom

Pr John Mack Constable

Note the other warant for S^{d} meeting was Rade and Ex-emened and found word for word So Not Needfull to be put upon Record

attest Pr Mo^{s} Barnett town Clerk

Provance of Newhampshir

Lond^{ry} Oct^{br} ye 25th 1759

In obedence to the forgoing warant the freeholders and Inhabitance of S^{d} town Mate on the afor^{sd} Day and after Reeding the warant for S^{d} meeting thy made Choys of Coll^{n} Sam^{ll} Barr for to Moderat in S^{d} meeting then the town Clark unlocked the Box for the Superer Court and took out abilet which was Peeter Peeterson to Serve as a Peetit Juror and he was Notify^{d} accordingly

Provance of Newhampshir

Lond^{ry} Oct^{br} ye 10th 1759

By order of Court to me Directed you are hereby Requiered to warn all the freeholders and Inhabitance in your Respective Bounds Duly Quallify^{d} as the late acte of Law Directs to meet at their first Meetinghouse upon thursday the twintyfifth Day of this Instant at two of the Clock after Noon to Chuse one Good and lawfull man to Serve as Grand Jurour at his Maj^{tis} Superer Court of Judicature to be held at Portsmouth in and for S^{d} Provance on the Second tusday of Nou^{br} Next

and this Shall be your warant Given under My hand the Day and year above

Pr Mo^{s} Barnett town Cl'k

To Mr John Mack town Constable

Provance of Newhampshir

Lond^{ry} Oct^{br} ye 25th 1759

In obedence to the forgoing warant I have posted it acording to former Costom

Pr John Mack town Constable

Note the other warant for S^{d} meeting was Rade and Compared and found word for word So Not Needfull to be put upon Record

attest Pr Mo^{s} Barnett town Clerk

Lond^{ry} oct^{br} ye 25th 1759

In Obedence to the forgoing warant the freeholders and Inhabitance of S^{d} town Mate on the afor^{sd} Day and after Reeding the warant for S^{d} meeting thy made Choys of Coll^{n} Sam^{ll} Barr for to moderat in S^{d} meeting then by the Majer parte of the Electers present thy Chuse John Mitchell Survier of S^{d} town to Serve as Grand Juror at the afor^{d} Court and he was Notify^{d} accordingly

Provance of Newhampshir

Lond^{ry} ye 1^{d} of Noub^{r} 1759

By order of Court to me Directed You are hereby Requiered to warn all the freeholders and Inhabitance in your

Respective Bounds Duly Quallify^{d} as the late acte of Law Directs to meet at their first meetinghouse upon friday the 16th Day of this Instant at two of the Clock after Noon to Chuse one Good and Lawfull man to Serve as a Grand Juror at the Next Court of Jenerall Sessions of the peace to be holden at Portsmouth on the Second tusday of Dec^{br} Next and this Shall beyour warant Given under my hand the Day and year above

Pr Mo^{s} Barnett town Clerk

To Mr Isaac Cochran town Constable

Provance of Newhampshir

Lond^{ry} Nou^{br} ye 16th 1759

In obedence to the forgoing I have posted it according to former Costom

Pr Isaac Cochran Constable

Note the other warant for S^{d} meeting was Compard and found word for word So Not Needfull to be put upon Record

attest Pr Mo^{s} Barnett town Clerk

Provance of Newhampshir

Lon^{dry} Nou^{br} ye 16th 1759

according to the forgoing warning the freeholders and Inhabitance of S^{d} town mate on S^{d} Day and after Reeding the warants for S^{d} meeting they made Choys of John wallace the first to modrate S^{d} meeting and after Consideration then by the maj^{r} part of the Electers present thy made Choys of John Wallace the Second of S^{d} town to Serve as Grand Juror at the afor^{sd} Seshons and he was Notify^{d} accordingly

Provance of Newhampshir

Londonderry Feb^{ry} ye 7th 1760

To Mr Isaac Cochran Constable for the Easterly Side of Beaver Brook

You are hereby Requiered to warn all the freeholders and Inhabitance in your Respective Bounds to meet at their first meetinghouse upon friday the twenty Second Day of this Instant at ten of the Clock before Noon then and their

First to See what the town will Do in Regard of the Select Men being Sued by Thos Reid and David taylor wither thy will answer their Demands their Demands and pay all their Charges that thy have pute them Selves too or Stand the triall and Contend for their Right

2ly at the Requist of upwards of thirty Signers to See if the town will Clear Thos Reid and David Taylor from paying town and provance Taxes for the year one thousand Seven houndred and fifty Nine and to acte thereon

3ly To See if the town will approve or Not approve of the Select Mens Conduct in puting Said Reid and Taylor in Goal for Sd taxes and to acte theiron

and this Sall be your warant Given under our hands the Day and year above

Saml Barr
Samll Dickey
Thos Moreson
John Crombie
Select Men

Provance of Newhampshir

Londry Febry ye 22d 1760

In obedence to the forgoing warant I have posted it according to Costom

Pr Isaac Cochran town Counstable

Note the other warant for Sd meeting was Rade and Compared and found word for word So Not Needfull to be pute upon Record

attest Pr Mos Barnett town Clerk

Provance of Newhampshir

Londry Febry ye 22d 1760

In obidance to the within Warant the freeholders and Inhabitance of Sd town Mate on Sd Day and after Reeding the warants for Sd meeting thy made Choys of Insin James Mt Gregor to moderat Sd meeting then after Reeding and Considering the first artickell of Sd warants it was voted to pass it untill the Second and third Artickell be voted upon the Second artickell of the forgoing warant being Rade and Considered it is voted by S^{d} freeholders and Inhabitance to aquite the afor^{sd} Reid and taylor of their town and Provance taxes for the year one thousand Seven houndred and fifty Nine Voted one the third artickell of the forgoing warant by S^{d} freeholders and Inhabitance that thy Disaprove of the Select Mens Conducke in puting S^{d} Reid and taylor in Goll voted on the first Artickell of the forgoing warant by S^{d} free holders and Inhabitance to Chuse aCom^{tee} of five men to Inspect and See what Charges hes arisen Either on S^{d} Reed and taylors parte or the Select mens part by puting S^{d} Reed and taylor in Goll the Com^{tee} is as followeth Sam^{ll} Allosen Junr James Mt Gregor John Mt Keen John Humphra and Mo^{s} Barnett and if S^{d} Com^{tee} or the Majer parte of them thinks that the Charges is Resonable then the town is to pay S^{d} Charges

voted Also by S^{d} town that if the Select men proside any forther in that Case Relating to them and the afor^{sd} Reid and taylor that the town will not pay the Charge but S^{d} Select men must pay it out of their own Estat

Coll^{n} Sam^{ll} Barr John Crombie and Sam^{li} Dickey Enters their Desent against that vote whereas the town Disaproves of the Selectmens Conducte the afor^{sd} Barr and Dickey Enters their Desent against the last vote past in the afor^{sd} meeting

Willm Blair Enters his Desent against the Second artickell voted in the afor^{sd} meeting upon the accounte of the Counsequances that May arise in Quiting men of their Reats

Provance of Newhampshir

Lond^{ry} Feb^{ry} ye 7th 1760

To Mr Isaac Cochran Constable for the Easterly Side of Baverbrook

You are hereby Requiered to warn all the freeholders and Inhabitance in your Respective bounds to meete at their first Meetinghouse upon wadensday the fifth Day of March Next at ten of the Clock before Noon then and their first to Chuse all their town and old parish oficers for the Corant year

2ly To here the Pitition that the Select Men for the year past Prosecuted agreeable to their vote in Regarde of taverns and Retalers and the order of the Jenerall Court thereon

3ly at the Requist of anomber of Subcribers to see what Mathode the town will take to have abridg made aCross Baver brook on the Recorded Rode Nigh Banj^{mn} willsons Mill

4ly at the Requist of anoumber of Subcribers to see what the town will Do in Regarde of aRode that thy Disier from the house of David Cochrans heirs to Com out near Hugh Mountgoumbreys

5ly to here the towns accounts Rade and approven or Not approve of them

and this Shall be your warant Given under our hands the Day and year above

Sam^{ll} Barr
Sam^{ll} Dicky
Thos Moreson
John Cromey Junr
Select Men

Provance of Newhampshir

Lond^{ry} March ye 5th 1760

In obedence to the within warant I have posted it according to Costom

P^{r} me Isaac Cochran town Constable

Provance of Newhampshir

Lond^{ry} March ye 5th 1760

In obedence to the forgoing warants the free holders and Inhabitance of S^{d} town Mate on S^{d} Day thy being legelly Call^{d} and after Reeding and Considiring the forgoing warants thy Chuse for moderater for S^{d} meeting Coll^{n} Andrew Todd then after Considiring Said warants thy proposed to Chuse their town and old parish oficers by vote for the Insuing year as followeth

Chosen for town Clerk Mo^{s} Barnett

Voted for five Select men for the Insuing year and their Names is as followeth John M^{tt} Keen will^{m} Renken Ja^{s} Ramsey Robt Moore Coll^{n} Andrew Todd

Chosen for Constables Willm Rogers in the peek Joseph Hogg

Colacters for the old parish Colecters Willm Beetey John Paton

Chosen taything men Joseph Scobey Ja^{s} Aiers Ja^{s} Cochran Junr Ja^{s} Cochran in Cannade

Surveyrs for the Easterly Side of Baverbrook and westerly Side Sam^{ll} Alleson Junr Sam^{ll} Huston John Cromey Junr Lif^{t} Robt wallace Sam^{ll} Dickey Sam^{ll} Allies Robt Alex^{dr} Willm Smith Robt Mt Clure Abr^{m} Moreson Coll^{n} Andrew Todd Thos Hilands John Dunken Willm Cochran Insin Senter Sam^{ll} Clark Mathew Clark Mathew Taylor John Hopken Gorge Reide David Mungombrey James Stell Robt Ferservice Robt Archabald James Tagart Jonathan Adams

Lather Sealers James Cromey David Clendinin

Hogg Rives James Miller will^{m} Dickey John Hogg Willm Allet Willm Dunken Junr

fence vewers and praisers David Stell John Cromey Junr

Counters with the Select Men and Counstables James Mt Keen Sam^{ll} Alleson Junr Mo^{s} Barnett

Invice Men the west Side is to have 15 pounds and the East 12 old tener John Mt Keen John Cromey Junr

Chosen for Sealer of weights and Mishers John Mitchell Junr

Vote on the Second atickell by S^{d} freeholders and Inhabitance as followeth by the Majority to Prosecute their Pitition agreeable to the prayers

This meeting is ajorned untill wadensday the twinty Sixth Day of aprill Next at ten of the Clock before Noon

Lond^{ry} Aprill the 26^{d} 1760

Then the freeholders and Inhabitance of S^{d} town Mate on S^{d} Day according to S^{d} ajornment and after Considering the forth artickell of the warant for S^{d} meeting they voted to pass it in the Negitive

The towns accounts was Rade and approven of Excepting the Select mens having one pound ten Shillings appeace for apploting the Reats and allowing two pounds to will^{m} Dunken padler for the wants of aformer year as the order Said

Provance of Newhampshir

Lond^{ry} Aprill ye 5th 1760

By order of Court to me Directed You are hereby Required to warn all the freeholders and Inhabitance in your Respective bounds Duly Quallify^{d} as the acte of Law Directs to meete at their first Meetinghouse upon wedensday the 23^{d} Day of this Instant at four of the Clock after Noon in order to Chuse one Good and lawfull man to Sarve as aGrand Juror at his Maj^{tis} Superer Court of Judicature to be held at portsmouth in and for S^{d} provance on the third tusday in May Next and this Shall be your warant Given under my hand the Day and year above

Pr Mo^{s} Barnett town Clk

to M^{r} will^{m} Roger town Constable

Provance of Newhampshir

Aprill ye 5th 1760

In obedence to the forgoing warante I have posted it acording to former Costom

Pr Willm Rodger town Constable

Note the other warant for S^{d} meeting was Compar^{d} and found word for word and Not needfull to be put upon Record

attest Pr Mo^{s} Barnett town Clerk

Provance of Newhampshir

Lond^{ry} Aprill ye 5th 1760

according to the appointment of the forgoing warant the freeholders and Inhabitance of S^{d} town attended and Chuse Mr Robt Clark to moderat S^{d} meeting then by the Majority of the Electers present thy Made Choys of Lif^{t} Willm Dunken to Sarve as Grand Juror at the afor^{sd} Court and he was Notify^{d} accordingly

Provance of Newhampshir

Lond^{ry} Aprill ye 5th 1760

By order of Court to Me Directed you are herby Requiered to warn all the freeholders and Inhabitance in your Respective bounds Duly Quallify^{d} as the law Directs to Meet at their first Meetinghouse upon wadensday the 23^{d} Day of this Instant at four of the Clock after Noon in order to Dravft one Man as the law Directs Quallify^{d} to Serve as a Petit Juror at his Maj^{tis} Superer Court of Judicatour to be held at portsmouth in and for S^{d} provance on the third tusday of may Next

and this Shall be your warant Given under my hand the Day and year above

Pr Mo^{s} Barnett town Clk

To Mr Willm Roger town Constable

Provance of Newhampshir

Lond^{ry} Aprill ye 5th 1760

In obedence to the forgoing warant I have posted it according to former Costom

P^{r} me will^{m} Roger Constable

Note the other warant for S^{d} meeting was Compared and found word for word and Not Needfull to be put upon Record

attest Pr Mo^{s} Barnett town Clerk

Provance of Newhampshir

Lond^{ry} Aprill ye 5 1760

According to the appointment of the forgoing warant the freeholders and Inhabitance of S^{d} town atended and Chuse Mr Robt Clark to modrat S^{d} Meeting and the town Clak Shuck the Box and unlocked it and Drue out James Nesmith Ju^{r} to Sarve as Petit Jurer at the afor^{sd} Court

Provance of Newhampsher

Lond^{ry} May ye 13th 1760

By order of Court to me Directed You are Requiered in his Maj^{tis} Name to warn all the freehorlders and Inhabitance in Your Respective bounds Duly Quallify^{d} as the law Directs to Meet at their first meetinghouse upon tusday the 27th Day of this Instant at four of the Clock after Noon in order to Dravft two Good and lawfull men of S^d^ town to Serve on the petit Jurey at the Next Inferer Court of Common plls to be holden at portsmouth on the first tusday of June Next and Court of Jannerell Seshons of the peace to be holden at portsmouth on the Second tusday of the Same Month and this Shall be your warant Given under My hand the Day and year above

Pr Mo^s^ Barnett town Clk

To Mr Joseph Hogg town Constable

Provance of Newhampshir

Lond^ry^ May ye 27th 1760

In obedence to the forgoing warant I have posted it according to former Costom

P^r^ me Joseph Hogg town Constable

Note the other warant for S^d^ meeting was Rade and Exemn^d^ and found word for word So Not Needfull to be put upon Record

attest Pr Mo^s^ Barnett town Clerk

Provance of Newhampshir

Lond^ry^ May ye 27th 1760

according to the appointment of the forgoing warant the freeholders and Inhabitance of S^d^ town Mate and Chuse for Moderater for S^d^ meeting John Cromey Junr and as the law Directs the town Clerk unlocked the Box and Dray^d^ oute the Names of Robt Alex^dr^ and Arther Archibald to Serve at his Maj^tis^ Court of Common plls and Court of Jenerall Seshons of the peace as petit Jurers as above

Provance of Newhampshir

Londonderry June ye 15th 1760

You are hereby Requiered In his Maj^tis^ Name to warn all the freeholders and Inhabitance belonging to your Respective Bounds to meete at the old Meetinghouse upon tusday the first Day of July Next at two of the clock in the after Noon then and their first to See what Money the town will allow to be Sased to Defray the Debts of S^{d} town for S^{d} year

2ly To See what the town will Do in Regard of the Gravyard and pound both wanting to be Repaired

3ly at the Disier of upwards of thirty Subcribers to See wither the town will vote to purtches Roade betwixt the late David Chochrans and Hugh Ramseys at any Rate and open it

4ly To See what the town will Do in Regard of Dividing the highways according to alaw Latly Made

and this Shall be your warant Given under our hands the Day and year above Mentioned

Andrew Todd
John McKeen
Robt Moore
Willm Renken
Ja^{s} Ramsey
Select Men

To Mr Joseph Hogge town Constable

Provance of Newhampshir

Lond^{ry} July ye 1^{d} 1760

I have posted this warant according to former Costom

P^{r} me Joseph Hogg town Constable

Note the other warant for S^{d} meeting was Rade and Compar^{d} and found word for word So Not Needfull to be pute upon Record

attest Pr Mo^{s} Barnett town Clerk

Provance of Newhampshir

Lond^{ry} July ye 1^{d} 1760

The freeholders and Inhabitance of S^{d} town Mate on S^{d} Day according to the apointment of the warant for S^{d} meeing and after Reeding S^{d} warant thy made Choys of Coll^{n} Sam^{ll} Barr to Moderate S^{d} meeting

the first artickell of the forgoing warant being Rade and Considered it is voted by S^{d} Inhabitance to pass S^{d} artickell untill the Rest of the artickells of S^{d} warant be voted upon

voted on the Second artickell of the forgoing war^{t} to Repere the pounde at forty fute Squire and the Select men is Chosen to buld the pounde and Repare the Grave yarde Gate at the old meetinghouse

Voted that Sam^{ll} Alleson Junr and Lif^{t} John wiar is Chosen as aCom^{tee} to take Care of S^{d} Grave yard when it is Repared

The third artickell of the forgoing warante being Rade and Considered is voted by S^{d} Inhabitance that thy will Rase no money to pay for land to Make ahighway in that place

Voted on the forth artickell to leve it with the Select men to Regelat any Difirance that arises betwixt Sirviers of highways where there is any Dispute

Voted on the first artickell of S^{d} warant by S^{d} town to Raise Seven houndred pounds old tener to Defray the town Debts for this present year

Provance of Newhampshir

Lond^{ry} August the 18th 1760

By order of Court to me Directed you are hereby Requiered to warn all the freeholders and Inhabitance in your Respective bounds Duly Quallify^{d} as the late acte of law Directs to Meet at their first meetinghouse upon tusday the Second Day of Sep^{tr} Next at three of the Clock after Noon to Chuse one Good and Lawfull Man to Serve as Grand Juror at the Next Court of Generall Seshons of the peace to be holden at portsmouth on the Second tusday of Sep^{tr} afors^{d} and this Shall be your warant Given under My hand the Day and year above

Pr Mo^{s} Barnett town Clerk

To Mr Joseph Hogg town Constable

Lond^{ry} Sep^{tr} ye 2^{d} 1760

In obedence to the forgoing warant I have posted it according to former Costom

P^{r} Me Joseph Hogg town Constable

Note the other warant for S^{d} meeting was Rade and Compared and found word for word So Not Needfull to be put upon Record

attest Mo^{s} Barnett Ck

the freeholders and Inhabitance Mate on S^{d} Day and after Reeding the warants for S^{d} meeting thy Chuse Thos Cristy for their Moderater

then after Reeding and Considering S^{d} warants thy made Choys of David Mungoumbrey to Serve as Grand Juror at the afor^{sd} Seshons and he hes been Notify^{d} accordingly

Provance of Newhampshir

Lond^{ry} Sep^{tr} ye 15th 1760

By order of Courte to me Directed You are hereby Requiered to warn all the freeholders and Inhabitance in your Respective bounds Duly Quallify^{d} by law to meet at their first meetinghouse upon Monday the 29th Day of this Instant at two of the Clock after Noon in order to Chuse one Good and lawfull Man of S^{d} town to Sarve as Grand Juror at his Maj^{tis} Supereour Court of Judicature to be held at portsmouth in and for S^{d} provance on the Second tusday in Nou^{br} Next and this Shall be your warant Given under My hand the Day and year above

Pr Mo^{s} Barnett town Clk

To Mr Willm Rogers town Constable

Provance of Newhampshir

Lond^{ry} Sep^{tr} ye 29th 1760

In obedance to the within warant I have posted it according to former Costom

Pr Willm Roger town Constable

Note the other warant for S^{d} meeting was Rade and Compared and found word for word So Not Needfull to be pute upon Record

attest Pr Mo^{s} Barnett town Clerk

the freeholders and Inhabitance of S^{d} town Mate on S^{d} Day and after Reeding the warants for S^{d} meeting thy made Choys of Mr Thos Campbell to moderat S^{d} meeting then after Reeding S^{d} warants thy made Choys of John Hilands to Serve as Grand Juror at the afor^{sd} Court

Provance of Newhampshir

Lond^{ry} Sep^{tr} ye 15th 1760

By order of Court to me Directed You are hereby Requiered to warn all the freeholders and Inhabitance in your Respective bounds Duly Quallify^{d} by law to meet at their first Meeting-house upon Monday the 29th Day of this Instant at three of the Clock after Noon in order to appoint one person Duly Quallify^{d} to Serve as petit Juror at his Maj^{tis} Superer Court of Judicature to be held at portsmouth in and for S^{d} provance on the Second tusday in Nou^{br} next

and this Shall be your warnt Given under my hand the Day and year above

Pr Mo^{s} Barnett town Clk

To Mr Willm Roger town Constable

Provance of Newhampshir

Lond^{ry} Sep^{tr} ye 19th 1760

In obedence to the forgoing warnts I have posted them according to former Custom

P^{r} Me will^{m} Rogers town Constable

Note the other warant for S^{d} meeting was Rade and Compar^{d} and found word for word So Not Needfull to be put upon Record

attest Pr Mo^{s} Barnett town Clerk

The freeholders and Inhabitance of S^{d} town Mate on S^{d} Day according to the appointment of the forgoing warants thy being legelly Call^{d} and after Reeding the warants for S^{d} meeting thy Made Choys of Lif^{t} John wiar for to moderat S^{d} meeting then after Reeding S^{d} warant for S^{d} meeting the Clerk Shakt and unlocked the Box that had the petit Jurors for the Superer Court and Dravfted out Capt John Ramsey to Serve at the afor^{sd} Court

Provance of Newhampshir

Londonderry Feber^{y} the 17th 1761

You are hereby Requiered in his Maj^{tis} Name to warn all the freeholders and Inhabitance belonging to your Respective bounds to meete at the old meetinghouse upon thorsday the fifth Day of march Next at ten of the Clock in the fornoon then and their

first to Chuse all the town and old parish oficers for the present year

2ly to See what price the town will allow the people for the land p^r acre that is tacken of them for highways

3ly To See if the town will vote to open ahighway from the late late David Cochrans to Hugh Ramseys a Number of Inhabitance Desiering the Same and Says that thy will make applecation to the Sessions for it if not Done

4ly To See what the town will allow the Constables P^r houndred for Collecting their town and provance Rates for the year past also for paying their provance Rates to the treassure

5ly at the Desiere of upwards of ten Subcribers to have aRoad from John Andersons Stone house formerly Stright to the old meetinghouse in Londonderry

6^ly to See if the town will alter the Rode that Goes aCross John Pattons lote to the line betwixt him and Capt John Gregg or as Near as Good Ground will allow S^d patton Ingaging to make the New Roade as Good as the Road Now is at his own Cost

7^ly to heare the towns accoumpts Read and approven or Not approve of them

and this Shall be your warant Given under our hands the Day and year above

Andrew Todd
John McKeen
James Ramsey
Robt Moore
Willm Renken
Selectmen

To Mr Willm Rogers town Constable

Provance of Newhampshir

Lond^ry March ye 5th 1761

I have posted the forgoing warant according to former Costom by me

Willm Rogers town Constable

the other warant being word for word it is Not Needfull to be pute upon Record

Pr Mo^{s} Barnett Clk

Provance of Newhampshir

Lond^{ry} March ye 5th 1761

In Obedence to the forgoing warants the freeholders and Inhabitance of S^{d} town mate on S^{d} Day according to the appointment of the forgoing warants and after Reeding Said warants for S^{d} meeting thy Chuse Coll^{n} Andrew Todd to Moderate S^{d} Meeting

then after Reeding and Considering the forgoing warants thy made Choys of their town and old parish officers as followeth

Chosen for town Clerk Mo^{s} Barnett

Chosen for town Clerk protemporay Lif^{t} John wiar

five Select Men Chosen for the Insuing year and thy are Coll^{n} And^{w} Todd John Mt Keen James Ramsey Willm Renken Robt Moore

Chosen for Constables Sam^{ll} Care Hugh young David pinkertown John Cromey Junr Robt Anderson S^{d} young pay^{d} his fine S^{d} pinkertown pay^{d} his fine S^{d} Cromey pay^{d} his fine S^{d} Anderson pay^{d} his fine and Non of the above men that pay^{d} their fins wold Serve

Then thy Chuse for Constable for the westerly Side of Baver Brook Ruben Senter Moses Senter and Moses Senter appered and offered to Serve Constable in his Brothers place for S^{d} Ruben but not for Mo^{s} for the Insuing year and he was Excepted accordingly

Chosen for Colecters for the old parish James Alex^{dr} Peeter Peterson

Chosen for taything men for the Insuing year Andrew Clendinin Ja^{s} Nickells Danill Mt Nell Willm Wallace John Highlands

Surviers for the Easterly Sid of Baver Brook Lif^{t} John wiar Capt John Gregg Robt Moore South Joseph Moreson Robt Mt Murphy Willm Taylor Thos Cristy David Doge David Craige

Surviers for the westerly Side of Baver Brook Robt Logan Willm Aires Gorge Clark John Hollms Alex^{dr} m^{t} Coloster Robt willson Junr Francis Graims John Aiken Hugh Moore Sam^{ll} Miller James Juings will^{m} Dunken Junr John Barnett John Hunter James Doake Ja^{s} paterson Thos Nesmeth

Chosen for Lather Sealers for the Insuing year James Cromey Robt Mt Nell

Chose for Hogg Rives for the Insuing year John M^{t}Kertney Alex^{dr} Nickolls Robt Coningham Hugh Thompson Eleis Sargant John wadell

Chosen for fence vewers and praisers for the Insuing year Robt Clark John Mt Keen

Chosen for Counters with the Select Men and Constables for the Insuing year John Cromey Junr Coll^{n} Sam^{ll} Barr Mo^{s} Barnett

Chosen for Invoice Men for the Insuing year the wages as usuell John Mt Keen John Cromey Junr

Chosen for Deer Keepers for the Insuing year Ins^{n} Ja^{s} Mt Greger Jonathan Adams Ja^{s} Nesmith Junr will^{m} Renken

Chosen for Sealer of weights and Mishurs for the Insuing year John Mitchell Junr

Voted by S^{d} freeholders and Inhabitance upon the Second artickell as followeth to Give fifteen pounds old tener for the best of land that must be pay^{d} per acre for highway land in S^{d} town and the best of Situation and So to fall according to the badness of the land and Sittiuation

this meeting is ajorned untill the first wadensday of aprill Next at twelve of the Clock

Lond^{ry} April ye 1^{d} 1761

The free holders and Inhabitance of S^{d} town mate accord- to the afor^{sd} ajorinment and after Reeeding the warants for the afor^{sd} meeting Robt Anderson pay^{d} his fine for being Chosen Constable and then they made Choys of Ruben Senter to Serve Constable for the westerly Side of Baver Brook for the Insuing year

Voted on the third artickell of the forgoing warant as followeth to allow the peeke people and those that Joyns with them that wants the Rode through from the heirs of David Cochrans house to Hugh Ramseys two houndred and thirty pounds old tener when they open Said Rode and Repers the Same in Good order and those that wants S^d^ Rode is to Recive the afor^sd^ Money in order to pay for the land of S^d^ Rode When they Give in Good Security to our Select men to Keepe S^d^ Rode in Good Repare for Ever here after besides their proportion of the Roads that thy have to work in other parts

Voted on the forth artick of the forgoing warant to allow the Constabels no more for Listing the Reates then what was formerly voted

Voted on the fifth artickell of the warant Not to upon nor pay for S^d^ Roade

Voted on the Sixth artickell of the forgoing warant as followeth that when John Paton Makes the Roade on his line as Good and as Nigh as the old Roade to our Selectmens Exceptence and S^d^ paton will Ingage to Keepe the town Indamnify^d^ from any Charge that may arise by any person that Stands against the Change of S^d^ Roade if Changed

Capt John Gregg Enters his Desent against the sixth artickell of S^d^ warant

this meeting is ajorned untill friday the tenth day of this Instant at one of the Clocke after noon

Lond^ry^ Aprill ye 10th 1761

then mate according to S^d^ ajornment and after Reeding the forgoing warants thy voted to Recive Moses Senter to Serve Constable for the Insuing year for his Brother Ruben Senter

[Editor's Note. The balance of the Records for 1761 consists of the warrants and minutes of the meetings for the selection of jurymen, which resulted in the choice of Lieut. Robert Wallace, James Wilson (Curly so-called), and Samuel Thompson, grand jurors; Robert Adams, George Clark, and James Adams, Jr., petit jurors.]

Provance of Newhampshir

Londonderry Jan^ry^ ye 4th 1762

To Sam^ll^ Karr Constabl for the Easterly Sid of Baver Brook in S^d^ town

In porsuance of his Maj^tis^ write to us Directed from Thos Parker Esqr Shirif of the provance of Newhampshir you are hereby in his Maj^tis^ Name Requiered to warn all the freeholders Quallify^d^ by law to Elect Representives to meet at the old Meetinghouse upon Monday the Eighteenth Day of this Instant at twelve of the Clock on S^d^ Day then and their to Elect one parson Quallify^d^ by law to Represent S^d^ town in Generall assembley and Make a Due Retorn at time & place and this Shall be your warant Given under our hands the Day and year above

Andrew Todd
James Ramsey
Robt Moore
will^m^ Renken
John Mt Keen
Select Men

To Mr Samuell Kare town Constable

Provance of Newhampshir

Lond^ry^ Jan^ry^ ye 18th 1762

In obedance to the within presepte I posted the Same according to Costom

Pr Samuell Kare Constable

Note the other warants for S^d^ meeting was Rade and Exemen^d^ and found word for word So not needfull to be put upon Record

attest Pr Moses Barnett town Clerk

Provance of Newhampshir

Londonderry Jan^ry^ ye 18th 1762

in Obedance to the forgoing warants thy being legally Call^d^ the freeholders of S^d^ Lond^ry^ and Windham mate on S^d^ Day and Chuse for moderater to S^d^ meeting Coll^n^ Andrew Todd then after Reeding all the warants for S^d^ meeting the moderater Give them the vote to Know if thy wold Chuse their Representitive by ahand vote or awriten vote and it Carried by awriten vote and by the moderaters orders the Clerk Rec^{d} the vots and there was of S^{d} vots for Coll^{n} Sam^{ll} Barr Seventy Six and for Insin James Mt Greger Eighty Seven and for Robt Clark thirty Six

and then there arose aDispute in the Meeting that it was not afaire vote and after Some time the provance —— the moderater told them that he would Give them the vote over again and Disiered to Name by vote if thy wold be pold of on awriten vote and if Carred for awriten vote then the Clark Rec^{d} the vots as befor and there was of vots for Coll^{n} Barr Seventy two and for Insn James Mt Greger Six and for Mr Robt Clark two and after the afor^{sd} vots was Counted the Moderater Declared Coll^{n} Sam^{ll} Barr to be Chosen for Assembley Man to Represent Lond^{ry} and windham in Jenr^{l} assembley for S^{d} provance

then Dismis^{d} the meeting

Provance of Newhampshir

Londonderry Feb^{ry} ye 16th 1762

To Moses Senter Constable in the westerly Side of Baverbrook

I porsuance of his Maj^{ts} write to us Directed from Thos Parker Esqr Shiref of the provance of Newhampshir afor^{sd} You are hereby in his Maj^{tis} Name Requiered to warn all the freeholders Quallify^{d} by Law to Elect Representitives to meete at the old meetinghouse upon friday the fifth Day of march Next at ten of the Clock in the fore Noon on S^{d} Day then and their to Elect on parson Quallify^{d} by Law to Represent the S^{d} town and windham in Generall assembley

and this Shall be your Suficent warant Given under our hands and Seal the Day and year above

And^{w} Todd
John Mt Keen
Robt Moore
william Renken
James Ramsey
Select Men

Provance of Newhampshir

Lond^{ry} march ye 5th 1762

In obedance to the forgoing presept I have posted it according to former Costom

Pr Mo^{s} Senter town Constable

Note the other warants for S^{d} Meeting was Rade and Compared and found word for word So Not Needfull to be pute upon Record

attest Pr Mo^{s} Barnett town Clerk

Provance of Newhampshir

Lond^{ry} March ye 5th 1762

In Obedance to the forgoing warants thy being legelly Call^{d} the freeholders of S^{d} Lond^{ry} and windham Quallify^{d} mate on S^{d} Day and after Reeding the forgoing warants by the Majority of votters thy Chuse Coll^{n} Andrew Todd to moderat S^{d} meeting

then after the Moderater had Cased the forgoing warants to be Rade he Disiered the Electers to bring in their vots for afite parson to Represent them in Generall assembley and there was of Vots for Mr Robt Clark 132 and for Coll^{n} Sam^{ll} Barr 138 and the moderater Declared Coll Barr Chosen their Representitve and Dismised the meeting

Provance of Newhampshir

Londonderry Feb^{ry} ye 16th 1762

To Moses Senter Constable in the westerly Side of Baver Brook

Y!ou are hereby Requiered to warn all the free Holders and Inhabitance belonging to your Respective Bounds to meet at the old meetinghouse upon friday the fifth Day of March Next at twelve of the Clock on S^{d} Day then and their

first to Chuse all your town and old parish oficers for the Insuing year

2ly at the Disier of upwards of ten Subcribers to See what the town will allow Joseph boyes for Defending ye Cause with James Morrow or what thy will allow him for his land

3ly to hear the towns accounts Read and approven or Not approve of them

and this Shall be your warant Given under our hands the Day and year above

And^{w} Todd
John Mt Keen
Robt moore
Willm Renken
James Ramsey
Select men

Provance of Newhampshir

Londonderry March ye 5th 1762

In Obedince to the within presept I have posted it according to the former Costom

Pr Mo^{s} Senter town Constable

Note the other warant for S^{d} meeting was Rade and Compar^{d} and found word for word So not needfull to be put upon Record

attest Pr Mo^{s} Barnett town Clk

Provance of Newhampshir

Londonderry March ye 5th 1762

In Obedeance to the forgoing warants thy being legelly Call^{d} the freeholders and Inhabitance of S^{d} town mate on S^{d} Day according to appointment and after Reeding the warants for S^{d} meeting thy made Choys of Coll^{n} Andrew Todd to moderat S^{d} meeting then after the moderater had Caused the warants again to be Rade thy Chuse their town and old parish oficers as followeth for the Insuing year

Chosen for town Clerk Mo^{s} Barnett

Chosen for Clerk protemprey Lif^{t} John Wiar

voted for five Selectmen and their Names is as followeth Andrew Todd John Mt Keen Robt moore James Ramsey will^{m} Renken Select men

Chosen for Constabls for the present year as followeth John Gillmor and S^{d} Gillmor pay^{d} his fine

then thy made Choys of Willm Dickey and S^{d} Dickey pay^{d} his fine then thy made Choys of Robt Barnett and Sd Barnett payd his fine

then thy made Choys of Nathll Hollms and Sd Hollms Served

then thy made Choys of James Hopkens to Serve for the Esterly Side of Baver Brook and Sd James agreed with his Brother John Hopkins to Serve Constable for the present year year for the Sd James but Not for the Sd John and was voted in by the town accordingly and excepted

This meeting is ajorned untill the forth tusday of this Instant at ten of the Clock before Noon

Provance of Newhampshir

Londry March ye 23d 1762

Then mate according to the aforsd ajornment of Sd town and prosided as followeth

Chosen for Colecters for the old parish for the Insuing year Robt Alexdr Junr David Stell

Chosen for taything men for the Insuing year James Mt Keen willm Ower Robt Mt Nell John Aiken Adam Dickey James paterson

Chosen for Surveyers for high ways on the Easterly Side of Baverbrook Samll Alleson Capt John Gregg Samll Moreson Robt Moore John Durham Willm blair Elias Sargant Robt Archibald Samll Karr Samll Clark

Hugh mungoumbrey Chosen Surveyr in willm Blairs Roome

Surviers on the westerly Side for the present year James Campll Junr James Ramsey John wallace Junr Thos wallace Samll Dickey James willson Black Dn Samll Anderson Thos Mt Clery Samll Boyes Samll Miller John Bell Joseph Boyes James Cochran John Brown Willm Cochran Joseph willson Stephen Spalding

Lather Sealers Chosen James Cromey Robt Mt Nell

Hogg Reves Chosen Thos Campbell Arther boyd Willm Alexdr Thos Mt Glaughlen Jacob Hancok Robt Paterson

Fence Vewrs and prisers Chosen Robt Clark John Mt Keen

Counters with the Select men and Counstables Chosen James Mt Keen Samll Alleson Robt Clark

Invoice men John Mt Keen John Cromey Ju^{r} Mt Keen is to have 15—0—0 old tener and Cromey 18—0—0

Deer Keepers for the present year James Nesmith Junr Insn Mt Greger Jonathan Adams Willm Dunken Junr

For the tacking Care of weights and mishurs John Mitchell Junr

Voted on the Second artickell of the forgoing warant Not to pay any thing to Joseph Boyes for his Charges in Going to law with James Morrow

this meeting is ajorned untill the forth tusday of May Next at two of the Clock after Noon

Lond^{ry} May ye 25th 1762

then mate according to the afor^{sd} ajornment and after Considering the towns accounts was not fited to be Rade the moderater Dismised the meeting

Provance of Newhampshir

Londonderry July ye 29th 1762

You are hereby Requiered to warn the freeholders and Inhabitance belonging to your Respective bounds to meet at their old meetinghouse upon frayday the thirteenth Day of august Next at one of the Clock after Noon then and their

first to See what Money the town will vote to be Raised to Defray the Charges of Sd town the present year

2ly to here the towns accounpts Rade and approven or Not approve of them

and this Shall be your warant Given under our hands the Day and year above

And^{w} Todd
John Mc Keen
Robt Moore
will^{m} Renken
Ja^{s} Ramsey
Select Men

To Mr John Hopkins Junr town Constable

Provance of Newhampshir

Lond^{ry} August ye 13th 1762

I have posted the within warant according to former Costom

Pr John Hopkins Junr Constable

Provance of Newhampshir

Lond^{ry} august ye 13th 1762

The freeholders and Inhabitance of S^{d} town Mate according to the appointment of the forgoing warant the other warant for the S^{d} meeting was Rade and Compar^{d} and found word for word So Not Needfull to be put upon Record

attest Pr Mo^{s} Barnett town Clk

then the afor^{sd} Inhabitance maid Choys of Lif^{t} Robt wallace to moderat S^{d} meeting then after Reeding and Considering the aforsd warants thy voted to Rise Eight houndred pounds old tener to Defray the town Debts for this Corant year

2ly the towns accounts was Raide and approven of (viz) Sam^{ll} Karrs Mo^{s} Senters and James Ramseys Clerk to the Select Men

[Editor's Note. The balance of the Records for 1762 consists of the warrants and minutes of the meetings for the selection of jurymen, which resulted in the choice of Dea. Samuel Anderson, Samuel Fisher, and Robert McCurdy, grand jurors; Capt. John Gregg and James Anderson of Mouse Hill, petit jurors.]

APPENDIX.

Petition of the Inhabitants of Londonderry for a Charter, 21 Sept., 1719.

The Humble petition of the People late of Ireland now settled at Nutfield to his Excellency the Governor and General Court assembled at Portsmouth Sep^t^ 23^d^ 1719.

Humbly Sheweth, That your Petitioners having made application to the General Court met at Boston in October last and having obtained a grant for a Township in any part of their unappropriated lands took incouragement thereupon to settle at Nutfield about the Eleventh of Aprile last which is situated by Estimation about fourteen miles from Haverel meeting House to the North West and fifteen miles from Dracut meeting House on the River merimack north and by East. That your petitioners since their settlement have found that the said Nutfield is claimed by three or four different parties by virtue of Indian Deeds, yet none of them Offered any disturbance to your petitioners except one party from Newbury and Salem. Their Deed from one John Indian bears date March the 13th Anno Dom: 1701 and imports that they had made a purchase of the said land for five pounds, by virtue of this deed they claim ten miles square Westward from Haverel line and one Caleb Moody of Newbury in their name discharged our People from clearing or any wais improving the said land unless we agreed that twenty or five and twenty families at most should dwell there and that all the rest of the land should be reserved for them.

That your petitioners by reading the Grant of the Crown of Great Britain to the Province of the Massachusetts bay, which determineth their northern line three miles from the

River merrimack from any and every part of the River and by advise from such as were more capable to judge of this Affair, are Satisfied that the said Nutfield is within his Majesties Province of New Hampshire which we are further Confirmed in, because the General Court met at Boston in May last, upon our renewed application did not think fit any way to intermeddle with the said land.

That your petitioners therefore imbrace this opportunity of addressing this honourable Court, praying that their Township may consist of ten miles square or in a figure Equivalent to it, they being already in number about seventy Families & Inhabitants and more of their friends arrived from Ireland to settle with them, and many of the people of New England settling with them, and that they being so numerous may be Erected into a Township with its usual Priviledges and have a power of making Town Officers and Laws, that being a frontier place they may the better subsist by Government amongst them, and may be more strong and full of Inhabitants:

That your Petitioners being descended from and professing the Faith and Principles of the Establist Church of North Britain and Loyal Subjects of the British Crown in the family of his Majesty King George and incouraged by the happy administration of his Majesties Chief Governour in these provinces and the favourable inclinations of the good people of New England to their Brethren adventuring to come over and plant in this vast Wilderness, humbly Expect a favorable answer from this honourable Court and your Petitioners as in duty bound shall ever pray &c, Subscribed at Nutfield in the name of our people Sept ye 21st 1719.

By

JAMES GREGG
ROBERT WEAR.

CONCERNING THE CLAIM TO NUTFIELD.

A Petition of *Joseph Pike,* in behalf of himself and others, that Purchased a Tract of Land of *John* an *Indian,* Heir of *Penicook,* in the year 1701. which Tract is Ten Miles Square, Lying to the Westward of *Haverhill.* Presented to the House, and Read

Shewing That sundry *Irish* People have Settled thereon and call it *Nutfield.*

Praying, That the said Purchasers may have the said Tract Confirmed to them, or so much as falls within this Government.

Ordered, That Mr. *Cooke,* Capt. *Gardner,* and Col. *Dudley,* be a Committee to consider of the said Petition, and of the affair of *Nutfield,* and make a Report to the House what they think proper to be done.

[*Mass. House Journal, Nov. 15, 1720.*]

Mr. *Cooke* from the Committee appointed, made Report on the Petition of *Joseph Pike,* Committed the 15th Currant, which was accepted by the House, And accordingly

Ordered, That whereas *James MacGregor, James MacKeen,* and *James Gregg,* on behalf of themselves, and sundry others, by their Petition to this Court, at their Sessions in *May,* 1719. set forth that the Court in *October* foregoing, Granted them a convenient Tract of Land, of six miles square, and appointed a Committee to Lay it out for them in the *Eastern* Parts; and upon further Inquiry the Petitioners found a more convenient Tract of Land, about fourteen Miles from *Haverhill*; and that they had begun a Settlement there, and had increased to the Number of Fifty Families; and therefore *Pray'd,* that in case the Land should Lye within this Government, they might be formed into a Township, and till then, quietly possess and improve the said Lands unappropriated, free and clear from any Disburse. Which Petition was rejected.

And that some time since they have applied to the Government of *New-Hampshire,* and are made by them a Township, and have Civil Officers among them, for Governing their Affairs; which is a great and open breach upon the Jurisdiction of this Government, and may tend to deprive them of their just Rights, and Proprieties, if not speedily prevented.

And whereas Joseph Pike, *on behalf of himself, and others Inhabitants of this Province have made application, for a Grant of those Lands for a Township.*

Wherefore Resolved, That Capt. *Gardner,* Capt. *Kimball,* and Mr. *Sanders,* be Desired and Impowered (taking with them the Sheriff of the County of *Essex*; and such a Number of Men from *Haverhill,* or those Parts as may be needful) to Repair to the aforesaid Land, and view the several Houses, and other Improvements that have been of late made by those people thereon; and report the same to this House, & at the same time signifie to the said *James MacGregor, James MacKeen,* and *James Gregg,* That they without delay come to the Court, and render the Reasons that induced them to proceed so far in their Settlements, without the leave or consent first had of the General Court. That this Court may take such further steps in this Matter, as they shall then think fit.

[*Mass. House Journal, Nov. 17, 1720.*]

A Message from the Board, by *John Wheelright,* Esqr. and Mr. Secretary *Willard. Viz.*

His Excellency observing a Mistake in the Votes of this Honourable House, of *November* 17. relating to *Nutfield,* in these words, *And that some time since they have applied to the Government of* New-Hampshire, *and are made by them a Township,* has directed us to acquaint you, that upon application made to him, and the Government of *New-Hampshire,* That they might be made a Town ; his Excellency absolutely refused ; giving them for reason, that it was doubtful, in which Province the Lands they were Settled on would fall.

And Col. *Wheelwright* acquainted the House, That he was present when the *Nutfield* People, Addrest themselves to the Governour and Council at *New-Hampshire,* to be made a Town, and that they were denied.

[*Mass. House Journal, Dec. 2, 1720.*]

Petition for Bills of Credit, &c.

To his Excellency the Governour and Honourable Council of New Hampshire in General Court assembled at Portsmouth Apr. 18th 1721.

The humble Petition of the People of Nutfield,

Humbly sheweth, That your petitioners are sensible of the Goodness of God and Care and Protection of his Excellency the Governour and Council of New Hampshire in supporting and defending their plantation for which they render them unfeigned Acknowledgments of duty and respect,

That your Petitioners are in a Growing condition having already Exceeded the number of three hundred and sixty souls of which there are one hundred and thirty Effective men capable to bear Arms for his Majesty King George, as his Excellency the Governour and Council may think fit to Employ them.

That altho' your petitioners have Exhausted their money in Subduing the wilderness yet they are Carrying on all the parts of good Husbandry and building a House for the worship of God;

That your Petitioners want to be incorporated, that the affairs of their settlement may be managed with greater advantage.

May it therefore please your Excellency and your Honours to give order that our people which are already so numerous may not be too much Confined in respect of room by any newer settlement in our Neighbourhood, that Bills of Credit May be lent out unto them upon due Security in some term of years to be paid again without interest in Hemp and other product of the land in such a summ as may incourage their Husbandry and especially their building of a meeting House, and that they may be duly invested with town Priviledges by Royal Authority, And your Petitioners as in duty bound shall ever Pray &c.

David Cargill	Arch : Clendinen
Abram Blair	Alex Walker
Rob^{tt} Wear	Samuell Allisone
John Senter	Will. Campbell
James Nesmith	Allen Andrews
Samuel Moor	John Coghran
John Moor	Will Coghran
Joseph Symons	Alex^{r} Macneall
Joseph Crosbee	William Cambell
Ronald Alexander	David Morison
Abel Merrill	John Archbald
Thomas Bogell	James Aiken
Robt Doke	Will. Aiken
James Nikels	John Bell
Alex^{r} Nickels	Will : Caldwell
Williame Nikels	John Barnet
John Barnet	William Eayrs
Ja: Archibald	Ja : McGregor
James Alexander	David Cargill
Thomas Steel	James M^{c}keen
Will. Wilson	James Gregg
Will. Thomson	Robert Willson
Edward Aiken	Samuel Graves
Ramin Willson	John McNeall
John Richey	John Mitchell
John Wallace	James Leslie
Andrew Todd	Silas Creyes
William Humphry	John McMorphy
James Lindsey	James Anderson
Matthew Clark	John Blair
James Clark	James Blair

Rob[t] M[c]Keen	John Shilder
Jo: Bar	Beniamin Kidder
Gabral ? Bar	John Anderson
Hugh Montgumery	Robert Morisone
Samuel Morison	Stephen Peirce
Abraham Homs	Edward Proctor
John Blair	John Goffe
James Morison	John Goffe, Jr
John Morison	Henery Green
James Moore	John Cromey
Andrew Spavid ?	John M[c]Conochey ?

Provincial Oaths.

I ——— Do sincerely promise and swear that I will be faithfull and bear true allegiance to His Majesty King George the second.

I — — Do swear that I do from my heart abhor detest and abjure as impious and heretical that damnable doctrine & position that princes Excomunicated or deprived by the Pope or any Authority of the see of Rome may be deposed or muther'd by their Subjects or any other whatsoever. And I do declare that no foreign Prince Person prelate State or Potentate hath or ought to have any Jurisdiction power authority preeminence or authority ecclesiastical or spiritual within the realm of Great Brittain.

So help me God.

I ——— - - do truly and sincerely acknowledge profess Testify & declare in my conscience before God and the world, That our Sovereign Lord King George the second is lawfull & rightfull King of the realm of Great Britain and all other His Maj[ties] Dominions and Countrys thereunto belonging, And I do solemnly and sincerely declare that I do believe in my conscience, that the Person pretended to be Prince of Wales during the life of the late King James, and since his decease pretending to be and taking upon himself the Stile & title of King of England by y[r] names of James the third or of Scotland by y[e] names of James y[e] eighth or the stile & title of King of Great Britain hath not any right or title whatsoever to the crown of the realm of Great Britain or any other the Dominions thereto belonging. And I do renounce refuse and Abjure any Allegiance or obedience to him. And I do swear that I will bear faith and true allegiance to His Majesty King George the second and him will defend to the utmost of my power against all traitorous conspiracies and attempts whatsoever which shall be made against his Person Crown or Dignity: And I will do my utmost endeavour to disclose and make known to his majesty and his successors all treasons & traitorous conspiracies which I shall know to be agst him or any of them, And I do faithfully promise to the utmost of my power to support maintain and defend the succession of the crown ag^{t} him the s^{d} James and all other Persons whatsoever, which succession by an act Entitled an act for ye further limitation of the crown and better securing the rights and liberties of ye subjects is and stands limited to ye Princess Sophia Electress & Dutchess Dowager of Hanover, and the heirs of her body being Protestants, and all these things I do plainly and sincerely acknowledge and swear according to these express words by me spoken and according to ye plain & common sense and understanding of the same words without any Equivocations mental evasion or secret reservation whatsoever. And I do make this recognition acknowledgm^{t}, abjuration renunciation and promise heartily willing and truly upon ye true faith of a Christian.

So help me God.

Names of persons who took the above Oaths.

David Cargill
James McKeen
James Harvey
John Goffe
Hugh Montgomery
James Morison
John Mitchell
Jesse Criste
James Rodgers
John Adames
Thomas Wilson
James Wallis
Alexander Walker
James Reid
John Macmurphy
David Macduffie
John Morison
Jonathan How?

James Leslie
John Goffe, Jr
Solomon Hopkin
James Adams
James Tagart
John Tagart
Samuel Houston
Patrick Douglas
Robert Cochran
his
Alexander ⅄ Renkine
mark
John X Conahie
mark
Peter Coghran
Thomas Watte
John Blair
James Lindsey

Alexander Macneall
Thomas Mackelme
Robtt Wear
Archiball Clendenin
William Moor
John Barnet
Archibald Mac Murphy
Robert Kennedy
Moses Barnett
Samuel Morison
James Blair
James Taggart
John Barnet
Andrew Clendenin
Jon. Woodburn
Thomas Cochran
David Hunter
Allen Anderson
Petter Cochran
James Gillmor
Robt Morison
Alexander Kelsey
David Cargill
Andrew Todd
James Calwell
James Caldwood
James Alexander
William Gregg
John Barr
John Cromey
William Nickell
John Gregg
John
James Nesmith
James Thompson
Matthew Clark
Robert McKean
Samuel McKeen
John Cochran
Charels McClarey
his
John £ Neale?
mark
his

John Douglas
John Archibald
John ——?
John McClourg
Rus. Buron
Robt Thomson
Thomas Seiell?
Gab: Bar
James Rueys
Nathaniel Aiken
Jon. Hollms
Hugh Wilson
Robert Arbuckel
John Hopkin
John Archibel
David Anderson
John Anderson
Samuel Renkin
Wilam Cochran
Wimen Cochran
John Moore
William Aiken
James Clark
Jon Harvey
Abner Nickels
Sam: Todde
James Moor
Samuel Allison
William Gillmor
James Andrews
John Craig
William Eayrs
James Willson
Robert Gillmore
Samuell Gregg
Angus Brown
his
Willm X Adams
mark
Benjamin Kidder
Thomas Bogall
Benjamin Willson
John Anderson
Abraham Holme

Willm & Kellso
mark
William Thomson
David McGregore
Christopher Airs
Samuel Greaves
Hugh Rogers
William Coghran
James Aiken
—— Blair
William Eayrs
Alexander McMurphy
John Blear
James Smith
David Morison
James Campbell
Benjamin Chamberlain
John McNeill
Samuell Barr
Joseph Irrvine

Londonderry 7ber 9th 1727.

The severall persons above mentioned took their oaths according to act of Parliament.

Relative to Boundary Dispute.

House of Representative.

Wednesday May the 10th A. D. 1732.

The Committee bro't in an Answer to his Excellys Speech, which was read & voted, accepted and sent up in the words following, viz.

May it please your Excellency

We beg leave to assure your Excelly, that we are now met to attend his Majties service in this Sessions and to do every thing that may tend to his Majties service and the Prosperity of his good subjects within this Province whom we represent; and this we shall do with chearefullness, and hope with unanimity, having no sinister ends or double views, and hope there will be no strugles nor contentions.

As to the affaire of the Lines, we apprehend this Govermt has done every reasonable thing to accomodate that matter in a Peace between the two Govermts, and in order to do this have exceeded his Majties Instruction to your Excelly in that affair; tho' this House thinks it absolutely necessary that something should be speedily done in compassion to the Poore People that inhabit neare the controversy; for sundry suits have been commenced agt the People of Londonderry and Kingstown, and the people carried into the county of Essex in the Massa Govermt to be tried for Trespass comitted at least twelve miles north from Merrimack, and this at their last Court at

Ipswitch; and those suits upon the controverted lands have already cost one of those Towns, by a moderate Computation, at least Eight hundred pounds: Wherefore we humbly pray that your Excelly would put a stop to these proceedings until the Lines shall be settled at home, which we hope will not be long, seeing it could not be accomodated here; and to this end, this House did empower Capt. John Rindge to represent that affaire to his Maj^tie in Council and [P. 368] humbly pray his decision.

TWO SETS OF TOWN OFFICERS CHOSEN, 1737.

To His Excellency Jonathan Belcher Esqr Governour & Command^r In Chief In and over His Majestys Province of New Hamp^r the Honble His Majestys Council, and the House of Representatives in General Court assembled—

The Petition of Sundry the Inhabitants of the Town of London-Derry in the Province of New Hamp^r—Most humbly shews—

That It hath been the Custom in said Town, ever since they have acted as a Town, at their General Town Meetings in March yearly to allow all persons that payed rates in said town to Vote in chusing town officers until at the town meeting held in said Town on the fifth day of March Instant when the Select men for the last year produced a list of Persons names who the select men said should be voters only.— That notwithstanding a Considerable majority of the persons present proceeded according to the usual method of said Town to Chuse a Moderator, and then to chuse a Town Clerk, selectmen and other town officers, and that the two Justices in said Town refused to swear any of said officers so chosen, and that a minor part of the persons then present in a by-part of the meeting-house made choice of another set of Town officers, which last sett the Justices in said Town have since sworn, which has already occasioned much disorder strife and confusion in said Town, and will We fear tend to the utter ruin and destruction of the peace and good orders of said Town unless something be done by the General Court to redress our Grievances.—

Therefore Your Petitioners most humbly Pray Your Excellency the Honble the Council and House of Representatives In your Great wisdom to ratify & Confirm what was done at the last meeting in said Town according to the former usage and Customs of said Town, or to Explain that paragraph in the Act for regulating Townships, choice of Town officers and setting forth their power relating to the qualification of Voters in said Town meetings, and order that There be another Town meeting in said Town to Chuse Town officers, and your Petitioners as in Duty bound, Shall Ever Pray—

John Moor
Saml Allison
Ronald Alexander
John Stewart
Robt Cochran
James Boyes
Hugh Rogers
Wm Cochran
Wm Candinon
Thomas Morrison
Joseph Wallis
Hugh Wilson
Abrm Holmes
John Givian
Robt Wear
Saml Miller
John Craig
Patrick Duglas
Wm Humphrey
Alexandr Macdorn
Robert Givian
Saml Mitchel
Saml Morrison
Alexandr Rankin
John Morrison
Thomas Cochran
Archd Miller
John Steel
James Morrison
Danl Anderson
Thoms Mellavy
James Cochran

John Reade
Saml Morrison
Thomas Steel
John Barnet
John Durham
Thos McMaster
Archd Candinon
Jesse Cristi
Wm Holmes
Robert Boyes
James Dalop
John Wilson
John Cochran
Robert Mccurdy
Wm Gregg
Moses Barnet
James Mccurdy
John Holmes
John Mclary
Benja Willson
John Smylel
Hugh Bolton
Thoms Wallace
Peter Cochran
Saml Morrison
Henry Comee
John Cromey
Patrick Fisher
David Morrison
John Humphry
John Ware
John Ramsey

Halbert Morrison
Wm McNeal
Peter Cochran
Robert Wallace
Wm Moor
James Wilson
Saml Kinkerd
John Alexandr
Thoms Hoag
James Patterson
John Duncan
David Vance
John Mckonoihy
Saml Morrison
John Stewart Junr
Wm Kelley
Thoms Bogel
John Mitchel Junr
Andrew Clandinen
Wm McMaster
Alexandr Parks
John McCleary
Francis Smaley
John Wallace
James Calwel Junr
Wm Cochran
Joseph Ball
James Glines
Allen Anderson
Wm Murdoch

Mem° I have copyed the names as well as I could read them but am not certain that they are right

R. Waldron Sec^{y}.

Proposals for Peace, 1737.

The civil and religious quarrels anent the division of the town waxed so bitter and vigorous that we find eighty of the leading citizens making proposals for peace.—Editor.

To our Christian friends and Brethren of ye old Congregation in London Derry; proposals of peace

Breth^{n}

It is a lamentable Truth, Too evident To be denyd, y^{t} the Scandalous divisions, both in Civils and Ecleseaiticks, which have Too long Subsisted among us, are a stain to our holy profession; that they have a Natural tendency, to provoke God; to procure Judgments and to render us a hissing a reproach and a byword to our Neighbours and that these are aggravated from our circumstances, we being Strangers which ought to excite us to a stricter amity and unity among our Selves.

but then Seing it is not Complaints & lamentations only, but proper remidys also, that are Necessary to effect an accommodation among us; we therefore out of a Sincere and Disintrested view To peace, do Chearfuly & unanimously make ye following proposals.

Proposal 1st whereas it has been (as we are Inform'd) Suggested or Insinuated, that The design of us who belong to the New Congregation, is To draw away the Strength of ye old Parish, and Consequently To build upon its Ruins; we propose that we who are already Incorporated in the new parish, with Those who are at present willing to joyn us, who in all are not one half of ye town, will oblige our Selves to maintain the Gospel in Our own Congregation, without demanding any help from our Neighbours in the Other parish; or if this will not Satisfie, we propose that the Salary's of both Ministers be asess'd in common, and equaly levyd from ye whole town in general.

As to the Ecclesiastick part of our divisions, we wou'd be heartily glad that this also were Accomodated: that which renders a reconciliation in this particular more difficult, is the want of a Synod, To whose Judgment all partys Consonant To presbyterian principles behoof'd to be Subjict: but Since we have not this Superior Judicature To have Recource To, in this part of the world: Since appeals to a foreign Church, in our present Scituation and Circumstances is Impracticable even in the Opinion of Several of ye ministers of y^{r} own party, whose disent against Such Apeals, is extant in ye minutes of the presbytery; and Since there is a Schism among the Members of presbytery, So that they being partys cannot be admitted as proper Judges, what must be ye Consequence, as Things are thus Circumstanced, but that Except Some other methode be found out, Our uncumfortable Debates be protracted time without End: for Remidy wherof we propose.

Proposal 2^{d} that a number of ministers, of ye Congregational perswasion, Such as you and we can mutualy agree upon; Shall be Invited To meet on this affair; and that haveing heard the whole of what is To be Said Pro and Con by the Respective partys, they Shall then draw up in writing their Result: whether Sd Result Shall be finaly deciseive or Not, we leave to be Considered. Note, ye S^{d} Ministers Shall be Obliged to judge the affair agreeable to presbyterian Rules. We for see no objection of any Seeming weight that can be made against this last proposal but Such as follows; to which by way of anticipation we Return Some Answer.

Objection 1st the persons whom you propose as Judges are of a diffarent perswasion; we Answer by Concession we grant they are So, but the Difference is not So wide, but that Some of ye greatest Divines of ye presbyterian perswasion, and even of those who have wrote against them, particulerly the judicious Mr Rutheroord, has Adress'd them with the friendly Epithet of Dr Brethren; for our part we firmly believe, that NotwithStanding the Difference in principle, there are To be found among them, Many men, of Learning, Goodness, Candor, Impartiality, and Every qualification, which may Render them very fit Judges in this affair.

Object^{n} 2^{d} this proposal if Complyed with, wou'd cast a Reflection on the Presbyterian Government, as if it were not Sufficient to answer all the Ends of Governm^{t}, without being beholden To another perswasion: we Answer ye objection has no weight in it; for 1st let it be Concidered that presbyterian Goverm^{t} Consists in a Subordination of Judicatures, The Inferior To the Superior; Now if we had a Synod To apply too and yet this Remidy were Necessary, it wou'd then Argue a Defect in the Constetution; but otherwise the Objection is of No weight. 2dly let it be Concidered, that the judges we propose, tho of another perswasion, are bound to judge by Presbyterian Rules: the Salutary Medicin is Still the Same, though the Application be made by Other hands.

we are far from being So premptory or wedded to Our own proposols, as to Say that these and these only are the terms on which we will be at peace; but these Are what we look on as Resonable and Christian; and if you think them Not Such, we wou'd be glad to hear Some from you that are more So.

In the Conclusion we beseech you Brethren, Seriously To Consider that 'tis your as well as Our Duty if it be possible, as much as lies in you, To live peacably with all men. to Seek peace, and pursue it. to lay Down your Gift at the Alter, and go be Reconcil'd with your Brother: and that Ecept we Do so Our Religion is Vain, that tho we had all faith to ye Removing of mountains and have Not Charity, we are as A Sounding Brass and tinkling Cymbal. and that he who Says he loves God and hates his Brother is a lyar: let the Serious Concideration of these Awful and weighty truths, leave Such a deep Impression on us, that we may be willing for peace, on the most Reasonable terms; and let us look on All Such as wou'd diswade us from hearkning to Reasonable proposals of accommodation, to be publick Nusances, the Bane of Civil Society, ye obstructers of Brotherly love, and the Active Instruments of Satan, and as Such let us Avoid them with detestation. we are your friends and Brethren in Christ.

London Derry April ye 19th 1737

Relative to West Parish, 1739.

To his Exelencey Jonathan Belcher Esq[r] Governor and Comander in Chief in and over his Magiestys Provence of Newhampshier the Honarebl his Magiestys Councel for Sd Provence and the hous of Represenitive in General asembley Convened

the Pitition of Sundrey of the Inhabitence of the Westrly part of Londondery in the Provence of new hampshier humbly Shueth—

That at the General Court at Portsmouth in and for the forsaid Provence in aprel 1736 ther was a Pitition preferred to the General Court of Said Provence that ther Might be a Parish Set of in said town in the westerly part of Said town AGreeable to a vote of Said Town that the General Court was pleased by a vote to Set of for a Parish In the Westerly part of Said town acording to the folouing Bounds Beginning of the Southerly part of the toun at a place kown by the name of Ston Dam thence Runing up Bover Brook to the South west part of Charels mclorgs lot thence Runing a Straight line by the Norwest Cornar of ninen Cochrans home Lote to amascige Road thence Runing alongst the Sd Rod to a place none by the Name of the twelve acer mido Brook thence Runing a noRth to the toun Line then torning westerly and roning Round the toun line till Bover Brook then Runing to the Bounds firs menshoned and that the miting hous Should be Wher it then Stod in the Westerly Part of Sd toun and that to the Number of thirty five in Said westerly parish might Remain to the old Parish and as Maney of Said Number as Should go from the Newe Parish to the old So maney of the old Should go to the new parish and that Befor the Said vote of the Generall Court was Redused to one act the Secriterys hous was Consumed by flaims and the vote amongst other papers was burnt Wherfor your Petitioners most humbly pray Your Excellency the Honorabl the Councel and hous of Representitive to Set of a Parish in the westerly part of Sd town Agreeable to the former vot of the Genarel Court and your Petishoners as in Duty bound Shall ever pray &c

Dated at Londondery October 12th 1737

John Mcleriee
Robart Bell
Thomas mclire
William holems
Thomas BoGel
Samul thomson
William thomson
Angus Mcalester
William mcalester
John Care
Thomas wollace
James ares
Robart Gaye
David mcalester
James thomson
michel mclinton
Joseph Boys
William wollac
John Blair
Thomas Hog
david BoGel
Joseph BoGel
John Wallace
iohn Crage
John willson
BenJamen willson
Andrue todd
Aalexander Crage
Aalexander mc : olom
Samul morison First
Nethaniel willson
Robart Gifen
John m.lorg
Abram holms
Robart Wallace
David morison
Samul morison
John morison
John holems
Ninin Cochran
Petter Cochran
Samul Tood
william hairs
Thomas Wallace
Joseph Wallace
John Barnat
Joseph Bell
James muray
James wollace
James Paterson

PETITION OF INHABITANTS OF OLD AND NEW PARISHES OF LONDONDERRY.

To his Excellency Benning Wentworth Esq. Governor and Commander in chief in and over his Majtes province of New hampshire the Honourable his Majesties Councill for said Province and the house of Representatives in Generall Assembly Convened.

The Petition of Sundry of the Inhabitance of Londonderry in the province of New hampshire belonging to the old and new parishes humbly Sheweth.

That whereas in february in the year 1739-40 there was a new parish sett off in this town by the Generall Court, Granting Liberty to fourty famelyes that lived within the Bounds of the said new parish still to Remain members of the old parish with their estates and at the same time granted Liberty that fourty famelys that lived within the Bounds of the old parish Should become members of the new parish With their estates if they saw cause.

Which accordingly was performed and that still their was some few famelys and single persons in Both parishes that was not contented because they were obliged to pay there parish Tax where they properly belonged and went to the contrary parish to the publick worship, and that whereas freedom and Liberty is most to be Desired especially in Religious affairs and whereas every christian ought chiefly to study those things That will be most for the advancement of the Redeemers Kingdom out of a consious consern for those persons that they might obtain their freedom and liberty as well as the Rest of the people of this town the Two parishes chose each of them a committee to see to accomodate that affair who is the Subscribers to this petition and was legaly chosen for Said End, and accordingly we meet and after some conversation about the affair we came to a mutuall agreement that all persons who had a mind to become members of the new parish should on a certain day then appointed meet the two committees and sign their names to said agreement which is two tedious here to Insert and those that had a mind to become members of the old parish had the same liberty and accordingly at the Day appointed the people came and signed their names only their is a saving clause in said agreement that we did not Intend any Infringement on the Court Act Relating to the fourty famelys belonging to each parish: Wherefore your petitioners humbly prays your Excellency the Honourable the Councill and house of Representatives that you would be pleased to pass an act to establish this our agreement, & that those persons, with their estates who hath already signed their names with us may become members of the old and new parish as they have signed, and that you would be pleased to Incorporate the new parish into a town & have priveledges as other towns except it be about highway work and taking the Invoice for the payment of the publick tax. Likewise that you would be pleased to explain the former act Relating to the fourty famelys that is to say whither on the sale of any of those fourty estates the purchaser shall be obliged to pay his parish tax where the estate was signed unto, or whither he may be at his Liberty to go to the other parish if he sees good. Also that all trangent persons who shall come to sojourn in this town shall have liberty to sign there names in three months after there arrivall with the Selectmen of the parish where they design to Belong and shall be oblidged to pay there taxes there and your petitioners as in Duty bound ever shall pray.

James Gregg	Hugh Millson	Committee
Moses Barnett	Robt Cochran	
James Nesmith	James Clark	
Thomas Willson	James Aiken	
Samuell Barr	Archibald McCormick	
Jon Wallace	James Taggart	

In the House of Representatives 9br the first 1741. The within Petition read and parties heard, and Voted that the Prayer of the Petition be so far Granted as concerns the signers mentioned in the agreemt mentioned in the Petition and that the new Parish be made a perticular Precinct by the name of —— —— and yt they have the prevelidges as other towns or Parishes have by the Laws of this Province excepting the choice of assembly man which shall be chosen as formerly By the whole Town, and as to the forty familys formerly Polled off in either new or old pish, that their persons or estates stand as they are and likewise their successors in the several estates either by Descent or purchase to Remaine the same having signd according as the Petition mentioned and as to any new Comers that is Tradesmen or ministers &c that Shall Signifie to the clerk of the Town within 3 months after they come there to live, where they will belong, and that all children & Servants when they become Rateable shall pay where their parents or Masters pay, and that the Petitionrs have liberty to Bring in a Bill accordingly.

James Jeffrey Cler. Assm

In Coun. March 13th 1741-2

Read and Concurred.

R. Waldron

Same day Assented to,

B. Wentworth.

Province of New Hamp^{r}. In ye House of Representatives June 23^{d} 1743.

Whereas for want of knowledge of the True bounds of the Districts of Methuen & Dracut how it interfered on the Bounds [P. 178.] of Londonderry Township when the Act was past last year for Proportioning the Towns & Districts within this Province the within persons were Doubly returned viz. By the Districts of Methuen and Dracut and by Londonderry, Whereby the within named Persons has been rated for their Province Tax to Londonderry and alsoe to Methuen & Dracut District—It being agst Reason that they should be rated to Both places,

Voted That they pay their respective rates for the Province Tax for the year 1742 to the constable or collector of the Parish of Windham as rated in Windham and that the District of Methuen and Dracut be abated the sum of nineteen pounds seven shillings & four pence part of the Proportion they were to pay for the Province Tax for the year 1742. And that the Collector of the District of Methuen & Dracut has rec^{d} of the Persons within named shall all such money so rec^{d} be repaid by s^{d} collector to the persons from whom the same was collected.

And that the s^{d} sum of nineteen pounds seven shillings & four pence Equal to old Tenour be taken out of the money put into the Treasury for contingencies and to ly in the Treasury as a Fund to Exchange the old Bills of Cred^{t} of this Province in order that they may be bro't in & burnt.

James Jeffrey Cler. Ass^{m}.

In Council July 2^{d} 1743 read and concurr'd.

Theodore Atkinson Sec^{y}.

Eod^{m} Die. Assented to

B. Wentworth.

Relative to Indian Troubles.

House of Representative.

Monday 24th August 1747 P. M.

The House met. Upon Information made to ye House of

ye Indians having kill'd sundry Persons at Notingh^m & a motion made by Coll. Pet^r Gilman for a scout of men to be marching continually across ye Frontiers,

Voted That his Excell^y ye Govr be desired to give orders for inlisting or impressing thirty good effective men to be imploy'd in scouting on ye Frontiers from Londonderry to Barrington & so up to Ipsom for six weeks making Nottingham their Head Quarters [P. 515.] & that they scout in a Body together or be divided some times into smaller scouts as shall appear most for ye safety of ye People & for ye discovery of ye Enemy. Sent up by Mr. Macmurphy.

House of Representative

Saturday 12th March 1747—8 A. M.

The House met according to adjournment.

Voted That for the Incouragement of such as shall inlist themselves for ye Defence of the Frontiers agreeable to ye vote of this House of yesterday that they be paid one Month's Pay advance ye Commanding or inlisting officer to receive ye Money out of ye publick Treasury for this End & to take Care to have effective Men & to be accountable to ye Genl Assembly for what money he shall so receive. Sent up by Mr. Macmurphy.

A Bill for Taxing ye Lands in Notingham West read three Times &

Voted That it pass to be enacted. Sent up by Mr. Macmurphy.

Relative to Taverns, 1758.

To His Excellency Benning Wentworth Esq. Captain, General, Governor, & Commander, in Chief, in & Over his Majesty's, Province of New-Hampshire, The Honourable his Majesty's Council, & House of Representatives, in General, Assembly, Convened.

The Humble Petition, of the Subscribers Inhabitants of Londonderry & Province aforeSaid, Humbly Sheweth, That the Number, of Taverns, are so Multiplied, in Londonderry Aforesaid, they are become a Snare to the Youth, & of Evil Tendency, to every Age of Injudicious persons, & if they are All Continued (or which is worse Increased) we fear they will More & More Debase, & Debauch, the Manners & Morals of All such persons as Abovesaid.

Therefore Your Petitioners Humbly pray, that for the future there may be but four Taverns, & Retailers, Alowed in Londonderry, aforeSaid, & the Inn-holders, to be Chosen by A majority, of Votes at the Annual Meeting, & so Annually Untill the Circumstances, of the Town Requires a greater, Number, & them that are pro Tempore, to be under such Regulations, in Respect to Travellers, Towns-Men, Sabbath-Days, & every night, as in your Great Wisdoms you think Most Convenient, & most Conducive, to Incourage Virtue & Discourage Vice, & your Petitioners, as in Duty Bound, Will ever Pray.

Samuell Gregg	Robert Boyes	James Blair
Samll Alison Junr	Mathew Thornton	John mckeen
Samll miller	William Wallace	John moor
his	Thomas Gregg	Hugh Montgomery
Soll o Alls	James Ervins	David mountgumrey
mark	James Campbell	Robert morison
hugh young	Robert Logan	David anderson
James Taggart	William humphra	Jno Wiear
James Anderson	Samuel morrison	Thomas Morison
Robert Craig	John Ramsey	Samll Mitchel Jur
James Doack	Samul moore	thomas Creaige
Nathaniel Aiken	Samul Alison	David Steel
Nathanel Holms	John morrison	Mos Barnett
Jon Wallace	Robt Wallace	Andrew Clendinin
Robt Parkeson	James Wallace	James wallace
Joseph Cochran	Thomas Willson	Thomas Wallace
John gillmore	Jas McGregore	

INDEX.

INDEX OF NAMES OF PERSONS.

B

C

H

Y

GENERAL INDEX.

V

W

www.ingramcontent.com/pod-product-compliance
Lightning Source LLC
LaVergne TN
LVHW020520100826
845148LV00010B/1291

* 9 7 8 1 5 5 6 1 3 6 8 2 5 *